# THE CAMBRIDGE
# COMPANION TO
# W. H. AUDEN

EDITED BY
## STAN SMITH

CAMBRIDGE
UNIVERSITY PRESS

CAMBRIDGE UNIVERSITY PRESS
Cambridge, New York, Melbourne, Madrid, Cape Town, Singapore, São Paulo, Delhi

Cambridge University Press
The Edinburgh Building, Cambridge CB2 8RU, UK

Published in the United States of America by Cambridge University Press, New York

www.cambridge.org
Information on this title: www.cambridge.org/9780521829625

First published 2004
Reprinted 2006

*A catalogue record for this publication is available from the British Library*

*Library of Congress Cataloguing in Publication data*
The Cambridge companion to W. H. Auden/edited by Stan Smith.
p.   cm. – (Cambridge companions to literature)
Includes bibliographical references (p. 240) and index.
ISBN 0 521 82962 3 – ISBN 0 521 53647 2 (pbk.)
1. Auden, W. H. (Wystan Hugh), 1907–1973 – Criticism and
interpretation – Handbooks, manuals, etc.   I. Smith, Stan, 1943–   II. Series.
PR6001.U4Z634   2004
821′.912 – dc22        2004051853

ISBN 978-0-521-82962-5 hardback
ISBN 978-0-521-53647-9 paperback

Transferred to digital printing 2008

# CONTENTS

CONTRIBUTORS

JOHN R. BOLY teaches modern literary theory and contemporary British literature at Marquette University, Milwaukee. He is the author of *Reading Auden: The Returns of Caliban* (1991) and sundry essays on the poet, and is currently at work on a study of Seamus Heaney's adaptations of romantic genres.

RICHARD R. BOZORTH is Associate Professor of English at Southern Methodist University, Dallas, Texas, and the author of *Auden's Games of Knowledge: Poetry and the Meanings of Homosexuality* (2001).

NADIA HERMAN COLBURN, a recipient of both Mellon and Javits Fellowships, recently completed a PhD from Columbia University, *The Surface of What's There: The Paradox of Authority*, which examines the work of Auden, John Ashbery and James Merrill. She was editor of the *Auden Society Newsletter* from 1999–2003. Her poetry has appeared in numerous publications, including *The New Yorker*, *American Poetry Review*, *The Harvard Review* and *Boston Review*.

RICHARD DAVENPORT-HINES is a historian and biographer whose biography *Auden* was first published in 1995 and republished in 2003. He has contributed to *Auden Studies* and to the *Auden Society Newsletter*. His other books include *Sex, Death and Punishment: Attitudes to Sex and Sexuality since the Renaissance* (1990) and *The Pursuit of Oblivion: a Global History of Drugs since 1500* (2001). He is a trustee of the London Library. *A Night at the Majestic*, a study of Marcel Proust, will be published in 2005.

PATRICK DEANE is Provost and Vice-President (Academic) at the University of Winnipeg, Canada, where he is also Professor of English. His publications include *At Home in Time: Forms of Neo-Augustanism in Modern English Poetry* (1994) and *History in Our Hands: A Critical Anthology of Writings on Literature, Culture, and Politics from the 1930s* (1998).

RAINER EMIG is Professor of British Literature at the University of Regensburg in Germany. He is the author of *Modernism in Poetry: Motivations, Structures and Limits* (1995) and *W. H. Auden: Towards a Postmodern Poetics* (2000) and of books and essays on nineteenth- and twentieth-century literature and culture, especially modernism, war, gender and sexuality. His most recent project is a study of eccentricity, provisionally entitled *Eccentricity: Culture from the Margins*. He is currently working on a course book on *Literary Masculinities* and planning a monograph on *Treasure Hunts in Literature*.

CHRISTOPHER INNES is a Fellow of the Royal Society of Canada, a Fellow of the Royal Society of Arts (UK), and Distinguished Research Professor at York University, where he holds the Canada Research Chair in Performance and Culture. His most recent books are: *Avant Garde Theatre* (1993); *The Theatre of Gordon Craig* (1997); Sourcebooks on *Naturalist Theatre* (2000) and on *Hedda Gabler* (2003); and *Modern British Drama: the Twentieth Century* (1992). He is editor of *The Cambridge Companion to Bernard Shaw* (1998), as well as the General Editor for the Cambridge 'Directors in Perspective' series, and has been co-editor of the quarterly journal *Modern Drama*. For more information see www.moderndrama.com

NICHOLAS JENKINS teaches English at Stanford University. He has contributed essays and reviews to the *London Review of Books*; *New Republic*; *TLS*; *The New Yorker*; *New York Times Book Review*; and *Yale Review*. He is co-editor, with Katherine Bucknell, of *Auden Studies*, and editor of Alan Ansen, *The Table-Talk of W. H. Auden*. He is currently completing a book entitled *The Island: W. H. Auden and the Making of a Post-National Poetry*, and a critical edition of Auden's *The Double Man*. He is General Editor of the Princeton University Press translation series *Facing Pages*, and literary executor of one of Auden's closest friends, the ballet impresario Lincoln Kirstein.

JOHN LUCAS, Emeritus Professor of English at the Universities of Loughborough and Nottingham Trent, is the author and editor of many books of criticism, including *England and Englishness: Ideas of Nationhood in English Poetry* (1990) and *Dickens: The Major Novels* (1992), and of six collections of poetry. Recent books include *The Radical Twenties: Writing, Politics and Culture* (1999); *Ivor Gurney* (2001); *Starting to Explain: Essays on Twentieth-Century British and Irish Poetry* (2003); and *A World Perhaps: New and Selected Poems* (2002). Since 1994 he has been the publisher of The Shoestring Press, Nottingham.

PAOLA MARCHETTI teaches at the Università Cattolica in Milan, Italy. She is the author of *Landscapes of Meaning: From Auden to Hughes* (2001), a study of the twentieth-century short story, *Fiction and Reality: Percorsi del Racconto Contemporaneo in Lingua Inglese* (1999) and articles on Auden, Dylan Thomas and Thom Gunn. She is currently completing a study of Auden's libretti.

EDWARD MENDELSON is the literary executor of the estate of W. H. Auden and Professor of English and Comparative Literature at Columbia University, New York. His books include *Early Auden* (1981) and *Later Auden* (1999). In addition to the *Collected Poems, Forewords and After-words, The English Auden* and many other collections and selections of Auden's writings, he is the editor of the Faber/Princeton *Complete Works of W. H. Auden*. He has recently completed a book tentatively titled *The Thing That Mattered: Birth, Childhood, Growth, Marriage, Parenthood, and the Future in Seven English Novels*.

ROD MENGHAM is Reader in Modern English Literature at the University of Cambridge, where he is also Curator of Works of Art at Jesus College. He is the author of books on Charles Dickens, Emily Brontë and Henry Green, as well as of *The Descent of Language* (1993). He has edited collections of essays on contemporary fiction, violence and avant-garde art, and the fiction of the 1940s. He is also the editor of the Equipage series of poetry pamphlets and co-editor and co-translator of *Altered State: The New Polish Poetry* (2003). His own poems have been published under the title *Unsung: New and Selected Poems* (1996; 2nd edition, 2001).

PETER PORTER was born in Brisbane, Australia in 1929. He is the author of many volumes of poetry and the two volumes of his *Collected Poems* were published by Oxford University Press in 1999. He won the Duff Cooper Prize in 1983 and the Whitbread Poetry Award in 1988, was awarded the Gold Medal for Australian Literature in 1990, and in 2002 the Queen's Gold Medal for Poetry and the Forward Prize for Best Poetry Collection of the Year for his volume *Max is Missing*. He is a prolific reviewer and broadcaster on both literature and classical music. He is a Visiting Professor of Poetry at The Nottingham Trent University and his collection of literary essays, *Saving from the Wreck*, was published by Trent Books in 2001.

GARETH REEVES is Reader in English at the University of Durham. He is the author of *T. S. Eliot: A Virgilian Poet* (1989); *T. S. Eliot's 'The Waste Land'* (1994); two volumes of poetry; and with Michael O'Neill, of *Auden, MacNeice, Spender: The Thirties Poetry* (1992). He has also published essays on more recent poets, including Donald Davie, Thom Gunn, Seamus Heaney, Robert Lowell and Charles Tomlinson.

IAN SANSOM is a freelance journalist, reviewer and critic whose Oxford DPhil examined Auden's influence on a range of British and American poets. His essay on Randall Jarrell and Auden appeared in *Auden Studies III*. He is the author of *The Truth About Babies* (2002) and *Ring Road* (2004).

TONY SHARPE teaches at Lancaster University, where he specialises in modern and American literature and formerly headed the Department of English. His published books include studies of Vladimir Nabokov, T. S. Eliot and Wallace Stevens, and he is currently writing the *Complete Critical Guide to W. H. Auden*. Alongside this he is working on a project exploring Auden's references to locations in the North of England and his lead-mining interests.

STAN SMITH is Research Professor in Literary Studies at Nottingham Trent University, previously held the Established Chair of English at Dundee University and has been Visiting Professor at Florence and Zaragoza Universities. He has published two books and many essays on Auden. Other work includes *Inviolable Voice: History and Twentieth-Century Poetry* (1982); *Edward Thomas* (1986); *W. B. Yeats: A Critical Introduction* (1990); *The Origins of Modernism: Eliot, Pound, Yeats and the Rhetorics of Renewal* (1994); an edition of Storm Jameson's *In The Second Year* (2004); and numerous essays on modern and contemporary literature. *Ireland Between Fantasy and History: Irish Poetry and the Construction of Modern Identity* will be published in 2005. He is currently preparing a variorum edition of *The Orators*; a book on *The Descent of Modernism*; a survey of modernist poetry; and various collections.

TIM YOUNGS is Professor of English and Travel Studies at The Nottingham Trent University. He is the author of *Travellers in Africa* (1994) and has co-edited with Peter Hulme *The Cambridge Companion to Travel Writing* (2002) and with Glenn Hooper *Perspectives on Travel Writing* (2004). He is founder editor of the journal *Studies in Travel Writing*.

# ABBREVIATIONS AND TEXTUAL NOTE

Unless otherwise indicated, poems quoted in this volume are from W. H. Auden, *Collected Poems*, ed. Edward Mendelson (London: Faber and Faber; New York: Random House, 1976; revised and reset edition, 1991). See also chapter 19 in this volume, Bibliographic essay. All quotations from Auden's published work are © The Estate of W. H. Auden. Extracts from unpublished writings are © 2004 The Estate of W. H. Auden.

| | |
|---|---|
| Ansen | Alan Ansen, *The Table Talk of W. H. Auden*, ed. Nicholas Jenkins (London: Faber and Faber, 1991) |
| *ASN* | *The W. H. Auden Society Newsletter*; currently published from Department of English, Columbia University, New York, N.Y. 10027, USA. |
| *ASI, ASII, ASIII* | *Auden Studies*, vols. I, II, III, ed. Katherine Bucknell and Nicholas Jenkins (Oxford: Clarendon Press). For details of individual volumes, see chapter 19 in this volume, Bibliographic essay. |
| *AT* | W. H. Auden, *Another Time* (London: Faber and Faber, 1940) |
| Berg | The Henry W. and Albert A. Berg Collection, New York Public Library (Astor, Lenox and Tilden Foundations) |
| Bodleian | The Department of Western Manuscripts, Bodleian Library, Oxford |
| Carpenter | Humphrey Carpenter, *W. H. Auden: A Biography* (London: Faber and Faber, 1981) |
| CW | W. H. Auden, *A Certain World: A Commonplace Book* (London: Faber and Faber, 1970) |
| *DH* | W. H. Auden, *The Dyer's Hand and Other Essays* (London: Faber and Faber, 1963) |

| | |
|---|---|
| *Dogskin* | W. H. Auden and Christopher Isherwood, *The Dog Beneath the Skin or Where is Francis?* (London: Faber and Faber, 1935) |
| *EA* | *The English Auden: Poems, Essays and Dramatic Writings 1927–1939*, ed. Edward Mendelson (London: Faber and Faber, 1977) |
| *Early Auden* | Edward Mendelson, *Early Auden* (London: Faber and Faber, 1981) |
| *EF* | W. H. Auden, *The Enchafèd Flood* (London: Faber and Faber, 1951) |
| *F&A* | W. H. Auden, *Forewords and Afterwords*, selected by Edward Mendelson (London: Faber and Faber, 1973) |
| *F6* | W. H. Auden and Christopher Isherwood, *The Ascent of F6* (London: Faber and Faber, 1936) |
| Fuller 1970 | John Fuller, *A Reader's Guide to W. H. Auden* (London: Faber and Faber, 1970); revised and extended as |
| Fuller 1998 | John Fuller, *W. H. Auden: A Commentary* (London: Faber and Faber, 1998) |
| Haffenden | John Haffenden, *W. H. Auden: The Critical Heritage* (London: Routledge & Kegan Paul, 1983) |
| *JTW* | W. H. Auden and Christopher Isherwood, *Journey to a War* (London: Faber and Faber, 1939) |
| *Later Auden* | Edward Mendelson, *Later Auden* (London: Faber and Faber, 1999) |
| *LFI* | W. H. Auden and Louis MacNeice, *Letters from Iceland* (London: Faber and Faber, 1937) |
| *Lib* | W. H. Auden and Chester Kallman, *Libretti and Other Dramatic Writings, 1939–1973*, ed. Edward Mendelson (London: Faber and Faber; Princeton N.J.: Princeton University Press, 1993) |
| *Light Verse* | W. H. Auden (ed.), *The Oxford Book of Light Verse* (Oxford: Oxford University Press, 1938) |
| *New Verse* | *New Verse Auden Double Number*, nos. 26–7, November 1937, ed. Geoffrey Grigson |
| *NYL* | W. H. Auden, *New Year Letter* (London: Faber and Faber, 1941) |
| Osborne | Charles Osborne, *W. H. Auden: The Life of a Poet* (London: Macmillan, 1980) |
| *Pilgrims* | J. A. Pike, ed., *Modern Canterbury Pilgrims* (Oxford: A. R. Mowbray & Co., 1956) |

| | |
|---|---|
| *Plays* | W. H. Auden and Christopher Isherwood, *Plays and Other Dramatic Writings, 1928–1938,* ed. Edward Mendelson (London: Faber and Faber; Princeton N.J.: Princeton University Press, 1989) |
| *Prose I* | W. H. Auden, *Prose and Travel Books in Prose and Verse, Vol. I: 1926–1938,* ed. Edward Mendelson (London: Faber and Faber; Princeton N.J.: Princeton University Press, 1996) |
| *Prose II* | W. H. Auden, *Prose, Vol. II: 1939–1948,* ed. Edward Mendelson (London: Faber and Faber; Princeton N.J.: Princeton University Press, 2002) |
| *Poet's Tongue* | W. H. Auden and John Garrett (eds.), *The Poet's Tongue* (London: G. Bell & Sons, 1935) |
| RD-H | Richard Davenport-Hines, *Auden* (London: Heinemann, 1995) |
| Smith | Stan Smith, *W. H. Auden* (Oxford: Basil Blackwell, 1985) |
| *Spain* | W. H. Auden, *Spain* (London: Faber and Faber, 1937); published in a revised version as 'Spain 1937' in *Another Time* (1940) |
| *SW* | W. H. Auden, *Secondary Worlds* (London: Faber and Faber, 1968) |
| *The Orators* | W. H. Auden, *The Orators: An English Study* (London: Faber and Faber, 1932; revised editions 1934, 1966) |
| *Tribute* | Stephen Spender, ed., *W. H. Auden: A Tribute* (London: Weidenfeld & Nicolson, 1974) |

| 1907 | | Wystan Hugh Auden born, 21 February, in York, third son of George Augustus Auden (1872–1957) and Constance Rosalie Bicknell (1870–1941). His older brothers were Bernard, in later life a farmer, and John, who became a geologist. |
| 1908 | | When he was six months old, the family moved to Birmingham, where his father became Chief Medical Officer for Schools and Professor of Public Health at Birmingham University. |
| 1914–18 | | The 'Great War'. War declared, 4 August 1914. Dr Auden served in the Royal Army Medical Corps, in Gallipoli, Egypt and France. |
| 1915–20 | | Boarder at St Edmund's Preparatory School, Hindhead, Surrey. Met Christopher Isherwood, a fellow pupil who became a lifelong friend and, in the 1930s, a regular if occasional lover. |
| 1917 | October | Revolution in Russia. |
| 1918 | | Great War ended, November 11. Father returned from the Army ('Father and butter to the table came'). World-wide epidemic of 'Spanish Influenza' killed more people than the whole war. |
| 1920–5 | | Boarder at Gresham's School, Holt, described in his essay 'Honour'. First read Freud and in 1922 fell in love with a fellow pupil, Robert Medley, at whose suggestion he began to write poetry. (Medley contributed a memoir of their schooldays to the *Tribute* edited by Stephen Spender in 1974.) First poem published in the school magazine, attributed to 'W. H. Arden'. |

| | |
|---|---|
| 1925 | Brief, obscure engagement to a nurse in Birmingham. Accompanied his father to Europe, staying in Kitzbühel, Austria, with his father's wartime friend Frau Hedwig Petzold. |
| 1925–8 | Exhibitioner at Christ Church, Oxford, studying Natural Sciences, then PPE (Politics, Philosophy, Economics) under Roy Harrod, and finally English, tutored by Nevill Coghill, graduating with a Third Class degree. Among undergraduates he met there were Stephen Spender, Cecil Day Lewis, Louis MacNeice and Bill McElwee, for whom he developed an unrequited passion. |
| 1926 | Revisited Austria. First heterosexual experience (probably with paternal encouragement) with the considerably older Frau Petzold. During the General Strike, unlike most undergraduates, supported the TUC, driving a vehicle for the strikers. Fellow undergraduate and Strike supporter, Tom Driberg, introduced him to modernist writing, particularly Eliot's *Waste Land*, and to Edith Sitwell, Laura Riding, Virginia Woolf and Gertrude Stein, whom Driberg brought up to speak in Oxford. In later years Driberg was a society gossip columnist on the *Daily Express* (as 'William Hickey'), a war correspondent, Labour MP and peer, and Chairman of the Labour Party, posthumously exposed as a Soviet double agent. In 1926 and 1927 Auden co-edited the undergraduate annual *Oxford Poetry*, first with Charles Plumb and then with C. Day Lewis. |
| 1928 | Auden's *Poems* published privately on a small hand-press by Stephen Spender. August: began a year in Berlin, in company with Isherwood, where he encountered for the first time serious left-wing politics, in the strife-ridden last days of the Weimar Republic. Brief affairs with working-class youths, most of them male prostitutes, including Kurt Groote and Gerhart Meyer, named in the poem later called '1929'. |

| | | |
|---|---|---|
| 1929 | | In Berlin, John Layard tried to involve him in his bungled suicide attempt. Returned from Germany to teach in London. October: the Wall Street Crash inaugurated the Depression years. '1929', begun in Germany, ended in October with auguries of economic and social collapse and the 'death of the Old Gang'. |
| 1930 | | T. S. Eliot arranged publication of 'Paid on Both Sides' in the *Criterion*, and of *Poems* (1930) with Faber and Faber. While teaching (1930–2) at the Larchfield School, Helensburgh (later Larchfield Academy) wrote *The Orators: An English Study*, drawing on many local figures and places. The *Helensburgh and Gareloch Times* records that at the annual Prize Day in 1932 pupils performed a play specially written for them by Auden, *Sherlock Holmes Chez Duhamel* (now lost). Had an intense and ill-starred affair with the son of a Clydebank iron-founder, the prototype of 'Derek my chum' in *The Orators*, with whom he visited the Shetland Islands. |
| 1931 | January | Oswald Mosley left Labour government to form the New Party. 24–5 August: Ramsay MacDonald resigns and forms National Government, with Labour, Conservative and Liberal members. He was expelled from the Labour Party. October 27: MacDonald's National Government wins 558 seats to the Labour opposition's 56 in general election. |
| 1932–5 | | Taught at the Downs School, Colwall, Malvern. |
| 1933 | | Hitler elected German *Reichskanzler*. *The Dance of Death* published, to be performed a year later by the avant-garde experimental Group Theatre under the direction of Rupert Doone. |
| 1934 | | A summer vacation motoring in Germany and Central Europe, penetrating as far as the Carpathians, accompanied by two former pupils of the Downs School, Peter Roger and Michael Yates, with whom Auden was in love, celebrated in the poem 'A Bride in the Thirties'. (A lifelong |

friend, Yates contributed a moving memoir to Spender's *Tribute* volume.) Auden's camp narrative of the expedition published as 'In Search of Dracula' in the Downs school magazine, the *Badger.*

1935            Married Erika Mann, the anti-Nazi, lesbian daughter of the Nobel Prize-winning novelist Thomas Mann, to provide her with a passport to leave Germany. Worked with John Grierson and the GPO Film Unit, writing 'Night Mail' for the documentary film of that name. *The Dog Beneath the Skin*, written jointly with Christopher Isherwood, performed by the Group Theatre.

1936   January    Death of George V and accession of Edward VIII. *The Ascent of F6*, written jointly with Isherwood, performed by the Group Theatre. *Look, Stranger!* published (US title: *On This Island*, 1937). Summer: with Louis MacNeice and Michael Yates, travelled around Iceland. Popular Front governments formed in Spain (February) and France (June). July: Spanish Civil War began with General Franco's insurrection against the elected Republican government. Britain and France declared a policy of 'Non-Intervention'. December: abdication of Edward VIII, succeeded by his younger brother, George VI.

1937            Published *Letters from Iceland*, written jointly with MacNeice. Spent January–March in Valencia, Spain, where he broadcast for the embattled Republic. Published the pamphlet poem *Spain*, all proceeds to Medical Aid for Spain (later reprinted in *Another Time* in revised form as 'Spain 1937'). On his return to Britain, met the writer and theological scholar Charles Williams, who was soon to have an enormous influence on his thought. Taught at the Downs School.

1938            With Isherwood visited a war-torn China, recently invaded by the Japanese Imperial Army, returning via Japan and USA. March: the

*Anschluss*, incorporating Austria into Hitler's Third Reich. September: the Munich Agreement. On behalf of Britain, Prime Minister Neville Chamberlain agreed to the cession of Czech Sudetenland to Hitler. November: the play *On the Frontier*, written jointly with Isherwood, performed by Group Theatre in Cambridge.

1939     The travelogue *Journey to a War*, jointly written with Isherwood. January: Spanish Civil War ended with victory for the right-wing Falangist rebels and a nationwide massacre of supporters of the Republic. Auden and Isherwood left Britain for the United States, where Auden lived in Brooklyn Heights, New York, from 1939 to 1941. Isherwood moved to Hollywood, to work as script-writer for Metro-Goldwyn-Mayer. March: taking advantage of the Munich Agreement and the mood of 'Appeasement', Hitler occupied Prague, the Czech capital. April: in New York, Auden met the eighteen-year-old student Chester Kallman, an aggressively 'out' and promiscuous homosexual who, though Jewish, had the stereotypical 'Aryan' good looks Auden favoured. They were to remain partners, with several turbulent interruptions, for the rest of their lives.

24 August     The Nazi-Soviet Pact between Germany and the Soviet Union agreed the partition of Poland. 1 September: Hitler invaded Poland, followed shortly by Stalin. 3 September: Britain and France declared war on Germany. Widespread disillusion on the Left led to divisions both within and outside the Communist movement, reflected in the poems of *Another Time*.

1940     *Another Time*, technically his first American volume, but with poems primarily written in Europe. Taught at the New School for Social Research, New York. Met Reinhold and Ursula Niebuhr, Christian Socialist Americans of German extraction, who were to have a profound influence on his later thinking. Under their guidance, he came to reject the pacifism towards which he had been drifting, and redis-covered a politically and socially committed Christianity.

| | |
|---|---|
| 1941 | His first real American book, *The Double Man* (published in Britain as *New Year Letter*). Benjamin Britten's operetta *Paul Bunyan*, for which Auden wrote the libretto, performed at Columbia University. Taught at Olivet College, Michigan, and Michigan University, Ann Arbor. |
| 1942–5 | Taught at Swarthmore and Bryn Mawr Colleges. |
| 1944 | *For the Time Being* published in the USA. Met Rhoda Jaffe, with whom he was to have an intermittent and intense sexual relationship between 1945 and 1948. |
| 1945 | The Second World War ended with the fall of Berlin, followed by the atom-bombing of Japan. Labour Government elected in Britain. Death of Roosevelt. Auden returned to Europe (via the UK) as a major in the US Airforce Strategic Bombing Survey, charged to monitor the effects of civilian bombing and to contact anti-Nazis known before the war. Moved to 7 Middagh Street, in Brooklyn Heights, New York. *Collected Poetry* published in USA. |
| 1946 | Became US citizen. Taught at Bennington College and New School for Social Research. Prolonged affair with Rhoda Jaffe. |
| 1947 | Taught religion at Barnard College. *The Age of Anxiety* published. |
| 1949 | Gave the Page-Barbour Lectures at University of Virginia, published as *The Enchafèd Flood* (1950). Communists under Mao Tse Tung seized power in China. |
| 1949–57 | Rented each spring and summer a villa on Ischia, a small island off Naples, Italy. |
| 1950 | *Collected Shorter Poems 1939–1944* published in UK. Taught at Mount Holyoke College. Korean War began, focusing the new |

Cold War with the Soviet Union which succeeded the wartime alliance against Hitler.

1951    Labour Government ousted in Britain. Auden's old friend and possible former lover, Guy Burgess, for many years undetected as a Soviet spy in the Foreign Office, sought to use Auden's Ischian villa as a staging-post on his flight to Russia. *Nones* published in the USA. Stravinsky's *The Rake's Progress*, for which Auden and Kallman wrote the libretto, performed in Venice.

1953    Death of Stalin. Berlin Uprising brutally suppressed. Lives (until 1972) at 77 St Mark's Place, Greenwich Village; Research Professor, Smith College.

1955    *The Shield of Achilles* published.

1956    Khrushchev's denunciation of Stalin's 'cult of personality' at 20th Congress of CPSU. Hungarian Uprising and Suez Crisis. Succeeded Day Lewis as Professor of Poetry at Oxford University, an honorary elective appointment (until 1961).

1958    With the proceeds of an Italian literary prize, bought a farmhouse in the village of Kirchstetten, Lower Austria, shared with Kallman until his death. In later years Kallman spent much of his time in Athens, where he had short-lived affairs with a series of young Greek men.

1960    *Homage to Clio* published.

1961    Hans Werner Henze's *Elegy for Young Lovers*, libretto by Auden and Kallman, performed in Stuttgart.

1962    *The Dyer's Hand* published in USA. October: a casual boyfriend, Hugerl, a young Viennese rent-boy and petty criminal, sentenced to fifteen months' gaol for a robbery in which he used Auden's Volkswagen as a getaway car, leaving it with a bullet-hole in the bonnet (see the poem 'Glad').

1963    Assassination of President Kennedy. Growing US involvement in Vietnam.

| | | |
|---|---|---|
| 1964 | | Revisited Iceland. Six months Ford Foundation artists-in-residence programme, Berlin. October: Labour Government elected in Britain, Khrushchev ousted, China's first atom bomb tested, all on the same day. |
| 1965 | | *About the House* published. |
| 1966 | | Henze's *The Bassarids*, with libretto by Auden and Kallman, performed in Salzburg. *Collected Shorter Poems* published. |
| 1968 | | Têt offensive in Vietnam. May Events in Paris. Soviet invasion of Czechoslovakia. *Collected Longer Poems* and *Secondary Worlds* published. |
| 1969 | | *City Without Walls* published. |
| 1970 | | Commonplace book, *A Certain World*, published in USA. |
| 1971 | | *Academic Graffiti* published. |
| 1972 | | While at All Souls, Oxford, robbed by a young labourer he had befriended. Lived in a cottage in the grounds of his old college, Christ Church. Published *Epistle to a Godson*, dedicated to Spender's nephew Philip. |
| 1973 | | Nicholas Nabokov's *Love's Labours Lost*, with libretto by Auden and Kallman, performed in Brussels. *Forewords and Afterwords*, edited by Edward Mendelson. |
| | 29 September | After delivering a talk in Vienna, died of heart attack in a small hotel in the Walfischgasse, close to the Staatsoper. Buried in the Kirchstetten churchyard. |
| 1974 | | Posthumous collection, *Thank You, Fog* published, edited by Edward Mendelson. |
| 1975 | January | Kallman died in Athens, aged fifty-four. |

# I

STAN SMITH

# Introduction

'Of the many definitions of poetry, the simplest is still the best: "memorable speech"', W. H. Auden wrote in the Introduction to his 1935 anthology, *The Poet's Tongue* (*Poet's Tongue*, p. v). Auden is one of the few modern poets whose words inhabit the popular memory. Long before the recitation of 'Funeral Blues' in the film *Four Weddings and a Funeral*, many of his phrases had passed into common use. His characterisation in 'September 1, 1939' of the 1930s as a 'low dishonest decade' has become definitive and ubiquitous, invoked even in quarters not normally associated with high literacy. Dan Quayle, for example, announcing his 1999 Presidential candidacy, applied it to the Clinton years. This poem alone has supplied titles for countless books, including studies of the economic origins of World War II (*A Low Dishonest Decade*), Soviet espionage (*The Haunted Wood*), the history of saloons (*Faces Along the Bar*) and a play about AIDS (*The Normal Heart*). Such diverse co-options indicate the range of reference Auden can pack into a single poem.

Ironically, a poem Auden rapidly disowned has become one of the most widely cited modern texts. Written in a 'dive' on New York's Fifty-Second Street on the day Germany invaded Poland, it took on a whole new significance after 11 September 2001. The *Times Literary Supplement*'s 'Letter from New York' after those events reported that Auden's words were now everywhere, reprinted in many major newspapers, read on national Public Radio and featured in hundreds of web chat-rooms. Students at Stuyvesant High, four blocks from Ground Zero, included the poem in a special issue of their newspaper distributed free by the *New York Times*, stressing its closing admonition: 'We must love one another or die.' Only rarely, however, did a country reeling from this assault on its security acknowledge the moral at the poem's heart: 'those to whom evil is done / Do evil in return'. Indeed, a nation in denial as well as in shock slapped down as un-American the few voices that dared draw the lesson which, the poem insists, all schoolchildren learn.

*The Concise Oxford Dictionary of Quotations* (1993) contains forty citations from Auden's work, shrewdly succinct observations such as that on Yeats ('silly like us'), and semi-aphoristic opening lines like those of 'Musée des Beaux Arts' or concluding ones, as in *Spain*'s reflections on an unforgiving history. Auden shares with Yeats (fifty citations) and T. S. Eliot (fifty-seven citations) a talent for turning the memorable phrase. But what distinguishes him is the *range* of his emotional and verbal reference. No one else strikes roots in such diverse areas of the collective linguistic unconscious as Auden. Even Yeats cannot match the range revealed by the *Dictionary of Quotations*, which extends from the lyric melancholy of 'Lay your sleeping head', through the gnomic utterances of the dense early poetry and the political intensities of the 1930s, to the brash demotic formula a former Tory Minister for Education, Kenneth Baker, adopted in 1980 as the title for an anthology of 'satirical and abusive verse': *I Have No Gun, But I Can Spit*.

Such responses testify to an ambivalent aspect of Auden's verse: its ability, as he put it in 'We Too Had Known Golden Hours', to sing from the 'resonant heart', with words that over the decades accrue new significances and establish new connections between some original complex of particulars and later ones. That poem also registered the dangers of such a talent: one's words may be hijacked, 'soiled, profaned, debased', 'pawed-at and gossiped-over' by the public, or concocted by meretricious editors into 'spells that befuddle the crowd'. In 1939, newly arrived in New York, Auden spoke at a dinner to raise money for Spanish refugees. The speech's success provoked a bout of self-contempt. As he wrote to a friend a few months later, 'I suddenly found I could really do it, that I could make a fighting demagogic speech and have the audience roaring. I felt just covered with dirt afterwards' (Carpenter, p. 256). Auden knew his poetry could have a similar effect. The self-loathing of the reformed sinner lies behind his expulsion of 'September 1, 1939', 'A Communist to Others' and even the revised 'Spain 1937' from his *Collected Shorter Poems* in 1966. A Foreword explained that such poems had been excised because they were 'dishonest', expressing feelings or beliefs he had never held, 'simply because it sounded to me rhetorically effective'.

This somewhat rhetorical attempt to wring rhetoric's neck echoes Yeats echoing Verlaine. There is some irony in this, since it was Yeats Auden blamed for what a letter to Stephen Spender called in 1964 'my own devil of unauthenticity . . . false emotions, inflated rhetoric, empty sonorities'. Yeats may indeed have made him 'whore after lies' (*Early Auden*, p. 206). But in 1941 he had explicated a punning line in *New Year Letter*, 'There lies the gift of double focus', with a note to the effect that the Devil is 'indeed, the father of

Poetry, for poetry might be defined as the clear expression of mixed feelings'. An equally emphatic pronouncement in 1968 in *Secondary Worlds* declared that 'It is with good reason that the devil is called the Father of lies', in the context of distinguishing 'the White magic of poetry' from the verbal 'Black Magic' of propaganda, which practises 'enchantment as a way of securing domination over others'. For millions of people today words like communism, capitalism and imperialism, peace, freedom and democracy, he wrote, have 'ceased to be words, the meaning of which can be enquired into and discussed', and have become instead 'right or wrong noises to which the response is as involuntary as a knee-reflex' (*SW*, pp. 126–9).

The situation is actually a little more complicated. 'Art poétique', Verlaine's poem denouncing rhetoric, commends the 'chanson grise' (grey song, neither black nor white) where ambiguity is joined to precision, opening itself to 'other skies' and 'other loves'. But this is only a different kind of rhetoric, posturing flamboyantly in the very refusal to take sides. Auden's gift of double focus performs a similar function. Indeed, his art is often at its richest when it testifies, rhetorically, to just such mixed feelings and nebulous horizons. With unabashed chutzpah, his 1939 sonnet about Verlaine's lover Rimbaud speaks of 'the rhetorician's lie' bursting like a frozen pipe to make a poet. As he wrote in his elegy for Yeats, 'the words of a dead man / Are modified in the guts of the living'. But it is in part rhetorical contrivance which ensures their resurrection as apparently direct responses to events they could not possibly have foreseen.

From his first public collection, *Poems* (1930), Auden was everywhere in the 1930s, both text and talisman. Naomi Mitchison in *The Week-end Review*, 25 October 1930, welcomed the volume as the harbinger of 'the New Generation', proof that 'the country is not going to the dogs after all'. Dylan Thomas carried around a copy of the volume until it fell to pieces. In 1932 John Hayward, the keeper of T. S. Eliot's critical conscience, wrote of *The Orators* as 'the most valuable contribution to English poetry since *The Waste Land*' (Haffenden, p. 114). The 'Auden effect' lay in that ability to catch the changing moods of the time in luminous images, magical phrases and breathtaking aperçus, expressing sentiments that people were unaware they shared until they read him. Such sentiments were often decidedly political, indicting a disintegrating social and economic system ripe for fascism, and propagating an alternative future in the form of a woolly, undefined 'communism' which bore little relation to the brutalities of Stalin's Soviet Union.

Auden's poems, however, also had a distinctive personal timbre, the sense of a vulnerable, embattled self which made them iconic to a generation whose psychic integrity seemed to be threatened by the impersonal forces of a history out of control. 'Consider this and in our time' defined the stance of a generation, looking down on its culture with disdainful detachment from the Olympian heights of hawk or airman. Another poem set that generation's agenda as the quest for 'New styles of architecture, a change of heart'. The question at the start of *The Orators* in 1932, 'What do you think about England, this country of ours where nobody is well?' was asked with varying degrees of anxiety throughout the decade. The title poem of his major collection of 1936, *Look, Stranger!*, invited its readers to look without illusions on contemporary Britain, 'this island now'.

If Auden was the unremitting critic of 'our time', a large part of his appeal lay in the verbal and imagistic ferocity, the rhetorical splendour, of his denunciations and dissections. His readers went to his poetry to make their flesh crawl. Auden was himself sufficiently shrewd to recognise and manipulate such impure motives. Thirty years later, in *Secondary Worlds*, the poet who in 1939 had written in *Journey to a War* of places 'where life is evil now: / Nanking, Dachau', argued that to write or attend a play about Auschwitz would be 'wicked', for 'author and audience may try to pretend that they are morally horrified, but in fact they are passing an entertaining evening together, in the aesthetic enjoyment of horrors' (p. 84). In a similar vein, *A Certain World* in 1970 observed that Christmas and Easter could be subjects for poetry, but, like Auschwitz, not Good Friday, the reality of which was too horrible even for many Christians to contemplate. Yet in 1951 the crucifixion had provided the subject for the title poem of *Nones*, and became part of a major sequence of poems about Good Friday, 'Horae Canonicae', in *The Shield of Achilles* (1955), a contradiction unpicked here by Gareth Reeves.

Auden's apparently tough-minded attitude towards the bad faith of art is focused in a much-cited and decidedly rhetorical axiom of 'In Memory of W. B. Yeats': 'poetry makes nothing happen'. This somewhat dubious claim has become a truism of debates about the social function of art. But Auden's poetry, modified in the guts of innumerable successors, has certainly made happen innumerable later poems, by writers as diverse as East European dissidents like Joseph Brodsky, postcolonial poets of exile and deracination like Dom Moraes and Derek Walcott, and playful postmodernists like New York's John Ashbery, Northern Ireland's Paul Muldoon or Yorkshire's Simon Armitage, for all of whom Auden's verbal 'polymorphous perversity' has been exemplary. By contrast, the plays he wrote in collaboration with Christopher Isherwood for the left-wing Group and Unity Theatres, widely admired in the 1930s, have had little subsequent influence, though Eliot learned much about Brechtian alienation techniques from their example.

The plays remain, nevertheless, the most significant British attempt to break with the traditions of bourgeois realism, as Christopher Innes demonstrates, drawing their models of dramatic artifice from 'charade' ('Paid on Both Sides'), 'tragedy' (F6), and 'melodrama' (*On the Frontier*), and giving a political edge, as Harold Hobson noted at the time, even to the forms of musical comedy. Auden's deconstructive dramaturgy incorporated song and dance (*The Dance of Death*) as well as parodying and pastiching other performative elements: a mock trial in *F6*, cabaret in *Dogskin*, mock sermons, perorations, encomia variously, devices from mummers' plays and Norse sagas in 'Paid'. 'For the Time Being' (1944), subtitled 'A Christmas Oratorio', contains a whole range of liturgical and religious forms, including those of miracle and nativity play. Its accompanying text, 'The Sea and the Mirror', is billed as a 'Commentary' on *The Tempest*, delivered as a series of dramatic monologues by characters from Shakespeare's play. *The Age of Anxiety* (1945), dubbed 'A Baroque Eclogue', for which Leonard Bernstein composed a symphony, intersperses dramatic monologues and dialogues with narrative, and contains a 'Masque'. Starting with *Paul Bunyan*, Auden wrote a series of libretti for operas, largely in collaboration with Chester Kallman. The latter works are now beginning to attract new critical interest, as speculatively 'postmodern' multi-media texts which subvert traditional genres.

Mould-breaking was Auden's forte. By the time of the Auden Double Number of *New Verse* in 1937, he was the undisputed uncrowned laureate of the age; and yet, as Geoffrey Grigson argued there, 'Auden does not fit', and his representativeness, his power to speak for his times, emerged from this very anomalousness: 'Auden is a monster', Grigson wrote, but he is 'an able monster', by definition therefore a being 'extremely difficult to measure up or confine'. 'The era in which Auden has grown up', Grigson concluded, 'has been one of bewildered mediocrity, triviality and fudge', justifying his refusal to 'obey the codes':

> But when a monster who writes so much is so fidgety and inquisitive, so interested in things and ideas, so human and generous, and so rude to the infinite, it does not matter at all if the lines of his development are twisted and obscure, if he writes plenty of verse which is slack, ordinary, dull, or silly . . .

By 1940 it mattered a great deal. The virtues of the past decade had become vices. Criticised by Christopher Caudwell in 1937, from an orthodox Communist position, as 'anarchist, nihilist and *surréaliste*', 'glorify[ing] the revolution as a kind of giant explosion which will blow up everything they feel to be hampering them',[1] Auden found himself attacked in 1940 by George Orwell, in 'Inside the Whale', for presenting in *Spain* 'a sort of thumb-nail sketch of a day in the life of "a good party man"', and giving callow approval to the politically 'necessary murder'.[2] The same year, Grigson's monster 'rude to the infinite' was cabined and confined in what sounds like an obituary in the Catholic journal *The Tablet* by Martin Turnell. If Auden spoke for a generation it was now because he was silly like them: 'For the tragedy of this generation was not the tragedy of too little faith, but of too much. It lay in the uncritical acceptance of all the revolutionary slogans of its time which led to the waste and destruction of its immense abilities' (Haffenden, p. 36). The ground has here been prepared for postwar constructions of a rather different Auden.

The foremost of these arose from what was almost universally seen at the time as Auden's 'desertion' to a neutral United States on the eve of war, which was coupled with an apparent abandonment of Leftist politics. It is difficult now to imagine the fury with which this was greeted not only by his regular detractors but by those who had previously been his most ardent fans. The early reservations of his friend Cyril Connolly set the tone for what was to become a critical orthodoxy in the postwar period. Connolly, who boasted of having invented the concept of the 'Homintern' and the characterisation of the Auden group as the 'Pylon Boys', was already in 1936 impatient with what he called 'the authentic rallying cries of homo-communism' in Auden's verse, and offered his considered conclusion – 'the point of view', he admitted, 'of the anarchic 1920s about the political 1930s' – that Auden was 'essentially an obscure, difficult, personal writer'. Reviewing *Spain* in 1937 he added that 'the Marxian theory of history does not go very happily into verse', and claimed that 'Lay your sleeping head', 'Auden's non-pamphleteering love lyric [was] by far the best thing' in his recent work, 'and utterly without political purpose' (Haffenden, pp. 187–8, 238–9).

Connolly's *Enemies of Promise* (1938), which Auden regarded as one of the best books of contemporary criticism, attributed the failure of the Auden generation to that state of 'permanent adolescence' induced by a British public school education. Stephen Spender, within a few years to renounce his own 1930s fellow-travelling in his autobiography, *World Within World* (1951), could still in a 1941 review of *Another Time* reproach Auden for running away from the 'struggle'. Auden's hurt response queried his old friend's 'assumption of the role of the blue-eyed Candid Incorruptible', which he found 'questionable', and replied that 'the intellectual warfare goes on always and everywhere, and no one has the right to say that this place or that time is where all intellectuals ought to be' (Osborne, pp. 206–7). Nicholas Jenkins in the present volume rightly stresses Auden's genuine patriotism.

But as John Lucas's chapter demonstrates, there is no reason at all why one praised by William Plomer in 1932 for 'a brilliant attack on English staleness, dullness and complacency' (Haffenden, p. 95), should after Munich have harboured any sentimental affection for a venal and hypocritical British establishment.

Postwar British critics tended to follow Spender in seeing expatriation as causing a decline in Auden's poetic powers. John Wain claimed in 1955, of 'the Auden line', that 'what smashed it . . . was Auden's renunciation of English nationality' (Haffenden, p. 40). The conviction of failing powers lies behind the rhetorical question asked in Philip Larkin's 1960 retrospective in the *Spectator*: 'What's become of Wystan?' For the younger Larkin, Auden 'was, of course, the first "modern" poet', not just in his ability to 'employ modern properties unselfconsciously' but primarily in the 'dominant and ubiquitous unease' at the heart of his poetry. Auden's 'outlook was completely dislocated', therefore, when prewar anxiety ceased with the outbreak of war and his simultaneous absconding: 'At one stroke he lost his key subject and emotion – Europe and the fear of war – and abandoned his audience together with their common dialect and concerns.' For Auden, Larkin argued, the damage was 'irreparable'. His work was taken over by 'a certain abstract windiness' which ensured that *New Year Letter* was merely a 'rambling intellectual stew', 'The Sea and the Mirror' 'an unsuccessful piece of literary inbreeding', and 'For the Time Being' 'too often chilly . . . or silly'. As for *The Age of Anxiety*, Larkin continued, 'I never finished it, and have never met anyone who has.' Larkin offered a vague hope for the future: 'If his poetry could once take root again in the life surrounding him rather than in his reading', then we might see a new Auden, 'a *New Yorker* Walt Whitman viewing the American scene through lenses coated with European irony'. But the 'poetic pressure' was not high in the recent work, which seemed little more than 'agreeable and ingenious essays'. Auden, he concluded, 'has not adopted America or taken root, but has pursued an individual and cosmopolitan path which has precluded the kind of identification that seemed so much a part of his previous successes'.[3]

A parallel case was argued by the American poet Randall Jarrell, who mourned the lost leader's resiling from a tough-minded secular humanism as a sign of 'the decline and fall of modernist poetry', 'a waste of . . . the greatest powers'.[4] The prevailing US consensus, however, saw Auden's reputation as an *American* poet grow apace, consolidated by his assumption of US citizenship in 1946. During the Cold War era, the increasing professionalisation of literary criticism in the American academy found in Auden a ready candidate for exegesis in scholarly dissertation and monograph. Much of this early enthusiasm for the later Auden drew sustenance from his return to a somewhat unorthodox Christianity inspired by Charles Williams, Kierkegaard and Reinhold Niebuhr.

Isherwood had written in *New Verse* in 1937 that, though 'the Anglicanism has evaporated . . . he is still much preoccupied with ritual', so that 'when we collaborate, I have to keep a sharp eye on him – or down flop the characters on their knees . . . If Auden had his way, he would turn every play into a cross between grand opera and high mass.' This is astute as well as prophetic. It was as much an aesthetic choice, the appeal of liturgy and ritual, of Kierkegaard's existentialist or Martin Buber's 'I / Thou' theology, that led to Auden's return to the Anglican faith after 1940. St Augustine's Heavenly City furnished opportunities to talk about the earthly city, and even that prolonged meditation on Good Friday, 'Horae Canonicae', has an odour of incense and play-acting about it. The parsonical tone was nothing new. His supposedly secular poetry of the 1930s carried its own freight of Christian, particularly Pauline baggage, the fruits of a pious Anglican upbringing. As late as 1965 he could write that 'I feel myself sufficiently close to Mr Waugh theologically and to Mr Woolf politically to act as a moderator' (*F&A*, p. 493), remaining what he had mocked in 'Letter to Lord Byron', 'a foolish pink old liberal to the end'. At times it almost seems as if the doctrine of Original Sin, like that of Historical Necessity before it, had been invented to get him out of moral scrapes. Auden was always a materialist, his theology centred in a radical conception of the Incarnation. The posthumously published 'No, Plato, No' could not imagine anything he would less like to be than 'a disincarnate Spirit', unable to chew, sip or touch physical surfaces. 'Whitsunday in Kirchstetten' (1962) draws a sceptical anthropological parallel between those in church on this holy day / holiday and the 'car-worshippers' outside who 'enact / the ritual exodus from Vienna / their successful cult demands'. Auden certainly underwent spiritual reinvention in the 1940s. A sense of the numinous pervades all his work, and he continued to deploy Christian motifs to the end. But they seem, to one critic at least, increasingly to resemble those 'metaphors for poetry' delivered by Yeats's spirit voices.

Auden's Americanisation was always a matter of playing at being what he had chosen to become. His Introduction to *The Faber Book of Modern American Verse* attempted to distinguish his new environment from a ruined Europe, at the level both of linguistic nuance and of the sociopolitical macrocosm, quoting Goethe's observation, 'things are easier for you, America, than for this old continent of ours; you have no ruins of fortresses, no basalt intrusions', glossing the latter as 'meaning, I presume, no violent political revolutions'.[5] In 'Prologue at Sixty' Auden spoke of himself not as an American but a New Yorker, though born in old York in Edwardian England – one 'whose dream images date him already'. He remained to the end what the US title of his first American volume had proclaimed him, a 'Double Man'.

That doubleness Auden had summed up, in the undergraduate magazine *Oxford Poetry* he edited in 1927, as 'the psychological conflict between self as subject and self as object' (*Prose 1*, p. 4). The Ode to his pupils near the end of *The Orators* depicted school as a kind of guerrilla warfare in which the frontier is everywhere and nowhere. The anguished retitling of the poem later, 'Which Side Am I Supposed To Be On?', indicates what is happening on this shifting frontier. A schoolmaster in a public school, only recently a schoolboy himself, Auden inscribes in the duplicity of the text's many voices the crisis of a consciousness belatedly recognising its own contradictory subject-position, as simultaneously patient, carrier and agent of power-relations that originate outside but penetrate every aspect of the self. This was the tenor of a shrewd critique by Irvin Ehrenpreis, which spoke of 'his habit of playing solemn games with his categories, especially with certain divisions between opposed sides', games with language and reality alike which allowed him to disclose 'the way the commonplace hides the extraordinary, and the outside of things grows from and yet misrepresents their inside' (Haffenden, pp. 499–500). Lincoln Kirstein, pursuing the analogy of guerrilla warfare in reviewing *Journey to a War*, thought this made him 'a really dangerous person', who 'threatens even our most recent and difficultly entrenched ideas' and 'employs pragmatic treachery to every preconceived poetic formula', recruiting allies from any English poet from Beowulf to Byron, and successively scrapping them, to open 'a new front' when it suited (Haffenden, p. 299).

Such a perception makes sense of that 'improvisatory' quality to which English moralist critics such as F. R. Leavis and Donald Davie have objected. Kirstein was right to link the moral and political positions to a stylistic one. Auden's use of pastiche and parody, his sleeping-around with poetic forms and his plagiarising of other poets' voices, constitute a deliberate assault on the idea of the autonomous authentic self, speaking with its own unique accents. All art is ventriloquism, he implies, and the discourses which shape our identity are impermanent, continually shifting. The poet always speaks from 'Another Time', the 'Double Man' remains a double agent, his heart set on the spy's career, and his playfulness, like that of the 'Flying Trickster' evoked in *The Orators*, an earnest of good faith.

*New Year Letter* announces that 'England to me is my own tongue', and a double relation to Englishness and the English language is central to both his British and American 'identities'. It is significant that Patrick Deane's chapter here views the 'English Auden' in the light of his American exodus, while Nicholas Jenkins examines Auden's American sojourn in the perspective of a continuing 'Englishness'. With characteristic slipperiness, Auden in later life deconstructed such binaries by adopting a third provisional location, reinventing himself as a European, taking up residence in Italy and then Austria, becoming, as he suggested in one poem, 'a minor Atlantic Goethe', and commuting between two worlds become much like each other in the accelerating logic of globalisation. Auden played self-consciously at being an English 'metic' in New York and an 'American abroad' in Europe, enjoying a double expatriation, in which each less than absolute allegiance simultaneously reinforced and yet relativised the other. While proclaiming his Americanness, he wrote of both Italy and Austria as places where he felt 'at home' as never before, and of his European residence as a kind of homecoming. Whereas the years of his exclusive American residence, years of world war and postwar reconstruction, are characterised by the fraught Kierkegaardian title of his 1947 work, *The Age of Anxiety*, there is a decidedly more relaxed tone from *Nones* (1951) onwards. There are poems of bitter disenchantment in *The Shield of Achilles*, but the volume closes with the complex and major harmonies of the sequence 'Horae Canonicae', working its way through to the absolution and self-reconciliations of his later years.

Traditional readings of Auden's sexuality concurred with Allan Rodway that, 'Its influence on his work, were it not known of, would be literarily imperceptible; known, it is negligible.'[6] The position coincided with Auden's own view and with the ascendant New Critical orthodoxy in the decades after the Second World War. Ground-breaking studies by Gregory Woods and Richard Bozorth[7] have reinstated Auden's homosexuality as a determining context of his poetry, underpinning its allusive infrastructure, informing his ideas about *Homo Ludens*, and adding a second order of discourse to many poems which can be read 'straight', revealing, as *F6* put it, that 'there is always another story, there is more than meets the eye'. Many of the early love poems encode homosexual as heterosexual relations, by a change of noun or pronoun, as for example the consummate love letter tricked out as 'A Bride in the Thirties'. While Auden's own critical pronouncements insisted that love poetry should be universal and not gender-specific, he also in '"The Truest Poetry is the Most Feigning"' reminds us of poets' traditional subterfuge in dissembling the addressee of a poem, with politic cunning converting a love lyric into a celebration of the dictator who has just seized power. According to Bozorth, 'practicing queer identity in all its contradictions between public and private, universality and marginality' (*Auden's Games of Knowledge*,

p. 254), Auden's work 'embodies a process of homosexual self-interrogation with few parallels in modernist literature', 'a staging of public and private selves through a range of codings of queer desire' (p. 3).

Not that Auden's ontology can be easily recruited to 'postmodern' ideas of 'performativity' and 'self-fashioning', aware as he was of the vast weight of social and cultural conditioning which determines individual identity. In *Journey to a War* he transformed into poetry Engels's blunt materialist credo that freedom is the recognition of necessity. But neither could that ontology be dissolved back into older Romantic and humanist ideas of the self. Coleridge's 'Dejection: An Ode' expresses an ambition 'haply by abstruse research to steal / From my own nature all the natural man', assuming that the end of all that intellectual effort will be the revelation of an essential and shared human nature. Such essentialism is precisely what Auden reacted against in his quarrel with Romanticism. His Introduction to the Romantics volume of the *Viking Portable Poets of the English Language* concludes that central to 'the Romantic definition of Man' is the conviction that the 'divine element in man' lies in self-consciousness: 'man can say "I": his ego stands over against his self, which to the ego is a part of nature'.[8] This makes the ego the hero of all its discourses, represented at its most extreme by Coleridge's famous definition in chapter XIII of *Biographia Literaria* (1817) of the Imagination as 'the living Power and prime Agent of all human Perception, and as a repetition in the finite mind of the eternal act of creation in the infinite I AM'.

Auden's idea of the self is quite different. In his Foreword to a young poet's first collection,[9] he denounced Stephen Dedalus's remark, in *Ulysses*, that history is a nightmare from which he is trying to awake as an impossible ambition, since 'it is precisely this attempt to escape being a historical creature that makes man's history a nightmare'. Trying to live 'the natural, unhistorical life' is simply foolish, for there is no 'natural man' to find. Sartre summarised existentialist philosophy with the aphorism that a waiter is only a man acting the part of a waiter. Auden would take this argument to its logical conclusion: a man is only someone acting the part of a man. '"The Truest Poetry is the Most Feigning"' picks up Shakespeare's dramatist's insight into the artifice of identity, when all the world's a stage, to cast 'Man' as a 'self-made creature who himself unmakes, / The only creature ever made who fakes', who has 'no more nature in his loving smile' than in all his 'theories of a natural style'. If 'Man' has a nature, it lies (a recurrent Audenesque pun) in this very capacity to make himself up, in a 'lying nature', inhabiting a universe of 'tall tales' and 'verbal playing'. Clues to a different conception of selfhood can be found, Auden's Introduction to the *Viking* anthology suggests, in Goethe's Faust, who seduces Marguerite and engages in humanitarian works not because he really wants to do this but because he 'wants to know what it feels like to be a seducer and a benefactor' (p. xvi).

Such beliefs were reinforced by Auden's extensive readings in anthropology, ethnology and psychology. For Auden, the writer, like the teacher described in 'The Liberal Fascist', 'must, to use a phrase of Mr Gerald Heard's, and I know no better, "be an anthropologist"' (*Prose I*, p. 61). The correspondences recent critics have discerned between Auden and the psychoanalytic theories of Jacques Lacan are not in the event entirely surprising, since Lacan's landmark paper on 'the Mirror Phase', first delivered at an international conference in 1939, owed as much to the same French surrealists who influenced Auden's early writings as it did to their other mutual mentor, Sigmund Freud. Auden's sense of the constructed nature of the self, and of the body's hegemony over consciousness, in such writings as 'Psychology and Art To-day' (1935), his essay in *Education To-day – and Tomorrow* (1939) and his review in 1960 of Erik Erikson's *Young Man Luther*, was in some ways more radical than Lacan's linguistic idealism, exemplified not only in the poetry of his avant-garde youth, but in such works of a supposedly conservative old age as 'A New Year Greeting' (1969), with its playful concern for the yeasts, bacteria and viruses for whom his ectoderm is the equivalent of 'Middle-Earth' for the poet. In Berlin in 1929, through the good graces of John Layard and Magnus Hirschfeld's *Institut für Sexual-Wissenschaft*, Auden had become persuaded of the psychosomatic origins of behaviour and identity, expressed notoriously in his reference to 'the liar's quinsy'. 'Letter to Lord Byron' went so far as to assert, following Freud, that 'No one thinks unless a trauma makes them', and urged the positive value of 'neurosis' in the creation of a robust ego. As a physical body endowed with sentience, the dualistic self occupies an interface between freedom and necessity, self-fashioning and biological and cultural determinism.

One of Auden's earliest poems foregrounds this liminality in an image he was to make his own, and to donate as a determining chronotope of all post-thirties writing: the frontier. 'On the frontier at dawn getting down' was written in Zagreb in 1927, on what was then the furthest margin of the Eurocentric world. A decade later, the play *On the Frontier* (1938) summed up the way in which this point of transit and return had become a symbol of the social and psychological condition of a generation. *Letters from Iceland* (1937), his first major attempt to look at Europe from (almost) the outside, found in the island's isolation from mainstream European culture an exterior viewpoint on all that had once been taken for granted, including the poet's own privileged middle-class status. Each decentring bred another. While he was sojourning in Iceland, civil war broke out in Spain. Going to Spain in 1937 meant crossing another frontier in time and space, to somewhere not really Europe at all but a 'fragment nipped off from hot / Africa', its Moorish past representing difference and danger. The opening of *Spain,* however, prefigured another decentring, its author's mind already elsewhere, assaying the language of size 'spreading to China along the trade-routes'. A year later, the trip to China with Isherwood which produced *Journey to a War* (1939), was similarly decentred. Looking for 'History' in Hankow, the travellers were chastened by news that Hitler had invaded Austria, making the prospect of death on the Yellow River as meaningless and 'provincial' as falling under a bus in Burton-on-Trent.

In *Look, Stranger!* it is pointedly the stranger who can look dispassionately 'on this island now'. This proleptically 'postmodern' sense of the decentredness of subject, place and history alike has led to renewed critical interest in the global perspectives of Auden's travel writings, explored here by Tim Youngs. Eliot and Yeats crossed the Atlantic between Old and New Worlds. Pound's Chinese obsessions largely projected the assumptions of *fin-de-siècle* Europe on to the Orient. Only Auden travelled at large in what came to be called the 'Third World', transgressing the European *limes* in pursuit of an insight into the accelerating logic of globalisation. His early fascination with the abandoned mineshafts and rusting machinery of an English industrial landscape in terminal decline, which found expression in the apocalyptic relish of such poems as 'Get there if you can', grew, in the postwar era, into an urgent sense of a whole planet confronting catastrophe. In this, Auden remained a far-sighted and radical witness. A 'small grove massacred to the last ash' in 'Bucolics' is now a metonymic warning that 'this great society is going smash'. 'Ode to Terminus' depicts a world 'plundered and poisoned' by 'our colossal immodesty'. 'Prologue at Sixty', considering our time, not from the supercilious detachment of hawk or airman but, empathetically, through the eyes of a helpless canine astronaut, looks down from space on 'our sorry conceited O' as a world where, for all the billions spent on such prestigious ventures, millions are still starving. 'Thanksgiving for a Habitat' contrasts the unimportance of the poet's personal death, surrendering his 'smidge / of nitrogen to the World Fund', compared with the collective 'giga-death' of nuclear holocaust.

Among the few volumes still gracing the residuary 'Poetry' shelves of popular bookstores, Auden's posthumous best-sellers, *Tell Me the Truth About Love* and *As I Walked Out One Evening,* sit for alphabetical reasons next to the kitsch light-versifier Pam Ayres. 'Mother' would have been amused. As *The Oxford Dictionary of Quotations* records Auden observing to Spender, 'Art is born of humiliation'. The first poet 'at home in the twentieth century', in Edward Mendelson's words, Auden is a singularly appropriate figure to preside over the beginning of the twenty-first.[10] Not only did he record the forces and obsessions that dominated that unlamented century, thereby setting the agenda for the present one; he also attempted to synthesise the intellectual and interpretative systems that might make sense of it. Trying to see Auden plain through the smoke haze, we may today, like the disconsolate drinkers of 'September 1, 1939', discern our own faces staring back from the saloon-bar mirror.

My work in this volume is part of a research project supported by the Spanish Ministry of Science and Technology (BFF 2002-02842), the Comunidad Autónoma of La Rioja (ANGI-2002/05), and the University of La Rioja, Logroño, Spain (API-02-35).

NOTES

1. Christopher Caudwell, *Illusion and Reality: A Study of the Sources of Poetry* (1937) (London: Lawrence and Wishart, 1946), p. 283.
2. George Orwell, 'Inside the Whale' (1940), *Collected Essays, Journalism and Letters*, vol. 1 (Harmondsworth: Penguin Books, 1970), p. 566.
3. Reprinted in *Required Writing: Miscellaneous Pieces 1955–1982* (London: Faber and Faber, 1983), pp. 123–8.
4. Randall Jarrell, *Kipling, Auden & Co* (Manchester: Carcanet Press, 1981), pp. 55, 226.
5. *The Faber Book of Modern American Verse* (London: Faber and Faber, 1946), p. 15.
6. Allan Rodway, *A Preface to Auden* (London: Longman, 1984), p. 18.
7. Gregory Woods, *Articulate Flesh: Male Homo-Eroticism and Modern Poetry* (New Haven: Yale University Press, 1987); *A History of Gay Literature: The Male Tradition* (New Haven: Yale University Press, 1998); Richard Bozorth, *Auden's Games of Knowledge: Poetry and the Meanings of Homosexuality* (New York: Columbia University Press, 2001).
8. W. H. Auden and Norman Holmes Pearson (eds.), *Viking Portable Poets of the English Language*, vol. IV ([1950] Harmondsworth: Penguin Books, 1978), pp. xii–xiv.
9. Robert Horan, *A Beginning* (New Haven: Yale University Press, 1948), pp. 7–10.
10. Preface to W. H. Auden, *Selected Poems* (London: Faber and Faber, 1979), p. ix.

# 2

RICHARD DAVENPORT-HINES

# Auden's life and character

Both Wystan Auden's grandfathers were clergymen: his last poems were haikus that described or took the form of prayer. There is a rounded integrity about his Christian antecedents and his Christian end. Yet many of his admirers mistrust, dislike or minimise the religious elements in his poetry, and celebrate him for his intellectual power, the profusion of his ethical ideas and the rich diversity of his creative output. He was an encyclopaedist who liked to collect, classify and interpret large amounts of information, and strove to integrate natural phenomena, spiritual experiences, human history and intimate emotions into a system in which both body, spirit, feelings and intellect cohered. His poems drew ideas from the work of other poets as well as from novelists, historians, theologians, psychologists, philosophers, political scientists and anthropologists. He was the first great English poet to be born in the twentieth century, and the first whose work was profoundly influenced by psychoanalytical and Marxist theories. As a child he trusted machines better than people, and when young was numbered among the 'pylon poets' who celebrated new technology. Yet experiences during the 1930s nudged him back towards Christian faith, which became more explicit after he moved from England to live in the USA in 1939.

His creative aims were pursued with such ruthless purpose, he was so prone to unforgiving self-rebuke and sometimes subjugated his emotional needs with such conscientious self-discipline, that he can be termed a spiritual masochist. He made testing, unequivocal and sometimes arbitrary choices about how he lived, worked and exercised his free will. Gratitude he thought was a duty rather than a virtue; though often unhappy, he was free of self-pity. Increasingly he spurned his previous poems as shoddy or boring, rewrote their lines and rejected his past intellectual notions as specious. Human speech was one of the enduring themes of his work. He was in love with language. Poetry was his chief achievement, but he also wrote plays and opera libretti in collaboration with men he loved. He was an omnivorous reader whose reviews and essays often foreshadowed ideas that he was later to develop in poems. Sometimes he embedded clandestinely self-revelatory reports on his current intellectual passions or volatile emotions in apparently neutral pieces of prose writing. He did so both to clarify his own mind and for the private edification of his intimate friends.

Wystan Hugh Auden was born on 21 February 1907, in York. His insulated and bookish background, as he often insisted, had a dominant influence on his outlook. Auden's father was a physician of intense intellectual curiosity and constructive humanitarianism who became School Medical Officer in Britain's largest industrial city, Birmingham, and Professor of Public Health at Birmingham University. From his father he gleaned his interest in psychology, disease and Nordic sagas. His mother was an intelligent but highly strung Anglo-Catholic who instilled in him a strong literary sense as well as a delight in theology and music. Her emotional intensity may have contributed to his retreat as a child into an imaginary world of limestone terrain emptied of human beings but containing lead mines, slag-heaps and mining machinery. This inanimate world is celebrated in such juvenile poems as 'The Traction Engine' (1924). In Auden's coded autobiography, his commonplace book *A Certain World* (1970), he hinted that he considered himself mildly autistic as a child, and conceivably diagnosed himself as manifesting what is now known as Asperger's Syndrome.

His boyhood reading was greedy, precocious and formative. A fellow pupil at his preparatory school was Christopher Isherwood, the future novelist who was subsequently his lover and literary collaborator. In 1920 Auden went to Gresham's School, a progressive Norfolk boarding school, where the headmaster's dismal, pompous piety estranged him from Christianity. There, in 1922, he experienced a sudden overmastering certainty that his vocation was to write poetry. His subsequent juvenile poems were imitative: Wordsworth, Hardy and Edward Thomas were successive influences.

In 1925 Auden entered Christ Church, Oxford on a natural sciences scholarship, but transferred to a course in politics, philosophy and economics. English literary criticism was just emerging as an intellectual discipline, and in 1926 he was admitted to the English school. He escaped from the overpowering influence of Eliot's *The Waste Land* by adopting Yeats and then Graves as poetic models to emulate. 'In Memory of W. B. Yeats' (1939) is his tribute to a master whose influence eventually disgusted him. His poems 'The Watershed' (1927) and 'The Secret Agent' (1928) were the earliest examples of his unique idiom – which sounded cryptic, ambiguous and menacing – that became called 'Audenesque'. He became a conspicuous leader of undergraduate opinion who held sway over his friends: they included, among the poets, Cecil Day Lewis, Stephen Spender and John Betjeman. He meddled in their love affairs, decried their pessimistic neuroses, dogmatised about their intellectual development, yet delighted them with his mimicry, clowning and elaborate jokes.

Auden was the first poet to use the ideas of twentieth-century psychology extensively in his work. Through his father, he became acquainted as a boy with W. H. R. Rivers's *Instinct and the Unconscious* (1920) and with Freud's psychoanalytical theories. From adolescence he would startle or bully his friends with Freudian diagnoses. In 1927 or 1928 he underwent a short trial of psychoanalysis, possibly administered by Margaret Marshall, who treated and unsuccessfully married his elder brother John. Either Marshall or John probably induced him to practise the techniques of self-improvement associated with the popular French psychologist Emile Coué. Later, in 1928, Auden became captivated by the ideas of an American quack psychologist, Homer Lane. Auden's subsequent intellectual mentors included the eccentric polymaths Gerald Heard and Eugen Rosenstock-Huessy as well as Wolfgang Kohler, an originator of Gestalt psychology.

In 1928 Auden went to live in Berlin, where he put himself through a ferocious course of reading, thinking and living, including energetic sexual adventures with other men. Homer Lane's belief that uninhibited sexual love was healing encouraged his eroticism. He broke his engagement to marry a nurse named Sheilah Richardson after returning from Berlin (having earlier had an affair with his Austrian landlady, Hedwig Petzold). Auden's bold homosexuality, which was subject to criminal sanctions in Britain until he was a man of sixty, contributed to his interest in delinquency and sense of exclusion. After returning to England, he taught at two boys' boarding schools, Larchfield in Dumbartonshire (1930–2) and the Downs in Worcestershire (1932–5). He proved a charismatic teacher who relished the company of young boys and enjoyed the gossipy community of boarding school life.

Eliot facilitated Faber's publication in 1930 of Auden's first book, *Poems*. The mood of Auden's work in this period was vital, apprehensive and diagnostic. He seemed to look down from a high altitude on the neuroses of Western civilisation and the sickness of capitalism. Overall his language and anxieties in the early 1930s entranced the young intelligentsia of Britain and the USA. They heard their most critical or terrifying concerns about political injustice and human pain clarified and amplified in his words. Each new poem was studied with eager, meticulous intensity. He became a totem for thinking dissent.

In 1932 Auden published *The Orators*. Using ideas and experiences from his year in Berlin, together with a scholarly article on anthropology by his former lover, John Layard, this extraordinary, minatory book mixes exciting poems with scrappy, elliptical notes and superb prose. *The Orators'* moods seem variously hectic, facetious, paranoid, guilt-ridden and disturbed;

a running metaphor represents homosexuality in terms of aviation. Auden put Christian images, including a martyred, self-sacrificing leader, to secular uses for, despite his rejection of Christianity, he could not evade its imaginative grasp. Then, in June 1933, while he was sitting on the lawn after dinner with three colleagues at the Downs School, he had a mystical experience during which he discovered the meaning of the Christian injunction to love one's neighbour as oneself. Auden celebrated this vision of *Agape*, as he termed it, in his poem beginning 'Out on the lawn I lie in bed', and later entitled 'A Summer Night'. This proved a transforming moment of his life, although some of its repercussions were deferred. His love poetry became eloquent and appealing despite his first experience of being in love – as distinct from sexual pleasure – involving Michael Yates, an adolescent schoolboy for whom equal reciprocation was impossible.

After 1932 Auden began contributing prose to literary periodicals and poems to influential anthologies. He himself compiled a total of twenty-two anthologies during his lifetime. In 1935, feeling too personally isolated and too creatively remote, he determined to reach larger audiences, and joined the General Post Office's documentary film unit, for which (among other work) he scripted a gripping monologue for the short film *Night Mail*. Working in partnership with Isherwood, he wrote two plays, *The Dog Beneath the Skin* (1935) and *The Ascent of F6* (1936), relating personal neurosis to political or revolutionary concerns. Their third play, *On the Frontier* (1938), also had a double plot of political satire and domestic melodrama. These verse extravaganzas were produced at the experimental Group Theatre under the direction of Rupert Doone, the partner of Auden's former lover, the painter Robert Medley. Another friend, Benjamin Britten, composed music to accompany Auden's lyrics. Despite compelling scenes, ambitious ideas and beguiling language, these plays (with their jarring mixture of tragedy and farce) have seemed too contrived to endure in the theatrical repertoire.

Auden was never a Londoner: Birmingham and Oxford remained his English, and deeply provincial, cities. Yet he was ambivalent about his roots and tested himself with outlandish journeys. He toured Iceland in 1936 with the poet Louis MacNeice, and together they assembled a rollicking book of prose and poetry reportage entitled *Letters from Iceland* (1937). Auden's witty, gossipy 'Last Will and Testament' (written jointly with MacNeice) closed with a prayer; henceforth all Auden's plays and long poems ended in prayer, although not addressed to a God until 1941. Despite the book's jollity, Auden saw in Iceland a spectacle of violence that served as a muted counterpart to his vision of *Agape* three years earlier. He watched a great whale being torn apart by winches and cranes worked by men who were indifferent to its suffering, and had a repulsive vision of humankind's inexorable, disciplined yet workaday ferocity. This incident provided a theme for 'Musée des Beaux Arts' (1938), in which people are too selfishly inattentive to notice the great harm happening near them, as well as for 'Memorial for the City' (1949).

In 1937 Auden volunteered to drive an ambulance for the Republican forces fighting fascism in the Spanish Civil War. Once in Valencia, however, he was cajoled into making futile propaganda broadcasts, and became dismayed by the Republicans' violence, harassment of priests and closure of churches. Although his most politically explicit pamphlet poem, *Spain*, confirmed him as the most famous British writer of his generation, Auden soon felt that it was meretricious, expedient and untruthful, and later repudiated it.

During 1938, accompanied by Isherwood, Auden visited China, which had been invaded by Japanese forces. This resulted in their joint book, *Journey to a War* (1939), containing 'In Time of War', a sequence of twenty-seven sonnets, which traces human history from the expulsion from Eden to the mechanised age and its neuroses. The sonnets' vision of human ferocity, unblinking ethical judgements and refusal to offer false comfort constitute Auden's supreme achievement of the 1930s.

He returned from China via New York, where he decided that he would settle in America and seek US citizenship. He made this choice because he was chafing at his celebrity as the cultural leader of young English partisans, which he found distasteful and creatively inhibiting. After a productive visit to Belgium, Auden reached New York again in January 1939. Many of his young, Leftist admirers felt betrayed by the departure of their putative spokesman. This resentment intensified after the outbreak of war in Europe nine months later, and scurrilous journalists and politicians tried in 1940 to brand Auden as a coward. The belief that he had deserted Britain during a dangerous crisis led to enduring hostility.

Although Auden avowedly went to New York seeking anonymous solitude, he soon fell in love with Chester Kallman (1921–75), a handsome, witty, blond college boy from Brooklyn. The two men exchanged vows during a honeymoon in New Mexico during the summer of 1939. As Kallman's wayward habits were impossible to ignore, Auden decided that a person's vices and weakness should be welcomed as potential opportunities and strengths. Unfortunately for two men who proposed spending their lives together, their preferred sexual acts were incompatible; Auden had an overwhelming commitment to fellatio and felt sadistic when satisfying Kallman's urgent anal passivity. Kallman had undeniable aesthetic sensibility, but was selfish and wilful; Auden (while regarding Kallman as a sacred being) was possessive, invasive and overbearing. There was a crisis in 1941, when Kallman declared that their sexual relationship must end, but they remained intimate companions, sharing summer homes in Europe (1948–73) and apartments in New York City (1951–63). In 1947 Auden rescued Kallman from obscurity by arranging their collaboration in providing the libretto for Stravinsky's opera *The Rake's Progress* (premiered 1951). After Auden (with Kallman) had provided the libretto for Hans Werner Henze's *Elegy for Young Lovers* (1959–60), he conceived the idea of an opera taken from Euripides. During 1963 Auden (abetted by Kallman) accomplished his finest work as a librettist in Henze's resultant opera *The Bassarids* (premiered 1966).

Auden suppressed a book he had drafted, *The Prolific and the Devourer*, because its progressive Christianity and wishful optimism became untenable after he visited a cinema in New York's Yorkville district during December 1939. The ferocity of the largely German-American audience, who chanted 'Kill the Poles' during a newsreel about the European war, destroyed his faith in liberal notions of human progress, and reinforced his burgeoning dislike of his poem written at the outbreak of the Second World War, 'September 1, 1939'.

In October 1940 Auden became a tenant in a famously lively literary and musical household at 7 Middagh Street in Brooklyn. His fellow lodgers in the house, which was leased by the fiction editor of *Harper's Bazaar*, included MacNeice, Britten, the tenor Peter Pears, Paul Bowles, Carson McCullers, the burlesque stripper Gipsy Rose Lee, and Golo Mann. Mann was the brother of Erika Mann, a lesbian whom Auden had married in 1935, at Isherwood's instigation, to provide her with a British passport needed to elude Nazi persecution. They never lived together or consummated the marriage.

*The Double Man* was Auden's preferred title for the book published in 1941 (under the UK title of *New Year Letter*). It contained his sonnet sequence 'The Quest', examining the existential choices of different human types, together with his witty didactic epistle 'New Year Letter'. This erudite metaphysical discussion of history, evolution and eternity has a modest, calm authority that was seldom heard in his more partisan or argumentative poems. In October 1940, as he finished revising *The Double Man*, Auden began attending an Episcopalian church in New York, and after two decades of religious ambivalence, chose to become a Christian poet. During 1941 he began drawing on theology as a poetic source just as previously he had been helped by the ideas of Lane, Freud and Marx. The existential Christianity of the nineteenth-century Danish philosopher Søren Kierkegaard impressed him. He befriended the German Protestant theologian exiled in the US, Paul Tillich, and the American-born Reinhold Niebuhr, and became convinced that Christianity and social justice were mutually related.

His first major explicitly Christian work, 'For the Time Being' (1941–2), describes the Christmas story through a medley of chorus, narrative, dialogues, songs and prose. Auden had resolved to use a light tone when discussing momentous subjects, and the exciting religious ideas of his 'Christmas oratorio', as it was subtitled, are approached with frivolity, irony and camp incongruities. It appeared in book form together with Auden's next long poem, 'The Sea and the Mirror' (1942–4), in which characters taken from Shakespeare's *The Tempest* depict the Christian conception of art, perfect divine love and imperfect human love. *The Age of Anxiety* (1947) is the least satisfactory of his eight major poetic sequences written after moving to the United States, although it won him a Pulitzer Prize. Auden also wrote notable shorter poems in this period, including 'The Fall of Rome' (1947) and 'A Household' (1949), in which the three protagonists are chilling self-portraits.

The apartment leased by Auden from 1946 until 1951 at 7 Cornelia Street in Greenwich Village was his first settled adult home. The Village in the late 1940s resembled Paris in the 1920s as a world centre of artistic innovation and intellectual development: he became a conspicuous local figure as well as a dedicated New Yorker who valued the anonymity and sounds of city life. In 1946, too, he became a US citizen. With married friends he had previously bought a holiday shack on Fire Island, a glorified sandbank off Long Island, where he spent several summers. It was one of the locations where, in 1946–7, he enjoyed a heterosexual affair with Rhoda Jaffe, a vivacious former Brooklyn classmate of Kallman. From 1948 he rented a house in the coastal village of Forio on Ischia, an island in the Bay of Naples which, like Fire Island, was developing as a gay resort. Both locations were celebrated in poems written during 1948, 'Pleasure Island' and 'Ischia'. After 1948 he chose to winter in New York, where he made money writing freelance prose, while his Italian visits were the privileged time in which he composed poetry.

Auden's Italian visit of 1948 transformed his poetic imagination as extensively as his private imaginary childhood world of derelict landscape and machines or his vision of *Agape* in 1933. It meant that in addition to the pre-1939 English provincial Auden and the post-1939 estranged New York Auden there was a stateless post-1948 Auden. Specifically, Italy inspired Auden with joy in the created world and fulfilled his need of a landscape symbolising the human body and connoting elemental happiness. 'In Praise of Limestone', an exquisite poem written in Italy during 1948, was explicit in comparing Italian landscape to a mother's flesh. It is significant not only for its lyrical beauty but because it inaugurated a new poetic phase in which he celebrated the human body for both its corporeal and sacred meanings.

To prove that in developing momentous new poetic ideas, he was not becoming pompous, he followed 'In Praise of Limestone' with a poem celebrating the human body's frivolity. 'The Platonic Blow, by Miss Oral' (1948) extols the rites of his preferred sexual act.

Auden also wrote a sequence of poems collectively entitled 'Bucolics' (1952–3) expressing his grateful pleasure at the earth's natural features. 'The Shield of Achilles' (1952) is amongst his most magnificent shorter poems. The high value that Auden attached to the hours of the clock (his insistent punctuality was sometimes annoyingly aggressive) underlay the sequence of eight poems about the Crucifixion and its aftermath that he wrote during 1949–54. Each poem was named after prayer services held by the Church at precise times of day. 'Horae Canonicae', as the sequence is collectively known, is Auden's most sublime achievement. It is the work of a humanist who never offered his readers false consolations but sought instead to disenchant. Human beings were born in sin, he thought; human history was criminal and pathological.

In New York Auden enjoyed friendships with Edmund Wilson, Marianne Moore and other writers. From 1951 he collaborated with Jacques Barzun and Lionel Trilling in managing a highbrow book club called Readers' Subscription, and contributed regularly to its circular magazine *Griffin*. He also supported the club's successor organisation, the Mid-Century Society (1959–62). As judge of the Yale Series of Younger Poets during the 1950s he chose for publication the first volumes of Adrienne Rich and John Ashbery. Other aspirant poets received his generous and shrewd advice. He also enjoyed happy, lascivious affairs, notably with Wendell Stacey Johnson in 1953. At other times he felt miserably secluded from human contacts, which prompted his inept marriage proposals to Thekla Clark (1952) and the political theorist and German émigrée Hannah Arendt (1970).

Prejudices against homosexuality exacerbated Auden's difficulties. After 1945 F. R. Leavis's critical magazine *Scrutiny* was unrelenting in denouncing Auden's ideas in terms which were a recognisable attack on his sexuality. In 1951, when the English diplomat and Soviet spy Guy Burgess defected to Moscow, he tried to telephone Auden, whom he was suspected of trying to visit in Ischia. Auden became entangled in the ensuing espionage scare, which led to a British police campaign against homosexuality; probably in consequence his application for a Fulbright scholarship at Rome University was rejected (1953). Both Leavis and Burgess damaged Auden's reputation in Britain, and contributed to his panic after being elected in 1956 as Professor of Poetry at Oxford University. His poem 'There Will Be No Peace' (1956) evokes his feelings of persecution at this time. His Oxford lectures, of which versions were included in *The Dyer's Hand* (1963), helped to restore his British reputation. Later, in 1963, *Time* magazine prepared a cover story about Auden only for it to be abruptly abandoned because its managing editor refused to honour a homosexual. He had never been secretive about his homosexuality, and became more candid in the 1960s, although paradoxically he also became more prudish after 1963.

For almost twenty years from 1938 Auden used a licit amphetamine drug, Benzedrine, which enhanced his power to make swift intellectual connections and his urge to communicate his insights. Changing medical and political attitudes to amphetamines, however, obliged Auden to renounce his Benzedrine habit in the late 1950s: withdrawal injured (temporarily) his creativity and (more enduringly) his social confidence. In contrast to his Greenwich Village and Italian periods, the five years of Auden's Oxford professorship mark the least interesting phase of his poetry.

In 1958 Auden forsook Italy with 'Goodbye to the Mezzogiorno' and marked his purchase of a cottage in Kirchstetten by writing 'On Installing an American Kitchen in Lower Austria'. This became the earliest of a sequence of poems, ultimately entitled 'Thanksgiving for a Habitat', mainly written in 1962–4. These serene celebrations of his Kirchstetten house could seem incongruous to those who knew the untidiness and squalor in which he lived. Nevertheless these poems (as it proved, they constituted the last of Auden's major poetic sequences) marked a creative revival, although the collection in which they were published, *About the House* (1965), was condemned as smug by some reviewers, who cavilled at its domesticated subject matter.

Kallman moved to Athens in 1963, where the sexual opportunities suited his tastes, although he continued to visit Kirchstetten for the summers. Auden's loneliness during their long separations was acute. His dependence on Kallman remained fierce, although his ex-lover's unhappiness, dipsomania and sexual escapades increasingly anguished him. His own health, too, suffered from chain-smoking, copious wine and strong martinis. His isolation during the six months of 1964–5 when the Ford Foundation paid for him to live in Berlin weakened his morale and physical health. Eliot's death in 1965 accentuated this deterioration. Thereafter his letters to friends were increasingly curt, repetitive and written on the backs of carbon copies of his latest poems, which were the only messages he wished to send. His reviews and prose writings are of diminishing interest after 1965, although his anthology *A Certain World* is a successful if allusive self-portrait.

An unscrupulous television advertisement for Lyndon Johnson's presidential campaign of 1964, which misused a phrase from 'September 1, 1939', shocked Auden into excising several early political poems, or deleting phrases, from future editions of his books. 'Partition' (1966), 'August 1968' (1968) and 'Rois Fainéants' (1968) however demonstrated his determination to remain a poet who deplored the misuse of power. As his health and social skills faltered, he remained ardent in his love of rare words and complex poetic metre. The vitality, wit, sumptuous vocabulary and wisdom of his poems did not recede. He strove to deny his enveloping despondency by insisting on his sense of gratitude, as in 'A Lullaby' (1972) and 'Thank You, Fog' (1973).

Great artists, Auden often said, die when they have done the work they are meant to do. He died in his sleep, on 29 September 1973, after giving a poetry reading in Vienna. For the rest of the twentieth century he was the poet about whom other poets wrote most.

# 3

PATRICK DEANE

# Auden's England

On 19 January 1939, the *Champlain* left Southampton for New York, with Auden aboard. In England, where national insecurity lingered corrosively despite reassurances purchased at Munich in September, Auden's departure was bound to be construed negatively. The impending European war meant that Auden's journey took on the character of betrayal in the public mind. To the 'either-ors', 'the mongrel-halves' (*NYL*, line 821) or 'the Lords of Limit' who set 'a tabu 'twixt left and right' (*EA*, p.115), there were no shades of motive or meaning, and 'facts' were harder when, paradoxically, life could be made to take on the bold lineaments of myth.

As a product of the twenties and thirties – a period, as Robin Skelton pointed out almost forty years ago, unusually prone to self-mythologising[1] – Auden did not distance himself from the myth-making impulse. His early poems are set in a world suffused with threat and mysterious urgency, yet oddly detached from history, and are in that sense mythic. Yet their preoccupation with liminality and transactions across borders made the secondary world of his imagination into an 'antimythological myth', to use his phrase from 'In Praise of Limestone'. In the decade before his departure for America, Auden certainly contributed in some measure to the discourse of the Lords of Limit and to the construction of the very myths according to which in 1939 he found himself alleged a traitor.

An unpublished poem written in 1932, which begins 'The month was April . . .', expresses the powerful urge to leave 'a world that has had its day', but ends with peculiar defeatism, arguing that you must 'go down with your world' (*EA*, p. 124). The speaker is a representative type – a member of what Frank Kermode has characterised as the 'politically amorous' bourgeoisie[2] – who must deal with the realisation that despite his handsome profile, public school education and modest investments, he is hopelessly cut off from the new world order and therefore doomed. There is pathos in his growing understanding that 'working boys . . . won't tell you their secrets', or that giving away one's money will not buy access to the working class. It is in fact 'no use turning nasty . . . no use turning good': you are identified with your world and you must live or die with it.

The poem considers an option Auden would actually choose to pursue six years later: 'I'll book a berth on a liner / I'll sail away out to sea.' But it recognises that the 'New World' does not exist for the liberation of citizens of the 'Old', indeed that refugees seeking redefinition in the 'New World' will find themselves rebuffed by natives who have 'sampled' their sort before. Auden's emigration was to bring him to the heart of what was then the 'ascendant imperialist power', an outcome with potentially vitiating effect on his left-wing credentials.[3] In itself, however, the poem represents a relatively uncomplicated cry from the heart of a doomed world. The speaker, his customs and habits, even his ideas for self-abasement, self-destruction and regeneration, are now simply irrelevant, so that the speaker is compelled to ask 'Why do I feel such a fool . . .?'

In Auden's early poems the decline of England is a recurring theme. Relics of an industry now 'comatose' litter the landscape, as in 'Who stands, the crux left of the watershed' (*EA*, p. 22), and human relationships are mysterious and enigmatic, played out within what seems a post-apocalyptic milieu. The formula, though, is not Eliotic: those relationships are oddly invigorated by their connection to dereliction and decline. Auden's speakers are stimulated by the thought of what elemental passions and instincts survive, what 'sap unbaffled rises'. 'Near you', runs the conclusion to 'The Watershed', 'taller than grass, / Ears poise before decision, scenting danger' (*EA*, p. 22).

In such poems Auden reverted to the style and setting of his schoolboy writings: in Mendelson's words, 'He frees himself from the manner of Eliot by reclaiming from Hardy what he later called Hardy's "hawk's vision, his way of looking at life from a great height"' (*Early Auden*, p. 33). While the speaker can allow himself the privilege of vatic authority over the figures in his landscape ('Go home, now, stranger'), his tone is also strikingly intimate, ambiguous pronouns and diacritical signs calling into question the very notion of an identity distinct from others or the landscape. If these poems are an index of Auden's sense of England in the late twenties, two points emerge. The first is that Auden was in a complex way attracted to the condition of dereliction, and thus might not be expected readily to abandon it. The second is that his poetic manner of rendering English life and landscape did not always follow the model of Eliot, whose view of England Auden said he shared: 'the England of 1925 when I went up to Oxford was *The Waste Land* in character'.[4] Notably absent from poems such as 'The Watershed' are Eliot's characteristic ironies, particularly those drawing on modified forms of the Browningesque dramatic monologue.

It is a measure of the ambiguity of Auden's attitude towards England, however, that in yet another substantial body of writings he does indeed resort to these and other techniques of the twentieth-century satirist. In this regard, *The Orators* is a *tour de force*, asking, in 'Address for a Prize-Day', 'What do you think about England, this country of ours where nobody is well?' (*EA*, p. 62). Much of what follows – an argument, a statement, a letter, a journal, diagrams, miscellaneous prose and six odes – seems intended to provide an answer, or several answers, to that question. The diagnosis is indebted, by turns, to Eliot and to Blake, 'unacted desires' being implied to lie at the base of a wider malaise afflicting the capacity to create art and to provide leadership. The fourth of the odes is dedicated to the infant son of Rex and Frances Warner, and comprises a somewhat tongue-in-cheek hymn to John Warner as saviour and deliverer of England. Auden, whose debt to Virgil is also apparent in 'Paid on Both Sides',[5] seems here to be working playfully within the tradition of the messianic fourth Eclogue. Warner's role is disclosed about halfway through the poem in a mock-heroic declaration – 'John, son of Warner, shall rescue you' (*EA*, p.103) – but in preparation for that moment 'first / We must have a look round, we must know the worst' (*EA*, p.101). The worst is that England is the Waste Land: 'our proletariat' lack vitality, consoling themselves with the vicarious excitements of sport and cinema, while those who might be expected to lead – 'our upper class' – are paralysed by caution and small-mindedness.

Auden's diagnosis differs from Eliot's in being leavened by humour. Certainly Auden's English malaise seems less a matter of illness in the soul than dysfunction in the body politic, a point underlined by his very un-Eliotic insistence on class as an analytic category. The advent of John Warner will bring spring, we are told, 'in the buds, in the birds, in the bowels, and the brain / Spring in the bedroom ventilator' (*EA*, p. 104). Through a change of heart it will yield a new socio-economic dispensation, featuring 'The official re-marriage of the whole and part, / The poor in employment and the country sound' (*EA*, p. 105). The mock-heroic tone, the complex ironies in almost every line, make it difficult to assess just what level of patriotic sentiment is at work here. But as the theme of national salvation reaches its climax, one is allowed to hear echoes of Rupert Brooke or Edward Thomas, alloyed with rather than corroded by the Audenesque: 'A birthday, a birth / On English earth / Restores, restore will, has restored / To England's story / The directed calm, the actual glory' (*EA*, pp. 105–6).

'Directed' suggests purpose and resolve as requirements for 'calm', and the primary context for this observation is psychological. Everywhere in Auden's writings at this time, psychic health is a prerequisite for social and political well-being. 'People cannot grow unless they are happy', he would write in the year of his departure for America, 'and, even when their material needs have been satisfied, they still need many other things.'[6] John Warner must get down to work on 'each unhappy Joseph and repressed Diana', whose passions and instincts, healthily directed, will lead them into a calm that is psychologically liberating as well as the proper basis for social and political equilibrium.

Whether he was right to see this as a problem that could be solved by appropriate leadership is unclear, but that he did so is apparent in *The Orators*, as in *The Ascent of F6* (1936). The analysis of leadership in that play tends to mirror Isherwood's concerns rather than Auden's. Isherwood had long cherished the idea that acts of apparent heroism are in fact the result of neurotic character flaws. However, a more distinctly Audenesque approach to leadership can be discerned in those parts of the play we know Auden wrote, in particular the utterances of Mr and Mrs A, who function as a sort of chorus to the mountaineering action.[7] Mr and Mrs A establish the context within which the heroic leadership of the mountaineer Michael Ransom must be read and evaluated. Mrs A speaks in a distinctively Eliotic way about the drudgery of suburban life: 'A slick and unctuous Time / Has sold us yet another shop-soiled day' (*F6*, p. 17). When her husband returns home from work he laments life in a waste land that is identifiably England in the thirties: 'All you can hear / Is politics, politics everywhere: / Talk in Westminster, talk at Geneva, talk in the lobbies and talk on the throne; / Talk about treaties, talk about honour, mad dogs quarrelling over a bone' (*F6*, p. 19). The year in which these words were written saw the formation of the 'Stresa Front' between Germany, France and Italy; the Italian attack on Abyssinia, and imposition of League of Nations sanctions on Italy; the Hoare–Laval Pact; the Anglo-German naval agreement; and, in Westminster, the resignation of Ramsay MacDonald as Prime Minister, his succession by Stanley Baldwin and the re-election of a National Government under Conservative leadership. Mrs A's utterances give us an indication of the psychological malaise that is both the cause and consequence of this social and political turmoil. Her husband's speeches concentrate on the public and historical dimensions of their situation. Thus there is both a personal and a national urgency in the simple plea with which Mrs A concludes the play's first choric section: 'Give us something to live for' (*F6*, p. 20). Leadership of the sort Michael Ransom can provide, and heroism such as he and his team demonstrate in climbing the mountain, are what the play offers in answer.

The sense of national crisis is strongest in those sections where Auden's hand is most discernible. Act II concludes with a choric section on the theme 'England's honour is covered in rust', where the nation is compared to previous imperial powers, Spain and Babylon. England 'has had her hour / And now must decline to a second-class power' (F6, p. 82). The rhyming couplet suggests some satirical intent in what seems an otherwise serious observation. A similar ambiguity hovers over the whole drama. England is clearly in some sense derelict; but redemption through some new colonial exploit is not the solution. The climbing of F6 provides an opportunity for Ransom and his team to demonstrate human qualities that might well alleviate the condition of England; but their actual errand – to extend British influence over Ostnian Sudoland – is tawdry and unworthy.

Notwithstanding the haze of irony, these two works quite seriously evoke an England waiting upon its deliverer, a 'national symbol' that Mrs A later comes to dismiss as 'a threadbare barnstorming actor' (F6, p. 82). In this respect, these works typify a time in which the preoccupation with leadership lured some of the age's most gifted thinkers into dubious political endorsements. Ezra Pound's Jefferson and / or Mussolini (1935) presented Mussolini 'as a wise and benevolent tyrant'.[8] Wyndham Lewis, in Hitler (1931), argued that the Führer could be expected to unite a disparate and dispirited German nation with 'increasing moderation and tolerance'.[9] David Jones, the Anglo-Welsh poet whose Anathemata Auden was to pronounce 'one of the most important poems of our time',[10] in 1939 wrote approvingly of Mein Kampf: 'there is much in both the Fascist and Nazi revolutions that demand our understanding and sympathy. They represent, for all their alarming characteristics, an heroic attempt to cope with certain admitted corruptions in our civilization.'[11] Lacking Auden's lightheartedness, Jones's words provide a dark indication of the crisis into which English culture and society had come, as well as the likely cost of deliverance. But it is important to recognise the similarity between Jones's words and the choric sections of F6. That Auden used theatre to present the spectacle of people longing for a leader suggests that he was both immersed in and distanced from this national obsession, and sceptical about the likely prospect of any deliverance.

However obscure the motives and appetites that brought Wallis Simpson of Baltimore, Maryland, into intimate relationship with Albert Edward Christian George Andrew Patrick David of Windsor, they were assuredly human and in that sense timeless. That the liaison between these two people would create a national stir was inevitable. Indeed, the controversy that arose in 1936 was at once unique, extraordinary and profoundly predictable. Less predictable was the sheer acuteness with which the abdication crisis would be felt, and across how many sectors of English society. The King's wish to marry Mrs Simpson was a threat to the British constitution, in all senses of that word: to the traditions and legislated instruments of the nation, but also to its overall health. The greater threat, though, was to what Edward Prince of Wales had promised the nation ever since his investiture – the hope, desperately needed after the Great War, of new and youthful leadership.

Auden and Isherwood completed a first draft of *F6* on 17 April 1936, by which time Edward, now King, was actively seeking to publicise his relationship with Mrs Simpson, and questions about the future of the crown were being asked. It is telling in this context that for Michael Ransom 'the future of England, of the Empire . . . weighty political considerations, the government' (*F6*, p. 43) are nothing beside his personal imperatives. Public and national matters are the concern of his brother, Sir James Ransom, to whom Michael has already remarked 'Keep to your world. I will keep to mine.' Michael's heroism is qualified and in some ways interrogated. If he is the leader everyone seems to need, he nevertheless exemplifies the notion that leadership and heroism are always alloyed with imperfection, that, indeed, heroic acts often issue from unheroic motives and neuroses. In Edward VIII, England had a leader who would be as unlikely to redeem the likes of Mrs A as Michael Ransom. Like Ransom, Edward was the focus of enormous public expectation even while his real allegiance was to a world increasingly private and separate. Paradoxically, then, the abdication in December 1936 simultaneously demonstrated and betrayed, asserted and fled from, an idea of leadership that had become a national obsession.

Michael Ransom's personal motives are finally irrelevant. When he dies all of England mourns, 'but it is a sorrow tempered with pride, that once again Englishmen have been weighed in the balance and not found wanting' (*F6*, pp. 115–16). Extrapolated into a purely political context, this idea has exceedingly gloomy implications: leaders do not make society, but are instead made by it. As Stan Smith noted twenty years ago, Auden's work of the thirties is preoccupied with 'the power of ideology to recruit new subjects, to reproduce the given order of things by reproducing the subjects who produce it as willing, co-operative agents' (Smith, p. 16). If a leader is less an extraordinary individual than a means by which the prevailing ideology or world-order reproduces itself in a mere simulacrum of renewal, there really is no hope of deliverance for Mr and Mrs A. This recognition underlies the ode to John Warner. John puts to flight a host of rivals, including the 'piss-proud prophet' and the 'pooty redeemer'. The claim that 'This is the season of the change of heart', promising a golden age in which the whole and its parts will be remarried, the poor employed and the country 'sound' (*EA*, p. 105), is undercut by the mock-heroic context.

Auden's later intimations of human happiness are consistent with this: while one may be granted moments in which 'the change of heart' is apparent and efficacious, these quickly recede as the imperfect world reasserts itself. The archetype here is the poem he was later to call 'A Summer Night', which recalls the 'vision of *Agape*' Auden experienced while working at the Downs School in 1933. A casual outdoor conversation with three colleagues was, he wrote in 'The Protestant Mystics' in 1964, 'invaded' by a 'power' such that he knew for the first time 'what it means to love one's neighbour as oneself' (*F&A*, p. 69). In the poem the vision has an enduring effect through memory, but is itself supplanted by its antithesis, the 'crumpling flood' of violence and historic contingency. The poem provides a useful gloss on Auden's thinking about England, suggesting that plenitude is inseparable from imperfection. In this respect, Auden's real affinity here is with the later Eliot of *Burnt Norton*, written in the same year as *F6*. In Eliot's poem, the moment in the rose-garden points to 'one end, which is always present', disclosed without warning and as suddenly gone, 'Ridiculous the waste sad time / Stretching before and after.'[12] If any moment or place is in that way ambivalent – that it may as easily disclose a vision of discord as of *Agape* – what significance is there in location or nation? This is the second point raised by 'A Summer Night': the ambiguity of 'England'. The fourth ode in *The Orators* puts the issue more colourfully, in a naïvely linear conception of the relationship between plenitude and the prosaic: 'England our cow / Once was a lady – is she now?' (*EA*, p. 101).

Auden's 1930s writings delight in evocations of high 'Englishness'. *The Orators* opens with the culturally specific English *topos* of Prize Day at a boys' school. In typically Audenesque manner, the humour deriving from the resounding banality of such occasions is turned to serious purpose. The invited speaker poses a series of sonorous questions about the meaning of commemoration, and then in a bathetic moment that recalls the cricket field, remarks 'It's a facer, isn't it boys?' (*EA*, p. 61). It is typical of Auden to approach profound and timeless issues through the banal and historically specific. Thus, a little later in *The Orators*, we have a version of the responsory prayer that might be said in a school chapel. The versicles are abstract, metaphorical and capable of broad interpretation: 'In the moment of vision; in the hour of applause; in the place of defeat, and in the hour of desertion.' The responses, in contrast, are parodic in their specificity, their at best tangential relationship to what is being prayed for, and their pointed Englishness. To the versicle above comes the response, 'O Holmes, deliver us.' Sherlock Holmes is one of a series of fictional English detectives invoked in the responses, along with English heroes who double up as famous pub names, such as the Marquis of Granby and the Fair Maid of Kent. As this 'English Study' progresses, such references proliferate until in the closing odes there is an apotheosis of Englishness, in the celebration of those who played for Sedbergh School's Rugby xv in the spring of 1927, in a language drawing on the Anglo-Saxon alliterative tradition and Hopkins's 'sprung rhythm' (*EA*, p. 97).

There is an interesting modulation of tone towards the end of this ode, as the speaker turns to consider success and defeat in the context not of rugby but of life. In relation to the latter, the discourse of the public school – and indeed the whole distinctively English habit of finding metaphors for life in sport – acquires a peculiar pathos. We have seen a version of the same thing in the bemused speaker of 'I have a handsome profile', for whom good looks, a public school education and modest investments ought to bring happiness – but do not. The poem allows the foolishness of its speaker to stand fully exposed in its self-centredness, so that we feel that he, his class and his nation are justifiably doomed. In an earlier poem, Auden's approach was even more cutting: to the 'splendid person' with gun, spotless flannels, horse and retriever, he declared that when the future kissed him, called him 'king', she was a deceiver (*EA*, p. 121). In the second *Orators* ode, however, Auden's use of the class-inflected discourse of Englishness is less easily objectified, the tone more difficult to apprehend. The poem itself effects empathy, as the speaker turns from memories of 'our' team to meditate on the opponents, on whom defeat has fallen. The self-awareness and selflessness apparent in his phrase 'Easy for us to tell' exerts a leavening influence on the upper-class schoolboy language. The message seems to be that the speaker is a team-player in the broadest sense, and that his language signifies not exclusiveness but a spirit of generous inclusion.

It is a measure of Auden's ambiguous relationship with England that his thirties poems repeatedly assert the imminent and welcome demise of the imperial power while simultaneously making bravura use of a language inseparable from the country's imperial, class-bound history. In linguistic terms, 'we' and 'they' are both on the same side in what might be read as either a model for inclusiveness or a recipe for civil war and artistic defeat. If the former, we are invited to find non-contingent value – pleasure and consolation – in a cosy and almost entirely fictional version of Englishness. The truth, though, is that Auden never loses sight of the potential for civil war. He breathes deeply and with relish the atmosphere of 'a world that has had its day' (*EA*, p. 123), mindful of the potentially toxic effect of this exposure.

'A Summer Night' makes the point that 'Our freedom in this English house' is bought at a price. While he and his companions enjoy their vision of *Agape*, the 'creepered wall' obscures the 'gathering multitudes' outside (*EA*, p. 137). Auden speaks metaphorically of the 'river-dreams' of persons like himself, which hide the magnitude and power of the sea. England's glory, lamented as lost throughout *F6*, depends on her ability to overcome resistance within and competition without. While Auden was demonstrably vulnerable to the charms of English river-dreaming, his rejection of British chauvinism and economic predation was consistent. Beginning in the mid twenties, Auden had imbibed from Freud belief in the importance of the liberated unconscious, and in 1928 he assimilated John Layard's particularly powerful doctrine of psychological liberation. 'To those brought up on repression', he wrote, 'the mere release of the unconscious is sufficient to give a sense of value and meaning to life' (Carpenter, p. 89). While recognising that to live in society requires sacrifice of some of this meaning, he nevertheless insisted that societies are healthy only to the extent that they allow their members maximum freedom of instinct, will, action and thought. 'The individual *in vacuo* is an intellectual abstraction', he wrote in 1939, for individuals are the product of social life (*EA*, p. 373). But the psychologically coercive and limiting effects of social life must be curtailed. For that reason, the 'river-dreams' of England already contain potential for frustration and grief.

Richard Davenport-Hines observes that 'it was Auden's integrity, toughness and meditated purpose that took him abroad' (RD-H, p. 176). All three qualities were undoubtedly required: Auden had long known he could not realise his river-dream at the mouth of the Hudson. The rather gloomy conviction that 'you're what you are and nothing you do / Will get you out of the wood' (*EA*, p. 125) had remained with him, and if anything his one hope in the move was that he would find himself able to contemplate more clearly and directly this situation. 'An artist ought either to live where he has live roots or where he has no roots at all', he observed to Louis MacNeice in 1940. 'In England to-day the artist feels essentially lonely, twisted in dying roots, always in opposition to a group . . . in America, he is just lonely, but so . . . is everybody else; with 140 million lonelies milling around him he need not waste his time in conforming or rebelling' (RD-H, p. 180). America, perhaps, promised liberation but no relief from the basic Audenesque dilemma: how to bring on 'the season of the change of heart' (*EA*, p. 105), to unite all 'lonelies' in a new human architecture of which the vision of *Agape* gave intimation.

As early as 1932 Auden had envisaged a role for the writer in building the good society, asserting in a piece for Naomi Mitchison's *Outline for Boys and Girls and Their Parents* that 'you must use your knowledge of people to guide you when reading books, and your knowledge of books to guide you when living with people' (*EA*, p. 311). This is something different from literary didacticism. The act of reading is here seen as a rehearsal for human interaction – and, since rehearsal leads towards perfection, reading could contribute actively to successful human community. This conclusion is anticipated in another of Auden's observations, that language arose as a result of our desire to escape the condition of solitariness (*EA*, p. 303). Society answered a psychological need, as 'man felt the need to bridge over the gulf' between 'I' and 'not I', to 'recover the sense of being as much a part of life as the cells in his body are part of him' (*EA*, p. 303). Notwithstanding Layard, then, Auden did not regard society as inherently antipathetic to human well-being, or even to the expression of a liberated unconscious. The writer was bound by his profession to foster a desirable social order, one in which 'all the individual wills are assured complete freedom of moral choice and at the same time prevented from ever clashing' (*EA*, p. 377).

That writers had a social function was an orthodox notion in England during the 1930s. By the start of the Spanish Civil War it was indeed widely assumed that artists and writers *should* 'ransom' themselves, sacrificing their artistic aloofness in service to the communal good. As the title of a famous *Left Review* pamphlet in 1937 suggests, it was assumed that 'Authors Take Sides on the Spanish Civil War' or any other issue of national moment. The death in combat of the poet John Cornford was seen as exemplary. Auden's 'social' theory of language – and the politically efficacious art it implied – was superficially comfortable in such a context. Although in retrospect there was clear significance in his refusal to join the Communist Party even when many of his friends were doing so,[13] several poems from the period attempt to enlist in the political struggle. 'A Communist to Others' was at least partly provoked by a conversation Auden had with Edward Upward, whose membership of the Party had been the subject of his own recent writing. Carpenter notes that 'If it were not for the word "Comrades" in the opening line and the title ... it would be easy to imagine that the poem was not about Communism at all' (Carpenter, p. 149). Within four years Auden had replaced 'Comrades' with 'Brothers', a clear indication of his discomfort within an identifiably Communist camp. *Spain* might stand plausibly as Auden's strongest essay in political poetry – except for the fact that it was written less in response to events than in reaction to a book he was reviewing for *New Verse* – Christopher Caudwell's treatise in Marxist literary criticism, *Illusion and Reality: A Study of the Sources of Poetry*. Auden pronounced Caudwell's book 'the most important book on poetry' since those of Dr I. A. Richards (*Prose I*, p. 387).

*Illusion and Reality* signalled a decisive shift in literary criticism away from the dominant formalism of the 1920s – the decade which saw the publication of Richards's influential *Principles of Literary Criticism* (1924) and *Practical Criticism* (1929) – and towards approaches which saw literary texts as enmeshed in history, products of ideology, and interventions in the socio-political realm. Even F. R. Leavis, for whom Richards had served as mentor, partook of this new sensibility. His essay on *Mass Civilisation and Minority Culture* (1930) began the decade by declaring that English culture was in crisis, and asserted the social responsibilities of writers and critics. He even briefly entertained relationship with 'some kind of communism'.[14] One Communist critic, Ralph Fox, asserted in *The Novel and the People* (1937), that 'the future of the English novel and therefore the solution to the problems which vex the English novelist lies precisely in Marxism with its artistic formula of a "socialist realism" which shall re-unite and re-vitalise the forces of the left in literature'.[15] Alick West, at one time Caudwell's teacher, was the figure who worked most energetically to bridge the formalist twenties and the 'engaged' thirties. His *Crisis and Criticism* (1937) sought to disprove 'the belief that Marxist criticism ignores aesthetic values', and that 'the idealistic conception of aesthetic value is the only true one'.[16]

The Second International Congress of Writers for the Defence of Culture met in Valencia, Madrid and Barcelona during the summer of 1937. A *Manifesto* was issued at the end of the conference and printed in *Left Review* that September. The text appeals solemnly 'to writers of the whole world, to all those who believe deeply and sincerely in their human mission, in the power of the written word', and summons them 'to take up their stand without delay against the menace which hangs over culture and humanity'.[17] Not all writers who subscribed to the idea of an 'engaged' art did so exclusively from the Left. Wyndham Lewis, from a diametrically opposed politics, elsewhere told his fellow writers that '[S]ides have to be taken; but do not be ashamed of that. Whichever cause you adopt – the red cause of Moscow and materialism, or the Fascist cause of nationalist idealism, or whatever cause it may be – it is a game purely and simply . . . The only important thing is to be on the side to which you belong.'[18]

Auden appears to have begun reading Marx after going up to Oxford in 1925, and the effects are discernible almost immediately. At the same time, his understanding of Marx, like his understanding of Freud, was idiosyncratic. In fact, he saw the two thinkers as closely related, both 'right', as he was to say in 1935, because economic oppression and psychological repression are linked: 'as long as civilisation remains as it is, the number of patients the psychologist can cure are very few, and as soon as socialism attains power, it must learn to direct its own interior energy and will need the psychologist' (*EA*, p. 341). Layard's version of Freud occupied an intensely personal place in Auden's conception of self, and it should not be surprising to find that he had a similarly private investment in Marx – one which would not allow him to subscribe to the Marx of public discourse.

The factitiousness of *Spain*, the self-consciousness of 'A Communist to Others', betray the discomfort Auden evidently felt in responding to the demands of the age. The point is not that his belief in the social function of writing was ever questionable, but rather that his understanding of that function differed from that of others. In particular, the model of literary engagement endorsed by the Congress of Writers is simple where Auden's is complex, direct where his is oblique and rhetorical where his is psychological and experiential. To read the card-carrying Cecil Day-Lewis's *The Magnetic Mountain* (1933), dedicated to Auden, next to Auden's own 'In Time of War' sequence vividly brings home the contrast.

Auden's most frequent explanation for his departure from England is that he could no longer tolerate the demands placed on him as what Edward Mendelson has called 'Court Poet of the Left'. The credibility of the 'red cause' had no doubt been shaken by his experiences in Spain, but one should not over-emphasise the role of his changing political beliefs in this decision. The fact is that he was in no way suited to be a spokesman for any ideology that might be arrived at by Congress resolution. Under growing pressure to write a poetry that 'took sides', his art seemed in constant danger of becoming a travesty. There is evidence for this in his elegy for W. B. Yeats, well known for its declaration that 'poetry makes nothing happen', and the claim that a poem relates to society as 'A way of happening, a mouth' (*EA*, p. 242). Such effect as a text has, then, is linked to the way in which readers experience it, rather than to anything that it might 'say'. Evidently not satisfied that this demurrer was sufficiently clear, Auden addressed the issue also in 'The Public vs. the Late Mr William Butler Yeats', an inventive, court-room variant on the Platonic dialogue, published in *Partisan Review* in the spring of 1939.

The case for 'the Public' against Yeats is that he failed to demonstrate two of the three qualities of a great poet: 'a profound understanding of the age in which he lived', and 'a working knowledge of and sympathetic attitude towards the most progressive thought of his time' (*EA*, p. 389). Invested with the irony that pervades the language of government figures in *F6*, the Public Prosecutor's speech attacks Yeats for his failure to subordinate his personal interests – 'the virtues of the peasant', fairies and 'barbaric heroes with unpronounceable names' – to support the cause of socialism. Of Yeats's 'Easter 1916' he notes cuttingly that 'to succeed at such a time in writing a poem which could offend neither the Irish Republican nor the British Army was indeed a masterly achievement' (*EA*, p. 390). Auden's hostility to such easy dismissals is palpable. The Counsel for the Defence does not offer a caricature reversal of the Prosecution, but an artist's defence of much more complex loyalties and obligations. He states clearly the pressure of Auden's own age: 'we are tempted to judge contemporary poets because we really do have problems which we really do want solved, so that we are inclined to expect everyone, politicians, scientists, poets, clergymen, to give us what we want, and to blame them indiscriminately when they do not' (*EA*, p. 391). The temptation, however understandable, is at odds with the nature of art:

> For art is a product of history, not a cause. Unlike some other products, techni-
> cal inventions for example, it does not re-enter history as an effective agent . . .
> [I]f not a poem had been written, not a picture painted, not a bar of music
> composed, the history of man would be materially unchanged.   (*EA*, p. 393)

In 1933, when 'England to our meditations seemed / The perfect setting', he had noticed that it has no innocence at all: 'It is the isolation and the fear, / The mood itself.' Separate from the transforming imagination of the poet, England is 'the body of the absent lover' (*EA*, p. 142), visible but not effectively present, a carnal thing but in no way the object of desire. The landscape speaks of a civilisation in decline, as 'the customs of your society . . . / Harden themselves into the unbreakable / Habits of death' (*EA*, pp. 142–3). Humphrey Carpenter (p. 244) has suggested that as late as 1937 Auden perhaps still believed it would be possible to realise, in England, the kind of society presaged by his Vision of *Agape*, but that by 1938 he did not. In 1939 he was to write that 'what England can give me, I feel it already has, and that I can never lose it'.[19]

As a 'secondary world', a body of ideas, images and linguistic practices out of which Auden's identity was formed, England would travel with him. As the milieu in relation to which that identity would unfold historically, England would – must – be left behind, not only because it had 'had its day', but because Auden's ability to conceive of human plenitude depended on separation from the familiar natural and social landscape of his birth. Almost a year after his departure he would write, in *New Year Letter*, that in America, more than in Europe, the choice of patterns is made clear, revealing 'what / Is possible and what is not, / To what conditions we must bow / In building the Just City now' (*NYL*, lines 1521–4). One year later, 'Atlantis' notes that, being set on the idea of reaching this mythic place (for which, read the 'Just City'), 'You have discovered of course / Only the Ship of Fools is / Making the voyage this year.' Scholars, the poem says, have proved there cannot be any such place. But such subtlety betrays a 'simple enormous grief', teaching how 'To doubt that you may believe'. In order to be at home, you must move elsewhere, for 'Unless you are capable / Of forgetting completely / About Atlantis, you will / Never finish your journey.'

## NOTES

1. Robin Skelton (ed.), *Poetry of the Thirties* (Harmondsworth: Penguin, 1964), p. 13.
2. Frank Kermode, *History and Value* (Oxford: Clarendon Press, 1988), pp. 40–1.
3. See Smith, p. 1.
4. *Southern Review* (Summer 1940), p. 83. Quoted and discussed in Carpenter, p. 57.
5. See *Early Auden*, pp. 20, 63, 149–50.
6. *I Believe*, ed. Clifton Fadiman (1939). Repr. in *EA*, p. 377.
7. See Carpenter, p. 194.
8. Leon Surette, *Pound in Purgatory: From Economic Radicalism to Anti-Semitism* (Urbana and Chicago: University of Illinois Press, 1999), p. 72.
9. Percy Wyndham Lewis, *Hitler* (1931) (New York: Gordon Press, 1972), p. 48.
10. 'A Contemporary Epic', *Encounter*, 2:2 (February 1954), p. 67.
11. See Thomas Dilworth, 'David Jones and Fascism', *Journal of Modern Literature*, 13:1 (March 1986), p. 155.
12. *The Complete Poems and Plays of T. S. Eliot* (London: Faber and Faber, 1969), pp. 172, 176.
13. In the autumn of 1932 he concluded a letter to Rupert Doone: 'No. I am a bourgeois. I shall not join the C.P.'
14. See Francis Mulhern, *The Moment of 'Scrutiny'* (London: Verso, 1981), pp. 94–5.
15. Repr. in Patrick Deane (ed.), *History in Our Hands: A Critical Anthology of Writings on Literature, Culture, and Politics from the 1930s* (London and New York: Leicester University Press, 1998), p. 155.
16. Alick West, *Crisis and Criticism and Selected Literary Essays* (London: Lawrence and Wishart, 1975), p. 75.
17. *Left Review*, 3:8 (September 1937), pp. 445–6.
18. *English Review*, 59 (November 1934), p. 571.
19. Letter to Mrs A. E. Dodds, quoted in Carpenter, p. 244.

# 4

NICHOLAS JENKINS

# Auden in America

The classical route map for a great poet's career was linear and ascendant. Following the Virgilian example, it began with pastoral apprenticeship (*The Eclogues*), continued with works about subjects of greater significance in more complex forms (*The Georgics*) and ended with the loftiest achievement, a national epic (*The Aeneid*). By this standard almost all twentieth-century artistic lives, marked by lateral turns and ideological reversals, seem flawed beyond mending. But classicism's failings have become modernity's virtues, and, understood in this light, W. H. Auden's career, with its sudden departures, intense foreswearings and radical changes of direction, is prototypically unpredictable, prototypically modern.

It is 'my vocation to be a Wandering Jew', Auden, aware of this emblematic restlessness, told friends.[1] Of his many 'moves', the most fateful was his decision to leave England at the height of his early celebrity, to live in the United States and, before long, become an American citizen. It was also easily the most controversial.

On a freezing January morning in 1939, Auden and Isherwood came ashore in Manhattan, apparently intending to stay for a year and write a travel book about the States, to be titled *Address Not Known*. Auden was beginning his challenge, at first perhaps unintended but later certainly deliberate, to one of the most tenaciously held assumptions of post-Romantic culture, one so deeply embedded in current ways of imagining literary history that many critics hardly acknowledge its existence, let alone question its explanatory power.

The assumption is that a poet's work is significant to the extent that it identifies with, or represents, the modern socio-cultural collective of a 'nation'. In 1889 the nationalist Yeats put the relationship bluntly: 'there is no fine nationality without literature, and . . . there is no fine literature without nationality'.[2] Beliefs like these persisted as commonplaces far into the twentieth century, even after psychopathic variants of nationalism had served as the ideological motor for untold millions of deaths in war and revolution. Indeed, from the 1930s onwards, Anglo-American poetic modernism, alienated from its transcultural origins, became steadily more nationalistic, more deeply obsessed with roots, community, tradition and belonging. In 1945 T. S. Eliot wrote that 'No art is more stubbornly national than poetry', an assertion to which the early Yeats would have readily assented.[3]

Though Auden had emerged early in the decade as a late modernist poet with a specifically English national identity, by the mid 1930s he realised that he was living at an unprecedented historical moment, in which, as he put it in a 1940 letter to Golo Mann, his brother-in-law, 'les relations économiques et politiques du monde entier sont complètement interlacées'.[4] And yet, in spite of this globalising reality, nationalist exceptionalism continued to flourish in politics and art. Auden sombrely noted in his 1939 elegy for Yeats that 'In the nightmare of the dark / . . . the living nations wait, / Each sequestered in its hate' (EA, p. 243). In the United States, Auden began to explore the consequences of the belief that a new kind of world demanded a new kind of poem. In Auden's time, just as much as in Virgil's, every poet aspiring to major status needed a profound historical gesture. Virgil joined the poet's text to the national destiny. The de-linking of poetry from authentication by nationality, initiated when he came to the United States, was Auden's.

Late in life, Auden admitted that he 'had never in his boyhood known anything about America – it was all just a blur over there, and he still knew nothing after Oxford'.[5] For 1930s English intellectuals, history was being made to the East, in Europe and Russia. During the first decade of his career, Auden took an interest in a number of writers who came from America, including Robert Frost and Laura Riding, as well as Eliot. But their 'Americanness' does not seem to have been pertinent. In 1936, for example, he managed to write an entire essay on Frost without once referring to America (Prose I, pp. 137–41).

Like England, the young Auden wanted to look inwards. His reputation was initially made in a cultural context where the local, rural and rooted had far greater cultural prestige than the technologised or metropolitan – qualities then conventionally associated in the European mind with the United States. For a while, whatever his professed Leftism, Auden offered his readers an intensely realised lyric version of English belonging, subtly but indelibly tinged with the aura of a potentially violent, regenerative nationalism. Wholeness and integration, to the young Auden, were at once philosophical, social and imaginative ideals. Correspondingly, his work of this period is filled with emblems of social totality and cognitive completeness, of imagined 'wholes' or 'cells', sealed and private spaces such as rooms, gardens, clubs, bars, even poems, or closed communities like the boarding school celebrated in the 1932 poem 'A Happy New Year'.

Ultimately these numinous wholes derived from the political vision of a blessedly insular, insulated, internally integrated England, 'this island now' of the title poem to Auden's strangely patriotic volume *Look, Stranger!*. In the first two stanzas England is superlatively delineated as a harmoniously interdependent island of green fields, chalk cliffs, a shingle beach and contented human observers. Nonetheless, the poem's close suggests a fragility and impermanence to England's literal and metaphoric insularity. The 'full view / Indeed may enter', the poem allows, as if in passing. And in muted, seemingly involuntary ways Auden's 1930s poetry records the ambivalence intrinsic to the language of nationhood, a language never more assertive than in the face of imminent collapse. The national 'sign', as Auden's poetry from time to time manages to acknowledge, is always unstable. The national space is never the autonomous realm that nationalist mythologising desires. The cliff that 'falls to the foam' in 'Look, Stranger!' is, from one perspective, happily fixed in an eternal, unhistorical present – always falling but never fallen. From another, though, that iconic white bulwark of friable chalk is inexorably crumbling under the assault of the sea, time, history.

As part of an emerging, de-anglicising 'full view', America's first appearance in Auden's poetry comes in 'The Sphinx', written in early 1938. Marooned in a country that is like an 'anarchical Woolworth's', the Egyptian monument has an 'old actor's wig', 'pink' cheeks and 'thin lion lips', making the crumbling monument into an eerily displaced emblem of the mouldy, moth-eaten imperial British lion. It lies in the desert, 'turning / A vast behind on shrill America'.[6] The Sphinx faces away from America (like Auden and his generation until this point), its ancient, wounded silence the antithesis of that country's *nouveau* shrillness. But if to be oriented towards the past, as the Sphinx is, means to look *away* from America, then, at the level of poetic logic, Auden's poem silently insists that the future lies in looking *towards* America.

Auden and Isherwood saw the Sphinx en route to China. On their way back to Britain in mid 1938 they stopped off for a brief, exhilarating visit to New York. Back in Britain, Auden found himself enduring the painful culmination of a lengthy process. He believed he was running out of things to say as a poet and, simultaneously, he despaired at the failure of his political ideals in the morally debased climate of Neville Chamberlain's Britain. One evening in autumn 1938, sitting at the window of a friend's Birmingham flat, looking out over the homes of Chamberlain's Tory constituents, Auden was steeped in gloom. 'What a window at which to sit and watch "the lights going out all over Europe"', he said. Europe was 'finished' and he admitted that he was thinking of going to America.[7] That spring, in 'The Sphinx', America had just been 'shrill'. But in the second half of 1938 the United States was transformed in Auden's poem 'Commentary' into a place that was 'absolutely free' (*EA*, p. 267).

To understand what Auden's departure meant, we must see it within the larger context. The early twentieth-century English-speaking poetic sphere was a transnational cultural system. Poets, styles, little magazines, books and gossip circulated freely back and forth across the Atlantic. What had appeared in London was soon well known in New York. And, from the spring of 1939, plentiful rumours about Auden in New York filled the literary precincts of the British capital. The interrelationship of politics and poetry changed substantially for Auden in Manhattan, but his old literary identity and social engagement were not simply cast aside. They just got more complex and less conventional, harder and more rewarding, to 'read'. The Auden born in York in 1907 was not magically reborn in New York in 1939. To live in New York was not to live in a world where he had no reputation and so could be completely anonymous. Most of his writing to date had already been published there, and his fame in US literary circles was well established.

To see the English-speaking poetic world as a single, transnational system does not imply the identity of all its parts. The intellectual and cultural atmosphere in New York was different enough to unleash a new burst of energy. Auden later claimed that the 'primary freedom conferred by America has little to do with democracy: it is the freedom to make experiments'.[8] And almost as soon as he arrived in the United States, Auden's poetry began emitting signals on a new frequency. The first poem written there, 'In Memory of W. B. Yeats', elegises many things – a particular poet about whom he had decidedly mixed feelings; his own former style; a vatic, politically instrumental conception of the poet's role within culture; the links that bound Yeats's and his own poetry to collective national traditions. But, like all elegies, it is as much concerned with the future as the past. In it, Auden also announced his new uprootedness, his work's relocation in the 'fresh woods and pastures new' of a different cultural milieu.

The frozen, wintry world in the first part of the elegy harks back to Auden's earlier poems, 'Brussels in Winter', 'The Capital', about a nightmarish European landscape of desolation, cold and entropy where both metaphorically and literally the lights had 'gone out'. The landscape of the elegy's first section is criss-crossed by congealed and arrested flows: brooks (figuratively springs of creativity and desire) are 'frozen', 'snow' effaces physical contours, the thermometer's mercury becomes viscous and 'sinks' as the temperature drops. However, in its middle section, the sacred source of poetic language begins to flow again at the exact moment Auden makes his relocation to America explicit. Poetry, he writes, like a river 'flows south / From ranches of isolation and the busy griefs, / Raw towns that we believe and die in'. Unmistakably, this was not a poem written in Europe, where an American word like 'ranches' or a phrase like 'Raw towns' would have seemed, literally, out of place.

In modern poetry, profound ideological changes are manifested in perturbations of diction, rhythm and form as much as in new kinds of content. In the ensuing months Auden's writing consistently invoked non-'English,' non-'traditional' poetic techniques. He made many attempts to write in what were for him unfamiliar, and defamiliarising, forms. Along with the long, breath-based Whitmanian line in the first part of the Yeats elegy, and the free verse in its middle section, there are in other poems examples of calypso, blues, frontier ballad (in the *Paul Bunyan* operetta) and, in 'The Unknown Citizen', of Ogden Nash-style light verse, the poem's irregular line lengths and comical rhymes mixing Nash's stylistic trademarks with the political import of Brechtian satire.

Even one of Auden's gravest poems began as a kind of pastiche of the *New Yorker*-ish Nash. In August 1939 Auden had written to an English friend that Nash was 'one of the best poets in America', citing the jaunty opening of Nash's 'Spring Comes to Murray Hill': 'I sit in an office at 244 Madison Avenue.'[9] A few weeks later, the sombre, topographically specific beginning of 'September 1, 1939', 'I sit in one of the dives / On Fifty-Second Street' (*EA*, p. 245), transformed the first line of Nash's poem while preserving the teeming concrete-honeycomb feel of Manhattan which Nash had so vividly captured. Another new influence was Marianne Moore, whom Auden visited in Brooklyn for the first time just as he was completing his Freud elegy, his first successful poem in syllabics, a form Moore had made her own. It is the specifically non-English mode in which many of Auden's most important poems of the next few years – 'Music is International', 'Ischia', 'Prime' – were to be written.

In New York in early autumn 1939 Auden observed to Robert Fitzgerald that 'America is the place because nationalities don't mean anything here, there are only human beings, and that's how the future must be.'[10] As a result of this belief, Auden's lyrics of the time are recognisably no longer 'English' poems. But they are not 'American' either. They exemplify instead the new kind of hybrid 'mid-Atlantic' style Auden was feeling towards, an in-between of voices and forms that would refuse identification with a single poetic culture or nation. Whatever else it is, Auden's writing in the United States is not an attempt to 'assimilate' poetically, to become 'an American poet', as in the ideological fiction of the New World 'melting-pot'. The new poetic measure that Auden sought was not national, but grew out of a world in which 'nationalities don't mean anything'.

In the draft of 'New Year Letter' (written between January and April 1940), he launched an assault on nationalist sentiments, 'The patrias of civility', 'England', 'La France', 'Das Reich', whose fictions of national separateness were the catalysts for wars engineered for private profit under the guise of patriotism.[11] But in less blatant form the same sentiments are everywhere in his published poetry at this time. The title poem to *Another Time*, for example, speaks caustically of those who 'bow with old-world grace / To a proper flag in a proper place'. Auden's first poems written in America bowed to no proper flag, neither Union Jack nor Star-Spangled Banner.

Almost all critics have overlooked the depth and thoroughness of Auden's critique of that most modern marker of personal identity, nationality. The critique, located even at the smallest stylistic and verbal levels, determines what can be misperceived as merely technical matters. Discussing 'New Year Letter', critics often assume there is something odd about composing a pastiche of a neoclassical, eighteenth-century epistolary poem in the America of 1940. But 'New Year Letter' deploys an awareness of form precisely to position itself outside easy stylistic or generic definition. Like 'The Unknown Citizen' or 'September 1, 1939', the poem is another of Auden's hybrids, stylistically displaced both from 'Old World' clarity and restraint and from 'New World' inwardness and liberation.

Mirroring this formal indeterminacy, it contains endless thematic and verbal dualities. In a polyglot compound of languages, reflecting the cultural ferment of a New York full of European refugees, it seeks to bridge the terrains of 'versified metaphysical argument' and psychoanalytically inflected autobiography. It oscillates between the local and the ideal, the particular and the general, between its actual setting in Brooklyn and the world of war and turmoil across the ocean – an 'Old World' of firing squads, bombs, torture and mass poverty. Auden's intensely metropolitan poem also contains his lengthiest and most powerful description of the deserted landscape in the Northern Pennines which constituted his bleak personal version of the Garden of Eden. And – the poem's addressee like Auden an exile from Europe – its projected audience is both a private friend and the unnumbered, faceless readers 'Who wish to read it anywhere'.

Auden's lines, unlike those of the firmly delimited neoclassical couplet, are more often than not open-ended, his rhymes frequently inconclusive and unstable. To balance against his partial evocation of English eighteenth-century discursive poems, Auden borrowed earlier, impeccably 'New World' models for the cascading, unrelaxed tetrameter couplets that he found himself deploying. They recall, for example, the forms of Emerson's 'Each and All' and the panoptic vistas of his 'The Problem'. Just as in Auden's shorter poems of this period, then, the United States is present as much in 'New Year Letter' at the level of form as content, meditating on national belonging in a loosened, fluctuating structure that incarnates the fundamental European idea of America as a place of enigmatic unfinishedness.

In *Studies in Classic American Literature* (1923), a book Auden specially admired, D. H. Lawrence claimed that writers about the United States 'see what they want to see: especially if they look from a long distance, across the ocean, for example'.[12] Like Lawrence, Auden at first viewed the United States through conceptual lenses. His ideas often derive from a few central themes which have focused European perceptions of the country from the moment of its independence in 1776. Latent, for example, in the familiar notion of a 'New World', is the idea that the United States differs from the 'Old World'. In 1939, the American poet Richard Eberhart summarised a conversational remark of Auden's that his 'coming to America may prove to be as significant as Eliot's leaving it. Eliot sought a truly old world. Auden wishes to become a citizen of what he must consider the theater of new attitudes, a place for growth.'[13] In the same vein, 'New Year Letter', citing Henry Adams's indictment of American technology and Goethe's praise of America as historically unencumbered, speaks of a culture that 'had worshipped no / Virgin before the Dynamo', had no Nicea or Canossa and no ruins of 'fallen castles'.

If, unlike Europe, the United States was free from the nightmarish weight of the past, it was in America that the coming shape of the world would first and most clearly emerge. Alexis de Tocqueville's *Democracy in America* (1835–40), perhaps the most influential book ever written about the country, observed that 'the same democracy reigning in American societies appeared to me to be advancing rapidly toward power in Europe'.[14] In a word, America was Europe's and the world's future, a Tocquevillian belief shared by Auden with commentators as diverse as Bishop Berkeley, J. S. Mill, Hegel, Marx and, again, Lawrence.

For Auden, the future was being determined not by collective loyalties but by the supra-national impact of technology, hypostasised as 'The Machine', which had created a quite new historical complex, 'the Machine Age'. This idea became an obsession in Auden's early years in America. His 1940 review 'Tradition and Value' asserts that 'men no longer have neighbors tied to them by geography, only a far-flung association of personal friends kept in touch with by machinery', and argues that the 'effect of the machine on life overshadows completely any political effects' (*Prose II*, p. 52). 'New Year Letter' notes that 'the machine has now destroyed / The local customs we enjoyed' by annulling 'the bonds of blood and nation' in favour (the republican terminology is noticeable) of 'personal confederation'. Auden's freighted, often enjambed line-endings, pointing ahead towards the completion of a current thought in a fresh line, are beautifully oriented to an open future, never more so than when he writes of America in the Machine Age that:

> More even than in Europe, here
> The choice of patterns is made clear
> Which the machine imposes, what
> Is possible and what is not . . .

'At least I know what I am trying to do', Auden wrote to a friend, 'which . . . is to live deliberately without roots'.[15] 'New Year Letter' embodies American modernity in its rootlessness and endless mobility, just as, in *The Age of Anxiety*,[16] Auden's fourth major long poem from this period (written between 1944 and 1947), a character mournfully accepts the 'sad unrest / Which no life can lack'. Because modernity *is* movement and because movement *is* America (another Tocquevillian theme), America incarnates the real modern condition, the 'Aloneness' which now means that 'Each must travel forth alone' on a personal quest in a world where 'all real unity commences / In consciousness of differences'.

This destiny is by no means just a liberation from outdated constraints. Emotional isolation accompanies moral 'Aloneness'. 'To be free / is often to be lonely' Auden wrote in his elegy for Freud. As late as 1947 he was lecturing Cyril Connolly on the same theme: 'He is, of course, extremely lonely, but then so is every American; "you have no idea", he says, "how lonely even the married are".'[17] Set in Auden's New World of the uprooted, the exiled and the searching, 'New Year Letter's keynote word 'travel' returns in the poem's final phrase, on which the emphasis of the caesura falls most heavily: 'The world's great rage, the travel of young men'.

The unifying theme of all Auden's long poems from his first decade in America is that most morally loaded form of travel: exile. 'For the Time Being' (written 1941–2) sets the mythic dimension of the Nativity narrative in a modern-seeming world where 'Mankind is on the march', where kings are displaced from their kingdoms and where a god must be born in a barn. Echoing the close of *Paradise Lost* (like *The Age of Anxiety*), but estranged in time and mindset from Milton's faith in the poet's prophetic role, the poem ends with Joseph and Mary's flight into Egypt, retracing the exilic footsteps of Moses. In 'The Sea and the Mirror' (written 1942–4) an exiled Duke, newly alienated from his habitual imperious self, prepares to leave his island home along with the travellers he has steered off course. In *The Age of Anxiety*, set in Manhattan, the ultimately rootless modern conurbation, three of the four main characters inhabit a country where they were not born: Malin is Canadian, Quant is Irish, Rosetta a middle-class Jew from Britain.

Metaphorically speaking, each of these four long works is generically 'exiled'. 'New Year Letter', a long verse letter, is subtly out of place in an era of image-based, anti-discursive poetry. 'For the Time Being', 'The Sea and the Mirror'[18] and *The Age of Anxiety* are dramatic poems uprooted from their natural home in the theatre, just as most of their characters are personally displaced from their points of origin. Even Auden's God is in exile from us, or we from Him. He told a New York congregation in 1951: 'our dominant experience is of God's absence, of His distance'.[19]

Wartime, Auden wrote in *The Age of Anxiety*, reduces everyone 'to the anxious status of a shady character or a displaced person'. He was voluntarily displaced and alone in a country he once called 'the Great Void', a place that teemed with exiles, immigrants, searchers and refugees of all stripes.[20] To steady himself in this social vacuum, Auden found three fixed reference points, underwent three kinds of 'conversion'. One, as Auden's comment about an absent God implies, was religious. Writing to Charles Williams in early 1940 about the latter's *The Descent of the Dove*, Auden still described himself as 'no Christian' (Carpenter, p. 285). But 'New Year Letter' concludes with an enigmatically Christian invocation of a mysterious supernatural presence, with quotations from Origen and Augustine quarried out of Williams's book. By the summer of 1940 Auden had begun attending church services in Brooklyn, as a prelude to his return to the Episcopalian fold. Isherwood reported that Auden already had 'a whole new lingo of Christian theology'.[21]

Another reference point was Chester Kallman. After falling in love with Kallman, whose Jewishness offered access to a world entirely different from his own, Auden almost immediately wrote a number of serenely happy love poems, 'The Prophets', 'Like a Vocation' and 'Heavy Date', the latter rich in a newly discovered American argot. From Kallman he acquired the third new reference point: grand opera, in which he quickly became fanatically interested. In 1944 in a letter to Isherwood about Vedanta, Auden invited his oldest friend to come and stay with him, commenting only half ironically: 'You could try to convert me to the Eastern Way and I would try to convert you to music.'[22] By 1948 Kallman and Auden were at work on the libretto for Stravinsky's *The Rake's Progress*. Religion, love of a young Jewish man, opera – these seem very different kinds of passions from the ones that had animated the 'English Auden'. But in 1947 Auden told an interviewer: 'In the war years, a poet had to be other-worldly. At any rate, I did.'[23]

It is easy to misunderstand that 'other-worldliness'. Auden's apparently most abstract and intellectual interests are almost always historically situated and socially pertinent. Take his thinking about gender roles. Although a believer, Auden was no saint, and no more entirely devoid of all the typical prejudices of his age than anyone ever is. Yet a crucial element of interest to him beneath the surface of American life – and, for a major male poet of this period, a very unusual interest – was the enhanced status of women in the United States. In his early years in the country, Auden formed important friendships with a number of women writers, in particular with Marianne Moore and Louise Bogan. In 1942 he told Bogan that he considered her, Laura Riding, T. S. Eliot and Marianne Moore as the four best American poets, and he asked, rhetorically: 'is it significant that three of you are ♀?'[24]

For Auden, American nature was 'female'. But, anomalously, for him 'she' was indomitable and beyond possession: wild, rampant, sometimes terrifying. In a draft for *Paul Bunyan*, he warned his American settlers that with the 'virgin to whom you are about to be introduced, all etiquettes will be worse than useless'. This 'virgin' has 'made up her mind to destroy all suitors' (*Lib*, p. 545). The antithesis of American nature, American society, traditionally a male-dominated domain, was fragile, without strong central authority or social ties, threatened not by the authority of an overbearing patriarchal tradition but by the 'fluid irresponsibility of crowd opinion'.[25] He once defined an American as 'a person who is as reluctant to give orders as he is to obey them'.[26]

Auden claimed that this comparative indifference to traditional representatives of authority had altered the cultural balance of power between the sexes: 'in America the mother is all-important and the father has no position at all – isn't respected in the least' (Ansen, p. 85). This important 'American' theme is adumbrated in 'For the Time Being', where Jesus's father is a dim, anxious cuckold who 'must learn that masculinity, / To Nature, is a non-essential luxury'. It is developed too in 'The Sea and the Mirror', in which Prospero is an ageing magician renouncing his powers, and at the same time a father relinquishing his daughter. Auden, while coldly satirising Prospero's illusions, could not give up his own authority so easily. In 'The Sea and the Mirror' he is more than ever the poetic professional, writing with dazzling, almost brutal, competence in a profusion of different verse forms for a cast of characters that is almost exclusively male. Emblematically, the piece concludes with a huge pastiche Jamesian *tour de force* speech by a Caliban who, according to Auden, represents the solipsistic, amoral phallus (in a letter to the Shakespearean scholar Theodore Spencer he referred to Caliban as personifying 'The Prick').[27]

This intense ambivalence towards his own 'mastery' (Auden hated it when Kallman referred to him campily as 'Miss Master') set the stage for, and determined the stakes in, Auden's most important long work in the United States in the 1940s, *The Age of Anxiety*. The poem is set initially in a seedy bar on Third Avenue on All Souls' Night, some time after the USA has entered the war. Three men and a woman drift into conversation and gradually begin to share a sense of irrational connectedness. In one respect, the work is Auden's covert attack on the he-man of modern American fiction, Ernest Hemingway (also known as 'Papa'). 'Hemingway is terribly limited', Auden insisted while working on *The Age of Anxiety*. At issue was Hemingway's pared-down, tough-guy realism, only adequate, Auden believed, for 'short stories, for people who meet once in a bar very late at night, but do not enter into relations' (Ansen, p. 2). In *The Age of Anxiety* Auden deconstructs the materials of this imagined Hemingway story by rewriting it antithetically in baroque, allegoric, poetic form.

To do so was to act out the diminishment of masculine, macho authority, which Auden believed was an essentially American (and thus modern) phenomenon. But like so much in Auden's thought at this time, this bookish, intellectual theme has a directly social dimension. Commentary dating back to de Tocqueville emphasised the lessened status in the United States of the male authority-figure, prototypically represented by the father who, within the family circle, stands in for the general authority of the state. Auden's interest in gender relations in this period, and his tying of those relations to the deep structures of American society, cannot be separated from the massive redefinition of gendered spaces and roles in America effected by the war, a contemporary historical phenomenon in which women, 'Rosie the Riveter' and her sisters, took over many kinds of manual work previously reserved for men.

Lamented in the 'Dirge' section of *The Age of Anxiety*, the passing of the omnipotent patriarch, the 'didactic digit and dreaded voice / Which imposed peace on the pullulating / Primordial mess . . . / Our lost dad, / Our colossal father', opened up a new space for the 'female' in Auden's work. One of the two most important characters in this work is Rosetta, a Jewish woman, now living in Manhattan but originally from Auden's English home town. Her graceful, renunciatory monologue over the drunken young sailor, with whom she would have slept had he not passed out first, is one of the most poignant sections of the entire work. Auden's contemporary affair with Rhoda Jaffe has often been cited to explain the fascination with the female voice and experience in *The Age of Anxiety*. But just as crucial for the conception of Rosetta is Auden's idea (consolidated by his reading of de Tocqueville and contemporary social anthropologists) that the American patriarch is an insignificant figure, and that American women have stronger, more inter-esting characters than American men. 'Over here . . . the men are so dull', Auden complained to Ansen (Ansen, p. 65). And his friend Thekla Clark heard him say that 'the only interesting students' in the United States 'were women, Jews or blacks'.[28]

Auden in America was a WASP who nonetheless, as a foreigner and a homosexual (and perhaps as a poet), could never fully 'belong'. It was a predicament that gave him a strange but powerful outsider-at-the-centre vantage point. Perhaps this explains why, besides his unusual interest in women's social roles and in women poets, he also had unusually progressive attitudes to and relations with Jews (principally, of course, Kallman but also, among many others, Lincoln Kirstein, Rhoda Jaffe and Hannah Arendt) and with African-Americans. For example, in 1939 at a time when legislated or tacit segregation was in operation throughout the country, Auden made a point during a visit to New Haven of asking Owen Dodson, the young African-American poet, to breakfast in the dining room of the Taft Hotel in New Haven. Michael Yates, who was also present, remembered noticing 'the eyebrows of the waiter'.[29] Auden remained a figure of substantial importance in Dodson's life (they may even have had a brief fling around 1944), as he did too in the life of the African-American poet Robert Hayden whom he met in Michigan in 1941.[30]

In the United States, then as now, no-one could be friendly with mem-bers of a stigmatised group, such as Jews or African-Americans, and not be aware of the broader context of their lives: the country's profound, appar-ently intractable racial and economic tensions. Auden's letters contain many references to prejudice against Jews: he remarked to a friend in 1943 that 'I never knew, even in Germany, what Anti-sem[i]tism meant till I came to this country.'[31] Of the American situation, he commented that 'I simply can't understand why every Negro isn't a Communist. It's the only system that holds out any hope for them' (Ansen, p. 83).

In 'New Year Letter', he had at one point touched powerfully on an Amer-ica deeply compromised by the legalised injustices of racism and poverty. Longer acquaintance with the country made Auden's representations of the United States less visionary and abstract and more socio-culturally realistic. Indeed, a darkening of mood clearly set in during the mid 1940s. Lawrence's *Studies in Classic American Literature* returned repeatedly to the idea that 'America is tense with latent violence and resistance' and that the 'essen-tial American soul is hard, isolate, stoic, and a killer'.[32] Auden too became preoccupied with the violence which seemed to lie at the heart of American literature, focusing increasingly, as perhaps a Christian must, on the victims of that violence, what Caliban's monologue in 'The Sea and the Mirror' calls all those 'others who are not here . . . who have not been so fortunate . . . whose streets were chosen by the explosion or through whose country the famine turned aside from ours to go'.

By 1944 Auden was making frequent and hostile references to the bureaucratised modern state and the increasing centralisation of power and authority. This was no idle concern. Under the double impact of the New Deal and the war, the United States was becoming an intensely centralised, muscular and corporatised nation. The historian David Reynolds notes that the archetypal American businessman of the nineteenth century, the 'robber baron', was being replaced in the 1940s by the emergence of vast, faceless corporations run by innumerable professional managers.[33] Auden warned about a present age disturbingly like that of imperial Rome. The 'planned society, caesarism of thugs or bureaucracies, paideia, scientia, religious persecution, are all with us', he wrote, along with the danger of 'a new Constantinism' where Christianity would become 'a spiritual benzedrine for the earthly city' (*Prose II*, p. 231).

His postwar poems are filled with apprehensions over a new, heartless, military-commercial bureaucracy, run by what he designated in 'Under Which Lyre' as 'Apollo's children'. It is not only the citizens and servants of the state who are diminished by this new order. The world is more tightly managed; it is also drearier. 'The Managers' sees contemporary rulers as personally diminished successors to the theatrically violent heroes of yore: 'Men, working too hard in rooms that are too big, / Reducing to figures / What is the matter'. Throughout Auden's work of the mid 1940s 'the present stalks abroad / Like the past and its wronged again / Whimper and are ignored'. The poem from which these words come, 'A Walk After Dark', ends Auden's 'American period', the 'Age of Anxiety' as he had christened it, by anxiously enquiring 'what judgement waits / My person, all my friends, / And these United States'.

Auden's initial ideas about the United States had emphasised its approximation to the truly 'open society' as opposed to the 'closed', backward-looking societies of Europe. After the end of the Second World War, though, in poems such as 'Pleasure Island' the open-ended incompletion of the country began to turn, imaginatively at least, into a threatening indeterminacy; its future-orientedness into a disturbing indifference: 'Pluralist and experimental', Auden admitted, America may not have fallen castles but it certainly has numerous 'ghost towns and the relics of New Jerusalems which failed'.[34]

By 1948 something had changed in Auden's relation to America. His Christianity had moved him on an emotional and moral plane into a world in which, as he put it in his introduction to Emile Cammaerts's book *The Flower of Grass*, adapting St Paul, 'there is neither Jew nor German, East nor West, boy nor girl, smart nor dumb, boss nor worker, Bohemian nor bourgeois' (*Prose II*, p. 250). And yet, as he wrote to his friend E. R. Dodds towards the end of the war, practically speaking, 'One of the worst features of Hitler is that his horrible parody of internationalism and migration has made everyone nationalist and lovers of the dear old homestead.'[35] By 1948, in the wake of the partitioning at Yalta of the postwar world into US and Soviet 'spheres of influence', that ironic Hitlerian legacy was in full swing: the Cold War was beginning and the United States was starting to be swept by waves of apple-pie chauvinism and anti-Communist hysteria.

When he compiled his *Collected Shorter Poems 1927–1957*, Auden divided his poetic life into four 'chapters' loosely corresponding to the periods spent in each of the different places which was, for a while, his home. Part 3 comprised poems written between 1939 and 1947, when his base was America. It starts with 'In Memory of W. B. Yeats'. It ends with 'A Walk After Dark'. To signal the opening of the next poetic chapter, demarcated as '1948–1957', Auden placed first a poem titled 'In Transit'. His 'American period' had begun with a moment of creative limbo: the start of the elegy for Yeats in which the brooks were frozen solid, the statues of the great were swathed in snow and the iced-over airports 'almost deserted' (*EA*, p. 241). With a beautiful symmetry of motif, 'In Transit' took poetic leave of America in the limbo of an airport lounge, at a stop-off for fuel somewhere on the Atlantic crossing.

Inside this stylistically anonymous space, 'the pearly clouds of a sunset' look 'Oddly early' because Auden's body is still on East Coast time. But mentally he is already somewhere else, travelling east. The 'new' Auden would be a more 'European', more 'Catholic', more circumstantial and ludic writer. But, at the end of the 1940s as of the 1930s, he was still intent on writing the anti-Virgilian poem of a non-national future.[36] In the Yeats elegy, poetry had begun to 'flow' again as Auden made clear his presence in the New World. In 'In Transit', the plane soon takes off, and, free of architectural, juridical and temporal limbo as well as national soil, the poet gazes down at a world where suddenly 'Motives and natural processes are stirred by spring', the ice breaks up, and 'an ancient / Feud re-opens with the debacle of a river'.

## NOTES

1. Letter to Charles and Therese Abbott, 31 May 1946, Buffalo. All unpublished writings by Auden in this essay are © 2004 The Estate of W. H. Auden.
2. W. B. Yeats, *Letters to the New Island*, ed. George Bornstein and Hugh Witemeyer (Basingstoke: Macmillan, 1989), p. 12.

3. Eliot, 'The Social Function of Poetry', repr. in *On Poetry and Poets* (New York: Harcourt, Brace, 1957), p. 8.
4. Letter to Golo Mann, 8 January 1940, Golo Mann papers, Archives littéraires suisses, Berne.
5. Cited in Edmund Wilson, *The Sixties: The Last Journal, 1960–1972*, ed. Lewis M. Dabney (New York: Farrar Straus Giroux, 1993), p. 173.
6. The phrases about 'Woolworth's', the 'wig', etc., appear in a draft in the Huntington Library.
7. Letter from A. H. Campbell to Stephen Spender, 5 June 1975, private collection.
8. 'Transplanted Englishman Views U.S.', *St Louis Post-Dispatch* (13 December 1953), p. 21.
9. Letter to A. E. Dodds, *c.* 3–6 August 1939, Bodleian Library.
10. See Robert Fitzgerald, 'From the Notebooks of Robert Fitzgerald', *Erato*, 2:3 (Fall–Winter 1986), p. 1.
11. 'New Year Letter' draft ledger, Berg Collection, New York Public Library. As 'Letter', the published poem comprises the main part of *New Year Letter* (London: Faber and Faber, 1941), published in the United States as *The Double Man* (New York: Random House, 1941). Texts also appear in *Collected Longer Poems* (London: Faber and Faber, 1968) and in *Collected Poems*, ed. Edward Mendelson (London: Faber and Faber, 1976; revised edition 1991).
12. *Studies in Classic American Literature* ((1923); Harmondsworth: Penguin Books, 1971), p. 55.
13. Paraphrased in Eberhart, 'W. H. Auden' (draft of contribution to *We Moderns*), Berg Collection.
14. Alexis de Tocqueville, *Democracy in America*, trans. and ed. Harvey C. Mansfield and Delba Winthrop (Chicago: University of Chicago Press, 2000), p. 3.
15. Letter to E. R. Dodds, 16 January 1940, Bodleian Library.
16. *The Age of Anxiety* (London: Faber and Faber, 1948). A text appears in *Collected Longer Poems* and in *Collected Poems*, ed. Mendelson.
17. 'American Injection' (1947), repr. in Connolly, *Ideas and Places* (New York: Harper Brothers, 1953), p. 170.
18. 'The Sea and the Mirror' and 'For the Time Being' constitute the two parts of *For the Time Being* (London: Faber and Faber, 1945). Both texts also appear in *Collected Longer Poems* and in *Collected Poems*, ed. Mendelson.
19. Cited in 'Auden Outlines Role of Layman In Community', *New York Herald Tribune*, 22 October 1951, p. 22.
20. Letter to Naomi Mitchison, 14 November 1943, Berg Collection.
21. Christopher Isherwood, *Diaries*, ed. Katherine Bucknell, vol. 1: *1939–1960* (London: Methuen, 1996), p. 116.
22. Letter to Isherwood, March–April 1944, Huntington Library.
23. Cited in Maurice Cranston, 'Poet's Retreat', *John o' London's Weekly*, 57:1329 (6 February 1948), p. 50.
24. Letter to Louise Bogan, 17 November 1942, Amherst Library.
25. 'Introduction', *Poets of the English Language*, ed. W. H. Auden and Norman Holmes Pearson, vol. IV: *Blake to Poe* (New York: Viking, 1950), p. xxv.
26. 'Authority in America', *Griffin*, 4:3 (March 1955), p. 6.
27. Letter to Theodore Spencer, 24 March 1944, Harvard Library.

28. Thekla Clark, *Wystan and Chester: A Personal Memoir of W. H. Auden and Chester Kallman* (London: Faber and Faber, 1995), p. 96.
29. Cited in James V. Hatch, *Sorrow is the Only Faithful One: The Life of Owen Dodson* (Urbana: University of Illinois Press, 1993), p. 58. Auden later advised Dodson about his poetry (*ibid.*, p. 103).
30. See John Hatcher, *From the Auroral Darkness: The Life and Poetry of Robert Hayden* (Oxford: George Ronald, 1984).
31. Letter to Naomi Mitchison, 14 November 1943, Berg collection.
32. Lawrence, *Studies*, pp. 56, 63, 68.
33. David Reynolds, *One World Divisible: A Global History Since 1945* (New York: Norton, 2000), p. 20.
34. 'The Anglo-American Difference', *Anchor Review*, 1 (1955), p. 214.
35. Letter to E. R. Dodds, 23 April 1944, Bodleian Library.
36. See for example 'Secondary Epic' (1959), which begins 'No, Virgil, no'.

# 5

EDWARD MENDELSON

# The European Auden

In 1948 Auden began summering in Italy, partly because he wanted to write a different kind of poetry from the kind he had been writing in America. In 1958 he began summering in Austria, partly because he wanted to write a different kind of poetry from the kind he had been writing in Italy. From his arrival in New York in 1939 until he left for his first Italian journey in April 1948, his poems had focused on the existential crises of the inner life. A comment he later made about Søren Kierkegaard could apply with little exaggeration to his own work in the 1940s: 'a planetary visitor might read through the whole of his voluminous works without discovering that human beings are not ghosts but have bodies of flesh and blood' (*Pilgrims*, p. 42). The poems he wrote after he arrived in Italy for the first time celebrate human flesh, not for its beauty, in which Auden now takes almost no interest, but for its ordinariness. And because they celebrate human flesh they also mourn over human blood.

Auden's collection *Nones* (1951; UK, 1952) included a few poems written in 1946 and 1947, before his departure for Italy, but the shape and style of the book reflects his new interest in the body and in the injustices inflicted on it, and his new wish to write about great themes in a modest style, his renunciation of the Yeatsian powers of enchantment he had wielded in 'Spain' and 'September 1, 1939'. The dedication of *Nones* to the theologians Reinhold and Ursula Niebuhr (he had provided much of the intellectual underpinnings to Auden's work in the early 1940s, she was a close personal friend) justifies the style. In response to deep feelings of love or loss, he writes, he 'would in the old grand manner / Have sung from a resonant heart'; but journalism and mass-culture have debased 'All words like peace and love, / All sane affirmative speech' by transforming them 'Into spells to befuddle the crowd' or 'a horrid mechanical screech'. The only 'civil style' that survives is 'the wry, the sotto-voce, / Ironic and monochrome'.

That unassertive style was the medium in which he masked the epic ambitions of *Nones* and the collection that followed it, *The Shield of*

*Achilles* (1955). *Nones* opens with 'Prime', a poem about the act of waking into consciousness that is also, simultaneously about the dawn of day,
the birth of an individual, the founding of a city and the creation of the world.
The book closes with 'A Walk After Dark', a poem that meditates on the
ageing of poet and world, and that looks towards the final day of judgement,
'As I walk home to bed, / Asking what judgment waits / My person, all my
friends, / And these United States.' At the centre of the book, preceded and
followed by fifteen other poems, is the four-part sequence 'Memorial for the
City'. This begins with scenes of wartime ruin (prompted by Auden's visit to
Germany in 1945 attached to the United States Strategic Bombing Survey),
then proceeds through a clotted history of a thousand years of European
social and urban life leading to the barbed-wire and inner divisions of the
modern city – and ends with a speech presented as the words of the inar-
ticulate human body, stating its refusal to believe all myths of power and
exclusion, acknowledging its suffering, and foretelling its resurrection: 'At
the place of my passion her [the city's] photographers are gathered together;
but I shall rise again to hear her judged.'

'In Praise of Limestone', the second poem in *Nones* and one of the first
Auden wrote after his arrival in Italy, inaugurates the styles and themes of
his Italian years. He remarked in a letter to a friend that Italy resembled
his '*Mutterland*', the limestone Pennine hills of northern England,[1] and he
asked rhetorically in the poem, 'What could be more like Mother' than a limestone landscape: 'Mark these rounded slopes / with their surface fragrance of
thyme and beneath / A secret system of caves and conduits.' Limestone can
be shaped (the poem continues) into statues, temples and fountains, but only
on a moderate scale; those who prefer this landscape live on the ordinary
scale of the village, where no one has any important secrets. In contrast,
'Immoderate soils' like granite and gravel attract saints and tyrants.

A poem merely about a moderate landscape could easily be trivial, but
the half-concealed subject of this poem is the ordinary human body, with
its own rounded slopes and secret system of caves and conduits. The body
in most modern literature is either debased, wounded or ignored, or else
exalted beyond all plausibility, but the body that matters in this poem is
the body that quietly goes about its bodily work. So the poem ends by
acknowledging that the limestone landscape, like the body, is not the site
of great historical events, that (rather like the womb) it is a 'backward /
And dilapidated province, connected / To the big busy world by a tunnel, with a
certain / Seedy appeal'. Yet, without intending to, it fulfils 'a worldly duty' by
calling into question our temptation to value anything that exists on a larger
or smaller scale than the body of our ordinary lives, anything disconnected
from the body, like abstract ideas, political power or the mind's fascination

with its own working. The poem reasons that, 'In so far as we have to look forward / To death as a fact', we are right to wish to transcend the transient and decaying flesh. 'But if / Sins can be forgiven, if bodies rise from the dead', that is, if the promises of Christianity are true, then the body may be perceived in a different way. Auden wrote in a later essay, 'Whatever else is asserted by the doctrine of the resurrection of the body, it asserts the sacred importance of the body' (F&A, p. 68).

'In Praise of Limestone' is written in alternating lines of thirteen and eleven syllables, one of Auden's adaptations of the syllabic metre that he first learned from Marianne Moore and gradually adapted into forms more regular and less eccentric than hers. Auden used regular syllabic metres as a solution to a pervasive problem in modern writing: how to retain the virtues of traditional regular forms without sounding archaic. Because they are regular, Auden's strict syllabic metres, like the traditional accentual metres of English verse, signify shared common meanings, unlike the disconnected private meanings signified by irregular 'free' verse. But because they are a twentieth-century invention, Auden's metres do not suggest a nostalgic longing for a coherent past in the way that Ezra Pound's bursts of sixteenth-century pastiche do, or in the way that T. S. Eliot in his essays saw regular metres as the product of cohesive societies that no longer exist. Syllabic metre became Auden's favoured medium for writing about the human body. The shared meanings signified by the regular metre correspond to the bodily rhythms which everyone has in common and which cannot be imagined as belonging only to a lost past.

Auden's increasing interest in the shared ordinary body corresponded to his increasing interest in unique individual speech. Taking up suggestions in the work of Kierkegaard and Kierkegaard's followers such as Martin Buber, he began theorising in prose and verse about the difference between first- and third-person speech. First-person speech was the product of personal responsibility, of words spoken in one's own name by an *I* addressing a second-person *you*. Third-person speech reduced oneself and others to an anonymous *he* or *she* or *they*. The lyrics in *Nones* and Auden's later books tend to be meditations or variations on this theme. 'Their Lonely Betters' contrasts the noises heard in a garden with words spoken by human beings: 'A robin with no Christian name ran through / The Robin-Anthem which was all it knew', and, like all other non-human beings, was incapable of lying, and unaware of time and death. Like most of Auden's lyric writing, its half-hidden central subject is love. Flowers, the poem notes, do not choose their loves, but wait for 'some third party' to decide which pair will be mated. Human beings are 'their lonely betters', who 'count some days and long for certain letters' while awaiting the arrival of the loved one they have chosen. In both animal and human voices, emotional reactions are noises, not words: 'We too make noises when we laugh or weep.' Commitments, promises, voluntary and faithful loves are made with language: 'Words are for those with promises to keep.'

*Nones* takes its title from a poem with the same title, in the same syllabic metre as the book's opening poem, 'Prime'. 'Nones' is about the immediate aftermath of the Crucifixion, an event that occurs in the poem both in ancient Jerusalem and in Auden's Italian village where an 'empty blue bus in the empty pink square' fills with passengers and drives away. Its opening stanzas report on the isolation and emptiness that follow the event, the realisation that we willed the event to happen and the awareness it brings of the irreversible finality of murder. At the close of the poem, the individual will withdraws into a brief troubled sleep, while the body, 'our own wronged flesh', works to heal our own desolation, 'restoring / The order we try to destroy, the rhythm / We spoil out of spite'.

Auden wrote 'Nones' and 'Prime' as part of a sequence of poems set on Good Friday, with each poem taking its title from one of the canonical hours, the times of prayer in the Roman and Anglican churches. When he prepared *Nones* for publication, he had written only these two of the seven. In his next book of poems, *The Shield of Achilles* (1955), he placed the completed sequence 'Horae Canonicae' at the end, and another seven-poem sequence about the world of nature, 'Bucolics', at the start. The completed 'Horae Canonicae' sequence is epic and encyclopaedic in its ambition and scope but deliberately muted in manner. The apocalyptic plot that had been implicit in *Nones* is now explicit: each of the seven poems portrays a different stage in the history of a day, a life, a city and the world. The penultimate poem, 'Compline', occurs at sunset and looks forward to personal death, the fall of a city and the day of judgement; the final poem, 'Lauds', takes place at dawn on the morning after Good Friday, in a renewed world of community and forgiveness, in which everyone wakes 'In solitude, for company'.

The narrative plot of 'Horae Canonicae' includes the social differentiation that begins to occur in the second poem, 'Terce', where everyone is in transition between a private role and home and a public role at work, and is fully realised in the third poem, 'Nones', where everyone has separated into those with vocation, those with authority and those in the crowd. Unlike Yeats and Eliot in their poetry about social differentiation, Auden never imagines that anyone is born into an inescapable social position; no one's fate is determined by the astrological 'cradles' of Yeats's 'The Phases of the Moon'. The social differentiation that matters is either chosen voluntarily (those with authority and vocation) or imposed involuntarily and unjustly, as in all the forms of exclusion and murder exemplified in 'Nones' by the Crucifixion.

The setting of 'Horae Canonicae' is simultaneously the village of Forio, on the island of Ischia, where Auden rented a flat or a house during his Italian summers. Of the island's patron saint, Restituta, Auden wrote in his poem 'Ischia' that her 'annual patronage, they say, is bought with blood'. In the next line he added diplomatically, addressing Restituta herself: 'That, blessed and formidable / Lady, we hope is not true', but he added that 'since / Nothing is free, whatever you charge shall be paid', and acknowledged that the Mediterranean pleasures of his Italian journey come at a price to himself and others. This is a characteristic theme: at the end of 'Vespers', one of the poems in 'Horae Canonicae', he acknowledges the guilty and uncomfortable truth that 'without a cement of blood (it must be human, it must be innocent) no secular wall will safely stand'.

'Bucolics', written while Auden was still working on 'Horae Canonicae', expands on the themes of 'In Praise of Limestone' by meditating on various landscapes: woods, mountains, lakes, islands, plains and streams, with an opening poem on winds about the relation between human beings and weather. Like classical bucolics, these poems are less about nature itself than about the ways human beings interpret nature and choose different aspects of it as suitable for themselves. Islands are for hermits, prisons and pleasure-seekers; lakes are for those who like their nature benign. The sequence offers no fantasy of a Wordsworthian escape into a green world – 'For an uncatlike / Creature who has gone wrong, / Five minutes on even the nicest mountain / Is awfully long' – and it acknowledges that a preference for nature at its most benign 'Goes with a wish for savage dogs and man-traps' to keep others from intruding. The sequence ends in a vision of innocent Eros that it recognises as a fantasy; but because all human beings share, through their bodies, in the world of nature, the vision can lead to a new sense of sympathy with others, 'Wishing, I thought [the qualification is essential to the affirmation], the least of men their / Figures of splendor, their holy places'.

'The Shield of Achilles', the opening poem of the middle section of the book of the same name, has become an anthology piece thanks to its apparently straightforward sentiments against war, cruelty, impersonality and regimentation, but the poem is more subtle than its overt sentiments. Its hidden subject is the way in which impersonal speech makes possible inhuman actions. The stanzas in which Thetis watches Hephaestos create Achilles' shield report on actions for which neither is personally responsible: until the final stanza (where Hephaestos hobbles away from his creation and Thetis cries out in dismay at it), 'she' looks at what 'his hands' do, but neither is an 'I' or 'you' and neither chooses anything. The shield made by 'his hands' portrays equally impersonal scenes of a barren landscape with an army of 'A million eyes, a million boots', but no individual persons except for the 'ragged urchin, aimless and alone', who lives in a solitude where individuality is meaningless because it can imagine no relations to other individuals. The poem became popular partly because it could be read as flattering its readers with the assurance that they are not unjust like faceless authorities and violent youths; but, as always in later Auden, the poem is a deeply unflattering portrait of the reader as the passive, observing Thetis, and of the poet as the indifferent craftsman Hephaestos, each allowing the worst to happen by their failure to protest against it in first-person speech.

The overt themes of *The Shield of Achilles* are large matters of war and injustice, but the covert themes are Auden's arguments with himself about his art and his relation to it. A light-sounding lyric like 'Nocturne 1' ('Appearing unannounced, the moon') proves to be a subtle meditation on individuality. When the moon appears, 'my heart' worships her as a divinity who 'can make / Or break you as Her fancy choose', while 'my mind' responds that the moon is an indifferent barrenness. But the poem endorses neither view, acknowledging of heart and mind 'That both are worshippers of force', indifferent to individual persons, and that because they worship force, rather than participate in love between persons, neither can 'Complain if I should be reduced / To a small functionary whose dreams / Are vast, unscrupulous, confused' – that is, if my existence should seem meaningless while my fantasies are incoherent dreams of power. But 'Supposing, though, my face is real', and that my individuality is real, then the moon should look to me like an individual person ('should look like x'). It should look to me like 'My neighbor's face' – and Auden invariably used the word 'neighbor' to allude to the commandment to love one's neighbour as oneself. My neighbour may be unimportant in the public world, 'That gushing lady . . . That hang-dog who keeps coming back', but nonetheless a 'counter-image' to the images of force perceived by heart and mind, something that for all its smallness can 'balance with its lack of weight / My world, the private motor-car [an instrument of isolation] / And all the engines of the State'. A personal voice has no imposing power, precisely because it issues from one vulnerable person; but its individuality can balance all the impersonal powers that have no individuality at all. In a poem on the Soviet invasion of Czechoslovakia, titled with the date of the event, 'August, 1968', Auden portrayed the Ogre who can perform 'Deeds quite impossible for man', who can master everything except speech and stalks about the subjugated plain 'While drivel gushes from his lips'.

Auden was never shaken in his faith in the virtues of human speech, but near the end of his Italian episode he was shaken for months in his confidence in his own verbal powers. In 1956 he was elected Professor of Poetry at

Oxford, the only chair in that university (and perhaps in any other) chosen by a vote open to anyone with an Oxford Master of Arts degree. The duties of the Professor of Poetry are to deliver three lectures each year for five years. Auden had been lecturing to large enthusiastic audiences in America for almost two decades, and he was surprised to find himself terrified by the prospect of a public lecture at his old university to an English audience, many of whom would not have forgiven him for spending the war years in America.

His inaugural lecture, published under the title 'Making, Knowing and Judging', described poetry as an act of homage to beings that induce sacred awe in the poet, whether those beings are human or non-human, imaginary or real, concrete or abstract. Auden combined personal self-deprecation with a subtle celebration of poetry, not for any inherent aesthetic or moral values that might be claimed for it, but for its willingness to praise other things. The lecture was a triumph that, as Auden told Kallman, 'won over my enemies'.[2] The terror that preceded his triumph left a mark. 'There Will be No Peace', a poem about obscure, unseen enemies who 'hate for hate's sake', was the only explicit record of the experience that he wrote for publication, but much of his later work reflects his new sense that all individuality needs to live partly behind a protective wall against antagonists outside.

The following year, 1957, Auden took steps to leave the public, open world of his life on Ischia. He used the money from an Italian literary prize to buy a new summer home for himself, a farmhouse in the Austrian village of Kirchstetten, about an hour's train ride west of Vienna, and settled there late in the summer of 1958. 'Goodbye to the Mezzogiorno', one of the first poems he wrote after leaving Italy, explored his reasons for going there ten years earlier and his reasons for leaving now. He went there, he said, 'In middle-age hoping to twig [in the slang sense of "comprehend"] from / What we are not what we might be next'. The poem makes a distinction between what he is, one of 'those who mean by a life a / Bildungsroman', that is, a history of their own inner development, and what he is not, one of 'those to whom living / Means to-be-visible-now', who live in the moment, untroubled by inwardness.

He had known from the beginning, he told friends privately, that his Italian idyll could not last. In moving to Austria (while still wintering in New York) he was moving to a culture with much to feel guilty about; Auden frequently noted in conversation that the Austrians had been among the most enthusiastic of Hitler's followers. The poems he wrote in his Austrian years express a double sense of happiness in the first home he had ever owned and guilt over those excluded from his own security and status. The sense of guilt that pervades Auden's work – and that has its basis deep in his psyche rather than in any guilty actions – found a new focus in the recent history of his Austrian neighbours. 'Joseph Weinheber', a poem written in 1965, was a memorial to a poet from Auden's own village of Kirchstetten who had aligned himself ambivalently with the Nazis and killed himself in 1945.

Auden had always taken theology seriously, even in the years from 1920 through 1938 when he thought he had lost the Anglican faith of his childhood. In the first years after his return to the church in 1939, he had adopted a Protestant existential theology derived partly from Kierkegaard, partly from Reinhold Niebuhr, and he went to Italy partly to correct an excessively Protestant world view by surrounding himself with a Catholic one. The Austria to which he moved was mostly Roman Catholic, but Auden's theological interests shifted back to the German Protestant tradition, although with a different emphasis from the Protestantism that had interested him in the 1940s. Instead of Kierkegaard's existentialism, he focused of the work of Dietrich Bonhoeffer, who had explored what he called a 'religionless Christianity' that had now outgrown the mythical elements of its long childhood, and in which religion took the form of the believer's participation in God's own experience of suffering in the world – in the Crucifixion and in all other acts of injustice.

Bonhoeffer had been murdered by the Nazis, and Auden memorialised him in a poem, 'Friday's Child', written in 1958. In simple, almost singsong rhythms, the poem states a theology of absolute human freedom to do good or evil without any hope of intervention from a paternalistic God, a theology in which everyone is free to see in 'the insulted face' that is silent on the Cross either meaninglessness and emptiness or a sign that all individual suffering has a universal meaning, because the face is simultaneously that of each individual victim and that of the God who suffers together with each victim.

The book in which Auden gathered the poems from his last Italian and first Austrian summers was *Homage to Clio* (1960). The title pointed towards his sense of life as a *Bildungsroman*, a personal history. In the book's title poem, Clio, the muse of history, is the protector of uniqueness in the form of unique historical facts and unique individuals. She is entirely unlike the goddesses Aphrodite and Demeter, who embody impersonal forces like sex and fertility; they can be represented by ideal images ('One guesses at once from the perfect buttocks . . . Whom the colossus must be'), but because she embodies individuality, the arts have no icon for her. Instead, she looks like anyone whom one doesn't notice: 'I have seen / Your photo, I think, in the papers, nursing / A baby or mourning a corpse', valuing other unique human beings for themselves. Auden privately told his friend J. R. R. Tolkien that the poem was a homage to the Virgin Mary.

Early in his career, as soon as he discovered in himself Yeatsian powers of rhetorical persuasion, Auden began to think about a poet's obligation – or lack of one – to write truthfully. In his Austrian years, this concern became explicit. The greatest and most moving work in *Homage to Clio* is a work in prose, 'Dichtung und Wahrheit' ('poetry and truth', the title of Goethe's autobiography), subtitled 'An Unwritten Poem'. It comprises fifty meditations on the meanings of each of the three words 'I love you' and of various combinations of them, and on the way in which poetry, music and painting inadequately represent them. The opening states Auden's wish 'to write a poem which would express exactly what I mean when I think these words', and the ending concludes that the poem cannot be written because 'I cannot know exactly what I mean' and because 'words cannot verify themselves' – a poem cannot demonstrate its own truth.

The alternative, he concludes, is to write a 'slightly unpleasant' poem about sexual desire, which Auden personifies in the traditional figure of 'Dame Kind' (Nature), the title of the poem that immediately follows in *Homage to Clio*, a poem of gratitude for all 'the dirty work She did' in hundreds of sexual couplings that led to previous generations, and which now bring two lovers together. 'Dichtung und Wahrheit' is about personal speech, which Auden values absolutely, but which he knows derives its value partly from its source in the impersonal, instinctive realm of human flesh.

Auden's Oxford professorship ended in 1961, and without any visible change in his character or habits, some part of his psyche withdrew into a private inner world. Characteristically, he wrote and published a poem about this most private and inward experience. 'A Change of Air' seems to allude to Goethe's journey to Italy (and by extension to Auden's), but the journey in the poem is an invisible one, away from visible action: 'To go Elsewhere is to withdraw from movement, / A side step, a short one, will convey you thither.' The motive for the journey is an 'estrangement between your name and you', a dissociation between the public self known to others by name and the inner self that needs no name to know itself. (This is one of the first of many poems from Auden's later years in which Auden addresses himself in the second person.) One returns from such a journey cured and restored, but in ways knowable only to oneself: 'Your sojourn Elsewhere will remain a wordless / Hiatus in your voluble biography.'

Auden's new home, a place where he could bar or open the door as he chose, was the visible counterpart of his invisible journey, and he made it the subject of a sequence of poems that he wrote in Austria about a subject he had ignored in the encyclopedic Italian sequences. In his first summer in Austria, when he wrote 'On Installing an American Kitchen in Lower Austria', a hymn of praise to his remodelled kitchen (something unimaginable, he noted, in

Plato's Athens), he did not then realise that it belonged in a sequence. In the early 1960s he retitled the poem 'Grub First, Then Ethics' (a translation of a line by Bertolt Brecht) and added other poems in a fifteen-poem sequence called 'Thanksgiving for a Habitat'. He placed the sequence at the start of his next book of poems, *About the House* (1965). The first two poems, 'Prologue: The Birth of Architecture' and the sequence's title poem, are about the ways in which houses are projections of personalities, comforting those inside by excluding those outside. The remainder of the sequence celebrates rooms in the house with an exuberance that makes the small farmhouse seem enormous. (Auden regarded the poem about the lavatory, 'The Geography of the House', as the first serious English poem about excretion.) Auden deferred his deepest reasons to value domestic life until the end of the sequence, in 'The Common Life', a poem occasioned by the living room, the 'fortress' that protects the almost-married life he shared with Chester Kallman.

After his Italian years Auden, who had earlier been a prolific writer of lyrics, stopped writing lyrics almost entirely. He had become more interested in speaking to his audience in a conversational personal voice than in singing to them. He wrote meditative, gnomic and comic poems (he often ended his public readings with 'On the Circuit', a summary of the comic irritations and rewards of the lecture circuit), and devoted more of his energy to compact epigrammatic forms that made little overt emotional appeal, but that concentrated intense feeling into a few laconic words. One of the most gnomic, 'You', is a riddling address to his own body that reads like an unhappy love poem, but which makes full sense only when one guesses its unstated subject.

The form that Auden found most suitable for epigram and meditation was the haiku, which he began using around 1963, after discovering the form's possibilities in the journals of Dag Hammarskjöld, the Secretary-General of the United Nations who had recently died in an air crash and whose journals Auden was translating from the Swedish (with help from a collaborator who provided a literal text). Until the end of his life Auden wrote haiku on large and small themes, many of them in sequences, and in doing so, he enlarged the possibilities of the form, much as he had enlarged the possibilities of the sonnet in the great sonnet sequences he wrote on vast historical and religious themes in the 1930s and 1940s. The haiku in *About the House* include the dark 'Et in Arcadia Ego' (in which a grammatically linked series of haiku function like stanzas in traditional English verse), a poem about the persistence of murderous violence in the rational humanist present, and 'Symmetries & Asymmetries', a series of disconnected haiku and epigrams on topics from trees to liquor to perception to discontentedness. In his next book, *City without Walls* (1969), he wrote a more ambitious five-part series of haiku (and some five-line tanka) under the title 'Marginalia', which masks the coherence of the poem's themes of relationship, tyranny, political history, sainthood and self-knowledge.

As early as his public lectures on Shakespeare in New York in 1945–6, Auden was theorising about the late work of great artists, work in which, he said, the late artist tended to lose interest in the work of his contemporaries and the reactions of his audience as he pursued the themes that mattered to him most. *City without Walls* begins to show some of these characteristics: the book is one of the most inventive and exuberant of Auden's career, but it is also the most explicitly autobiographical, marked by recollections that are clearly his own, not concealed behind imaginative transformations into allegory and epigram as in much of his earlier work, even in such highly personal poems as 'There Will Be No Peace'.

The title poem in *City without Walls* is a conversation between three inner voices, the first exclaiming a late-night jeremiad in alliterative verse against the modern world; the second voice expressing amused contempt for the pleasure that the first takes in complaining; and a bored third voice telling the first two to go to sleep. Among the shorter poems in the book, 'Since' looks back to a love affair of Auden's youth, 'Amor Loci' to the landscape of abandoned mining machinery that he loved in childhood. 'Profile' is a self-portrait in haiku and tanka. The final poem in the book, 'Prologue at Sixty', is a more extended self-portrait in terms of Auden's origins and inclinations, with a list of the place-names on 'my numinous map' of 'sites made sacred' by his private experiences of them, experiences that can include 'something read there, / a lunch, a good lay, or sheer lightness of heart'.

After many years in which he treated political themes in terms of perennial problems of language and justice, Auden had begun again to write topical political poems, although not always about themes that invited posturing and sloganeering. 'August, 1968' was prompted by the latest news in the same way that *Spain* and 'September 1, 1939' had been, but Auden now began writing poems about political events from the past while leaving open to the reader's judgement any question of their relevance to the present. The political poems in *City without Walls* included 'Rois Fainéants', about the powerless child-kings of seventh-century France who were the public face of the real rulers, and 'Partition', about the makeshift procedure that divided India and Pakistan in 1947 and prompted the (unmentioned) warfare and massacres that followed.

*City without Walls* also contained perhaps the greatest poem of Auden's last years, the imposing and compact 'River Profile', in which twelve rapid stanzas about the course of a river from the mountain to the sea trace the course of a human life from conception through death without saying that a human life is the poem's subject – except in the epigraph from Novalis, 'Our body is a moulded river.' Each stanza is a rush of nouns and adjectives characterising the stages of life in terms of a river's movement, from a mountain storm (the act of conception: 'head-on collisions of cloud and rock in an / up-thrust') through open hill country to sophisticated cities, finally to its dissolution in a delta. The poem ends with the evaporated river condensing again into liquid: 'image of death as / a spherical dew-drop of life', and an allusive reflection on the religious doctrine of the resurrection of the body: 'Unlovely / monsters, our tales believe, can be translated / too, even as water, the selfless mother / of all especials'.

Until the late 1960s Auden published his new collections of poems at intervals of about five years; four years separated *About the House* from *City without Walls*, and *Epistle to a Godson* followed only three years later, in 1972. The language of the book is less concentrated than before, and a few poems seem more like exercises than completed works, but Auden was still writing memorably, with a new focus on non-human nature as a means of understanding – through contrasts, not parallels – the nature of human beings. This technique was deliberately opposed to the scientific fashion that emphasised the ways in which human actions are shaped by amoral evolution rather than by moral consciousness. 'A New Year Greeting' is a seriously comic address to the micro-organisms on his own body, prompted by an article in *Scientific American*. 'The Aliens' imagines the kind of temptation that could produce the nightmare societies of insects. 'Natural Linguistics' explores the ways in which the rest of the natural world uses languages different from human speech but with their own special powers.

'Natural Linguistics' closes by asserting that non-human creatures would surely 'prefer that they were rhetorized *at* than *about*', that is, treated as much as possible as persons not objects. The last three poems in the book take up this theme: 'Talking to Dogs' is about the languages that human beings and dogs share and do not share; 'Talking to Mice' explains as a matter of state policy the use of the mousetrap, but makes no pretence of justifying it; 'Talking to Myself' is the most extended of Auden's poetic addresses to his own body, with none of the sardonic riddling of the earlier address in 'You' a decade earlier.

Auden had described himself in 'Prologue at Sixty' as not an American but 'a New Yorker / who opens his *Times* at the obit page'. As he grew older, he increasingly hoped to return to his native England, and in 1972 left his New York flat for a cottage in the grounds of his Oxford college, Christ Church. As before, he summered in Austria, but spent the last winter of his life a few dozen yards away from the rooms where he had been an undergraduate.

He had withdrawn into a far more private self after his weeks in Oxford in the 1950s, and he found himself lonelier and more isolated than he had expected. When he died in Vienna in September 1973, on his way back to Oxford, he had put together about two-thirds of what would have been another collection of poems under the title *Thank You, Fog* (posthumously published in 1974). The title poem praised the isolating weather of an English winter, and much of the rest of the book had a valedictory quality, as if Auden were more aware than he realised of his impending death. Even a poem about the dawn, 'Aubade', is less about new beginnings than about an inner world of pronouns 'where I hold council with Me', and about an outer world where everyone's 'political duty' is to the past and future more than to the present. The matching evening-poem, 'Nocturne', suggests without saying that it is about other endings than that of a day.

Auden's poetry now tended to look across vast stretches of time, and the last poem he wrote for publication, 'Archaeology', is about matters too distant to be known, suitable for guessing, which is 'always / more fun than knowing'. One guess is that myths were always known to be tall stories, that their real purpose was to provide occasions for rituals by which human beings are made one with themselves and each other. Characteristically, Auden insists on taking personal responsibility for a myth about the escape from personality: 'I'd swear / that men have always lounged in myths / as Tall Stories.' As Auden withdrew into the timeless world of ritual and myth, his ethical and political vision was undimmed: while celebrating rituals, he remembers that 'some are abominable', that 'the Crucified' has no wish for 'butchery to appease Him'.

## NOTES

1. Letter to Elizabeth Mayer, 8 May 1948 (Berg Collection, New York Public Library); quoted in *Later Auden*, p. 290.
2. Letter to Chester Kallman, 25 June 1956 (Berg Collection).

# 6

TIM YOUNGS

# Auden's travel writings

> A travel book owes so little to the writers, and so much to the people they meet, that a full and fair acknowledgment on the part of the former is impossible.
>
> We must beg those hundreds of anonymous Icelanders, farmers, fishermen, busmen, children, etc., who are the real authors of this book to accept collectively our gratitude.

The radical force of these very first words of *Letters from Iceland* (1937, p. 9) still impresses; their insistence on group authorship is in keeping with Auden's left-wing politics of the time and markedly out of step with the predominant individualism of twentieth-century travel writing. Even in terms of its formal authorship, *Letters from Iceland* is a joint composition by two writers, as was Auden's other travel book, *Journey to a War* (1939).

The significance of Auden's co-authored works has been underlined by Stan Smith, who identifies them as those 'which most conspicuously insist on their status as texts, not representations of the real, but aware of their own artifice . . . They are also the works which most directly confront the artifice of a capitalist society in crisis' (Smith, p. 109). Auden's travel books were written in a decade when social and economic insecurity and political polarities saw 'abrupt and important changes in outlook and affiliation';[1] and when disorder and instability (for the middle class in particular) 'led to the radicalization of many intellectuals, and a crisis in outlook [that was] reflected in every aspect of art and culture'.[2] This much is commonly known, but less scrutiny has been accorded to the contemporary travel book, which Philip Dodd has described as 'the most important literary form of the 1930s', 'the most appropriate form for writers restless with inherited beliefs . . . eager to "explore" and "discover" new allegiances'.[3] More recently, Andrew Hammond has remarked that the period's widespread social change made it perhaps inevitable that 'a paradigm shift would occur in travel writing, as well as in the methods and aims of travel'. A new set of travellers emerged, who 'displayed gentler, more sympathetic and more intricate subject positions' than those of their predecessors, and whose work was at times linked to 'the complex and self-conscious writings of Anglo-American modernism'. Hammond's focus is on travellers to the Balkans and he does not mention Auden, but his observations about the travel writers whom he does discuss – their 'understanding of identity as fragmented, fluid and discontinuous', the dilution of brash masculinity, and 'an awareness of one's cultural intrusiveness' – apply to Auden's work also, confirming the importance of his historical and cultural context.[4]

Auden's travel books have generally been downplayed in studies of travel writing, even in some of those that focus on the 1930s.[5] They have been undervalued, too, by many Auden specialists and other literary critics. When Auden's travel books have been taken seriously, they have been admired on other grounds. As perceptive a critic as Tom Paulin, while acclaiming Auden's and MacNeice's 'extraordinary sensitivity to politics' in *Letters from Iceland*, has asserted that they were 'not writing a travel book' because they were writing about European culture.[6] Yet these are spurious grounds on which to rule out *Letters* as a travel book: travel writers, whether or not they admit to it, always reflect on departure points as much as on destinations.

Paul Fussell, concurring with Evelyn Waugh's judgement that there must be something wrong if it takes two men to write a book, observes of Auden's travel books that: 'the narrative is disturbingly discontinuous, interrupted by jokiness, nervousness over what literary mode is appropriate, and self-consciousness about the *travel book* genre itself. Both books give the unhappy impression of apologizing for themselves. In both, the narrative is eked out by poems that don't really belong, and nothing is rounded off.'[7] At least Paulin has understood that the form of *Letters from Iceland* advances its aim; that the device of letters to friends and relatives has them employing a suitably *social* form in keeping with their democratic interest in people rather than landscape, even though Paulin prefers to describe this in terms of a poetic rather than travel writing.[8] Fussell, on the other hand, seems insensible to the palpable energy of the works and to the wit with which *Letters from Iceland* exposes the limitations of other travel texts.

While Fussell advises that 'The way to imitate an early Auden poem is to get as many frontiers into it as possible',[9] the manifest connections between Auden's two travel books and his other writing has been appreciated by some. Stan Smith comments that 'Auden's journeyings constantly reflect back on that which he is ostensibly leaving behind', and writes of how 'All Auden's discoveries of the artifice of cultural identity, the source of that anthropological interest that runs through his work, occur at moments of dislocation' (Smith, p. 95).[10] As Smith observes, what Auden and his co-authors find they are reflecting back upon is the prospect of war in Europe.

Auden is preoccupied in his work with the motif of travel and sees in it (as in sex) a site and symbol of the interaction of private and public.

'No Change of Place' (1930) communicates the stultification of not travelling, but understands too that to journey is not a matter of choice alone:

> . . . no one goes
> Further than railhead or the ends of piers,
> Will neither go nor send his son
> Further through foothills than the rotting stack
> Where gaitered gamekeeper with dog and gun
> Will shout 'Turn back'.

In this poem the disinclination of Auden's subjects to wander is coupled with – produced by – warnings against trespass. No wonder the sense of 'much to be done, / Frontiers to cross' of which 'This Loved One' speaks in 1929 is present in all forms of his writing. Travel is a matter of intellectual growth, as well as a freedom. Other poems, such as 'A Summer Night' (1933) and 'A Bride in the 30s' (1934), show travel in that turbulent decade taking place under the threat of war. Most of the poems that deal with travel of various kinds, like 'Night Mail' (1935) and 'Dover' (1937), bring the personal and the public together.

Likewise the dramas. *The Ascent of F6* (1936) brilliantly dissects the meaning of travel and exploration for those who journey and those who stay at home; for the state and for the individual, whose changing attitudes towards the colonialist mountaineering expedition at the centre of the drama reveal the symbolic uses of travel. The ordinary clerk, Mr A, tells his wife, who is fed up with the ritual of their annual fortnight by the sea, that by cutting out photographs and maps, they can 'Follow the progress of this mountain mission, / Day by day let it inspire our lowly condition' (*F6*, pp. 50–1). After the death of the expedition member Edward Lamp has revived in Mr A horrible memories of the First World War, he asks: 'What is this expedition? He has died / To satisfy our smug suburban pride' (*F6*, p. 90). Later, when there is no more news of the expedition and fears grow for the safety of its members, Mr A tells his wife:

> Turn off the wireless; we are tired of descriptions of travel;
> We are bored by the exploits of amazing heroes;
> We do not wish to be heroes, nor are we likely to travel.
> We shall not penetrate the Arctic Circle.
> And see the Northern Lights flashing far beyond Iceland.
>
> (*F6*, p. 99)

They become reconciled to their lives that will never change; to the reality of their mundane forms of travel that, in proportion, can hold equal significance: 'Let our fears and our achievements be sufficient to our day' (*F6*, p. 100).

The plot of another Auden–Isherwood play, the extraordinary *The Dog Beneath the Skin or Where is Francis?* (1935), is propelled by travel and, in the course of its revelation of fascism in village England, its dialogue pithily expresses issues that have since underlain whole academic studies on travel and tourism: 'Such images of travel do not apply'; 'Places sometimes look different when one comes back to them'; 'man' sees 'others only in reference to himself' (*Dogskin*, pp. 33, 152, 156). A further Auden–Isherwood collaboration, *On the Frontier* (1938), has one character wondering, given the beastliness of war, whether 'Perhaps "country" and "frontier" are old-fashioned words that don't mean anything now.' For the generation *entre deux guerres* to which Auden belonged, borders were shaky things.

Notwithstanding the centrality to Auden's work of the idea of the journey, his most sustained treatments of it are still underrated. Valentine Cunning-ham, who confidently instructs us that 'the world has no more powerful body of travel literature' than the group of poems Auden wrote after his trip to Spain, derides *Letters from Iceland* and *Journey to a War* as 'oppor-tunistic rag-bags'.[11] (He does not seem to like the fact that writers produced travel books for money.) Samuel Hynes, who nominates travel as 'the most insistent of thirties metaphors' and recognises Auden's persistent use of it,[12] judges *Letters* to be 'a failure that is full of brilliant successes – disorga-nized and unresolved, uncertain and fluctuating in tone . . . It has almost no shape at all, not even the shape of the journey itself.'[13] While other art of the period is admired for its experimentation with shape, Auden's travel writing is strangely damned for it.

True, the statements of Auden and his collaborators have not always helped the cause of their travel books. Edna Longley quotes MacNeice's remark that: 'Our travel book was a hodge-podge, thrown together in gaiety', an admission she rightly declares to be 'half-disingenuous', but her remark that *Letters* satisfies the authors' conviction 'that poetry should be a kind of fun as well as a kind of journalism',[14] shows her, like others, to be reading the volume as poetry with some prose and not as a travel book. Yet the innovativeness of *Letters* can be appreciated only if it *is* read as a travel text.

Auden makes it quite clear that he aims to write a fresh, alternative kind of travel book. He finds the repetition of most travel books boring – 'the actual events are all extremely like each other – meals – sleeping accommodation – fleas – dangers, etc.' – and claims that he is neither clever nor sensitive enough to manage the usual alternative: the kind of essay arising from things seen that Lawrence and Huxley write (*LFI*, p. 142). Auden's innovation has, however, been quizzically and suspiciously regarded as 'one of the oddest of all travel books', and the kind of precedent from which he wished to depart, William Morris's *Icelandic Journals*, as 'a travel book in the purest sense – a diary of movement, describing a journey step by step or meal by meal'.[15]

Since Auden's unusual alternative travel book cleverly and continually draws attention to its own composition, it might be helpful to begin by listing its contents. After a Preface, its chapters are as follows: the first part of the verse 'Letter to Lord Byron'; the poem 'Journey to Iceland' and a prose letter, both to Isherwood; a letter to Graham and Anne Shepard; information for tourists; part II of the 'Letter to Lord Byron'; an anthology of Icelandic travel addressed to John Betjeman; a letter to R. H. S. Crossman; 'Letter to Lord Byron' part III; a letter from Auden to E. M. Auden; MacNeice's 'Eclogue from Iceland'; Auden to E. M. Auden number 2; Hetty to Nancy; 'Letter to Lord Byron' part IV; letter to Kristian Andreirsson; letter to William Coldstream; 'Letter to Lord Byron' part V; 'Auden and MacNeice: Their Last Will and Testament'; 'Epilogue' for Auden by MacNeice and an appendix with charts. There are also several photographs, taken by Auden.

In his opening verse letter to Lord Byron, Auden lists some of the features that we will encounter in the volume – photographs (out of focus and with wrong exposures), press cuttings, gossip, maps, statistics, graphs – and declares: 'I'm going to be very up to date indeed. / It is a collage that you're going to read' (*LFI*, p. 21). The travel book will give Auden what he wants: 'a form that's large enough to swim in, / And talk on any subject that I choose' (*LFI*, p. 21).

Auden's use of the collage as modernist technique has received serious attention from Marsha Bryant, who has also noted the marginalisation of *Letters* by critics of Auden's poetry and of travel writing. However, even Bryant's efforts to recuperate *Letters* have her rescuing it from the '"travel book" label [which] fails to address the purposeful disjunction that Auden achieves by mixing genres and dislocating perspective'.[16] But the book's label does not have to be switched and to do so can only perpetuate the prejudice against travel writing, which accommodates a number of genres anyway and can, though too rarely does, dislocate perspective.

*Letters* self-consciously displays from the outset its revisionism. In 'Letter to Lord Byron' Auden humorously explains his choice of rhyme royal for this poem instead of the *ottava rima* employed by Byron in *Don Juan* (1818–24), which Auden had been reading on the boat to Reykjavik, and which itself frequently draws attention to its own artifice. *Don Juan* provides Auden with a model for the literary journey as radical commentary on Europe and satire on Britain, as well as a precedent for parodying the forms on which it draws. What Byron's recent editor writes of *Don Juan* may well be applied to *Letters*: 'Running through the poem is not only a series of open commentaries on contemporary people and events, but also a set of coded biographical allusions meant for those whom he liked to call "the knowing ones".'[17] At the end of this first 'Letter' Auden apologises to his publishers lest the book be a flop, to his readers for pulling their leg and to the critics lest they be hard on him for leading them up the 'garden' (*LFI*, p. 24).

The second chapter (presented as a letter to Christopher Isherwood) is written part in verse and part in prose – the latter answering questions about Reykjavik, Icelandic authors, young Icelanders, the sex-life, Icelandic humour and his impression of life on small islands. Auden remarks that the Icelanders' pride in their country is free from 'the least trace of hysterical nationalism' (*LFI*, p. 30). This lack appeals to him, as, one infers, does the observation (in the verse) that 'Europe is absent' (*LFI*, p. 26), but Auden feels that it is too late for himself and Isherwood to escape Europe: they are both only really happy living among the lunatics. In fact, Auden and MacNeice bring Europe with them. As MacNeice remarks in his verse letter to Graham and Anne Shepard, he and Auden were travelling to find facts, not to escape them, and gain a focus from standing 'outside the crowd and caucus' (*LFI*, p. 33). Travel brings or intensifies a (sense of) detachment that affords a clearer perspective. The use that Auden and MacNeice make of their travel book could not be more apparent.

Chapter IV, 'For Tourists', written mainly by Auden with interjections from MacNeice, has short sections on many practical matters of travel in Iceland; a brief bibliography with titles on general information, language, history and literature, and a signpost to the travel bibliography in chapter VI. It will be complicated by the questioning (in chapter XIV, discussed below) of tourist perspectives. 'Letter to Lord Byron' is resumed in chapter V and nods at the restrictions of conventional travel writing:

> I've done my duty, taken many notes
>   Upon the almost total lack of greenery,
>  The roads, the illegitimates, the goats . . .
> (*LFI*, p. 49)

The plodding iambic pentameter and hard rhyme of that last line suggest the tedium of the models for travelling and writing that Auden is supposed to follow – and won't. Instead, supposing that Byron wants news about present-day England, he runs through for the dead poet's sake – and in homage to him – some tendencies and features of the modern age. He points to the existence of two Englands, remarking that in the north 'The scars of struggle are as yet unhealed' (*LFI*, p. 50), and criticises views of a showy

and comfortable modernity that may be true of Surrey but not of Warrington or Wigan. (Orwell's *The Road to Wigan Pier* appeared in the same
year.) This chapter includes Auden's memorable expressions of his preference
for industrial landscape: 'Clearer than Scafell Pike, my heart has stamped
on / The view from Birmingham to Wolverhampton', and 'Tramlines and
slagheaps, pieces of machinery, / That was, and still is, my ideal scenery'
(*LFI*, p. 51).

It is not just the physical landscape that attracts Auden's attention: the
cultural and ideological ones do, too. He is scathing about the shallowness
of democracy, amusing about snobbery, perceptive about the new, ordinary,
unremarkable middle-class hero and exercised by the rise of fascism. The
verse letter is picked up again in chapter VIII, combining immediacy with
bathos as he writes that he's back on shore in a 'warm bed-sitter' (*LFI*,
p. 99). The undercutting of the heroic tradition of exploration continues
with a wonderful rejection of the adventurous spirit as Auden hopes that
the expedition on which they are about to embark will not involve too
much walking (*LFI*, p. 99). Also in this chapter is confirmation of what
Paulin has admired in Auden's approach to his writing: 'To me Art's subject is the human clay, / And landscape but a background to a torso' (*LFI*,
p. 103).

In chapter IX, a prose letter from Auden to E. M. A., Auden confesses
that although he has been in Iceland for a month he still has no idea how to
begin writing the book, but that as the contracts are signed and the expenses
paid he supposes it will be done somehow. Perhaps it is this air of casualness
that fosters readings of *Letters* as an unplanned mélange. Auden's idea of
how to write his way out of his block is articulated in chapter XI, where he
describes having had the 'bright idea' of writing a chatty letter in light verse
to Byron, whose dislike of Wordsworth and his approach to nature he finds
sympathetic. Auden will write about himself, Europe, literature, anything
he can think of. Crucially, the letter he writes will, he announces, have little
to do with Iceland, and will describe how travelling in a distant place may
'make one reflect on one's past and one's culture from the outside'. He will
hang on this central thread letters to other people, who will be chosen to
allow each letter to deal with its subject in a 'different and significant way'
(*LFI*, pp. 141–2).

Chapter XIV, 'Letter to Kristian Andreirsson', presents itself as the fulfilment of a promise made by Auden while in Reykjavik that he would,
once back in England, send Andreirsson his impressions of Iceland. Auden's
several reasons why 'I question whether the reactions of the tourist are of
much value' (*LFI*, p. 213) – some of the same doubts that decades later exercise the new discipline of tourist studies – include the brevity of tourist visits

(including his own three-month stay), ignorance of the language, the tourist's social status and the 'glib generalisations based on inadequate and often incorrect data' (*LFI*, p. 213). Admitting the 'superficiality' of his impressions (*LFI*, p. 219), and, inviting Andreirsson to come to England and do likewise, he writes that he will be frank about what he disliked, though he says that he enjoyed his visit enormously. He then offers his observations under various headings. Under the second of these, 'Character', he writes that it is a 'silly thing to write about' and that he can't believe that the characters of nations differ much from one another or do not have the same variations: 'In any case the tourist sees nothing important' (*LFI*, p. 215).

This is a determined tilt at national stereotypes in a decade that employed them to genocidal effect. (The photograph on the facing page of a blond boy, labelled 'Germanischer Typus', represents a dig at the Nazi search for kinship.) Moreover, Auden's remarks undercut the authority of most travel writers, whose short-term visits peddle fixed ideas about national character. He underscores the point by exclaiming: 'I know that the day of a self-contained national culture is over' (*LFI*, p. 217). And of course he articulates this in a book that does away with self-contained genres.

Paradoxically, Auden's declaration of limited competence as spectator and recorder assumes an authority of its own. Thus his utterance (in 'Letter to Lord Byron', part IV) that 'what we see depends on who's observing' (*LFI*, p. 211) underlines his *awareness* of subjectivity, rather than the fact of that subjectivity itself. Indeed, the stanza from which that line is taken begins 'I know', and this is one of the things he does know. Auden is aware of this irony and has fun with it, captioning one photograph: 'What the Tourist does not see' (*LFI*, facing p. 218) – a laughing contradiction, given his self-designation as one.

The writing of the book is further addressed in chapter xv, a verse letter to William Coldstream. Here Auden addresses the problem faced by every writer of travels: how to present what one has seen. Taking an earlier suggestion of Coldstream's that an artist is both perceiver and teller, he begins as perceiver by pretending that he is the impersonal eye of the camera sent out by God to shoot on location, and they will look at the rushes together. After presenting (verbally) some images, he becomes the teller, chatting in a gossipy manner. Even here the noises from Europe are heard. Auden refers to the wireless announcer from Europe declaring, like a consultant surgeon, that 'Your case is hopeless. I give you six months' (*LFI*, p. 226).

There are more direct signals too. Chapter IX records a visit to Iceland of Goering's brother (whom Auden briefly meets), and notes the Nazis' theory that 'Iceland is the cradle of the Germanic culture' (*LFI*, p. 119). In the same chapter Auden notes that he has just heard for the first time of the civil war in Spain (*LFI*, p. 123), where he was to serve briefly as a broadcaster. The twin threats of Nazism and nationalism impinge increasingly on the book's consciousness. Chapter XVII, 'Auden and MacNeice: Their Last Will and Testament', written 'in the eighteenth year of the Western Peace' (*LFI*, p. 236), has a reference to Erika Mann, the wife he married to help her escape from Nazi Germany, with his hope that she will see the end of Hitler and his rule (*LFI*, p. 257). The same chapter also scorns the English fascist Sir Oswald Mosley and mocks the right-leaning Wyndham Lewis. In the 'Epilogue' by MacNeice addressed to Auden, there are further references to contemporary and impending conflicts, the cancellation of human rights and the final grim cheer: 'Still I drink your health before / The gun-butt raps upon the door' (*LFI*, p. 261). This is a ricochet from Auden's line that 'I'm home to Europe where I may be shot' (*LFI*, p. 212). As Hynes points out, events in Europe made this more than a rhetorical fear. *Letters* may be fun but it is deadly serious.

*Journey to a War* (1939) similarly uses a described space elsewhere to reflect on the imminent conflict in Europe. Auden and Isherwood had been asked by Random House in June or July 1937 to write a book about the East, and it was the war between China and the aggressor Japan which began in July 1937 that decided the authors to make this their subject. They left London in January 1938 and returned in July of the same year. In January 1939 they travelled into exile in the US, two months before the book was published.

The book's poems (also published separately, both before and afterwards) are by Auden. Its 'Travel-Diary', constituting the bulk of the book, was reworked by Isherwood from both men's diaries and from articles they wrote during and after the journey.[18] Auden also 'gathered his Chinese photographs into a "Picture Commentary" on the unique particulars that his poems treated in terms of allegory'.[19] The foreword to *Journey to a War* explains that this was the authors' first journey east of Suez, they spoke no Chinese and had no special knowledge of the region's affairs. They cannot vouch for the accuracy of many of the book's statements; some of their informants may have been unreliable, and they can only present some impression of what a first-time visitor to China would be likely to see and hear (*JTW*, p. 13). After the foreword the volume opens with half a dozen poems under the heading 'London to Hongkong'. This is followed by the prose 'Travel-Diary', then by the several photographs of the 'Picture Commentary', and finally by 'In Time of War: A Sonnet Sequence with a verse commentary'.

The amateur war correspondents maintain a detached, critical tone towards Britain. This is evident in their observations on, among other things, race and masculinity. They describe the football-playing crews of the British and American gunboats moored near the river-island of Shameen, as 'hairy, meat-pink men with powerful buttocks'. This after they have written of the British Consulate: 'For once, we had to admit . . . the British had shown some good taste' (*JTW*, p. 31). Auden and Isherwood take a critical view of their country and compatriots, empathising with the Chinese. This stance also generates self-deprecation. When the two travellers leave Sü-chow with their servant/translator Chiang on 27 March, and a large crowd laughingly watches them, they think of themselves as resembling some of Jules Verne's lunatic English explorers (*JTW*, p. 104).

Such moments of self-deprecation have been seen by Richard Johnstone as 'also self-congratulation', with Auden and Isherwood unable to understand the country through which they pass, taking 'refuge in their common background, in a whole network of jokes and references that protects them from whatever is outside'. Theirs is 'an assertion of personal identity, a declaration that [they] possess characters and habits of mind that are as incomprehensible to the Chinese as the Chinese are to them'.[20]

This interpretation seems harsh. If Auden and Isherwood shore up their sense of identity through not belonging, this applies to their standing back from British as much as from Chinese norms. (The several references in the book to having sex and being drunk seem designed to shock the British bourgeoisie.) They enthusiastically distinguish themselves from other traveller-correspondents, most notably Peter Fleming, and if their personal identities are bolstered by their journey, this is managed without resorting to the crude racism and near-misanthropy that infest their contemporary Evelyn Waugh's travel books and novels of Africa. They raise deep questions about war, travel and travel writing, and China in relation to the West.[21]

Auden and Isherwood's awareness of the lack of objectivity in travel observations extends to a recognition of how one's impressions may be affected by one's emotions and state of mind. In the city of Cheng-chow, 'In my jaundiced, sleepy mood, everything I noticed seemed miserable and corrupt' (*JTW*, p. 76). The limits of the visitor's understanding are explicitly addressed. Writing about the tiring social functions they have to attend, Isherwood asks whether, despite the warm goodwill on both sides, they are 'really communicating with each other at all' (*JTW*, p. 155).

Auden and Isherwood are not the only Western travellers in China to pose this troubling question. Agnes Smedley, the US journalist who did know the Chinese language and whose passionate commitment to the Communist Chinese Eighth Route Army is patronised by Auden and Isherwood – 'The Red Army, one sees, is [her] whole life – her husband and her child' (*JTW*, p. 166) – insists that 'The real story of China can be told only by the

Chinese workers and peasants themselves.'[22] On the face of it, Auden seems similarly concerned with those whose voices are not heard. In his magnificent sonnet XVIII of 'In Time of War', he writes of the anonymous dead Chinese soldier who 'will not be introduced / When this campaign is tidied into books' (*JTW*, p. 276), but this is Every-soldier, and his evocation an instance of Auden's movement from the particular to the universal, though no less compelling for that.

Auden's and Isherwood's degree of empathy with the Chinese should not be exaggerated. At one point, Isherwood applies as an absolute rule Western tastes, judging that, despite their attractiveness, the faces of Chinese women are generally too broad and flat to be really beautiful (*JTW*, p. 158). Such caveats apart, Auden and Isherwood move away from the values and behaviour of their compatriots. After an 'argumentative and political' lunch at the British Consulate, Isherwood writes of the Race Club buildings and the grounds around them that they might as well be in Surrey, for, as Auden had remarked, 'all trace of China has been lovingly obliterated' (*JTW*, p. 162).

A shift of perspective of another kind is recorded by Isherwood as he sits with Auden at the home of their missionary hosts at Paak Hok Tung, half a mile downriver from the gunboats. As they take tea, he hears an air raid outside and cannot share the calm of Auden, who has seen war in Spain. As Isherwood surveys the 'charming room' with its teacups, scones, copies of Chesterton's essays and Kipling's poems, and its photograph of an Oxford college, he tries to reconcile these sights with the sound of warfare outside: 'Understand, I told myself, that those noises, these objects, are part of a single, integrated scene. Wake up. It's all quite real. And, at that moment, I really did wake up. At that moment, suddenly, I arrived in China' (*JTW*, p. 32). The necessity for arrival of relating the domestic and the foreign, safety and danger, is fundamental to Auden's travel texts and is managed through a juxtaposition of forms that complements the process from disorientation to integration described by Isherwood above. Similarly, when Mr A. W. Kao, prior to a visit from General Ku's representative, explains to Auden and Isherwood the strategic situation, he talks as though 'Everything was lucid and tidy and false.' But Auden knows that war is not like that. 'War is untidy, inefficient, obscure, and largely a matter of chance' (*JTW*, p. 202). A uniform narrative would not be the most appropriate choice for the narration of their journey to it.

In discussing the relationship between the two authors' contributions to the book, Douglas Kerr has argued that Isherwood's prose is less certain, more questioning and less authoritative than Auden's verse. According to Kerr, whereas Auden's poems pull China into a more general and confidently expressed world view – 'a *grand récit* indeed' – Isherwood's prose is unable to get to grips with China. The result (on Isherwood's part) is 'a failure – a conscious, if not deliberate failure – to write a travel book. It is a failure of arrival, comprehension, integration, and closure.' Kerr appears to approve this failure as a kind of unexploitative and self-reflective 'narrative of disorientations'.[23] Once more, if by a different route, we are faced with a refusal to see a travel book for what it is.

Auden should not be blamed for drawing what he sees into a wider world view. Not only socialists but anyone wishing to understand general principles must do that. It does not mean that he cannot see the specific, but that he seeks to relate it (in the sense of telling and linking). In 'a world that has no localized events', he enforces upon us an understanding of our connectedness. The 'material context' that he has witnessed: 'Is but the local variant of a struggle in which all . . . are profoundly implicated' (*JTW*, pp. 291–2).

There is, in the powerful sonnet sequence and verse 'Commentary', from which the above lines are taken, an overwhelming sense of troubled enquiry into the human capacity for malefaction, and a vibrant tension between political and humanist explanations for it. A concentrated example of this is found in sonnet XIV:

> Behind each sociable home-loving eye
> The private massacres are taking place;
> All Women, Jews, the Rich, the Human Race.
> ( *JTW*, p. 272)

Behind that eye is the brain. Those private massacres are not only the ones that are carried out hidden from view but are those that take place in the mind; the prejudices and hatreds that enable the public massacres. The combination of the specific and the universal, of the political and the moral, is also apparent in the shocking ending of sonnet XVI, with the force of its terminal stresses:

> And maps can really point to places
> Where life is evil now:
> Nanking; Dachau.   ( *JTW*, p. 274)

In the twenty-first century, as we are taken on our own journey to a 'war on terror', Auden's travel books of the 1930s have as much to tell us not only about how we travel but about the relationships between nations, between individuals and the state, about our views on others and how to represent them, as any now being written. As he puts it in 'Hongkong', 'We cannot postulate a General Will; / For what we are, we have ourselves to blame' (*JTW*, p. 23).

## NOTES

1. Philip Dodd, 'The Views of Travellers: Travel Writing in the 1930s', *Prose Studies*, 5:1 (1982), pp. 127–38; quotation at pp. 127–8.
2. Noreen Branson and Margot Heinemann, *Britain in the Nineteen Thirties* (London: Weidenfeld and Nicolson, 1971), p. 257.
3. Dodd, 'The Views of Travellers', p. 128.
4. Andrew Hammond, '"The unending revolt": Travel in an Era of Modernism', *Studies in Travel Writing*, 7:2 (2003), pp. 169–89.
5. For example, Bernard Schweizer, *Radicals on the Road: The Politics of English Travel Writing in the 1930s* (Charlottesville: University Press of Virginia, 2001).
6. Tom Paulin, '*Letters from Iceland*: Going North', *Renaissance and Modern Studies*, 20 (1976), p. 74.
7. Paul Fussell, *Abroad: British Literary Traveling between the Wars* (New York: Oxford University Press, 1980), pp. 219–20.
8. Paulin, '*Letters from Iceland*', pp. 77, 80.
9. Fussell, *Abroad*, p. 32.
10. See also Stan Smith, 'Burbank with a Baedeker: Modernism's Grand Tours', special issue on 'Modernist Travels', ed. Stan Smith and Tim Youngs, *Studies in Travel Writing*, 8:1 (March 2004), pp. 1–18.
11. Valentine Cunningham, *British Writers of the Thirties* (Oxford: Oxford University Press, 1989), pp. 394–5, 391.
12. Samuel Hynes, *The Auden Generation: Literature and Politics in England in the 1930s* (1976) (London: Pimlico, 1992), p. 229.
13. *Ibid.*, p. 291.
14. Edna Longley, *Louis MacNeice: A Critical Study* (London: Faber and Faber, 1988, repr. 1996), p. 49. There is no countering Mendelson's exposure of the 'many errors of spelling, transcription, and fact' (*Prose I*, p. 773) in the manuscript that Auden and MacNeice gave their publisher; my argument rather is that their book is more accomplished and sophisticated than has been granted – and is a travel book.
15. James Morris, 'Introduction' to *Icelandic Journals by William Morris* (Fontwell: Centaur Press, 1969), pp. xv, xvi.
16. Marsha Bryant, 'Auden and the "Arctic Stare": Documentary as Public Collage in *Letters from Iceland*', *Journal of Modern Literature*, 17:4 (1991), pp. 537–65; quotation at p. 537. Bryant looks at the documentary and photographic features of *Letters* in the context of Auden's six-months' job with a documentary film collective just before he journeyed to Iceland.
17. Lord Byron, *The Major Works*, ed. Jerome J. McGann (Oxford: Oxford University Press, 2000), pp. 1043, 1044. *Letters from Iceland* has spawned its own imitators, most directly Simon Armitage and Glyn Maxwell, *Moon Country: Further Reports from Iceland* (London: Faber and Faber, 1996).
18. For a detailed account of the book's composition, publication and variants see *Prose I*, pp. 822–31.
19. Edward Mendelson, 'Introduction', *Prose I*, p. xxxiii.
20. Richard Johnstone, *The Will to Believe: Novelists of the Nineteen-thirties* (London: Oxford University Press, 1984), pp. 133–4.

21. See also Maureen Moynagh, 'Revolutionary Drag in Auden's and Isherwood's *Journey to a War*', *Studies in Travel Writing*, 8:2 (2004). Moynagh undertakes a serious examination of Auden and Isherwood's camp performativity, which she sees as both subversive and engaged.
22. Agnes Smedley, *China Fights Back: An American Woman with the Eighth Route Army* (London: Victor Gollancz, 1938), p. 158.
23. Douglas Kerr, 'Disorientations: Auden and Isherwood's China', *Literature & History*, 3rd series 5:2 (Autumn 1996), pp. 53–67; quotations at pp. 58, 56, 54. Kerr's comments on Auden's poems refer specifically to the sonnet sequence 'In Time of War'.

# 7

CHRISTOPHER INNES

# Auden's plays and dramatic writings: theatre, film and opera

Auden focused consistently on the opportunities for wider discourse and immediate emotional impact offered by various kinds of performance. He started writing his first dramatic script on leaving Oxford at the age of twenty-one, and was collaborating on an operatic libretto in 1973, the year of his death. There was hardly a year when Auden was not working on some kind of performance text. In addition to stage plays and libretti, he experimented with cabaret, liturgical drama, Agitprop, pageant and declamatory verses, the masque and (rejected) lyrics for the musical comedy, 'The Man of La Mancha' (1963). As new forms of media appeared he immediately adopted them, writing radio plays, scripts for early documentary films and movie scenarios.

This cultivation of a public poetic voice paralleled T. S. Eliot, who also turned to drama to reach a wider, more popular audience, and experimented with ritual theatre. Whereas Eliot gave up the stage after *The Elder Statesman* in 1958, Auden's involvement lasted throughout his life. Although he never managed to write anything as truly popular as Eliot's ritualised drama of martyrdom, *Murder in the Cathedral*, Auden maintained his poetic agenda by turning in his later years to opera.

Auden's connections with Eliot were particularly close on the theatrical level. Eliot published Auden's earliest play, 'Paid on Both Sides', which was performed in America in 1931 by Hallie Flanagan, who also staged Eliot's first play, *Sweeney Agonistes*, three years later. Both were centrally involved with the Group Theatre, which produced *Sweeney Agonistes* and Auden's *The Dance of Death* as a double bill in 1935. Auden belonged to a group of poets, including MacNeice and Spender, which aimed to revolutionise English theatre by restoring 'serious' drama, always seen as 'poetic', whether defined as spiritual, archetypal, symbolist, psychological or directly political. In searching for a more public – and more directly political – dimension for his poetry, Auden was fighting the general tide in British theatre. To measure his accomplishment, as well as to appreciate the experimental nature of this writing, it is useful to consider the context he was entering.

Nineteenth-century attempts to create poetic drama had set up an almost insuperable barrier, with any dialogue in verse being associated with empty declamation, fustian grandeur, artifice and archaism. The 'Bardolatry' which Bernard Shaw so vociferously attacked kept Shakespeare as almost the only serious drama performed on the English stage. Even when major poets turned to the theatre the Shakespearean influence seemed inescapable, as with Tennyson's *Becket* (1884). This dealt with exactly the same historical incident that T. S. Eliot was to treat very differently in *Murder in the Cathedral*, but Tennyson's play is characterised by a kind of neo-Elizabethan inflation that makes it almost unreadable. Theatrical attempts by more recent poets such as John Masefield, James Elroy Flecker or Yeats only confirmed the gulf between verse and modern experience. In using Noh conventions to establish the imaginative 'remoteness' that 'must be firmly held against a pushing world' if his poetic symbols were to 'inhabit . . . the deeps of the mind', Yeats withdrew from the public stage to present his hieratic dramas in drawing rooms, before an elite audience.[1] Masefield retreated from contemporary subjects to Roman and biblical themes. Following Yeats and Gordon Craig, he experimented with Japanese Noh and medieval Miracle Play models, but his poetic dialogue came to seem undramatic – a form of 'costume language'. The sensuous lyricism of Flecker's *Hassan* (first performed in 1923) has an exotic attraction, but it was immediately received as a period piece, its popularity due as much to the incidental music supplied by Delius and the ballets by Fokine, as to Flecker's romanticised Middle-Eastern scenario.

From the start Auden was forced to experiment radically if he was to find a viable form of poetry for contemporary drama. He certainly realised the problems. As he put it a few years later, referring specifically to the kind of drama represented by Tennyson and Yeats:

> [M]odern English poetic drama has been of three kinds: the romantic sham-Tudor which has occasionally succeeded for a short time on the strength of the spectacle; the cosmic-philosophical which theatrically has always been a complete flop; and the high-brow chamber-music drama, artistically much the best, but a somewhat etiolated blossom. And it is difficult to believe that the poets are really satisfied with this solution.[2]

Since poetry, the traditional language for tragedy, was relegated to verbal spectacle, Auden had to re-establish the very idea of using poetry as a dramatic expression for serious themes. The dominant influence of Ibsen had led to the slices of working-class life in D. H. Lawrence's plays, or the gritty realism of plays like R. C. Sherriff's anti-war drama, *Journey's End*, which was the hit of the year when Auden started writing his first play. For 'serious' themes, particularly dealing with current society or topical issues, 'everyday' prose dialogue was seen as the only viable mode, with any conventionally poetic elements like symbols relegated to the subtext of a play.

There was, however, one challenge to the naturalistic definition of modernism promoted by Shaw and Archer: German and Scandinavian Expressionism. This was introduced to London during the 1920s by the Gate Theatre, where the plays of Kaiser, Toller and Wedekind, as well as Strindberg's later and O'Neill's early work were staged by Peter Godfrey. Auden had more direct personal knowledge of the German theatrical scene than almost any other British playwright; and the initial source for his theatrical enthusiasm is clear.

Leaving Oxford, Auden went to Berlin; and in Germany he found a vibrant cabaret scene, Expressionist films and a strident political theatre filled with 'New Realist' (*Neue Sachlichkeit*) productions, as well as Brecht's didactic drama. Although the classical cabarets – Wedekind's *Elf Scharfrichter* (Eleven Hangmen), Rosa Valetti's *Grössenwahn* (Megalomania) – had long since closed, there was still a pro-Communist group that gave cabaret performances in union halls across Berlin, and 1928 was the year when Marlene Dietrich made her debut in one of Max Reinhardt's revues. Erwin Piscator's highly mechanised and filmic proletarian theatre reached one of its high points in the same year with his striking productions of *The Good Soldier Schweik*, as well as a constructivist piece about the oil industry with music by Kurt Weill, while the Brecht/Weill *Threepenny Opera* opened in August 1928. This artistic scene influenced even more explicitly Auden's first major collaborator, Christopher Isherwood, who made the heroine of his Berlin novel *Goodbye to Berlin* the cabaret artiste Sally Bowles.

In some ways Auden seemed to be harking back to the German scene far earlier in the twenties, when Expressionism was in full swing. Already by 1924 it had practically vanished from the stage, to be replaced by the *Neue Sachlichkeit* (thematic realism/objectivity) of Bertolt Brecht, Klaus Mann and Leon Feuchtwanger. The first major sign of German influence was the introduction of an Expressionist dream-sequence into the second draft of 'Paid on Both Sides'. Auden was later to devote a considerable amount of time to Brecht's work – collaborating with him on a Broadway adaptation of *The Duchess of Malfi*, translating songs from both *The Caucasian Chalk Circle* and Brecht's 'song-ballet' *The Seven Deadly Sins*, as well as the Brecht/Weill opera of *The Rise and Fall of the City of Mahagonny*. There were also more directly poetic models that appeared on the Berlin stage while Auden was there, such as Ernst Barlach's *Der Findling* (The Orphan). Barlach's religious symbolism would have appealed to Auden's combination of Christianity and socialism, as well as his use of surreal and charade-like figures.

Auden subtitled 'Paid on Both Sides' a 'Charade', and used Expressionist distortion in the central scene – in which Father Christmas appears as judge at a trial where a murder is replayed, and the victim is resurrected by a farcical doctor, a typical figure from Mummers' plays. As in a family game of charades, the characters are divided into two teams, but here these represent the two armies in an internecine war of assassination and revenge. The characters may superficially be representative English figures (with names like John Nower and Aaron Shaw), yet their story is related to Oedipus ('A greater, but not fortunate in all'), Beowulf (the title – 'no good exchange, that they should pay on both sides with lives of friends'), and the Anglo-Saxon poem *The Battle of Maldon* ('There he died. Nor any came / Fighters home'), as well as echoing *Wuthering Heights* in a moor setting resembling the Brontë country (*Plays*, pp. 30, 20).

The play is in many ways a rough version of Eliot's later experiments in merging mythical substrata with modern England, as in the appearance of the Aeschylean Greek Fates, the Eumenides, at the contemporary aristocratic homecoming of *The Family Reunion* (1939). A handwritten note on the cover to the 1950 edition of *W. H. Auden's Collected Shorter Poems 1930–1944*, which has been attributed to Eliot, indeed acknowledged this play as 'the forerunner of contemporary poetic drama' (*Plays*, pp. xvi, xxix). It is probably due to Auden's dream scene that Eliot included the figure of Father Christmas in one version of *Sweeney Agonistes*. But even here there are stylistic signs of the contrast between them. Eliot's dramatic tone, even in his first and most Audenesque drama, *Sweeney Agonistes* (with its use of masks and jazz rhythms, deliberately vapid verses and screams in the dark) is always fundamentally serious, while his characters are given a primarily mythological depth. In comparison, 'Paid on Both Sides' constantly verges on burlesque – Auden's great dramatic weakness – and can be interpreted as a Freudian psychoanalytic projection, with the various poles of conflict (Ego, Id, etc.) being represented by the antithetical forces of the two families, who are still 'Sharers of the same house / Attendants on the same machine' (*Plays*, pp. 21, 26).

Notably anticipating the critical label for Brecht's plays (which came to be identified as parable drama) Auden described 'Paid on Both Sides' as being 'A parable of English Middle Class (professional) life 1907–1929'.[3] 'Parable' exactly describes the three major plays he produced with Isherwood.

The parable elements are particularly clear in *The Dog Beneath the Skin*, where the action is based on the archetypal trope of a quest – with a naïve hero (Alan Norman) being chosen by lot to go in search of a lost saviour-prince (Sir Francis Crewe), hoping to win the promised reward of marriage to a virgin-princess (the heiress of Honeypot Hall). Reversing the title, the skin of the eponymous pantomime dog Alan takes along as a companion, turns out to conceal a man – and not just an anonymous stagehand, as in a pantomime horse, but the aristocrat who is the object of the quest, Sir Francis himself. Some of the scenes are played in masks (the half-mask of Brechtian theatre in the original 1935 production) and the conclusion is a standard transformation scene – though here in political terms. The rural England of the traditional village, as it had appeared at the start, is revealed as the base for a fascist movement, promoted and supported by the vicar, managed by the reactionary forces of an embittered war-widow and a general, with the fairy-tale heiress (rejecting her symbolic role and now engaged to an arms manufacturer) presenting the black-shirted Boys' Brigade with their new standard. In the final tableau, where these fascist figures line up for a press photograph, they are all transformed into animals, barking, quacking, grunting or squeaking – with the vicar as a goat and the general as a bull bellowing incomprehensibly against the sound of loud martial music.[4]

Alan is the proverbial innocent abroad. His journey, accompanied by the dog, through the sink-holes of Europe (a clear parallel to the 1930 Brecht/Weill opera, *The Rise and Fall of the City of Mahagonny*, which Auden was subsequently to translate) offers a symbolic survey of the moral state of capitalism which exposes its links with the rising fascist tide. We get 'a dog's-eye view' that strips away respectable façades to show 'people from underneath'. Their picaresque progress leads from a king's palace (Ostnia, where the wives of political prisoners are treated to a royal reception and light refreshments while their husbands are executed), through the red light district (meeting one of the previous questers from the village who never returned, now an addict enslaved by drugs) to a lunatic asylum (Westland, where Alan is incarcerated and the wall is decorated, according to the stage directions, with a large portrait of a man in uniform, beneath which is written 'Our Leader'. The man has a loudspeaker instead of a face, through which ranting speeches and orders are issued). Repeatedly rescued by the dog, Alan continues his search through England, first in a so-called paradise park (where the beautiful people turn out to be terminal hypochondriacs, and another of the earlier questers dies under the surgeon's knife) and finally the Nineveh Hotel, where the dancing chorus of Nineveh Girls are literally consumer-items, picked out of the line-up by a gross diner for his meal, with 'the finger-nails served separately as a savoury' (*Plays*, pp. 285, 225, 263).

Here Alan himself is corrupted (seduced by a beautifully dressed shop window dummy, on to which men project their desires) and bankrupted.

As the dog's skin itself (temporarily vacated by its human inhabitant) points out in a soliloquy to a clock during one of the more grotesquely surrealistic scenes: 'I'm an idea, you're an idea, everything's an idea' (*Plays*, p. 274). This solipsistic intellectual – or indeed spiritual – level of incorporeal existence is Auden's focus in his next collaboration with Isherwood, *The Ascent of F6*, where the plot – in the form of a *Boy's Own* imperialist adventure, underhand manipulations by politicians at home and exotic landscapes of mountaintops with monks and demons – stands revealed as the manifestation of social unreality. As the onlookers ask, when the deaths of the British climbing expedition are reported one by one:

> What is this expedition? He has died
> To satisfy our smug suburban pride.

In counterpoint to Mr and Mrs A (for 'Average'), waiting in quiet desperation to be redeemed by the success of the expedition, there is a solemn chorus aware of a deeper reality, pointing out: 'There is always another story, there is more than meets the eye' (*Plays*, pp. 337, 353). As with 'Paid on Both Sides', the true level of reality in the play is psychological and based on a Manichean duality between Ransom and his evil alter ego, his brother Sir James, who is an egotistical government minister.

Ransom, the protagonist, is heroic on every possible level. A natural leader of men, he is first encountered sitting on a spire of rock, alone above the world, reading Dante and contemplating what being a hero might mean, debating the figure of Ulysses as one of a band of 'seedy adventurers', 'a crook speaking to crooks' about Virtue and Knowledge. He is to be turned into precisely this sort of fake hero by the newspapers, with headlines like 'Young English Climber's Daredevil Attempt!' (*Plays*, p. 314). A paragon – philosopher, physically daring and handsome, broad-minded moralist, expert chess player, pacifist and voluntary martyr – Ransom is also cast as the hero of military melodrama, willing to die for the Empire, and a Christ figure, sacrificing himself to redeem the ordinary people and bring meaning to their lives. Indeed the major image at the end represents him as St George – on a white horse, slaying a dragon with a spear – patron saint of England.

Salvation, in its many manifestations, dominates the play. Although given physical existence by the scenery of steeply rising rock terraces, the 'haunted' mountain is more a liminal space: a boundary between rival colonising powers (dividing British from Ostnian Sudoland, with the first to reach the top winning a military as well as propaganda victory), between states of consciousness (quotidian and the depths of the psyche) and between modes of being (material and individual versus archetypal). More than anything else it is a moral boundary, containing both good – in the shape of the abbot, wise holy man with magic crystal – and evil, whose myriad forms are incorporated in a demon. This monster appears in the shape of Ransom's politician-brother, for whom power is all that counts, and then, more distressingly, as Ransom's mother. The climax transforms the action of scaling the peak, which has already been emphasised as a metaphor for achieving self-knowledge, into a signifier for attaining the spiritual heights of martyrdom. The struggle to the top turns into a heavily symbolic chess game, in which the masked figures of militarism, capitalism and colonialism confront the figures of Ransom's dead climbing companions, and victory becomes defeat. This modulates into a surrealistic court-trial, where acknowledging guilt establishes innocence, and a death sentence sets the accused prisoner free, culminating in a Freudian *pietà* with Ransom's corpse cradled on his mother's knees. As E. M. Forster perceived in his review of the first production: 'Mother-love, usually sacrosanct, becomes a very nasty customer.'[5]

Real-life analogues for this hero were clear to contemporary audiences. The international competition with the reactionary central European monarchy of Ostnia derives from Captain Scott's race to the South Pole against the Norwegian explorer Amundsen. The self-sacrifice of the sick Captain Oates, walking out into the blizzard to give his comrades a chance of survival, is repeated in the suicide of one climber in Ransom's party, while the deaths of Ransom and his last companion echo the tragic outcome of Scott's expedition. Ransom himself was based on T. E. Lawrence, a national hero who rejected society and combined a life of action with literary contemplation. The parallels were so obvious that Alec Guinness (later to re-enact the role more directly in his 1960 performance as the title figure of *Ross*, Terence Rattigan's dramatisation of Lawrence's life) researched Lawrence's biography as preparation for the part of Ransom in a 1939 revival of *F6*. But comparison with Rattigan's historical treatment shows the degree to which Auden and Isherwood's version is allegorised to bring out its spiritual focus.

This may be a signal of Auden's loss of control over the dramatic material, since religious themes were far more characteristic of the Group Theatre, while Auden's socialism gets buried beneath symbols. His voice comes through clearly in the parody figures of Mr and Mrs A, typical inhabitants of what Auden subsequently christened 'The Age of Anxiety', who live in fear and boredom, unable to find any meaning in their materialistic petty-bourgeois existence, and grasp at the substitutes manufactured by the capitalist news-media. The formal choruses of the second half of the play give powerful images of modern society as urban waste land. Yet the chorus itself is dressed in monks' habits (supposedly from a monastery on a glacier on the mountain) and forms a divine jury exercising life-and-death judgement over the hero. Isherwood recorded that there was a sharp division of writing responsibilities in this play, with each of them working quite separately on specific parts – it being 'understood throughout, that Wystan's speciality was to be the "woozy" and mine the "straight" bits'[6] – with true collaboration only in the final scene.

While *F6* is in many ways their most unique and expressive drama – with contemporary reviewers comparing Ransom to Hamlet – Isherwood clearly points to the creative problems that produced a confusion of allegories and the juxtaposition of conflicting levels of reality. Auden himself seems to have had serious doubts about the final scene, which he rewrote at least twice in 1939 for performances in America and at the Old Vic, and again for a 1945 performance. One of these alternatives shows the final scene (as printed in the Faber text) to be entirely a hallucination of Ransom's dying mind, since his evil brother James – who is apparently killed by Ransom – reappears in an epilogue to expropriate the dead hero for his imperial project. Others clarify the intended message with lines to the effect that 'There is no Demon', only human greed and hypocrisy, or suggest how the audience should respond: 'wake up . . . see the real world and find a true reason for being'.[7]

As Auden wrote to Stephen Spender, *F6* was like 'a cross between [Ibsen's] Peer Gynt and Journey's End' (Sherriff's grim picture of front-line trenches in World War I). Their third play, *On the Frontier*, subtitled 'A Melodrama', lacked the characteristic Audenesque Peer Gynt aspect almost altogether. Working on it, Auden recorded feeling 'uncomfortable. The subject is too contemporary for a semi-realistic play.'[8] By mid 1938 the urgency of current events was all but overwhelming, with the coming war against Hitler (despite Prime Minister Chamberlain's vain claim of 'Peace in our time') only too clearly unavoidable; and in Auden's early notes the sinister apologist for dictatorship in *On the Frontier*, Valerian, was called Ribbentrop, after Hitler's minister for foreign affairs. In this depiction of war breaking out between (once more) monarchist Ostnia and fascist Westland, the psychological or poetic aspects of the play are limited to just two scenes depicting the Romeo-and-Juliet children of families on opposing sides. Their love is initially presented as a saving force. But this is hardly meant as a realistic possibility since they come together in an imaginary no-man's-land of a small spot-lit space in the darkness between the two nations. In the final scene, in which they lament the violence that has made their union impossible, they meet in the limbo between life and death, early casualties of the war. In contrast, the solution proposed by the political action is union-organised strikes that shut down all the industry of war, mutiny among the common soldiers, who kill their officers instead of fighting the 'enemy', and assassination of leaders like Valerian. As a chorus of factory workers sings in a prologue:

> Stoke up the fires in furnace number three
> The day is coming, brother, when we shall all be free.
>
> (*Plays*, p. 362)

In *Dogskin*, in addition to the embedded poems, Auden wrote the dominant part of the play – the more Expressionistic and symbolic scenes, particularly the palace, red light and paradise park scenes, plus the more grotesque elements of the Nineveh Hotel episode – as he acknowledged in a letter to Stephen Spender, where he distinguished clearly between himself as 'a parabolic writer' and Isherwood as a 'realist'.[9] When they wrote *F6*, performed by the Group Theatre in 1937, Auden turned out to be responsible for only about one third of the script. The difference shows. Although the hero bears the heavily symbolic name of Ransom, while the peak he dies climbing is clearly allegorical, the overall mode of the play is quasi-naturalistic, which conflicts with the phantasmagoric style of the ending. *On the Frontier* explicitly dismisses humanistic poetry as a way of changing the situation, in favour of Communist revolution. In a very real sense too, the coming war represented a complete break with the ethos and literary modes of the 1930s. The Group Theatre, which had found its distinctive voice in Auden and Isherwood, closed with the war; and its final production in 1939 – the revival of *The Ascent of F6* with Alec Guinness – marks the end of symbolic Expressionism on the British stage.

Perhaps not surprisingly, even while working closely with Isherwood, Auden was also turning from stage drama to alternative forms that seemed to offer more scope for experiment. At first it might have looked as though radio offered an alternative for achieving a public voice and a mass audience for poetry. Freed from the physical limitations of the stage, and the crudity of visual symbolism, the direct appeal to the ear and the imagination made radio an apt medium for lyricism. As another of the Group Theatre poets, Louis MacNeice, described it, the advantages of a completely aural form were that it automatically created 'stream of consciousness . . . subordinating analysis to synthesis', and appealing 'to more primitive elements' in the listener. But this kind of radio drama, which reached its fullest expression in the musically structured dreaming-back of Dylan Thomas's 1953 'play for voices', *Under Milk Wood*, was the antithesis of the kind of socially involved writing Auden favoured. MacNeice was largely correct in describing the effect of the BBC style of radio play in this period as having the status of a dream, which 'does not admit of a completely rational analysis and still less adds up to any clear moral or message'.[10] So while Auden showed an interest in radio, he only wrote a single piece for the BBC, the 1937 script of *Hadrian's Wall*, an evocation of British history in the aftermath of the Roman conquest and its psychological effect, which is traced down to the modern voices who are now tourists for whom politics, bloodshed and barbarity are only curiosities (*Plays*, p. 362).[11] Instead Auden turned to a very different medium: film.

The style of cinema that particularly attracted him was the documentary – almost the exact opposite of all that BBC radio represented. Most of Auden's film work was with the brilliant British director John Grierson, who effectively defined documentary through the promotional pieces he shot for the new General Post Office Film Unit and later his significantly named Realistic Film Unit. One of these has become a classic of the genre, *Night Mail*, where Auden's voice-over poem exactly matches the thrusting rhythms of the clacking wheels over the track as the railway engine of the title surges northwards, and gives a strong human – and socialist – dimension to the images of pounding machinery and empty landscape by focusing on the cargo of letters picked up and distributed by the unpausing train. Each of the six verses is a single extremely extended sentence, exactly capturing the driving urgency of the journey from London to Glasgow and mirroring the sophisticated mechanics of mail delivery in effortless virtuosity. Made in 1935, the film came hard on the heels of *Coal Face*, Auden's first film experience, which experimented daringly with 'found poetry', alphabetical lists of job designations and statistics, chanted to the percussive beat of Britten's music, over pictures of coaldust-blackened miners in lifts and mineshafts.

It was followed in the same year by *Negroes*, completed in 1938, again with music by Britten, under the title of *God's Chillun*. The only film not made with Grierson, this was almost operatic, with the only spoken words brief single lines by a 'Negro Commentator', and all the rest of the voice-over mixing solos for tenor and soprano with chorus and calypso. It ends with a chorus that was to be reused as the final lines of *F6* – but has a far more direct meaning in the context of this film (*Plays*, pp. 422, 428).

However striking his contribution to Grierson's films, Auden must have realised that his words could play only a minor role in such a visual medium. Although he continued to write scripts for films, ending with *The Londoners* in 1938 – a strongly socialist propaganda piece made to mark the fiftieth anniversary of the London County Council, and urging its audience, 'Here then in London build the city of the free' – *Negroes* points the way to his next medium. It was a logical move for Auden, who had worked with Britten in almost all his plays and films from *Dance of Death*, to turn to opera, to

collaborate with him on a whimsical treatment of American mythology in
*Paul Bunyan*, an operetta for children first performed at Columbia University in 1941. After that, together with a new collaborator, Chester Kallman,
Auden wrote a series of libretti for two of the other leading modernist composers, Igor Stravinsky and Hans Werner Henze, as well as a notable translation of Mozart's *Magic Flute*.

Perhaps the most radical of the libretti is his second and grandest operatic
experiment with Henze, *The Bassarids*, written in 1964 and first performed
at Salzburg in 1966. Anticipating the avant-garde interest in the stark
tragedy of Euripides' *Bacchae*, the text's deliberate anachronism and mix
of different periods formed a model for subsequent postmodern stagings
such as Bogdanov's 1987 treatment of Shakespeare's history plays. The original Greek setting is presented as stiffening into statuary, with the 'traditional
white draperies of a generalized classical Antiquity' being worn by the chorus 'with a certain stiffness', while Agave's dress and hairdo are 'elaborate: in
the style of the Second Empire', the prophet Tiresias appears as an Anglican
archdeacon and a captain in the fourteenth-century armour of a Frankish
knight, while the bearded, barefoot bacchants and the maenads with 'hair
à la Brigitte Bardot' present the bacchic revellers as contemporary counter-
culture youths. There is also an element of conscious artifice, both distancing
the darkness of the tragedy and emphasising it by contrast. Dionysus openly
acts the part of a Byronic hero, but with a 'languor that is more "nineties"
than Byronic'; and Auden interpolates an intermezzo of eighteenth-century
aristocrats playing out a comic version of the 'Judgment of Calliope' in a
Boucher-like painterly scene. This underlines the nexus of myth and art, featuring classical groupings of statuary (Leda and the swan, Cupid and Psyche)
amid the painted shrubbery – all framed by 'the painted proscenium arch of
a Rococo theatre, with stage boxes on both sides' (*Lib*, pp. 251, 253, 271,
303, 272, 284). This entirely playful interlude of comic sexual seduction is
tongue-in-cheek –

> TIRESIAS A charade, you know.
> AGAVE, AUTONOE, AND CAPTAIN
>                         Oh . . .
> Why should candour lack
> In our happy Bac-
>    chic family?          (*Lib*, p. 286)

– yet obviously parallels the tragic action with the tune of the goddesses'
lament for the death of Adonis (a variant on music from Bach's St Matthew
Passion) being repeated as an accompaniment when Pentheus' dismembered

body is carried in at the end. Even so, the focus is not on these ancient Greek or rococo French aristocratic individuals, but on the chorus of the title, the Bassarids: a deliberately antique collective noun for followers of Bacchus, both male and female, with its weighty and exotic overtones. Their massed voices frame the action at beginning and end, while their chants ('Ayayalya' for dancing, a wordless humming that varies from reverence to menace or 'echoes' of lines sung by Dionysus that become increasingly prolonged) form an almost continual accompaniment to the singing of the principals.

But, even if *The Bassarids* is Auden's most complex undertaking, his most effective opera is undoubtedly *The Rake's Progress*, performed in Venice in 1951 and at the Metropolitan in New York in 1953, which he and Kallman wrote for Stravinsky. While explicitly based on Hogarth's series of satiric etchings depicting the downfall and ruin of a young man who inherits a fortune in eighteenth-century London, Auden transforms this into a quintessential myth of European (and specifically British) civilisation, by superimposing the archetypal Faust legend, and layering this with the biblical expulsion from Eden as well as symbolic figures from Mummers' plays. The opening is changed from the Hogarthian original to an idyllic garden, a prelapsarian paradise where 'The woods are green and bird and beast at play / For all things keep this festival of May' (*Lib*, p. 49). The garden is inhabited by Anne, the daughter of Truelove and the angelic fiancée of the title figure. In place of crooked lawyers and corrupt companions, Auden introduces the Devil, under the heavily symbolic name of Shadow, who tempts the still innocent but lazy Rakewell, presenting himself as Rakewell's servant and granting desires in exchange for his soul.

This Everyman's problem is that he wants something (money, happiness, public esteem) for nothing, and each time breaks out of the opera's closed discourse by speaking his wish. The temptation he succumbs to is that of solipsistic egoism, 'One aim in all things to pursue: / My duty to myself to do' (*Lib*, p. 5b), which leads to a rejection of all social duty or moral restrictions, and single-minded pursuit of the pleasure principle. These are, of course, precisely the sins that Auden sees as characteristic of the modern world; and in the opera they are rewarded by madness and death. Abandoning the Garden of Innocence and Anne, Rakewell lives up to his name, betraying her love for the immediate self-gratification of purely physical lust, marrying a seeming paragon of beauty who turns out to have a thick black beard beneath her veil. This hermaphroditic 'Baba the Turk' is yet another figure from the traditional Mummers' plays that interested Auden from the start. Auden takes the ending, in which Shadow plays a game of cards with Rakewell for possession of his soul, from the same folk repertoire. *The Rake's Progress* contains many echoes from Auden's earlier works, the 'Man-Woman' from

'Paid on Both Sides', and the illusory paradise park and corruptly grotesque Nineveh Hotel from *Dogskin*.

Reversing the Faust legend, in keeping with a less religious modern age, Anne cannot save Rakewell's life or sanity, but the memory of her image rescues him from being carried down to hell. Paralleling the final quintet in Mozart's *Don Giovanni*, the five main characters step in front of the curtain for an epilogue, which applies the moral lessons explicitly to the audience, and sums up the relevance of what they have been watching by adapting a popular proverb: the Devil finds work for 'idle . . . hearts and minds' (*Lib*, pp. 56, 92). The lush angularity of Stravinsky's score, together with Auden's limpidly clear verse and the allegorically rich but extremely simple plot, have made *The Rake's Progress* one of the most performed modern operas, as well as attracting major artists. David Hockney, who had himself produced a modern 'Rake's Progress' series modelled on Hogarth, designed the settings for a Glyndebourne production in 1975.

Shortly before the opening of *The Bassarids*, Auden noted that his 1930s plays 'seem to me now to be libretti *manqués*'.[12] The same could be said of such long poems as 'For the Time Being' and *The Age of Anxiety*, which contains dramatic dialogue between four distinct characters and was staged at Princeton in 1960, with Auden himself appearing on film to read the framing narrative. As with the contrast between Anne's light and the Shadow of the Devil, all Auden's libretti, as he remarked in the preface to his version of *The Magic Flute*, revolve around the 'change in relation between the Dionysian principle and the Apollonian, Night and Day, the instinctive and the rational, the unconscious and the conscious' (*Lib*, pp. 129–30).

## NOTES

1. W. B. Yeats, *Essays and Introductions* (London: Macmillan, 1961), p. 224.
2. W. H. Auden, *The Listener*, 9 May 1934, p. 808 (unsigned review of Priscilla Thouless, *Modern Poetic Drama* – a collection of plays by Yeats and the Georgian poets).
3. Handwritten note by Auden, dated 1942, in Albert Stevens's copy of *Poems* (1934). 1907 was the year of his birth, and 1929 of his final revisions to the play.
4. Following Isherwood's suggestions, Auden played around significantly with this ending. This reflects the original typescript which was revised to become the basis of the Group Theatre promptbook (and is printed in the Faber version of *Plays*). In the 1936 production Francis was shot dead – a variation on *The Chase* (the initial draft for the play), where Francis was the patient killed by the surgeon – instead of leading Alan and some of the villagers with consciences away to become the core of resistance, while the final version has his corpse sewn up again in his dog skin as a literal cover-up, while Alan shouts out from the back of the auditorium, having taken his place among the spectators, so aligning them with him.

5. Cited in P. N. Furbank, *E. M. Forster* (London: Secker & Warburg, 1978), vol. II, p. 214. For a more critical analysis of the symbolism in the play, see my *Modern British Drama: 1890–1990* (Cambridge University Press, 1992), p. 383.
6. Christopher Isherwood, diary, 17 April 1937, quoted in *Christopher and His Kind* (New York: Farrar, Straus and Giroux, 1976).
7. Printed as appendices in *Plays*, pp. 648, 651.
8. Auden letters, n.d., and July 1938: Berg Collection, New York Public Library.
9. 28 June 1935, Berg Collection.
10. Louis MacNeice, Introduction to *The Dark Tower* (London: Faber and Faber, 1967), pp. 11, 9, 21.
11. Auden later wrote two other radio plays for CBS, *The Dark Valley* – an expansion of a earlier cabaret piece written for the German actress Therese Giehse – and an adaptation of D. H. Lawrence's short story 'The Rocking Horse Winner', both with music by Benjamin Britten.
12. Auden, 'A Public Art', *Opera*, January 1961, p. 14, and BBC interview, 29 April 1966 (transcript, BBC Written Archives Centre).

# 8

STAN SMITH

# Auden's light and serio-comic verse

Responding in 1932 to an enquiry from Geoffrey Grigson, Wystan Auden asked 'Why do you want to start a poetry review [?]', adding 'I'm glad you like poetry but cant [*sic*] we take it a little more lightly . . . I hope you'll keep it gay.'[1]

There are enough instances of Auden's play with this last word to suggest that it already, by the 1930s, had some of its modern resonance, at least as a coded formula among those in the know. The satiric verse epistle, 'Letter to Lord Byron' (1937), for example, approved Byron's muse 'because she's gay and witty'. Byron's bisexuality would have been an open secret in Auden's circles, which included Harold Nicolson, author of a 1924 biography of the poet, and Peter Quennell, whose *Byron in Italy* would appear in four years' time. Certainly, in the 1930s many of the attacks on Auden's 'gaiety', his lightness and unseriousness of tone, linked it surreptitiously to a hinted moral 'deviancy'. Thus F. R. Leavis, reviewing *Poems* in 1931, wrote of Auden's 'combination of seriousness and flippancy' being in a mould 'so peculiar to himself and so eccentric in its terminology', displaying 'mental idiosyncrasies . . . extravagantly indulged', that it 'fails to make a living contact with us'. The revised *Poems* prompted him to reflect in 1934 on the 'profound inner disturbance, a turbid pressure of emotions from below' which leave the poet 'too immediately aware of the equivocal complexity of his material, and too urgently solicited by it to manipulate it with cool insistence'. His review of *Look, Stranger!* in 1936 spoke of a poet 'happily in love with expression' who 'certainly has a gift for words; he delights in them and they come', a snide echo, for the knowing, of Pope's self-parodically 'sissy' formula, 'I lisped in numbers, for the numbers came.' Leavis's strictures (collated in Haffenden, pp. 88–91, 100–1, 140–3, 222–5) laid down a pattern which was to persist through subsequent decades, in which, remarkably, to speak of the poet's linguistic virtuosity was usually to level, simultaneously, the charge of superficiality, immaturity, narcissism and, ultimately, moral failure and degeneracy.

It was *New Verse*, soon to become the most influential review of its day, that Grigson was mooting in that letter to Auden. In the Auden double issue in 1937, Grigson made the poet's 'monstrosity' into a virtue (see the Introduction to the present volume, p. 5), while conceding that he had written 'plenty of verse which is slack, ordinary, dull, or silly'. This last word is significant, in a decade remembered for its po-faced earnestness and unremitting political commitment. Auden was to use it himself a couple of years later in his elegy for that most solemn and sententious of poets, W. B. Yeats, spelling out what everyone may have thought but no one else felt appropriate to say at a wake: 'He was silly like us.' For Auden, silliness was part of the whole show. The poet, aloft on his high horse, was, after all, only human. Those, he wrote in the Introduction to his co-edited anthology *The Poet's Tongue* (1935), 'who try to put poetry on a pedestal only succeed in putting it on the shelf. Poetry is no better and no worse than human nature; it is profound and shallow, sophisticated and naïve, dull and witty, bawdy and chaste in turn' (*Poet's Tongue*, p. vii). In the poem 'Plains', from the 'Bucolics' sequence in *The Shield of Achilles* (1955), Auden purports to admit that 'I wish I weren't so silly.' He imagines himself ending up a disreputable old man, cadging drinks from unwary strangers in a decaying seaside port, and 'scribbling / Reams of edifying and unreadable verse'. The poem ends, however, with the acknowledgement that, though he cannot pretend that flat plains are 'poetic', it is good to be reminded sometimes that 'nothing is lovely, / Not even in poetry, which is not the case'. The recollection here of the (intensely serious) Ludwig Wittgenstein's aphorism, in the *Tractatus Logico-Philosophicus* (1922), that 'The world is everything that is the case', is for Auden part of the fun.

Many critics didn't get the joke. Donald Davie, reviewing *The Shield of Achilles* in 1955, deplored 'the latest Audenesque persona. Homo Ludens, incorrigibly playful, preferring the bad pun to the good one', linked the 'facetious diction' to the 'perversities' of the 'improvisatore', and tendered the line about being 'silly' as an instance of a 'playfulness' he found 'ponderously coy'. For Davie, this was 'Auden in short pants, acting the little horror' (Haffenden, pp. 401–3). Auden's camp double entendre in 'Streams' flirts with Huizinga's concept of *homo ludens* to make a serious point, one put explicitly in the same volume's '"The Truest Poetry is the Most Feigning"'. Insisting on the essential frivolity of poetry compared with 'real historical unhappiness', this poem self-reflexively observes that a poet's tears only 'have value if they make us gay; / O Happy Grief!* is all sad verse can say'. The duplicity of discourse is part of its gaiety. Seriously frivolous, poetic fictions inevitably dissemble and dissimulate, refuse to make unequivocal, monological, absolute statements, preferring instead what *New Year Letter* calls 'the gift of double focus'.

In *The Shield of Achilles*, the militaristic, totalitarian universe of its title poem, which opens the sequence 'In Sunshine and in Shade', finds its anti-type in the vision of the all-sustaining earth in the 'Ode to Gaea' which concludes it. In a world where the wise wilt, the stern advise paying tribute to political power and the 'large-hearted' already speak its gibberish, this poem envisages a last stand in the passes by those for whom Valhalla is not grandiosely Wagnerian but can be found listening to verses by Mackworth Praed or an aria by Rossini, 'between two entrées' by Carême. As if this inversion of the heroic Spartan stance at Thermopylae into some epicurean 'last stand' were not enough, 'entrées' compounds the playfulness. Following the reference to Rossini, it might sound like an allusion to some little-known minor composer – a trick that Auden turned variously in later life. Hedonistic resistance to the discourse of power, however, encompasses not only light verse and opera, but also food. Antonin Carême (1783–1833), was the grand chef to several of Europe's most powerful men, the French Talleyrand, the English Prince Regent and the Russian Czar Alexander I, who remarked to Talleyrand: 'What we did not know was that he taught us to eat.' Carême presided over the cuisine for the Congress of Vienna in 1815, at which the Great Powers, Talleyrand representing a defeated France, redrew the map of Europe for the next century. Along with Praed and Rossini, then, he stands in, metonymically, for the irresponsible sensuous pleasures of art in general, which simultaneously provides sustenance for and offers a modest critique of the discourse of power. What Auden said in 'In Praise of Limestone' might also define his idea of art and of his own 'inconstant' poetry: it exercises a 'worldly duty . . . in spite of itself', that 'calls into question / All the Great Powers assume'.

Even Philip Larkin, who acknowledged that Auden's modernity lay in making 'no theoretical distinction between *Paradise Lost* and "*The Young Fellow Called Dave*"' of ribald limerick, seems to have missed the point, writing in 1960 that, if Auden 'has now recovered a new dialect, it is all too often an extraordinarily jarring one, a wilful jumble of Age-of-Plastic nursery rhyme, ballet folklore, and Hollywood Lemprière served up with a lisping archness that sets the teeth on edge'. Objecting to such lines as 'Just reeling off their names is ever so comfy' ('Lakes') or, of 'Dame Kind' (Nature), 'She mayn't be all She might be but She *is* our Mum', Larkin asked exasperatedly, 'Are there people who talk this dialect, or is it how Auden talks to himself?'[2]

The refrain continued well into the era of modern critical theory. Terry Eagleton pronounced excommunication in the columns of the *Tablet* in 1976, indicting 'an overbred irresponsibility which threatens to dwindle the substance of a poem to empty technical acrobatics' and 'historically obsolescent postures' (Haffenden, p. 52). It has taken the emergence of postmodernist approaches to literature to revalorise the yokings and jokings of Auden's poetry, something Eagleton, having himself taken the poststructuralist turn, more generously acknowledged in his introduction to my own *W. H. Auden* in 1985, recognising that 'the playfulness and multiple ironies of the later poet can be read not as a defeatist political withdrawal, but as an instance of that "carnivalesque" spirit, subverting the solemnities of bourgeois authority with the iconoclasm of humour and the body' (Smith, p. viii). The first study to take the 'carnivalesque' Auden seriously, Edward Callan's insightful *A Carnival of Intellect* (1983), came from a traditional quarter, as the titular balancing act suggests. But in recent years Auden has attracted wide critical attention for the hermeneutic indeterminacy, ludic iconoclasm and polymorphously deconstructive nature of writings, in the words of a late poem, 'modern only in this – our lack of decorum'.

Auden's verbal indecorum burgeoned as he became more religiously orthodox and politically conservative. The later poetry ransacks the dictionary for nonce-words and neologisms, arcane or archaic usages, exhibiting a vocabulary by turns skittish, whimsical, hoydenish, haughty, polyglot and jargonish, ruminative and aphoristic, shocking and coy. It cuts short portentous polysyllables with sudden racy slang, and has little regard for that 'Purity of Diction' which Davie promoted in a major critical study in 1952. In the 'Bucolics' sequence, God is familiarly renamed as 'our First Dad', and 'holy insufflation' jostles 'teleost' and 'arthropod', human beings are defined as 'lower-ordersy' compared with trees, and Foreign Secretaries in conclave are imagined walking round a lake 'widdershins or deasil'. 'Epithalamium' speaks of marriage as a 'diffy undertaking', describes bride and groom as 'two idiosyncrasies', human beings as 'enantiomorphs' who are 'super-posable', and nominates 'a gangrel / Paleocene pseudo-rat' as the 'Ur-Papa' of princes and crossing-sweepers alike. 'Ode to Terminus' refers to the universe itself as a 'Thingummy' addicted to violence, the earth as a 'placid tump', unexpectedly able to 'cocker' life, and disowns poets who 'wow' an audience with 'some resonant lie'.

This last phrase, which concludes the poem, indicates what is going on. It follows the assertion that scientists can only be truthful, paradoxically, if they regularly remind us to assume that everything they say is a tall story. The poem had opened by speaking of apparently harmless scientific abstractions which go critical when 'translated / into the vulgar anthropomorphic / tongue'. All language, the poem suggests, involves translation into discourses which come freighted with presuppositions and prejudices. The polyglot impurity of Auden's diction, his manipulation of pastiche, parody, periphrasis, euphemism and jargon, the long-winded and whimsical circumlocutions and the verbal promiscuity which juxtaposes incongruous words from very diverse registers, alert us to the unreliability of all communication. The conspicuous artifice of such devices will not let us take language for granted as offering some unmediated, transparent, disinterested access to reality. Defamiliarising language, they teach the mind to look afresh, as 'Ode to Terminus' puts it, at the 'surround it is called on to interpret'.

Introducing the politically driven anthology *Poems of Freedom* in 1938, Auden rejected Shelley's claim that poets are the 'unacknowledged legislators of the world', a 'social force', but also their dismissal as 'introverted neurotics who find in infantile word-play an escape from the serious duties of life'. Both opinions are 'bosh'. Because language, the medium of poetry, is the medium of all social activity, he argued, more demands are made on it than any of the other arts. For Auden, poets are primarily people with a skill in handling words. Poetry reports on the experience of people in 'many different social positions', whether a peer like Byron or a poor priest like Langland, living in 'many different Englands'. Reading it will teach no one 'how to run a state or raise a revolution', won't, indeed, even establish what 'freedom' is. Poetry recognises no restrictions of theme or register, encompassing, he observes, both the high sententiousness of Milton's political sonnet, 'Avenge, O lord, thy slaughtered saints', and the rumbustious mockery of a ballad from the postbellum South, with a 'dislike of pompous authority' that will survive long after the American Civil War is forgotten.[3] Fusing the demotic and the abstruse, fashionable slang and philosophical high talk, thieves' cant and Immanuel Kant, Auden's poetry effects a democratic levelling of discourse, bringing down the mighty from their seats and exalting the humble and meek. Whether recruiting the Burns stanza for the roistering polemic of 'A Communist to Others', engaging in Skeltonic flyting in 'A Happy New Year', or hurling lampoon insults at newspaper barons in 'Beethameer, Beethameer, bully of Britain, / With your face as fat as a farmer's bum', it never ceases to wage class war on the terrain of language.

In ' "The Truest Poetry is the Most Feigning" ', Auden brought together *Paradise Lost* and the hapless rail passenger of the music-hall song 'Oh, Mister Porter', to present a picture of 'Man' as a creature made in God's image who has 'forgot his station'. 'Light verse can be serious', he had claimed in 1938 (*Light Verse*, p. ix). His own approach might be summed up by James Joyce's coinage: it is 'jocoserious'. 'Get there if you can' epitomises the method. It presents an apocalyptic 1930s scenario of industrial dereliction, political failure and economic collapse in the gung-ho metre of Tennyson's 'Locksley Hall'. It also supplements its angry satire with a list of those who have 'betrayed us nicely' that descends into bathos when such 'high', public figures as Cardinal Newman, Plato, Pascal are mingled with names from Auden's private address-book. It plunges into absurdity with the claim that his guru Homer Lane was 'killed in action by the Twickenham Baptist gang'. We may hear doom's approaching footsteps in these ominously prophetic tones, but Auden can't refrain from giving them a comic inflexion, with a vision of workers blowing up monster stores and intellectuals, and his indictment of the latter, presumably including himself, 'Lecturing on navigation while the ship is going down'.

His Introduction to the 1935 anthology *The Poet's Tongue* insisted that 'We do not want to read "great" poetry all the time, and a good anthology should contain poems for every mood' (*Poet's Tongue*, p. ix). Poetry, he suggested, may address birth and death, the Beatific Vision, hatred and fear, the pleasures and pains of desire, 'the unjust walking the earth', etc., but also 'Everything that we remember no matter how trivial' (*Poet's Tongue*, p. vi). Auden's democratic, levelling impulse led him to explore all the non-canonical forms of poetry: ballad, blues, invective, curse, prophylactic, cautionary tale, nursery jingle, riddle, limerick, clerihew. But he also infiltrated 'low' and 'trivial' moments into the high canonical forms of love lyric, elegy, philosophical meditation, dramatic monologue.

That reworking of traditional ballad quatrains, 'As I walked out one evening', opens with a recollection of folk song's formulaic encounters. The poem is full of motifs from oral popular culture, the hyperbole of Burns's 'Till a' the seas gang dry', the American hobo ballad 'The Big Rock Candy Mountain', the Jack and Jill of nursery rhyme and the 'Lily White Boys' of the campfire counting song, 'Green grow the rushes O'. At the same time, it indicates what is distinctively original and modern in Auden's work, taking for venue a contemporary urban setting, Birmingham's Bristol Street, fusing traditional imagery with a specifically twentieth-century idiom, depicting a world of headaches and worry in Kafkaesque terms as 'the burrows of the Nightmare', where 'Time watches from the shadow, / And coughs when you would kiss', like a dirty old man whose prurient voyeurism mutates into the killjoy's prudish interruption.

The *Oxford Book* Introduction asserts (*Light Verse*, p. xviii) that 'The Border ballad could be tragic; the music-hall song cannot.' Auden's practice disproves the dictum, combining both with echoes of Thomas Hood in 'Miss Gee', 'James Honeyman' and 'Victor'. The latter adapts the opening formula of the John Henry ballads, with Victor a little baby on his father's knee. 'Miss Gee' begins, familiarly, 'Let me tell you a little story.' Mingling pathos and bathos, farce, caricature and pseudo-psychoanalytic platitude, the gallows humour of these cynical cautionary tales is at once sad, nasty and absurd. Their themes are serious enough: weapons of mass destruction, uxoricide and psychosomatic cancer. But the treatment, recalling the satiric grotesquerie of Georg Grosz's cartoons, is flippant and gloating, and, in the case of the spinster 'Miss Gee', spitefully misogynist. The irony of the name 'Victor' is deliberate. All of these figures, even Honeyman, the technocrat who invents a more effective poison gas, are not victors but victims.

The interpenetration of high and low, tragic and comic modes, cuts both ways. 'Now the leaves are falling fast' begins in a Betjemanish world of nurses pushing out prams that roll on for ever, but segues into images of Nazi stormtroopers, starving trolls, dumb nightingales and an angel that 'will not come'. That consummate lyric of love and faithlessness, 'Lay your sleeping head', deploys the fairy-tale motif of Cinderella as its most plangent metaphor, post-coital joy reverting to ordinariness at the stroke of midnight. 'Roman Wall Blues' presents a sadly comic picture of any soldier a thousand miles from home, wanting his girl and his pay. 'Refugee Blues' uses the same stoical popular form to evoke the plight of German Jews fleeing Hitler. Even a poem like *Spain* has its comic moments, as in the Mayakovsky-style image of poets exploding like bombs with poetic *joie de vivre*. 'September 1, 1939' qualifies its reflections on the outbreak of war with *New Yorker* social observation of subway commuters, reiterating their daily resolve to be true to the wife and devote more time to their work.

Approaching a rueful sixty, Auden almost seemed to have accepted the censure of his critics, admitting in the Foreword to a revised edition of *The Orators* in 1966 that 'To-day I find "Auden with play-ground whistle", as Wyndham-Lewis called him, a bit shy-making.' But he then offers a self-justification which allows him the last word: 'I realise that it is precisely the schoolboy atmosphere and diction which act as a moral criticism of the rather ugly emotions and ideas they are employed to express', adding that his own 'juvenile' discourse was intended to 'make it impossible to take them seriously'. 'In one of the Odes', he says, 'I express all the sentiments with which his followers hailed the advent of Hitler.' Typically, late as early Auden has it both ways, claiming that such sentiments ought to be rendered innocuous 'by the fact that the Führer so hailed is a new-born baby'.

Wyndham Lewis clearly did understand what Auden was getting at. In *Blasting and Bombardiering* (1937) he commended 'the technique of a new guy', observing that 'I like what he does. He is all ice and woodenfaced acrobatics', and adding that 'Mr Isherwood, his alter ego, is full of sly Dada fun, too. Both pander to the unuplifted, both flirt robustly with the underdog, but both come out of Dr Freud's cabinet.'⁴ Only someone as integrally serious as Auden himself could recognise the seriousness of these flirtations with the underdogs of discourse. In *Modern Poetry* (1938) Louis MacNeice noted that Lewis 'maintains that satire is the proper genre for this age', but with the 'important qualification that satire, as he conceives it, can be non-ethical, non-partisan. It is satire for its own sake *and allied to tragedy*.' MacNeice linked Lewis and Auden in their reversion to Augustan satiric modes, both recently producing 'long poems of serious criticism in the lighter manner', in 'the grand critical tradition of Pope or Byron'.⁵

Auden's poem is 'Letter to Lord Byron', first published in *Letters from Iceland*, and undoubtedly his major exercise in comic verse. In pre-emptive mock self-deprecation the poet wearily acknowledges that he 'Must hear in silence till I turn my toes up, / "It's such a pity Wystan never grows up." ' Imitating the picaresque mode of Byron's *Don Juan*, this auto-referential, 'self-conscious' text, dubbing itself a 'collage', 'very up to date indeed', repeatedly stops to reflect on what it's doing, raise an eyebrow at its own procedures and comment on its own antecedents and contemporaries, even down to the aside that it contains 'samples of MacNeice's art'. 'Up to date' artfully recalls MacNeice's comment, reviewing *Poems* in 1931, that 'Mr Auden . . . uses an up-to-date technique to express an up-to-date mood', deploying 'a bathos which still comprehends the dignity of its precedents [and] is thereby raised to tragedy' (Haffenden, pp. 86–8). The poem's opening section refers, knowingly, to the 'modern methods of communication' by which a culture propagates itself, about which we learn from documentaries from the GPO – a self-regarding allusion to the film *Night Mail* for which Auden wrote the soundtrack. One stanza offers snippets from several languages, then admits that it doesn't know what they mean, but is simply emulating Ezra Pound. The reason for choosing Byron as addressee is equally flip. He has heard it rumoured that Icelanders have little sense of humour, and, while that rumour may be 'only silly', in a terrain which rhyme requires to be described as 'hilly' and 'chilly', he has pounced on Byron as one whose style is 'light and easy', but also – the forced French rhyme making his culturally relativising point – 'warm and civilisé'. The style of the poem, that is, imitates its author, 'travelling, as they call it, light'.

Admitting that he daren't use Byron's ottava rima lest he come a cropper, the poet invites us, impressed by his facility in rhyme royal, not to believe him. Similarly, explaining why he'd decided against Jane Austen as addressee, he claims to find this 'English spinster of the middle-class' far too intimidating, shocking him with her proto-Marxist insight into 'The economic basis of society' and the 'amorous effects of "brass" '. The rhyme here would cause a middle-class reader to stumble, for, after the Received Pronunciation long 'a' of 'grass' and 'class', this word, recalling the boast of the Yorkshire industrialist that 'Where there's muck there's brass', requires for comic effect to be uttered with a short northern 'a'.

The poem repeatedly manipulates rhyme to subversive effect. Speaking of the home counties vision of a chromium-plated future, all Aertex underwear, plate-glass windows and sound-proofing, it concludes that, for the inhabitants of northern industrial towns like Warrington and Wigan, this is not a white lie but 'a whacking big 'un'. Rejecting the idyllic Romantic landscape represented by Wordsworth's Lake District, a bathetic rhyme tells us that (as with a trademark), his own heart has 'Stamped on / The view from Birmingham to Wolverhampton'. In this poem, 'scenery' rhymes more than once with 'machinery'. Trisyllabic rhymes usually have a comic effect in English verse. When those three syllables are also bathetically unpoetic names, the effect is compounded, as in the rhyme of 'Birmingham' with 'confirming 'em', which recalls a scurrilous limerick about an elderly Bishop of Birmingham. In later life Auden published a host of limericks and clerihews, artfully improbable rhymes on the names of people and places (see his *Academic Graffiti*, 1971). Other 'Byronic' rhymes here include 'Duke of Wellington' with 'Duke Ellington' ('duke' causes a further hiccup), 'apparatuses' / 'afflatuses', 'properer' / 'opera' and ones which require some syntactical contortion: 'quietus to' / 'status to', 'Atta boys' / 'hatter, boys' or deliberately arch pronunciation ('long' / 'Continong').

Byron is a model because he never aspired to serious thought, making himself the 'master of the airy manner' in a style where 'meaning does not need a spanner'. Inevitably, such a self-reflexive text contains a manifesto for its own practices:

> By all means let us touch our humble caps to
>   La poésie pure, the epic narrative;
> But comedy shall get its round of claps, too.
>   According to his powers, each may give;
>   Only on varied diet can we live.
> The pious fable and the dirty story
> Share in the total literary glory.

Auden cannot avoid the serious undertone even here, linking 'poésie pure' and heroic epic to the inequalities of a class society with that gesture of cloth-capped homage, and suggesting also, in the echo of the *Communist Manifesto*, a revolutionary alternative. The point was made even more explicitly in an article for the Workers' Educational Association journal *The Highway* in 1936, 'Poetry, Poets, and Taste', which argued that pure poetry cannot exist, just as 'pure chemicals do not react', and concluded that the secret of good art is to find out what interests you, 'however strange, or trivial, or ambitious, or shocking, or uplifting, and deal with that . . . "To each according to his needs, from each according to his powers", in fact' (*Prose 1*, pp. 163–5).

Comparing poetic and sartorial styles (Dryden's lounge suit, Wordsworth's Harris tweed, Byron's roué's dressing-gown, Auden himself in a cotton frock), the poem matches such succinct stereotypes with brilliant historical and cultural metonymies, summarising the whole century since Byron's death, for example, in a single line: 'Crying went out and the cold bath came in.' It takes perverse pride in baring the device of narrative, interrupting the flow to bemoan, parenthetically, the fact that it can find no other rhyme except the totally irrelevant 'anoint'. Such deliberate bathos repeatedly reminds us that language is not a transparent medium for the truth but has its own anfractuosities and resistances, and that a poet is only as good as his rhyming dictionary. The technique is most bare-faced when, having recalled Yeats's conviction that great art enshrines 'The fascination of what's difficult', a stanza plunges from the sublime to the ridiculous, outdoing Byron's own inverted pride in a deliberately banal line by proclaiming:

> Et cetera, et cetera. O curse,
> That is the flattest line of English verse.

For a poet with such facility with words, the 'flattest line of English verse' is, possibly, the most difficult achievement of all, and therefore consummate art.

'Letter to Lord Byron' makes a political statement in its inversion of the genre hierarchy. It regards 'light verse' as a weapon in the class war, temporarily dragooned into a misalliance:

> Light verse, poor girl, is under a sad weather;
>   Except by Milne and persons of that kind
> She's treated as démodée altogether.
>   It's strange and very unjust to my mind
>   Her brief appearances should be confined,
> Apart from Belloc's *Cautionary Tales*,
> To the more bourgeois periodicals.

Rhyme-royal stanzas demand a strong rhyme in their clinching couplet. Here, the final syllable of 'periodicals' has to bear an uncustomary stress and, for the sake of the rhyme, be pronounced effetely as 'cales'. Such dubious stretching of normal pronunciation is often a deliberate trick of popular comic verse, making a joke of the author's incompetence in having to strain for the rhyme. But this poem doubly disrupts expectations, since it has already set up a scenario in which a word such as 'periodicals', particularly in a closing couplet, would normally be a double (feminine) or even triple rhyme.

In a diminished world, this 'Letter' proposes, where the robust archetype of John Bull has given way to the wimpish Chaplin or Mickey Mouse, the proper style for poetry may well be the whimsies of Lewis Carroll, Edward Lear, Beatrix Potter or Ronald Firbank, with all of whom the poem professes its solidarity. In a similar move, 'A Bride in the Thirties' imagines Europe's totalitarian states as 'lands of terrifying mottoes' transformed by love into 'worlds as innocent as Beatrix Potter's'. The strained, unsatisfactory rhyme suggests a certain lack of conviction, even while the poem proceeds to turn the dictators into figures of Dadaist absurdity, recruiting them to the wooing voices of love 'saying lightly, brightly – / Be Lubbe, be Hitler, but be my good / daily, nightly'. Auden's Marxist tendencies in the thirties, one might say, owed as much to Groucho as to Karl.

The originality of Auden's mixed modes was recognised by Harold Hobson in reviewing *The Dance of Death* (1933), with its song and dance routines and general knockabout:

> He takes that most frivolous of entertainments, the musical comedy, and transforms it so that it becomes an instrument for the serious drama of which the potentialities, in his skilful handling, seem illimitable. It is an extraordinary achievement, as though one were to see *No, No, Nanette* taken, without incongruity, as the mouthpiece for a twentieth-century *Contrat Social*.
>
> (Haffenden, pp. 154–6)

The entry of Marx at the end of the play to the tune of Mendelssohn's Wedding March, to announce the Dancer's death, is pure Dada. 'The instruments of production have been too much for him', Marx proclaims, in the final lines of the play, 'He is liquidated.' In the same vein, the Father Christmas of the old Mummer plays irrupts into the Cornelian high rhetoric of 'Paid on Both Sides' to hand out presents and judgements.

Behind such confusions of high and low lies a saturnalian impulse to see the world turned upside down. Not for nothing is one of Auden's finest pieces of criticism a reading of Shakespeare's Falstaff, whom he subversively identifies with the figure of Christ as a Lord of Misrule. In a similar vein, 'Under Which Lyre', written in 1946 as Phi Beta Kappa Poem at Harvard University, takes its conspicuously public occasion as the opportunity for uttering what its subtitle calls a 'Reactionary Tract for the Times' that is personal and anarchic. The poem contrasts Falstaff, the figure of folly and carnal indulgence, with the 'prig' Prince Hal, eager to assume his public destiny. The poem's title reinforces the contrast, recalling the question put by Falstaff's boozing crony, Pistol, to Justice Shallow in *Henry IV, Part II*: 'Under which king, Bezonian?' According to *Brewer's Dictionary of Phrase and Fable*, a 'bezonian' was 'A new recruit; applied originally in derision, to young soldiers sent from Spain to Italy, who landed both ill-accoutred and in want of everything.' In Auden's poem, the raw recruits to Harvard's postwar campus, funded by the GI Bill, are serious young men out to improve themselves. They have to choose between the demands of Apollo, learning to do boring jobs which they need to think important, and the injunctions of the Hermetic Decalogue, foremost of which is 'Thou shalt not do as the dean pleases' nor 'bow down before / Administration'. The poem downgrades the lyre of the god of macho epic, Apollo, in favour of the wistfully androgynous, mercurial Hermes, whose acolytes 'love to play / And only do their best when they / Are told they oughtn't'.

Hermes is the god of thieves and travellers, liars and conmen, an appropriate patron for a poet who stole some of his best tricks from other writers, and made them his own. Hermes is also the father of another classical archetype with whom Auden identifies in 'Forty Years On', that Autolycus resurrected in Shakespeare's *Winter's Tale*, who was in turn the grandfather of the wily Odysseus. Autolycus has the pickpocket's magical ability to make things vanish. He is also a wandering minstrel, that symbol of the bohemian artist which Auden's generation inherited from the *fin de siècle*, in an Oxford forever associated with youthful wild oats. Returning late in life to this landlocked 'Bohemia', and contrasting himself with useful technicians and bureaucrats, Autolycus takes pride in at least possessing 'the courtier's agility to adapt / my rogueries to the times'. As is fitting, the poem's vocabulary lacks all decorum, joining the colloquial 'thwacks', 'oggle', 'glib', to the literary and esoteric 'havocking', 'oppugnant', 'eloignement', 'whelking'. Confronting the prospect of death as a black cave through which he must make his final exit, forced to duck awkwardly as no tragic hero ever would, he concludes by asking irreverently whether it will really be so shaming: 'When has Autolycus ever solemned himself?' The archaic usage of 'solemn' as a verb fulfils two functions. It cocks a snook at seriousness by using not only a solemn word but the word 'solemn' itself ironically, and in refusing solemnity it also mocks death as no more than, in the Shakespearean cliché, a stage exit from a theatre of illusions.

The arbitrariness of all cultural practices, ideological or material, for coping with death is comically relativised by the dry anthropological updating of Stone Age burial rites which opens 'Thanksgiving for a Habitat': 'Nobody I know would like to be buried / with a silver cocktail shaker, / a transistor radio and a strangled / daily help.' If the sting of death can be drawn by such verbal strategies, so too, can that of love, whether in the homespun

Frostian aphorism that closes 'First Things First', 'Thousands have lived without love, not one without water', or the Freudian psychobabble of 'Heavy Date', qualifying the claim that 'Love requires an Object' with the observation that 'Anything will do', disarmingly telling the beloved that as a child he 'Loved a pumping engine, / Thought it every bit as / Beautiful as you'. The verbal slapstick of 'The soldier loves his rifle' works in the same way, listing the many perverse and obsessional forms that 'love' can take. The closing analogy, followed by the refrain which ends each stanza, is all the more demeaning because the speaker apparently does not realise what it reveals about his attitude towards his beloved: 'And dogs love most an old lamp-post, / But you're my cup of tea.' The 'truth about love' for which the jaunty 'Some say that love's a little boy' pleads is hardly likely to be flattering either to the lover or the beloved. Inevitably, the poem speculates as to whether love will come without warning just as he's picking his nose, or tread in the bus on his toes.

'Epistle to a Godson' tells the young Philip Spender that poetry's function is to provide 'a stunning / display of concinnity and elegance', of which the 'dominant / mood should be that of a Carnival'. 'Elegance' and 'Carnival', apparently antithetical values, frequently consort in Auden's light verse, as the poem itself exemplifies, ending on the 'serio-comic note' it recommends to others, with 'some worldly maxims':

> Be glad your being is unnecessary,
> then turn your toes out as you walk, dear,
> and remember who you are, a Spender.

Toes are silly. Toes R Us. As such, they are more than a footnote to Auden's deconstructive rhetoric. Another late poem, 'Encomium Balnae', imagines him sitting in his bath, singing a *Lieder Abend* to a 'captive audience of his toes'. This poet afflicted with fallen arches, like many cultures described by anthropologists, sees feet as simultaneously sacred and unclean, the point at which human aspirations come literally down to earth. 'Letter to Lord Byron' attributes the poet's 'flat feet' and 'big behind' to the mysterious workings of the unconscious, Georg Groddeck's 'It'. In similar vein, Auden's lavatory humour in 'The Geography of the House' addresses, in doubly distanced euphemism, what 'Arabs call *the House where / Everybody goes*'. The poem moves between infantile and vulgar idiom ('potty', 'a satisfactory / Dump') and refined speculations on Luther, Freud and St Augustine, conflating the different timetables of mind and body in the image of Rodin's Thinker, 'Crouched in the position / Of a man at stool'. It revels in the prospect that, on the point of taking up 'Higher Thought', we will be kept in our station by some 'deflating image like the pained ex- / pression of a

Major / Prophet taken short', the enjambment reproducing the straining of which it speaks. Auden's scatological zest in raising 'a cheer to Mrs Nature' for such primal pleasures as the body affords lies close to the carnivalesque heart of his serio-comic gaiety. As he wrote in 'Concerning the Unpredictable':

> Carnival celebrates the unity of our human race as mortal creatures, who come into this world and depart from it without our consent, who must eat, drink, defecate, belch, and break wind in order to live, and procreate if our species is to survive. Our feelings about this are ambiguous ... We oscillate between wishing we were unreflective animals and wishing we were disembodied spirits, for in either case we should not be problematic to ourselves. The Carnival solution of this ambiguity is to laugh, for laughter is simultaneously a protest and an acceptance. (*F&A*, p. 471)

## NOTES

1. Letter to Grigson (11 October 1973 ), Harry Ransom Humanities Research Center, Texas, cited in RD-H, p. 127.
2. Philip Larkin, *Required Writing: Miscellaneous Pieces 1955–1982* (London: Faber and Faber, 1983), pp. 127–8.
3. *Poems of Freedom*, ed. John Mulgan (London: Victor Gollancz, 1938), pp. 7–9.
4. Wyndham Lewis, *Blasting and Bombardiering* (London: Eyre and Spottiswoode, 1937), pp. 304–5; rev. edn (London: John Calder, 1982), pp. 340–1. On the Auden–Wyndham Lewis connection, see Stan Smith, 'Re-Righting Lefty: Wyndham and Wystan in the Thirties', *Wyndham Lewis Annual* 2002–3, vols. IX–X, pp.34–45.
5. Louis MacNeice, *Modern Poetry* (London: Oxford University Press, 1938), pp. 27, 187–8; emphasis in the original.

# 9

TONY SHARPE

# Auden's prose

A striking feature of Auden's prose is its accumulated quantity. Two volumes have appeared so far in Edward Mendelson's ongoing edition of the *Complete Works,* and his preface to the latest indicates that at least four will be needed to contain Auden's total output in the medium. This prediction seems amply justified. *Prose* vols. I and II, at 836 and 556 pages respectively, have only reached 1948, and thus exclude much – though not all – of what was collected during Auden's lifetime in *The Enchafèd Flood* (1951), *The Dyer's Hand* (1963), *Secondary Worlds* (1968) and *Forewords and Afterwords* (1973). *A Certain World* (1970) must also come into the reckoning, that autobiography disguised as a commonplace book, in which Auden's own reflections intermingle with a preponderance of material drawn eclectically from other sources; and since the edition so far has included the work of his literary collaborators, the likelihood is that its subsequent volumes will contain this book, as well as the others listed above and all post-1948 prose previously uncollected. There is, then, a great deal of material: Auden's prose will constitute the largest generic component, when the edition of his *Complete Works* stands finally, and magnificently, completed.

Auden himself, who was notoriously non-reverential in his treatment of books as artefacts, as well as emphatic that the image of 'the Master's study with its vast mahogany desk' and its busts of literary greats was terminally obsolete (*Prose II,* p. 347), might smile to find himself enshrined as Man of Letters, in a set of volumes bulkily reminiscent of some outmoded predecessor. He might also be surprised to observe how much prose he had ended up producing: for he valued his output in this medium much less than his poetry, tending, for example, not to keep copies of essays and reviews, while subjecting his poetic corpus to constant and even ruthless revision. If, as he asserted, art creates its 'secondary' world out of elements found in the 'primary' phenomenal one (*SW,* p. 144; *CW,* p. 424), then writings about writing might be deemed to offer no more than a tertiary world. His publicly expressed attitude towards his prose was dismissive in the foreword to *The Dyer's Hand*, where he offered that book as evidence of the distortions implicit in a culture where a poet could earn much more money by reflecting on his [*sic*] art than by practising it. Whereas all his poems had been written 'for love', his prose was, he asserted, written on commission, fulfilled because he needed the money. The bad faith implicit was deepened by his belief that aspiring poets should avoid reading literary criticism altogether.

Such work, then, proceeded from and returned to the fallen world of getting and spending, and represented (to continue Wordsworth's sequence) a laying waste of poetic powers; for whatever Auden's prose pieces might achieve, they could hardly aspire to the condition he predicated as the end of every poem that he wrote: to be a hymn of praise to the English language. Usually obliging him to work within a predetermined format, such exercises enforced – he grumbled in his foreword – an arbitrary relation between form and content; and his title's allusion to Shakespeare's Sonnet CII seemed to hint at a shameful and even self-harming collusion:

> Thence comes it that my name receives a brand,
> And almost thence my nature is subdu'd
> To what it works in, like the dyer's hand.

But Auden's depreciation of what Philip Larkin called 'required writing' need not dictate the terms on which we value it. Although setting the essay-done-for-money against the poem-done-for-love offered the sort of binary division he always found seductive, implicit in that opposition is a sacramental elevation of art that Auden more characteristically abjured. Could they have managed it, he and Isherwood would have happily achieved their goal of a West End hit with their play *On the Frontier*; nor did he despise the financial success of Alexander Pope, whom he cited as an important influence, who had made good money from his poetry. Nor, as he half-conceded, was 'love' absent as an animating force from his prose: his 1954 piece in *Vogue* titled 'England: Six Unexpected Days' proposed to its readers an itinerary taking in some of the North Pennine locations he loved above all others in the world.

On occasions Auden took great pains with his prose: he told Ursula Niebuhr in 1944 that he thrice rewrote a review of Cochrane's *Christianity and Classical Culture*. Even after such meticulousness, this work was much more subject to editorial alteration than his poetry; but for all that, prose-writing did not invariably signify demeaning servitude. The 'dyer's hand' passage contains the sly word 'almost', to acknowledge that his nature was *not* completely subdued by this employment – and in any case Auden, whose first literary love was for Thomas Hardy, knew from the latter's

Diggory Venn (the reddleman in *The Return of the Native*) that there were honourable ways of taking a stain from one's livelihood. As with William Carlos Williams in his surgery, Wallace Stevens in his insurance office or even Larkin confronting the toad work as a university librarian, symbiosis rather than parasitism offers the appropriate model. Prose-writing surely played its part in that regime of spiritual hygiene Auden outlined in a letter to his friend James Stern in 1942, when he declared that unless he wrote 'something, anything, good, indifferent, or trashy, every day', he felt ill (*ASIII*, p. 72). His was hardly the predicament he outlined in his essay on Tennyson as that of the lyric poet, 'perpetually confronted with the problem of what to do with his time between the few hours when he is visited by his muse' (*F&A*, p. 225), and therefore resentful of any prose he wrote for implying a poetic impotence.

However different the motives by which he was led to write one or the other, Auden accepted that it was pointless to attempt any absolute formal distinction between prose and poetry (*DH*, p. 23); and in his own case, his poetry contains a significant amount of what resembles prose. The obvious example, which he on occasions suggested as the poem of which he felt most proud, is Caliban's long speech at the close of 'The Sea and the Mirror'; but there are also prose elements in *The Orators*, 'For the Time Being', *The Age of Anxiety*, 'Vespers', while 'Dichtung und Wahrheit' is a prose 'apology' for an unwritten love poem. In the essay on Poe collected in *Forewords and Afterwords*, Auden made clear his sense of the importance of 'Eureka', that lengthy prose disquisition Poe insisted was not only a poem but also his finest achievement and which, Auden admiringly noted, contravened every definition of poetry Poe had previously argued for. It is also interesting to note that Auden's 1945 tribute ('A Toast') to his father-in-law Thomas Mann, which he described in a letter as a 'very equivocal poem', is to be represented both as prose and as poetry in the *Complete Works*.

There are various parallels between Auden's prose and his poetry. Each offered its provocative stances and its implied recantations of earlier positions; in each we can find prejudicial categorisations, and observe the waxing and waning of named authority figures; in each we can find the autobiographical traces that, he felt, would make any subsequent biography redundant. In the case of his prose, this last aspect develops from the brief aside in 1934 on the changing economic circumstances of the class his family represented, to the sustained comparison between his own personal history and those of Evelyn Waugh and Leonard Woolf, offered in 1965 in 'As It Seemed to Us' (*F&A*); it would also include those considerations of other poets where he covertly meditated on his own career (as in his 1942 review of Louise Bogan). In both Auden's poetry and his prose there was an abandoned major project: in poetry, this was his ambitious epic modelled on Langland, 'In the Year of My Youth' (1932), which he set aside after having written 1,300 lines of alliterative verse; in prose, this was the work titled (after Blake) 'The Prolific and the Devourer' (*Prose II*, pp. 411–58[1]), largely written during his first summer in America in 1939, which seems to have been abandoned after the onset of war in Europe. Just as some of 'In the Year of My Youth' re-emerged in *The Dog Beneath the Skin*, so bits of 'The Prolific and the Devourer' went into the notes in *The Double Man*, and outcropped elsewhere. Both projects may have foundered because each implied an untenable role for their author.

A large proportion of Auden's prose consisted of reviews. Sometimes these fed into the poetry, as when, soon after his arrival in America, reviewing books on Voltaire and Matthew Arnold provoked poems on those writers: but it is noteworthy that the prose view of Arnold as a failed rebel against his times was less pointed than the poem's psychobiographical diagnosis of his relations with an overbearing father. Even so, Auden's set-piece reflections on illustrious predecessors still read engagingly, from the 1937 survey of Pope in his time to his 1944 introduction to Tennyson which, similarly offering an unexpected comparison to Baudelaire, also offended some by its animadversions on Tennyson's stupidity. If occasionally disrespectful to the canonised dead, Auden's response to contemporary writing, whether creative or scholarly, was characteristically generous. Sometimes this could verge on the parodic, as in the final sentence of his 1934 review of Liddell Hart's biography of T. E. Lawrence ('No one who is interested in anything at all should fail to read this book'), or in his ecstatic response to *The Book of Talbot*, a memoir by Violet Clifton of her husband which, he affirmed in the *Criterion* (October 1933), had the 'glory' of 'great art' (*Prose I*, pp. 62, 44). In this spontaneous overflow of powerful feelings he went so far as to confer on 'Lady Clifton', as he termed her, a title she did not actually possess.

Mendelson suggests that this piece was another consequence, along with 'Out on the lawn I lie in bed', of the 'Vision of *Agape*' Auden had experienced earlier in 1933 (indirectly described in his 1964 foreword to *The Protestant Mystics*). But beyond such extravagances, there is in his reviews a consistency of positive attention to the work under consideration, evidenced in the introductions he was required to provide (albeit against his inclination) for the Yale series of *Younger Poets* he had responsibility for selecting in the 1940s and 1950s. There, a poet already of international stature turned an uncondescending eye on the work of his juniors in the craft. Robert Lowell paid an appropriate tribute: 'Much hard, ingenious, correct toil has gone into inconspicuous things: introductions, anthologies, and translations.

When one looks at them closely, one is astonished at how well they have been done.'[2]

Auden the prose-writer was made, not born; Lowell's word 'toil' may suggest why he found his voice there later than he found it as a poet: 'Who stands, the crux left of the watershed' was written in the same summer that he and Day Lewis assembled the stilted formulations of their preface to *Oxford Poetry* (1927). The broad phases of Auden's development in prose were that between then and 1938 he progressed from early work that was on occasions marked by self-conscious over-emphasis to a more confidently wide-ranging style; the move to America saw an initial retrenchment which was followed by partial displacement of his political and psychological concerns by overtly theological interests; his style became more relaxed and his own presence within it more evident, and the range of publications in which he appeared broadened, embracing the popular and scholarly. He made money out of compiling anthologies; but these also enabled him to proselytise for kinds of writing he valued, such as light verse or aphorisms, and had an obvious congeniality for one who enjoyed making lists and mapping out intellectual territory.

At the outset of his career he had actively solicited book reviews, and tended to adjust his tone to the house style of the periodical for which he was writing – a tactic which was also in evidence when he moved to the USA and was picking up commissions there. His first piece for *Scrutiny* (September 1932), reviewing some books on education, offered a Lawrentian perception of the dangers for children of being subjected to the 'love-smarm'; here and in other *Scrutiny* pieces he mimicked the selectively disrespectful asperity that was a hallmark of its approach. *Scrutiny*, however, proved impervious to Auden's own love-smarm, and the relationship did not prosper. Although four months later a Lawrentian apocalypticism was audible at the close of a *Criterion* review of books on sexual roles – 'we must hurry or it will be too late' – generally Auden's work for Eliot was less extravagant in its phraseology, and at times almost ventriloquial. The formulation 'I am only uncertain firstly whether the appreciation of poetry can be taught', in the July 1934 *Criterion*, could have been written by the poet of 'If and Perhaps and But' himself (*Prose I*, pp. 31, 71). A talk 'In Defence of Gossip' given for the BBC in 1937, and published that year in *The Listener*, was appropriately colloquial in tone. Whereas it seems that only once, in a 1941 review of Gertrude Stein's *Ida*, did Auden write an actual pastiche of the style of the author under consideration, writers like D. H. Lawrence and Henry James, in particular, seemed to resonate audibly in his style when he wrote about them. His 1946 address on James, which contained some observations on artistic expatriation of close relevance to Auden's own situation, also contains many

Jamesian locutions, and ends with a pseudo-Jamesian flourish (see *Prose II*, p. 303).

Friends remembered Auden as one capable of speedy assimilation of the contents of a book; and the generosity already referred to was in part derived from an intellectual porousness that made him quick to absorb and register the times he lived in. Thus, in November 1939, words like '*Anschluss*' and '*Lebensraum*' crop up in a review having nothing otherwise to do with Hitler. The downside of this was, some have suggested, a magpie acquisitiveness in respect of the ideas he entertained and then rejected; but on balance one prefers an Auden to whom Hitler was no mere footnote (as with Joyce, of whose mandarin stance in *Finnegans Wake* Auden grew increasingly critical), and who responded to the attempted extermination of European Jewry with more than Eliot's slightly eerie taciturnity. (*A Certain World*, for example, includes a section on concentration camps.) Eliot offered the most influential contemporary model of a poet's engagement with prose for an English writer of Auden's generation; but just as part of Auden's distinction as a poet consisted in the speed with which he outgrew Eliot's influence, so his prose was different: he was prepared to be more experimental, or simply messier. To borrow James's definitions of 'art' and 'life' from the Preface to *The Spoils of Poynton*, Eliot's prose seems 'all discrimination and selection', whereas Auden's, while not precisely 'all inclusion and confusion', does show in the range of its concerns a characteristic impulse to inclusiveness. Like Eliot he rebelled against the belletrism of the late Victorian literary climate, but his more immediate critical influence was the I. A. Richards who attempted to introduce 'scientific' principles into the business of literary criticism. This was congenial to Auden's own temperament, formed as it was in a household where his father was a classicist as well as a medical scientist. Late in his life, he declared that the only two magazines to which he regularly subscribed were *Nature* and *Scientific American*; as an undergraduate he had gone up to Oxford to read Natural Sciences before changing to English, and was subsequently scathing about the classically influenced snobbery then prevalent in the educational establishment, which dismissed science as 'Stinks' (see, for example, 'The Cave of Making'). An approach aware of scientific method came to him naturally; and although he could – as in his first *Criterion* review (April 1930) – use its terminology in a deliberate attempt to sound imposing ('Is there in any sense a Thalamocortical rivalry?', *Prose I*, p. 5), more generally his deployment of this mode carries greater conviction than Eliot's allusion to the cerebral cortex and digestive tracts in 'The Metaphysical Poets' (1921), or his stage-managed introduction of a chemical analogy to 'Tradition and the Individual Talent' (1919).

'Let me count the ways' might stand as motto for Auden's prose. His preference was for a taxonomic approach which categorised, listed and labelled,
and whose enumerations combined briskness with absoluteness: 'A poet may
write bad poetry in three ways' (*F&A*, p. 224); 'There are four things which
Lawrence does supremely well' (*Prose II*, p. 318); 'To a situation of danger
and difficulty there are five solutions' (*Prose I*, p. 96); 'For a complete life a
man requires six kinds of love' (this also from his 'Notes' on Lawrence, who
often caused Auden to put out more flags; *Prose II*, p. 321). Such multiplicities
were, typically, justified by his ensuing argument; but beneath them tended
to throb the groundbass of an underlying dualism, dividing the world into
'prolifics' and 'devourers', enunciating art's functions as 'escape' or
'parable', its practitioners as likely to be either 'Alices' or 'Mabels', and –
when not asserting the schizoid nature of the individual life, as in 'Jehovah
Housman and Satan Housman' or a dark poem like 'A Household' – insisting
on there being 'two eternal classes of men'. This phrase comes from his 1944
review of a biography of Gerard Manley Hopkins, where Auden clinched
his case with a type of rhetorical accumulation also encountered in his pieces
on Pope and Tennyson:

> He didn't matter: he had a silly face; he was a martyr to piles; he bored his
> congregations and was a joke to his students; he fiddled around with Egyptian
> and with Welsh and with Gregorian music; he wrote a few poems which h[is]
> best friends couldn't understand and which would never be published; after
> forty-four years he died. Yes, like Don Quixote.          (*Prose II*, p. 220)

Although the flippant irreverence of this is intentionally subversive, what it
subverts is not the importance of Hopkins's poetry so much as any unquestioning veneration of it or its writer. Schoolmaster Auden had felt his pupils
needed to be startled into knowledge; similarly, the idiosyncrasy of this
sequence and its conclusion induces (in Wallace Stevens's phrase) 'a laughter,
an agreement, by surprise'.

Detractors might argue that this merely exemplifies Auden's irritating mannerisms, his never-adequately-suppressed schoolboyishness. But it can also
be viewed as part of a tactic followed with some consistency, whose aim
was less to undermine the seriousness of serious writing than to assert the
validity of 'unserious' writing – the importance, if you like, of not being
earnest, so that, in *The Enchafèd Flood* and *The Dyer's Hand*, writers like
Edward Lear, Lewis Carroll, Jules Verne or P. G. Wodehouse furnish examples alongside those from more canonical authors. Its justification is to be
seen in the case he mounted in his preface to *The Oxford Book of Light Verse*
(1938), arguing that the inspirational seriousness that was the chief legacy
of Romanticism eclipsed a longer tradition in which the poet felt entitled to

assume a community of interest in the social world with his readership. Our trivialisation of the meaning of 'light' verse was the sign of an unhealthily over-exalted individualism in the understanding of literature and its proper subjects. Poets like Walter de la Mare and John Betjeman, about each of whom he wrote appreciatively, seemed to Auden to exemplify a more desirable integration with the community of their readers than any *poète maudit*; and his poetic tribute that Lear had become a 'land' settled by delighted readers described a more benign assimilation than that envisaged, the following month, in the elegy he wrote for Yeats.

His method was also part of an overall strategy of disruption working to prohibit the 'rehearsed response': 'In Lawrence's case, one enemy was the conventional response, the laziness or fear which makes people prefer second-hand experience to the shock of looking and listening for themselves' (*DH*, p. 280). Auden's prose mounted a series of diversionary manoeuvres to obstruct that impulse, operating by means of structure, range of reference or tone. Obtrusive enumerations reminded the world of letters about the world of numbers, and the lists, charts and elaborately interrelating tabulations deployed were a means also of spatialising his argument, rather than temporalising it in the sequences of discursive prose. This is similar to the tactic used in his schools anthology *The Poet's Tongue* (with John Garrett, 1935), as well as his own *Collected Poetry* (1945). In each, poems were arranged by first-line alphabetical order, which prevented the reader bringing to them expectations generated by notions of literary history or authorial development; but also, in such de-chronologising, Auden made the book a simultaneity rather than a sequence, a living immediacy more than an accumulated retrospect.

A notable instance of his chart-making occurs in the essay 'Psychology and Art To-day' (1935), written under the intellectual aegis of Freud but already alert to the limitations of the psychoanalytical approach; and a much more complicated example was given by Auden to his university class in the USA in 1943, by which time he had formally rejoined the Christian faith (reproduced in *Later Auden*, p. 240). As well as owing something to his scientific education, this methodology may go back to the books about mining in which he steeped himself in boyhood. With their tabular listings and diagrammatic presentations of the types of rock through which a vertical shaft would sink, these described location through schematic depiction of underlying structural geology rather than in terms of visible landscape, conducing to a sense of place radically unpicturesque. The intricately elaborate chart he gave his American students offered the components for a working model of the moral universe, as systematic as anything in Dante; and here is possibly seen an effect of the books of mining machinery that the boy Auden greedily devoured (and retained into adulthood), which copiously illustrated the turbines and pumping-engines by which he was fascinated, and diagrammatically represented how they worked. In *The Dyer's Hand* Auden referred to the poem as a 'closed system' and a 'verbal contraption' about which his first question was always technical – how does it work? While not as self-consciously Futurist as Williams's definition of the poem as a 'machine made out of words', the mechanical analogy helps explain Auden's penchant for initial classification in terms of type and function, and illuminates the pleasure he could take in the strict beauty of poems as well as of locomotives.

It is significant that the second of these charts was created in a classroom context; for education was an area with which from early in his writing career Auden had both practical and intellectual involvement, as a schoolmaster, as reviewer of books on the school system and as commentator on the educational system. As a teacher, he was remembered for the unorthodoxy of his methods – getting pupils to write an essay in which every sentence was a lie, for example, or proposing an examination question in which they had to unscramble two intermingled sonnets – which had the object of subverting rather than inculcating rehearsed responses. He was capable of overestimating the power of education, whether in asserting its revolutionary duty – 'Educationalists must always be revolutionaries' (*Scrutiny*, 1934; *Prose 1*, p. 66) – or in his willingness to take the English public school as model for a fascist state. He came to doubt the contribution he could make to social change by teaching the offspring of the well-heeled middle classes in comfortably isolated schools; just as he came to doubt the power of poetry to make much happen. Although in favour of the rote-learning of poems, he was consistently sceptical that anyone could be *taught* to appreciate literature; and his denunciations of the bookishness of too much education had a practical outcome in the embodied challenges he mounted to received ideas of what a book should be. *The Orators*, *Letters from Iceland*, *The Dyer's Hand* and *A Certain World* all offer resistance to the simply generic anticipations which a reader brings to them: none conforms exactly to what a volume of poetry, a 'travel book', a collection of critical prose or a 'commonplace book' might, ordinarily, be expected to amount to.

The principal books of prose Auden conceived were *The Prolific and the Devourer*, *The Enchafèd Flood*, *The Dyer's Hand* and *A Certain World*. *Forewords and Afterwords* was rather more a means of preserving uncollected essays, and *Secondary Worlds* is of considerably less interest than all these others. During his own lifetime he was probably best known in prose through *The Enchafèd Flood*, consisting of the Page-Barbour lectures delivered at the University of Virginia in 1949, and *The Dyer's Hand*, based on lectures given during his later tenure of the Oxford Professorship of Poetry. In certain aspects these reflected their times, as in their titles' Shakespearean allusiveness (somewhat snootily unexplained in each case; the first is a particularly obscure reference to *Othello*, II. i). *The Enchafèd Flood* was the nearest approach Auden made to producing a conventionally sequential book-length treatise about literature, but even here his appetite for subdefinitional groupings is strongly to the fore. Subtitled 'The Romantic Iconography of the Sea', the book sets out to explore the nature of Romanticism by examining its use of the theme of the sea – although almost immediately that term calls into being a thematic opposite, the desert. It starts, somewhat surprisingly for readers recalling the impatience with Wordsworth expressed in 'Letter to Lord Byron', with the dream passage from *The Prelude* (Book v) that presents a visionary encounter with a figure who seems a composite of 'an Arab of the Desert' and Don Quixote, carrying a stone in one hand and a shell in the other. From this passage, quoted at length from the 1805 version, Auden immediately derives three pairs of symbols which become important structuring devices for the rest of the book: the desert and the sea; the stone of abstract geometry and the shell of imagination or instinct; the double-natured hero. From these in turn follow the subcategories and enumerated lists that are a feature of the rest of his argument, plotting the distinctive differences between the Romantic and the neoclassical temperaments, illustrated by quotations from a variety of sources – including much Melville, in tribute to his adopted country. This derivation of large consequence from selective quotation was of its time, and the book is also of its era in its literary enclosedness, its taking for granted the iconic and representative status of literary texts (though high seriousness is mitigated by the attention paid to Lear, Carroll and Verne). The study ends in a way that develops the argument advanced in Auden's *Oxford Book of Light Verse*, asserting that the asocial vision of the Romantic artist is obsolete, and has been replaced by the figure of the 'builder, who renews the ruined walls of the city' (*EF*, p. 126) – an image especially resonant for one who had in 1945 undertaken a survey in Germany of the effects of Allied bombing.

*The Dyer's Hand* ('and other essays', as subtitled) is a less integrated book, although Auden claimed to Stephen Spender that its unifying subject was art and Christianity. In the foreword he made clearer than ever his aversion to 'systematic criticism', and declared that in revising his essays he had reduced them wherever possible to notes, preferring a critic's notebooks to his treatises. The Prologue, consisting of two sections, 'Reading' and 'Writing', adheres to that aphoristic principle, and offers by implication a set of instructions to the would-be consumer of the book – who had already been advised to read it in proper sequence. Asserting that a writer's particular 'dream of Eden' should only concern his reader once he sets up as a literary critic, Auden punctiliously answers his own odd questionnaire on that subject; in 'Making, Knowing and Judging', however, he confesses that his 'technical' question (what kind of verbal contraption a poem is) is always followed by a 'moral' one about the poet's human nature and 'notion of the good life or the good place' (*DH*, pp. 51–2). He denounced a biographical approach to an author's work almost as invariably as he practised it himself, often internalising Freudian presumptions he elsewhere disputed. At a minor strategic level, he signalled his new nationality to his Oxford audience by inserting slightly ostentatious Americanisms into the basically 'English' English usages of his style; and this was part of a more pronounced autobiographical element, starting with the book's dedication, by which he positioned himself in respect of his readership.

'The Guilty Vicarage', collected in *The Dyer's Hand*, was first conceived as a lecture to a theological seminary round about January 1946, and subsequently delivered at other venues before its publication in *Harper's Magazine* in May 1948. It exemplifies Auden's mature style; just as he felt that a true poem would improve for being read aloud, so the sense of an immediate audience generated by its origin survives into the essay. Relaxedly first-person in its address to the reader, it takes for subject the 'Whodunit' – expressly defined as a sub-artistic literary genre – which is scrutinised in a series of short separately titled sections, including a diagrammatic comparison of the mythic structures of the detective story with Aristotelian tragedy, and a sociological speculation about its typical readership. The essay's loosely theological perspective and analytical classifications create a potentially comic disproportion between the gravity of the enquiry and this lightweight subject; but its purpose is to define by default those qualities which true art has and the detective story lacks. Amongst them is re-readability; for Auden concludes that each detective story casts an unrepeatable spell, in a fundamentally escapist fantasy of return to a lost Eden – in which conclusion the essay's link to overall themes of the book becomes explicit.

*The Prolific and the Devourer* and *A Certain World* may at the time of composition have been closer to Auden's heart than either *The Enchafèd Flood* or *The Dyer's Hand*, which one way or another were written to commission. By contrast, it is not clear that *The Prolific and the Devourer* was written at a publisher's request; and although he told E. R. Dodds that he had been commissioned to produce what became *A Certain World*, Auden clearly had considerable latitude in determining contents and format. Thus each has in common that, to revert to his dichotomy, it was written at least as much to please himself as to please other people. *The Prolific and the*

*Devourer*, as it stood when he left off (when, presumably, it had ceased to please him), consisted of four sections, the first pronouncedly aphoristic, dealing mainly with issues relating to the role of the artist in a politically defined world, and containing passages of autobiographical reflection which included a retrospect on the 'follies' of the political writing of the 1930s. The middle two sections were more discursive in character. Although broken up into discrete paragraphs, these were more extended than in the first section; the main thrust was a semi-secularised consideration of the force of Christianity, with Jesus being regarded more as a teacher of ethics than a divine personage. The final section was an interrogation of the author, in a question-and-answer format, by an unsympathetic interlocutor possibly modelled on Edward Upward, inclined to challenge what he saw as the deluded disconnection from the crises of contemporary history embodied in Auden's position.

Given the circumstances of its composition, it is not surprising if Auden felt the need to take stock, and to assess the seriousness of charges that could be laid against him – in much the same way as earlier that year he had imagined Yeats on trial for his reputation, in 'The Public v. the Late Mr William Butler Yeats' (March 1939). When war broke out in Europe, however, there may also have seemed a vaingloriousness in imagining that his own particular predicament was of much consequence. Moreover, his beliefs were evolving in ways and at a speed that would soon make it unacceptable to treat Christianity merely as a set of ethical hypotheses propounded by one Jesus. The self-questioning, the autobiographical elements (including Auden's early interest in mines) and the engagement with theology were more elegantly set forth in 'New Year Letter': attached to which remnants of his book survived in the form of notes, like a vestigial appendage, before disappearing altogether from subsequent editions.

Nevertheless, in its aphoristic nature and its autobiographical impulses, *The Prolific and the Devourer* can be seen as an early forerunner of *A Certain World*, although the differences between them are as instructive as the similarities. What Auden turns away from, there, is precisely that attitudinising self-centredness which he came to feel had disfigured his early poetry, and which remained audible in *The Prolific and the Devourer* (and perhaps also in 'September 1, 1939'). *A Certain World* is structurally more democratic: its alphabetical arrangement, whilst not unusual to the genre of commonplace book, offers a simultaneity that can be entered or left at any chosen point. It enacts a modest quasi-effacement of the Auden whose planet it maps, by largely ventriloquising his experience through the words of others. It is no accident that the final entry on 'Writing' (before the 'Addenda'), which is in his own voice, closes by returning to his early mining fantasies and their link with his art, and ends resonantly quoting St Augustine on the communality of truth.

Reviewing *The Book of Talbot*, Auden had identified love with 'intensity of attention' (*Prose I*, p. 43); *A Certain World* – where 'certain' implies specificity and therefore partiality, as well as assurance – modifies this, endorsing 'a view of reality common to all, seen from a unique perspective' (*CW*, p. 425), and attempting in that formulation to resolve the tensions between individual and collective, with which his prose had been continuously concerned. There may be less 'intensity of attention' than in his poetry, but the 'unique perspective' of a good Auden essay can surprise us into seeing things differently. Poetry was more important to him than prose because he associated the latter with the realm of necessity rather than freedom: the compromised and compromising world of the Trolls or Sancho Panza, not the visionary gleams of Peer Gynt or Don Quixote. But he knew that freedom unconditioned by necessity is unearthly, dangerously magical; and just as the undergraduate aspiring to be a 'great' poet became the older writer who distrusted the airs poetry could put on in its pose of greatness, so he reconciled himself to the prosaic: Caliban has (nearly) the last word. 'Since the Word was made Flesh', Auden declared in *Secondary Worlds*, 'it is impossible to imagine God as speaking in anything but the most sober prose' (*SW*, p. 136). Auden's prose, however, does not embody a divine sobriety – or even self-consistency; he could be silly, like us. But in the variety and evolution of its interests through successive episodes of attention, its aphoristic fragmentariness, its charts and diagrams, the *sprezzatura* of its enumerations and its lively reachings after truth, it reminds us, rather, that his favourite stop on the harmonium was the *vox humana*.

## NOTES

1. Posthumously published as a separate volume, ed. & introd. Edward Mendelson (Hopewell, N.J.: The Ecco Press, 1981).
2. Robert Lowell, 'Auden at Sixty', *Collected Prose* (London: Faber and Faber, 1987), p. 74.

## 10

PETER PORTER

# Auden's English: language and style

Style in any writer is more than quirkiness of manner or some notable bias of usage or direction. This is especially the case with W. H. Auden, as few writers in any century have emerged into public view so fully fledged in recognisable plumage. The thirties produced for him an early apotheosis, 'The Auden Double Number' of Geoffrey Grigson's *New Verse* (1937), decently adorned with a Faber advertisement for 'Vin Audenaire' and collecting a host of tributes to the thirty-year-old poet from the established and famous as well as the neophyte tastemakers. Here, bringing their offerings, were such unexpected Magi as Edwin Muir, George Barker, Dylan Thomas, Herbert Read, Sir Hugh Walpole and even Ezra Pound (jokey but impressed). Just before this, Auden's celebrity was capped by Wyndham Lewis's questioning, 'Who's this new guy who's got into the landscape?' By the time of the publication of *New Country* (1932), the poetry community was coming out in an Audenesque rash – as in the tribute from Charles Madge in 'Letter to the Intelligentsia':

> But there waited for me in the summer morning
> Auden fiercely. I read, shuddered and knew.
> And all the world's stationary things
> In silence moved to take up new positions . . .

Although slightly his elder, Cecil Day-Lewis hailed Auden as the true leader: 'Look west, Wystan, lone flyer, birdman, my bully boy!' Some of this Audenesque imitation was embarrassingly unconscious of its derivativeness. The literary world was much more tightly knit then, and a reputation made in Britain travelled untrammelled across the Atlantic. Faber and Faber and Random House sold scarcely more than a thousand or so copies of most of Auden's collections during the thirties, but his notoriety and that of the misnamed 'Pylon Poets' got into unliterary places such as newspapers while reaching legendary status in senior common rooms. When Edmund Wilson mocked the celebrity of Archibald MacLeish in 'The Omelette of

A. MacLeish', he specified, among his Coleridge-like marginal annotations, that the poetic dish had become subject to the influence of 'British schoolboys flying over', an acknowledgement of the public school language of Auden's 1930s writings.

Auden's Minerva-like precocity seems the more extraordinary now that we have Katherine Bucknell's edition of *Juvenilia: Poems 1922–1928* (1994). The first part of this assembly not only fails to hint at what was to come but falls below even the most ordinary level of beginner's skill. His maturing was incredibly speedy, and three-quarters of the way into the book we encounter such defining first lines as 'Who stands, the crux left of the watershed' and 'Control of the passes was, he saw, the key'. How did this voice manoeuvre itself out of the Edward Thomas and Yeatsian imitations and the Hardy taciturnity into that Auden dawn? Perhaps we should conclude that talent does not always announce its impending arrival; it simply bursts on the scene.

There is, however, within this rag-bag of juvenilia, one anticipation of a different order indicative of a tone never to be dispersed in Auden's work. This is his fondness for aphorism – not any sort of general maxim-making but a specific set of paradoxes and chidings intended to do everybody a power of good. Soon after, at the time of *Poems* and *The Orators*, such couplet-rhyming squibs as 'The friends of the born nurse' started to pile up in Auden's notebooks, though they had to wait until his life's work was assembled before appearing in print. One poem sums up this manner more bleakly, since it doesn't share the self-healing monstrance of its fellow apophthegms. This is 'Uncle Henry', an openly homosexual satire, and one of the rare examples of Auden's callous approach to *de-haut-en-bas* knowingness. Uncle Henry, who goes south on pederastic jaunts, hails the female sex only as the provider of the young boys he's looking for:

> All they have they bwing,
> Abdul, Nino, Manfwed, Kosta:
> here's to women for they bear such
> lovely kiddies!

Such jokey seriousness is the opposite side of the coin to the powerful and portentous poems which made his name at the beginning of the thirties. Even today the shock of this poetry can be felt, hardly diminished. Stephen Spender has testified to Auden's 'powerful intelligence and personality' and to his pervasive influence in the thirties. Spender's privately printed book of Auden's work in 1928 was quickly expanded to the Faber edition of *Poems* (1930). So began a run of extraordinarily prescient verse, the *fons-et-origo* of what has ever since been recognised as the characteristic Auden tone. In fact, it is only the first Auden tone, to borrow from musical terminology, and was followed by some very dissimilar ones. Yet its primacy once established remains unquestioned. It permits of some degree of linguistic analysis, though much which has been offered by critics has been too blunt and prescriptive. Omission of the definite article, minatory muttering and threatening images, often transmuted from the sagas in near comic-book brevity, gang warfare rituals and prep school argot, psychosomatic identification with healers such as Groddeck and Layard, the dismantled English landscape standing for mental bankruptcy, ruined oracles. Just to list such characteristics is to signal that there is no accurate terminology for stylistics. Nor will the impulse to codify Auden's procedures explain the originality and authority of this poetry. Auden himself soon became afraid of his originality. Newly settled in America, he split his output up and his first *Collected Poems* (1950) redistributed the contents by alphabetical order of first lines throughout the book, and equipped them with usually facetious titles. Originally they were untitled. Fortunately the definitive *Collected Poems* (1976), edited by Edward Mendelson, restored chronological precedence to these first-begotten masterpieces, though it retains the titles.

Spender described Auden as an aloof commentator, endowed with great cleverness and a lucid gift, adding that 'with Auden one is aware of the Audenesque mood and the Audenesque attitude . . . but not of Auden'. This has become an orthodoxy of Auden criticism, but the opposite is just as true. The clinical objectivity, the categorising knowingness, the private references, do not impede the reader's sense of the poet's individuality, the almost tangible feeling of physical and mental presence conveyed by the verse. This, as much as any quirk which might appeal to a parodist, accounts for the recognisability of an Auden poem at any stage of his creative process. He may not consciously evoke emotion but he seldom fails to present it as central to his poetic strategy. It remains good advice to the reader, if not to ignore, then at least to discount the influence of such healers, early on, as Homer Lane and John Layard, and later of theologians and philosophers, such as Charles Williams, Niebuhr, Eugen Rosenstock-Huessy, Loren Eiseley and Oliver Sacks. Auden, as co-editor of *The Faber Book of Aphorisms*, knew how much trust to place in ex-cathedra rulings. In poem after poem he warns against believing that poetry and dogma are the same thing, or even that art's service to truth carries any guarantee of authority. 'But poets are not celibate divines: / Had Dante said so, who would read his lines?' he asked in ' "The Truest Poetry is the Most Feigning"'. 'Friday's Child', a poem in memory of Dietrich Bonhoeffer, murdered by the Nazis, observes that

> Since the analogies are rot
> Our senses based belief upon,
> We have no means of learning what
>         Is really going on,
> And must put up with having learned
> All proofs or disproofs that we tender
> Of His existence are returned
>         Unopened to the sender.

The riddling locutions, the sense that Auden is taking a scalpel to language itself, which is so marked a quality in his early poetry, can seem almost to make him an anticipator of today's 'language poetry'. Though the threat which many of these works poses is palpable, their verbal game-playing element is equally strong. Admirers in the thirties noticed the linguistic emphasis but, though this was the age which gave birth to logical positivism and to various incursions into verbal analysis, they interpreted his poetry in political and psychological terms. John Fuller's admirable *W. H. Auden: A Commentary* (1998) is aware of the influences on Auden's thinking at each turn of his changing convictions, but concentrates on the language and technique of the poetry, always aware of the artist, not the advocate.

Fuller identifies a young German as Auden's love in the poem, 'Love by ambition' (later entitled 'Too Dear, Too Vague'), but his examination of the poem initiates an analysis of what the unbearably elasticated term 'love' means for Auden which continues throughout 500 pages of his commentary. The peculiarity of the close rhymes, the short lines and general sense of a nursery rhyme in this poem do not conflict with the poet's seriousness. The poem's disillusion with the selfishness of love is not, however, the final conclusion drawn from the poem by the reader. Instead, the simple actions – 'the shutting of a door', 'the sofa's creak' – create a feeling of predatoriness impinging on truthfulness, of the staccato action of conscience forced to confront feelings in as few words as possible. Familiarity is broken into sharp and constituent parts. 'Love' is subject to some of Auden's most slippery codifying – 'O Love the interest itself in thoughtless Heaven' – recurring in his verse like the chord of the diminished seventh. Yet to state this is not necessarily to accuse Auden of lying or even of prevarication. Love, he seems to have decided, is the bridge between psychology and ethics. Fuller quotes Emily Dickinson's 'Love is over there', glossed in 'Too Dear, Too Vague' as 'Love has moved to another chair'. He reminds us that both Laura Riding and her lover Robert Graves accused Auden of stealing from Riding. This accusation underlines a major paradox, that Auden borrows from many poets but always stays himself. Like Stravinsky, who claimed that he was not influenced by other composers but simply stole from them, Auden can absorb almost any style but never seem a pasticheur; his personality shows through each disguise. He is supremely the analyst who becomes a synthesist. His dismantling is a mode of construction.

Flanking *Poems* (1930) are two compositions which point in opposite directions. One is a *via negativa* of formality, and the other the closest Auden ever came to inventing an apocalypse. 'Paid on Both Sides' describes itself as a charade and does indeed exhibit some embarrassing house party games-manship, or, at its worst, seems like a board-set from Waddingtons, with the rules inside the lid. Because it was his first appearance in public it has been overestimated. It is also the only work of his approved by F. R. Leavis. Auden's obsession with the topography of Yorkshire, the Lake District and Northumberland and their lead mining sites gives him his scene, and a minia-turised version of saga feuding provides the action. What works over the span of a short poem becomes otiose in this over-extended farce. It is a poor guide to his prevailing style as it is *all* style: the lack of seriousness obliges its many quiddities to be little more than attitudinising.

*The Orators* (1932) is a very different case. This remarkable work shows Auden, still in his mid-twenties, practising to become the mid-Atlantic Goethe he wanted to be in later years. Topped and tailed by some of his most daring ode-shaped Pindarics, and prefaced by the lines about private faces and public places which became his carrying-card, *The Orators* is a mad-house study of the failing land England had become after the First World War. It is Auden at his most undisciplined – an *omnium gatherum* into which mass observation, studies in psychology from Freud to Spengler and Hirschfeld, joky odes to public school virtue, 'Magic Mountain' inti-mations of the social pathology of disease, the Farnborough Air Show and much else are woven. It is as if an oracle had swept the historical airwaves and left an utterly confused but enormously panoptic set of data on the desk of one highly imaginative student.

An account of *The Orators* here can do no more than merely assert its crucial importance in terms of subject matter and language. 'Letter to a Wound' and 'Journal of an Airman' include many semi-Surrealist notions central to the paranoid landscape of European thinking between the wars, decorated with Auden's utterly original, Lewis Carroll-like flourishes. The Auden atmosphere is being created before the reader's eyes in this study, and the poet himself found that he could not breathe in it. When he reissued *The Orators* in 1966, he prefaced it with the words, 'My name on the title-page seems a pseudonym for someone else, someone talented but near the border of sanity, who might well in a year or two become a Nazi.' He did nothing of the sort, of course, and he never abandoned the force-field which animates his 'English study'. Outcroppings, often of a comically exaggerated sort, recur: 'Destructive Desmond' and the scene in the lunatic asylum in *The Dog Beneath the Skin*, the Notes to *New Year Letter*, the Seven Ages section of *The Age of Anxiety*, 'Dichtung und Wahrheit', Caliban's speech from 'The Sea and the Mirror' and a fair quantity of criticism in *The Dyer's Hand* carry the imprimatur of this ur-text. It is all the more English for its recognition of how modern England has shrunk from its imperial confidence.

Auden's style, as much as his reputation, has always been open to the charge of irresponsibility. He seemed to rejoice in paradox. The excitement of his originality passed among his early readers as the epitome of modernism. But restoration was quite as powerful an innate drive in his work and personality as anything revolutionary. Whether he ever did say, as he has been reported, that 'the only thing in the world which never changes is the avant-garde', he was not a paid-up modernist of the sort of Eliot and Pound. His use of language made him an experimenter all his life, but he hated obscurity posing as profundity, and he loved tradition and sought ways of realigning modern poetry with its inheritance. His great tradition was wider and more natural than F. R. Leavis's. In an early poem he spoke approvingly of 'new styles of architecture, a change of heart', but his admirers should have guessed that he really disliked such things and would one day repudiate them.

Contemporary with *The Orators* are the sonnets of psychological pressure, poems which are almost mini-biographies – 'A shilling life will give you all the facts', 'Fleeing the short-haired mad executives' and 'The fruit in which your parents hid you, boy'. They are knowing enough but reveal how his poetry was beginning to look more traditional by the day. Auden stressed the popularising function of verse. Eliot could be smutty and could gloomily enjoy rebuking the modern world in verse, but he had none of Auden's instinctive fondness for popular forms. It was at this time that Auden began his campaign to lead modern poetry away from the arcane difficulty of progressive modernism. That a writer perceived to be 'difficult' himself should be doing this is another paradox, one perhaps explained by the suggestion that what Auden wanted to avoid was any sense that modernism was a uniform or restrictive orthodoxy. Looking back sixty years further on, we can appreciate that he took poetry up to the great quartermaster's store of inherited forms, devices and structures, and borrowed whatever suited his purpose. He is the great reviver of past disciplines within modern times. Sonnets, sestinas, rhyme royal, Pindaric odes, catalogues, threnodies, *terza rima* and *ottava rima*, cabaret songs, ballads, aphorisms, alliterative verse, sapphics, villanelles, American syllabics – the roll-call is prodigious. Only the triolet, he believed, was not worth the effort.

Auden's temperament was radically opposed to Pound's famous instruction, 'Make it New!' Pound's own poetry is often based on past forms, but these are not as widely chosen as Auden's. Pound has a fondness for the hierarchical and despotic; there is too much stained-glass medievalism in his poetry right up to the last of the *Cantos*. Auden's way of making something new is to observe the shape of the bottle before pouring in the wine. It will be new wine however much it is going to be shaped by its container. Auden gives no credence to the idea that form must be governed historically, or should spring mysteriously but inevitably from contemporary necessities. He was sceptical that 'the age demanded' any style just because it *was* the age. Language changes, but its preoccupations stay the same. You cannot write like Keats, but you can make a thoroughly up-to-date poem using the blank verse renovation Keats employed in *Hyperion*. Consciousness of history is instinctive and needs no special imperative.

Auden's 'low dishonest decade' was the most politicised since the Napoleonic era, and he seemed to his audience at the time a political poet. Close examination of his thirties writing will demolish this notion. He was always a Freudian rather than a Marxist. Mr Marx may dismiss the contending forces with a wave of his hand at the end of *The Dance of Death*, but this is a joke in the way that the dilemma of Ransom, Auden's mountain-conqueror in *The Ascent of F6*, confronted and destroyed by his vision of the spirit of the peak becoming his mother, is not. The best of Auden's directly political writing is in his comic verse and in the Shavian situations he and Isherwood worked into their Group Theatre plays. *The Dog Beneath the Skin* is a repository of left-wing skits as well as a gathering place for many of Auden's fugitive lyrics of the time. *On the Frontier* contains some of Auden's broadest propaganda pieces. 'Two hundred miles behind the Line / The GHQ sits down to dine' is doggerel of the sort which Thomas Hardy surprised his admirers with at the end of his life in such terse observations as 'Christmas 1924': 'After two thousand years of Mass / We've got as far as poison gas.' Like so many of his class drawn to Communist politics by the Depression and the pall of guilt which Europe inherited from the Great War, Auden was happier satirising the faults of bourgeois capitalism and the corruption of international politics than in finding prescriptions for social justice. His Freudian leanings kept him from too much faith in human reformation or working-class solidarity. When he propagandises for Communism, a schoolboy exaggeration turns his more preposterous poems into pieces of Surrealist theatre. He becomes the Ubu Roi of political satire in 'A Happy New Year', for example:

Churchill was speaking of a battleship.
It was some little while before I had guessed
He wasn't describing a woman's breast.

. . .

Lord Baden-Powell with a piece of string
Was proving that reef-knots honour the King.

. . .

The Sitwells were giving a Private Dance
But Wyndham Lewis disguised as a maid
Was putting cascara in the still lemonade.

(*EA*, pp. 447–8)

A few years later, this threat-filled fantasising attained a sleazy apotheosis in 'Auden and MacNeice: Their Last Will and Testament', the coda to their volume *Letters from Iceland*. Ambiguity can hardly go further than this all-too-knowing countdown to apocalypse. Edmund Wilson noticed that, however much its authors were hoping for revolution, the poem is a show-case for the English establishment, a power circuit where everybody seems to know everybody else. In 'A Communist to Others', the crudest of the propaganda poems, Auden seems close for once to abandoning his facetiousness for a species of solemn warning:

Because you saw but were not indignant
The invasion of the great malignant
　　　Cambridge ulcer
That army intellectual
Of every kind of liberal
Smarmy with friendship but of all
　　　There are none falser.

(*EA*, p. 122)

His recommendations of a new order of health and fairness are so unconvincing that you see why he felt, rereading *The Orators*, that he had been briefly closer to fascism than to Communism. His briefly maintained political populism, however, encouraged one of his greatest gifts, the writing of lyrics, ballads and choruses. Here his lyrical bias is joined to a talent for the internal drama of short poems as natural as Browning's. Has any poet composed more haunting lyrics since the heyday of the Earl of Rochester, even Blake or Tennyson? Auden's independent lyrics resemble Rochester's by plunging us *in medias res*. So many of these brief poems start memorably, their authoritative and magical openings engaging attention at once, often with attention-grabbing vocatives, 'Look, stranger, on this island now', 'Let the florid music praise', 'Lay your sleeping head, my love', 'Deftly, admiral, cast your fly'. Often, attention is engaged by the single unexpected word in an opening line: 'Fish in the *unruffled* lakes', 'May with its light *behaving*', 'Now through night's *caressing* grip', 'Underneath the *abject* willow', 'The piers are *pummelled* by the waves' (emphasis added).

The plays can be mustered under the rubric of popular art, as joky as they are didactic. So may his many ballads, including such hard options as 'Victor' and 'Miss Gee', and the thirties ballad 'Stop all the clocks' unexpectedly popularised by the film *Four Weddings and a Funeral*. Alongside these, 'As I Walked Out One Evening' and 'The Witnesses', stand such quasi-musical numbers as songs from plays, radio features and collaborations with Benjamin Britten, especially those from *Our Hunting Fathers* and the cabaret songs for Hedli Anderson. In his opera libretti he displays a similar ability to combine *coups de théâtre* with lyric definition. '"Gold in the North" came the blizzard to say', 'The Single Creature leads a partial life' from *Paul Bunyan*, the chorus of whores and roaring boys and Anne Truelove's lullaby from *The Rake's Progress*; the 'servants of the Servant of the Muse' duet from *Elegy for Young Lovers* and 'Feed the brute with eggs and fruit' from *Moralities* (Henze), all illustrate Auden's unfailing touch as a lyricist.

Auden the educator was seldom silent throughout his career. As compiler of anthologies he is rivalled only by Geoffrey Grigson. *The Poet's Tongue* (1935), edited with John Garrett, acquainted generations of readers with the rich bequest of popular and proverbial verse in English from medieval times onwards. Equally influential was *The Oxford Book of Light Verse*, whose introduction contains the observation that up till Milton all English poetry had something 'light' about it. In the United States Auden became an occasional university teacher, acknowledged by students as a disturbingly original setter-aside of academic shibboleths. His five-volume *Poets of the English Language* speaks against many special pleadings of the canon while remaining properly inclusive in scope. *The Faber Book of Aphorisms*, edited with Louis Kronenberger, allots more entries to neglected masters of the genre such as Halifax and Lichtenberg than to Rochefoucauld, Wilde and the more slippery maxim-makers.

Auden's didacticism has to be considered in any discussion of his use of language. The moral insistence of much of his poetry is alleviated by his constant questioning of ethical seriousness. That so culturally aware a writer should, ultimately, make a stand against the obligations of history is as much a hopeful gesture as a revolutionary one. His notorious withdrawal of approval from some of his most admired poems is not due only to fastidiousness of moral conscience but to a horror of becoming the complacent celebrator of doom, a species of contemporary Spengler. He admonishes himself on this in 'City Without Walls', reporting a doom-laden dream at the centre of the poem:

> What fun and games you find to play
> Jeremiah-cum-Juvenal,
> Shame on you for your Schadenfreude.

To persist in the dystopian prophecies of his early poetry would have been intolerable not merely to his own sense of good taste but might have disturbed his serious allegiance to Christian hopefulness. Christians are not permitted an excess of Manicheism. It hurt and disappointed many admirers when he disowned *Spain* with its 'History to the defeated / May say Alas but cannot help nor pardon.' This rejected sentiment does seem truer than the gloss he puts on it as 'immoral'. Even more upsetting to some people was his priggish rejection of the line 'We must love one another or die' in 'September 1, 1939'. His suggestion that 'or' should be replaced by 'and' is notably crass. Joseph Warren Beach's *The Making of the Auden Canon* takes the reader through a compendium of verbal and structural alterations imposed on already published work, most of the changes being examples of 'the removal of detonators'. Ambiguity is at the heart of any Auden poem. What history says to the defeated in 'The Fall of Rome' is no more comforting than its remonstration in *Spain*. Perhaps the problem is how to write dramatically and yet remain loyal to truth. Taking up public responsibilities came to involve expectations far exceeding the capabilities of the art he was practising. ' "The Truest Poetry is the Most Feigning" ' observes that 'love, or truth, in any serious sense, / Like orthodoxy is a reticence'. But how is he to be a truthful reporter of the human condition? One way is to reprimand his own mental tendencies. He warns us that 'the occupational disease of poets is frivolity', and he has Prospero ask in 'The Sea and the Mirror', 'Can I learn to suffer / Without saying something ironic or funny / On suffering?' There is a constant desire in him to be affirmative and escape the voices of scepticism. Sometimes he sees the way forward, as in the conclusion of 'In Memory of W. B. Yeats', or in the movement from aspiration to human fallibility in 'At the Grave of Henry James'.

The 'lexically sweetened' late Auden, with its fondness for raiding the dictionary for archaisms, technical terminology and nonce words – 'the baltering torrent sunk to a soodling thread' and 'insurrected eagre' of 'Under Sirius', 'King Arthur's rundle', 'the cloop of corks', 'flosculent speeches', 'tiddle and curmurr', 'dapatical fare' in 'Tonight at Seven Thirty', plus the camp locutions ('silly sausage', 'get her') – is not so different from his wantonness with words while he lived in Britain. Philip Larkin admired the brilliant deviancy of 'English Auden', but disliked the academic usage in

'American Auden'. He felt a vernacular poet with his pulse on modern life had become a boringly mandarin one – and foreign to boot. In truth, the change was simply from one vernacular (British) to another (International American). The Horatian tone which Auden believed was characteristic of his later work is already perceptible as far back as *Look, Stranger!* and *Another Time*.

There is, however, a genuine watershed in the Auden canon traceable to his removal to the United States. His long poems belong to his American years. He told Louis MacNeice in 1940 that America had enabled him to make himself into a truly professional writer. In New York he could tackle the big themes of his life's obsessions. It is true that 'Letter to Lord Byron' is of a reasonable social length, that the Group Theatre plays are decently extended and also that *The Orators* is not short (though it is only partly in verse). But the American challenge was felt to be more serious, and received from him a more concentrated response. His first decade in America resulted in *New Year Letter* (1940); 'For the Time Being' and 'The Sea and the Mirror', published together in one volume, *For the Time Being*, in 1945; and *The Age of Anxiety* (written between 1944 and 1946, published in 1948). None of these is a long poem in the sense that *Paradise Lost*, *Don Juan* and *The Ring and the Book* are. Twentieth-century long poems tend to come in modules, like Pound's *Cantos*, Carlos Williams's *Paterson* and Olson's *Maximus Poems*. But the four extended Auden works of the forties are considerable achievements of organisation. Most popular is 'The Sea and the Mirror', his Shakespearean fantasy in which the dramatis personae of *The Tempest* return to explain their somewhat loquacious selves. Browning had already reintroduced Caliban and given him some very Victorian doubts in his poem 'Caliban upon Setebos' or 'Natural History on the Island'. Auden too is very theological in his several dramatic monologues and lyrical intermezzi. Prospero's self-justification is markedly Browningesque, and is interspersed with brilliant lyrics, especially 'Sing first that green remote Cockaigne'. The song of 'Master and Boatswain' ('At Dirty Dick's and Sloppy Joe's') is as authoritative a popular interjection as any ditty in Shakespeare, and Miranda's introspective *canzone* lights up the more lucubrative verse around her. But the most audacious part of this richly embroidered tapestry is the prose monologue 'Caliban to the Audience'. Once readers have congratulated themselves on spotting the Henry James syntax, they can go on to appreciate that never before or after did Auden sustain so formidable and prolonged an excursion into convincingly stylised soliloquy. Seeking insight into his prodigious control of the English language, an analyst must give time and energy to the voice of Caliban/Auden. Every sort of metaphorical extension, thrasonical labouring and comic audacity Auden is capable of finds utterance here. The miracle is how such indirectness leads to so brilliant a clarity of argument. Caliban's speech is the glory of Auden's game-playing with the vernacular.

'For the Time Being' is frisky enough, but having been intended as an oratorio for Britten, it must be held to be a failure. As reading matter it is another of his grand pot-pourris, a gallimaufry of ideas about the incarnation of Christ. *The Age of Anxiety*, the longest continuous poem Auden wrote, is an elephant's graveyard of applied mannerism. To bring off two thousand-odd lines of largely alliterative verse of varied lengths is a tour de force, though one which even enthusiasts find vitiating eventually. It is, however, well plotted and from time to time finds Auden's muse in full sail. Each of its four characters, three men and a woman who meet by chance in a New York bar in wartime, is equipped with several monologues. Though these speeches are largely self-contained the poem is in some ways a return to the eclogue form popular in the thirties, particularly with Louis MacNeice. Indeed, its subtitle is 'A Baroque Eclogue'. These monologues are like arias in some *opera seria*, or perhaps *opera giacosa*, since their text is enlivened with some of Auden's most irrepressible humour. A critic of style would be badly advised to look to *The Age of Anxiety* to isolate the central intensity of what makes any poem 'Audenish' or even 'Audenesque'. Being an advertisement for his virtuosity, it will always be relished by devoted Auden hands, but it does not reach to the heart of his genius.

*New Year Letter*, surprisingly, is the long poem which does. A special galvanism entered Auden's spirit as soon as he arrived in America. He had already changed gear on his trip through China with Isherwood, the fruits of which were published in their account of their pilgrimage to the Sino-Japanese conflict, *Journey to a War*. The sonnets and other pieces included in this book show Auden adopting a very *de-haut-en-bas* attitude to history, an approach which came under pressure immediately in New York. He had left England largely to escape his admirers ('Family are wonderful but you can't live with them'). He plunged into the life of a hard-working and relatively lonely professional writer. Poems such as 'Law Like Love', 'September 1, 1939', the villanelles and lyrics printed in *Another Time*, dramatic monologues such as 'Voltaire at Ferney', 'Herman Melville', and 'Anthem for St Cecilia's Day' are Auden at high noon.

Much of what we might call 'Auden in language and play' turns on *New Year Letter*, the pivotal poem of this period. It consists of some 1,300 lines of tetrameter rhyming couplets, predominantly in iambics, and is supplemented with notes which are a forest of brilliant notions and devices, some of them in doggerel verse. But the poem itself is not doggerel, for all that it is conducted in the simplest verse form possible in English, one used in greeting cards and jingles by Mabel Lucie Atwell, attaining its previous apotheosis in Belloc's *Cautionary Tales*. In Auden's hands this verse speeds up apprehension and makes effective connections; it promotes the fusing of ideas and enables antithetical emotions to illuminate each other. He had used tetrameter before, in lyrics in his plays and for interpolated lyrics in longer forays, but nothing could have anticipated so remarkable a performance as this – a philosophical and witty poem touching on the most serious issues of faith, politics and art. Like some oracular river, it carries forward an existential concern with life at its crisis point in mid-century. It also demonstrates how well Auden can dissolve his aphorisms in the general argument of a poem, speaking, for example, of Tennyson's talent for 'an articulate despair', and of Rilke as 'The Santa Claus of loneliness', and in a roll-call of native places, of 'The wreck of Rhondda', or 'squalid beery Burton', which stands symbolically for 'shoddy thinking of all brands'.

There is also a confession which fits many people's perception of Auden, or at least of his commonly perceived failings. He is aware of why his detractors scorn him as a loose journalist and commentator, a glib Theophrastian and not a pure poet:

> For I relapse into my crimes.
> Time and again have slubbered through
> With slip and slapdash what I do,
> Adopted what I would disown,
> The preacher's loose immodest tone.

Auden, his more dogmatic opponents say, doesn't argue, he harangues; doesn't observe but categorises; pelicanises the past and gives it nothing more than modern chic in return; has no still centre but only a noisy parleying. To which those who love his work, warts and all, reply: his preaching is witty and does not serve any easy orthodoxy; his sympathy profound; and his recognition of the human condition unparalleled among poets of his time. Above all, he has returned to poetry its ancient privilege as a major component of world literature. He has made verse interesting and restored to language its birthright of play and dazzle. His fondness for quoting in German and other languages, his familiarity with arcane diction, his apparent pedantry and concentration on works of art rather than the latest manifestations of modern mores, may earn him the suspicion of doctrinaire democrats and Little Englanders. But we may presume that *homo ludens* is assured of a welcome in the long boredom of heaven, and that nobody in the past hundred years has shown better how English can be a fitting vehicle for intellectual illumination. Auden has fought to limit the destruction of our inheritance. As not only practising poets know, the 'short views' he prescribed in 'Under

Which Lyre' allow for a cleansing of the rot of jargon and spin. Such is the nature of poetry as Auden describes it in 'The Cave of Making', his elegy in memory of Louis MacNeice:

> After all, it's rather a privilege
>     amid the affluent traffic
> to serve this unpopular art which cannot be turned into
>     background noise for study
> or hung as a status-trophy for rising executives,
>     cannot be 'done' like Venice
> or abridged like Tolstoy, but stubbornly still insists upon
>     being read or ignored: our handful
> of clients at least can rune.

# 11

JOHN R. BOLY

# Auden and modern theory

Auden discusses only two theoretical systems at any length, Freudianism and Marxism, though he does glance at myth criticism. This leaves out two important contemporaries, the rhetorically based formalism known as New Criticism, and the linguistically based formalism which runs from Saussure through Jakobson to structuralism, Lacanian psychology, poststructuralism and deconstruction. In the period since Auden's death, critical trends have put less emphasis on such text-based theories and favoured the greater historical and social orientation of post-Marxism, cultural poetics, reader response, critical discourse theory and multiculturalism. While the descendants of Saussure's linguistic formalism can produce valuable readings, they require the acquisition of a highly technical apparatus and, in the case of Lacan and Derrida, the conquest of perplexing idiolects. To avoid equally perplexing because overly compressed explanations, this group must be relegated to passing references. More accessible are the culturally based approaches of the last three decades. Because these readings derive many of their premises from Freud and Marx, Auden's comments on those authors can furnish a basis for drawing inferences about the later theories. That leaves New Criticism, which Auden seldom addressed and might be set aside, except that it dominated literary studies in America for most of the poet's lifetime. On the related grounds of supporting enquiry into recent critical thought and illuminating the relatively hostile theoretical environment in which Auden worked, this introduction will focus on his three main contemporaries, New Criticism, Freudianism and Marxism.

## Auden's theoretical foundations

Had he never written a single poem or play, Auden would still be a renowned critic, though of world culture more than English literature. In addition to his poetic genius, he possessed a synoptic intelligence that could almost instantly visualise the system of codes which shaped a work, or, to borrow his term from *New Year Letter*, its paradigm. A threshold concept, 'paradigm' articulates a general theory of understanding-as-interpretation into the more immediate cultural frameworks which humans rely upon to assemble raw data into meaning. Among its tasks, a paradigm selects which elements in the field of experience must be noticed or ignored; which names must be revered or despised; which organising patterns must be accepted or refused; and which narratives must be believed or condemned. Modern philosophical, scientific and political thought offers a rich array of differing enquiries into the nature of paradigms. The origins of Auden's cultural theory belong to an intellectual tradition that includes Kant's categories of the understanding, Marx's superstructure, Heidegger's *Dasein*, Gramsci's hegemony, Saussure and Lévi-Strauss's *langue*, Foucault's *épistéme*, Raymond Williams's dominant discourse and Fredric Jameson's political unconscious.

A brief guide to the interpretative systems that most interested Auden could simply thumb through his essays for the charts, diagrams, lists, headings or outlines which resemble the notes of an architect or engineer. In an early self-parody, the 'Journal of an Airman', he borrowed a cartoon device, heuristic graffiti, to caricature his protagonist's attempts to visualise 'the mechanism of the trap' (*EA*, p. 335), the assemblage of codes that construct his world. A more serious version of these can be found in Auden's schemata for political ideologies such as liberalism, communism, nationalism, fascism and institutional Christianity. Sometimes he took a synecdochical approach and listed only a few elements. If necessary, though, he drew elaborate maps. The encyclopedic chart in 'Psychology and Art To-Day' includes the categories of First Cause, World View, End of Life, Means of Realization, Personal Motives, Mark of Success, Worst Sinner, Scientific Method, Power Sources, Manufacturing Materials, Social Organization, Economic System, and Political Structure (*EA*, p. 338). Significantly, no two of these analytical devices are identical. Intellectual throw-aways, they are meant only as aids to understanding the invisible systems which ensnare the passive 'man-in-the-street' (*EA*, p. 395), who accepts whatever prescribed truths he is fed.

Had Auden mapped one of his own poems, 'In Praise of Limestone', it might resemble figure 11.1.

As the column under 'Romantic hero' indicates, Auden found elements in the paradigm of Romanticism which prefigured the nihilistic totalitarianisms of his own age. Indeed, one of the consistent concerns of his criticism, from the 1929 journal to *The Dyer's Hand*, is to resist if not overcome the cultural aftermath of Romanticism and its many descendants. But a few provisos are essential. Auden considered Romanticism one of several contributory factors to the politics of despair, not the main cause. He further believed that while

|  | Prehistoric tribe | Romantic hero | Modern American poet* |
|---|---|---|---|
| Supreme being | skittish deity with well-deserved inferiority complex | the void, unrealised possibility | the intricate workings of one's own mind |
| Nature | schizophrenic mood swings | treacherous garden vs. absolving sea | obtuse, insipid, tedious external reality |
| Primary commandment | to be overawed by deity | to reject the finite | to reject first impressions |
| Main ritual | self-abasement before enraged and highly incompetent god | the quest for oblivion | to write poetry that transforms the literal into brilliant figurations (e.g. metaphor) |
| Greatest success | anonymous conformity | annihilation of self, along with anyone else who is handy | replace myth of external reality with anti-myth of animate, pleasurable, ever-changing imaginings |
| Greatest fear | any ability or talent that might threaten the deity | ordinariness | objectivity |
| Worst sinner | individualist | a happy person | empiricist, sceptic |
| Ideal society | trembling on edge of extinction | Führer and expendable herd | poet surrounded by his tragically short-lived creations |

*I am indebted to Edward Mendelson for the suggestion that it is probably Wallace Stevens.

Figure 11.1. 'In Praise of Limestone': a diagrammatic representation.

literature could expose and critique a society's leading paradigms, it did not *directly* 're-enter history as an effective agent' (*EA*, p. 393). Lastly, he readily distinguished a work's aesthetic merit from the worth of its ideas. As his anti-polemical polemic 'The Public v. the Late Mr William Butler Yeats' illustrates, a brilliant poet might nonetheless espouse facile or absurd beliefs. Other instances would be Shelley, Tennyson and, as 'In Memory of W. B. Yeats' proposes, Kipling and Paul Claudel.

Auden's respect for the power of environment and culture led him to trace Romanticism's material source to the ironic consequences of the Industrial Revolution. Breakthroughs in technology and science had potentially at least freed humans from back-breaking labour and bondage to the land. But they also increased inequalities of wealth, destroyed traditional communities, concentrated populations in slums and left most people alienated from their work, one another and themselves. Romanticism attempted to make this situation tolerable to an ambivalent middle class. 'With the increase in wealth appeared a new class who had independent incomes from dividends, and whose lives felt neither the economic pressure of the wage-earner nor the burden of responsibility of the landlord' (*EA*, p. 365). While alarmed by squalor, disease and child labour, they had no wish to give up their rentier's profits and leisurely life-style. Hence they needed a paradigm to reconstruct the social scene in a way that distracted them from their angst but otherwise left things unchanged. Romanticism achieved this by sending its new hero, the artistic genius, into the 'relatively unexplored field' of his 'private world' (*EA*, p. 366). Despite occasional revolutionary aspirations, it diverted attention from actual living and working conditions, and grew beguiled instead with the labyrinth of its one-sided version of human identity. In Auden's somewhat technical revision of Coleridge's Primary and Secondary Imaginations, Romanticism tried to restrict its focus to the predicate ego (the awareness of possibility), at the expense of the subject self (the awareness of a complex personality living with others in a material environment). But, to adapt a metaphor from 'The Ancient Mariner', a person might as easily outrun his own shadow. Eventually the flight from tedious self to hollowed ego, corrupt city to purifying sea, must end in failure or annihilation.

Having framed the problem of the disaffected individual in a way that made it insoluble, Romanticism then designated the resulting condition as the authentic human lot. Its heroes had to be in mourning, embittered, guilt-ridden, cursed, filled with rage or bent on revenge, but above all, isolated from a contemptible society. As a respite from its mandatory torments, Auden noted, Romanticism elevated fantasy to the new status of vision: Wordsworth's nature, Mallarmé's *poésie pure*, Shelley's utopia, Baudelaire and Hölderlin's innocent origins (*EA*, p. 366). When reversed, its idealisations turned into the paranoia that drives Melville's Ahab to defy the demonic universe created by his tortuous misreading of the whale, as examined in *The Enchafèd Flood*.

## New Criticism

A distant child of the French Symbolists, New Criticism began with the influence of T. S. Eliot on a small group of American poets and critics, and grew into the most widely accepted critical orthodoxy of the twentieth century. Much of its success stems from an efficient division of labour between its theorists, the academics William Wimsatt, Monroe Beardsley and Cleanth

Brooks; and its textual critics, many of whom were gifted poets, John Crowe Ransom, Allen Tate and Robert Penn Warren. The theorists have earned the lion's share of the attention by shrewdly portraying their claims as disproofs of logical fallacies. That move let them shield their own positions behind a bristling defence of pre-emptive refutations. Because New Criticism venerated Eliot's preference for the verbal and tonal ironies of Metaphysical poetry, it is often mistaken for an anti-Romantic movement. Yet from the perspective of Auden's cultural critique, its debt to the late Romanticism of the French Symbolists becomes more apparent.

The best known and least observed of New Criticism's doctrines, the intentional fallacy, holds that a poem's interpretation must not be fixated on reconstructing from a text the personal intentions of a specific individual. The intentional fallacy's near relative, the biographical fallacy, argues the separate point that the speaker of a poem must not be confused with the author. Whereas the inward-looking intentional fallacy protects a poem's meaning from being restricted to a particular intention on the part of its author, the outwardly focused biographical fallacy frees meaning from being determined by a particular set of events in that author's life. Both offer valuable correctives. The concept of 'intention' derives from communication theory, and if narrowly construed can require that a poem, like an ordinary speech act, must be guided by a single, clear idea. Auden certainly agreed that poetry must not be reduced to some message or meaning, nor did he dispute that interpretation must not be confined to a recitation of events from an author's life and times. In his 'Introduction' to *The Poet's Tongue* (p. v), he noted that reading poetry requires 'exactly the opposite kind of mental effort' from understanding ordinary uses of language. He went on to describe the 'aura of suggestion' that surrounds the words of a poem in a way that anticipates deconstruction's *différance*, or continuous deferral of signifieds (meanings) into chains of signifiers (words).

Yet unless carefully applied, both the intentional and biographical fallacies can lead to unnecessary restrictions. The biographical fallacy sets up a binary (determinism/freedom) which potentially severs a text from the author's historical situation, even when that situation functions as a source of pressure to be resisted. This unhelpful and unnecessary revocation too closely mimics the Romantic disregard for social conditions and tacitly sympathises with a retreat into some 'ideal order', akin to the one Eliot ordains in 'Tradition and the Individual Talent'. The intentional fallacy implies a similar misstep in that its binary (intention/ambiguity) also oversimplifies a plurality. A poem must encompass the varied intentions of its author, poetic persona, audiences or even, if 'intention' can be attributed to non-individual agents, its culture, literary traditions and linguistic medium. Each is composed of varied and often unconscious impulses which are too numerous, too contradictory and too unstable to be known in full.

New Criticism's long ascendancy, disdain for history, hostility to other theories and patriarchal self-righteousness persisted through the mid-century decades that witnessed the Second World War, the atom bombs dropped on Japan, the Nuremberg Trials, the McCarthy hearings and the Civil Rights march on Selma. Its fall from grace during the cultural upheavals of the late 1960s ended what many still consider an era of intellectual tyranny. It currently endures a penitential afterlife, and considerable value, as the sacrificial object of an academic bonding ritual in which it plays the one safely impugnable critical approach. But New Criticism's techniques of close reading, the invention of its poets rather than its theorists, can be applied independently, or even in opposition, to its overtly restrictive doctrines. For proof-text one can take any Auden poem and develop the tension between its evident statement and the complexities introduced by its poetic uses of language. The Audenesque (or post-New Critical) objective, however, is not to resolve that tension into a moralised paradox, but to illustrate how its complexity brings into focus a particular paradigm's construction of a world.

Like many of Auden's characters, the speaker of 'On This Island' seems to spring from nowhere, though he actually belongs to a well-established tradition, the *genius loci* or spirit of the place. His monologue insinuates a prior narrative in which his audience is cast as quest heroes who have arrived at a crucial turning point. The setting's chalk cliffs, harbour and distant ships suggest Dover. As if the travellers had hit a trip wire on the bluffs overlooking the sea, the *genius loci*'s voice begins to warn of dangers ahead. But Auden replaces the traditional figure of guide and helper with its Romantic counterpart, the artist as quest hero. Because this new protagonist must substitute a world of his own making for any further explorations by the audience, the expected helper turns into a boundary guardian. He begins by neutralising the England of 1935 to 'this island', archetype of a private world. He ends by contemplating the clouds' aimless drift of pure possibility.

Unlike Auden, who possessed a detailed knowledge of character codes, this particular dramatic speaker shows little understanding of the directives which compel his behaviour. One requires his total control of the audience. Accordingly, he orders them where to stand, when to listen, what to notice and how to name it. Another requires him to empty himself of anything that might curb an infinite potential. Strictly speaking, he is not a character at all but only a voice, anonymous, invisible, disembodied, lacking a past and without social moorings. This phantom-entity projects an equally spectral audience, which has no purpose except to listen and no existence outside the moment of his utterance. His transcendent aspirations tolerate only the hollowed-out shell of a timeless world. History disappears when the ships and artefacts that might date the scene are left vague enough to include any era from neolithic to modern times.

While New Criticism generally turns poetic complexity against rhetorical statement, its master tropes of tone, irony, ambiguity and metaphor can also be brought to bear on the paradigm that guides a poem's rhetoric. We have seen how Romantic codes oblige the speaker to suppress his human attributes, in pursuit of an ideal of pure possibility. But the language refuses to play along. It is difficult to arrange words into syntax without producing a tone of some kind. (Tone includes the range of a speaker's attitudes to audience, topic, language and self.) Since tone enables inferences about character, so by extension must the syntax-dependent actions of writing and speaking. In the first stanza of 'On This Island', the clustered imperatives, direct but generalised address, rapid pace and clipped rhythms intone the features of a concrete personality. Auden creates a character who keeps at a safe distance, doubts the authority he usurps and fears his audience. It is also very difficult to avoid variations in tone, which in turn reveal developments in character. In the last stanza, the optative mood, relaxed pace and more variable stress disclose a character who has lost sight of his original intent, forgotten his audience and fallen captive to his own meditation. Development, however, requires a motivating force which, because the speaker has banished nearly everything else from his world, most likely originates in his language. The audience can only guess what so enthralls him. But more important than any answers is that in prompting this speculation, the poem introduces an ambiguity, which in turn shifts control of its meaning from the intentions of the speaker to the interpretations of his audience. Like the shingle at the cliff's base, the words keep rushing back to the humanity the speaker would forsake. 'Swaying sound' mimes the way language rhythms alternately mystify and set in motion. 'Ships' and 'errands' presuppose communities and obligations, mirrors show the necessity of rehearsing social roles. Ironically, the instrument of the speaker's power and control, his command of language, becomes his undoing. The poem's personifications animate the words with an energy of their own. Light leaps and discovers, tides pluck and knock, ledges oppose, shingles scramble, ships run errands, a view enters like an actor and clouds saunter. Each verb initiates numerous sequels by transforming the now humanised words into characters awaiting a future which the speaker cannot control.

## Freud and psychological theory

Auden found his earliest ally in Freudian psychology. The two shared a common opponent, in the cultural manipulation of individuals to act against their own interests, and a common strategy, 'to dissipate a reaction by becoming conscious of it' (*EA*, p. 318). ('Reaction' here means any automatic response or unreflective behaviour.) Elsewhere he added that psychology and poetry share a common mood, disillusionment, and a common hope, that individuals can become more free and thus more human by discovering the hidden forces that rule them without their knowledge or consent. But Auden also detected, though less in Freud's writings than in popular psychology, traces of Romantic isolation and nihilism. By concentrating on personal neurosis, while neglecting its social contexts beyond the family, psychology fashions a world from private experience. Even though it views this world as pathologically distorted by repression, it has little interest in the underlying cultural problems that require and enforce those distortions. To take Auden's example, psychology's theoretical bias permits it to study the complexes of the clinging child, but not the economic circumstances and political beliefs that produced his doting mother (*EA*, p. 352). Freud's theory of the death-wish as the basis of desire particularly irked Auden, who followed Dante in believing that the deepest human motive is creative joy (*EA*, p. 345). Both the 'romantic Death' of *Spain* and the sinister oceanic voice of 'In Praise of Limestone' link the death-wish to Romanticism's doomed quests and blighted heroes. But Auden reserved his harshest criticisms for the judgemental and thus normalising tendencies of common psychiatric practices, which he carefully distinguished from Freud's analytical methods. As the parodically self-resignifying cure-seeker of the early couplet-sonnet 'Petition' illustrates, Auden quickly realised how the pretext of healing neurosis could be turned into an excuse for mutilating individuality.

Although Auden extended psychology's theoretical field to include history and culture, he retained much of Freud's topography of the self. Like the neurotic individual, a society can be torn by opposing codes of knowledge, value, authority, law, duty and purpose. In a traditional or closed culture, a single system of codes can prevail indefinitely. But as societies become more diverse in their living and working conditions, they develop the equivalent of a cultural unconscious. Rival or alternative discourses begin to emerge which threaten the official versions of reality. While rules and punishments can keep sceptics and blasphemers in check for a while, coercion is not always feasible on a large scale. So a dominant discourse eventually develops effective mechanisms of repression. These have the task of keeping would-be competitors out of sight, or if that fails, construing them into whatever the dominant powers want to designate as criminal or unthinkable. Unfortunately, the new technologies of the later Industrial Revolution enabled journalism, radio and television to become irresistibly efficient in marketing these distortions. Few would expect the quiet voice of poetry to surpass the collective din. But were the participants in Freud's analytical model transposed from the therapist to the literary work, and from the personal to the cultural unconscious, then poetry could conceivably serve as an instrument of social critique. Its objective would be to help unveil and thus diminish the resources of cultural repression.

Auden's cryptic revision of an Anglo-Saxon poem, 'The Wanderer', offers a likely site for such an adaptation of Freud's clinical practices. The lucid uncanniness of its image-driven development bears the stamp of misrepresented desire. Yet the poem's provenance at the very beginnings of English literature, particularly when linked to its early religious function as an allegory of the soul, also gives it a broad cultural reference. Unlike the speaker of 'On This Island', a hero-visionary who becomes a threshold guardian, the dramatic monologist of 'The Wanderer' suggests Auden's account of a different archetype, Coleridge's Ancient Mariner, or the accursed returnee (*DH*, p. 24). Having survived the fatal journey and suffered its forbidden knowledge, he must thereafter accost the unsuspecting and rehearse his warning fable. Like Coleridge's character, Auden's persona has both individual dimension and symbolic scope. He personally assumes the role of social superego by attempting to stifle and abnormalise resistance from the cultural unconscious. Repression often relies on reverse-logics which, according to 'the law of the negation of the negation' (*EA*, p. 347), faithfully mirror what they would conceal. The dramatic speaker, for example, piles up rationales for why no one should follow in his path. He tells of a malevolent doom that afflicts the unlucky. Out they go on their futile journey, crossing into hostile lands and risking capture or death, but only to bring vengeance and shame on those left behind.

Much like an analyst, the language of a poem, which for present purposes should be thought of as an agent independent of its speaker, can use misemphasis, feigned solemnity and bare-faced lies to expose structural patterns of repression. Auden organises 'The Wanderer' around a series of well-marked but unstable inversions. The need for so many excuses (plural/singular) shows dissident urges coalescing (strength/weakness) in what becomes a logical motif. The sterility of rock-face, sea and wasteland (to take one meaning of 'fell') distorts the real promise of renewal and creativity (life/death). The ill-suited details of spring's light-seeking flowers, clement weather and newly returning landscapes assume a logic of conscious/unconscious which, when righted, tells of emergent impulses from the oblivion of nature. Were anyone to risk the unknown, the oppositions individual/group and growth/regression would condemn them to a mindless collective, figured in Auden's purposely ludicrous kenning, 'Houses for fishes' and the nameless bird flocks. The even more aggressive reversals, self/other and reward/punishment, project the speaker's forbidden desires on to others who can be punished in his stead, the 'stranger to strangers', the shocked eavesdropper and the tiger-ambushed wretch. Some inversions are emotional rather than cognitive. The love of home forges the bars of a terrible prison. The plaintive petition disguises a bitter curse. In the most telling reversal of all, an initially distant and impersonal 'Doom' eventually fuses into the thunderbolts of a vindictive deity Auden borrowed from Hardy and Dr Johnson (*EF*, p. 52). But this ominous development actually rephrases the poem's paradoxical theme, that repression intensifies the resistance it seeks to vanquish.

The myth and archetype criticism of Freudian psychology's early schismatic, Carl Jung, also influenced Auden's thinking, but as a means of differentiation. Jung's primary concept, the collective unconscious, promotes a quasi-religious faith in the existence of a universal archive that contains the essential narratives and images of all cultures and indeed, of every personality. Although Auden found Jung's system useful in his criticism, he rejected its cross-cultural and anti-historical pretensions. Through his poetry he brought archetypes into human time by showing how they become unrecognisable from their earlier versions as a result of social adaptation, as, for example, when the Roman goddess becomes a demented boys-school nurse in 'Venus Will Now Say a Few Words'; or by suggesting that archetypal characters' prior roles leave them ill-suited to modern life, as when Thetis' fond expectations for 'The Shield of Achilles' are dashed by Hephaestos' Capra-like techniques of photo-journalism.

Apart from his doctrine of the collective unconscious, however, Jung's secondary claims about the process of individuation appealed to Auden. Individuation reconstructs Romanticism's fragmented self as a problem, not a privileged condition. But while Auden valued the struggle towards individuation, he thought its goal unattainable and, even were it reached, without social impact. In *The Age of Anxiety*, the characters Malin, Emble, Rosetta and Quant, in part allegorical figures for Jung's faculties of reason, sensation, feeling and intuition, embark on a post-Romantic quest to overcome the solitude and emptiness of modern life. However, Auden puts their Jungian dream-journey immediately after 'The Seven Stages', Malin's account of human disappointment and failure. As the stage directions put it, this sequence contextualises their prior efforts as 'one long flight' from the tougher world of New York in wartime.

Still, Auden did write one of the great examples of modern myth criticism, *The Enchafèd Flood*. Its three lectures anatomise Romanticism into opposing archetypes of quest destination (sea and desert), modes of truth (stone and shell) and types of hero (Ishmael and Don Quixote). But this gathering of so much nineteenth-century English, American and European literature within the span of a few contraries enacts a silent indictment. Unlike Jung, who thought a single master-plot could hold the secret of life, Auden regarded the cohesive structures of myth as necessary to a culture's early development, but later becoming a dangerous force. To counter the culturally compelled signifieds of modern myth, Auden turned to an antithetical narrative form, the parable. By disconnecting its concrete imagery from any compulsory references, a parable strongly motivates an audience's efforts at interpretation yet offers them little guidance. 'You must never tell people what to do – only tell them particular stories of particular people with whom they may voluntarily identify themselves, and from which they may voluntarily draw conclusions' (*EA*, p. 347). The Jungian critic Northrop Frye fitted myth and genre into a single grand scheme, but Auden set one against the other. The poet uses the manifest, even intrusive nature of literary form to expose and target the concealed paradigms of culture. As with shock therapy, the oddities of versification, figure, diction, rhetorical context, point of view, characteristic problems, permissible solutions and a host of other genre devices can startle and disorient readers. The aim is to prod them into discovering the surreptitious metaphors and narratives which, without their knowledge or consent, purport to reveal a final and comprehensive reality. Always attentive to readers who were not professional critics, Auden often chose titles that specified the relevant genre: ode, legend, epitaph, memorial, nursery rhyme, letter, duet, eclogue, bucolic, nocturne, marginalia, prologue, doggerel, lullaby. This is not mere traditionalism or antiquarianism, however, but a design to break the trance of an unquestioning passivity.

## Marxism and Brecht

Auden was not taken in by the utopian promises of Communism, unlike many English and American intellectuals during an age of relative innocence, before the revelation of Stalin's mass murders. But he did find in Marxist social theory an ally against Romanticism, one which addressed many of the problems ignored by psychology. Marxism's forthright critique of economy-driven injustices provided him with something better than vision or prophecy, a coherent explanation of why modern culture would fail to achieve a human community. To the discomfort of some churchmen, Auden traced parallels between Marxist ideals and the Gospels' theme of an 'absolute equality in value of every individual, and the evil of all State restraint' (*EA*, p. 353). Although one of his best known lines accepts 'guilt in the fact of murder' (the revised 'Spain 1937') that phrase supports the theory of a just war which allows self-defence if attacked, a position defended by both Aquinas and Augustine. It does not advocate a revolutionary's faith in violence as the only hope of sweeping away social formations too corrupt to reform themselves. Yet unlike its social critique, Marxism's literary theory is absent from Auden's writings, at least in the thirties versions now sniffily labelled as 'vulgar Marxism'. Given the rise of fascism and its virulently nationalist and racist propaganda and practices, it is understandable that some writers would advocate subordinating art to ideological ends. Nonetheless, Auden steadfastly rejected any suggestion that poetry should champion some cause. Whereas a propagandist must conceal the contradictions of his pet paradigm, the poet must expose precisely such discontinuities, a task that endears him to few true believers.

Although Auden left few doubts concerning his poetic intentions, he said little about how to put them into practice. Aside from a few tantalising passages about parable art, his remarks on poetic ways and means typically explore the complex effects of versification. This relative silence has led Auden's critics to his contemporary, Bertolt Brecht, because the German playwright specifically designed his stagecraft to unmask cultural indoctrination. The hope is that these dramatic practices might offer parallels to Auden's poetic strategies. Brecht drew his primary inspiration from the Marxist tenet that social economies evolve a superstructure (intellectual systems such as history, religion, education, etc.) whose collective versions of truth justify the concentration of wealth and power in a ruling class. To implement his dramatic critique of the slanted reality produced by these systems, Brecht developed the Russian Formalist Viktor Shklovsky's concept of *ostranenie* or defamiliarisation into the distinctive techniques of his *Verfremdungseffekt*, or alienation effect.

Unfortunately, the word 'effect' indicates a result rather than a process. The alienation Brecht had in mind consists of ushering an audience from its habitual mystification into the phases of insight, acquisition, and transference. People arrive at the theatre well entrenched within a largely unnoticed because already familiar assemblage of beliefs and perceptions. The alienation effect uses an array of strategies to undermine this conditioning. It satirises the hypocrisies and contradictions of accepted truths. It reveals the sly beneficiaries of pious and solemn doctrines. But mainly, it dispels the illusion of a pristine, external or natural reality by turning the world of the play, which must be brought into being through a complicated apparatus that controls how the audience sees each set, into an analogy for the similarly contrived worlds outside the theatre. Brecht hoped that the audience's shift from naïvely accepting the truth of a stage scene to noticing the intrusive devices needed to create that impression, could then be transferred to the harder task of tracing the codes and components of a paradigm in the world at large.

Auden was probably paraphrasing Brecht when he remarked that if poetry does have an external purpose, it is 'to disenchant and disintoxicate' (*DH*, p. 27). But whatever an artist's objectives, his tactics must fit the specific aesthetic form. Auden's most evident parallels with Brecht occur in his manipulation of dramatic genres. Brecht designed his songs to deflate sentimentality and nostalgia by counterpointing the topic with an inappropriate rhythm. The chaplain in *Mother Courage* recites the hideous details of a crucifixion, but in the cadence of a nursery rhyme. Similarly, Auden's 'Heavy Date' glosses the weighty topics of random thinking, Malinowski's matrilineal cultures and Spinoza's *amor intellectualis*, but in a clunky trochaic whose comic rhymes are made even more prominent by the trimeter beat and abcdabcd octaves. A good actor, however, can recapture a sense of realism with an impassioned performance and powerful voice, despite a poor or non-existent set. To counter such intensity, Brecht encouraged his actors to overplay or otherwise distance themselves from their characters. In a parallel move, Auden frequently undermined his speakers by having them begin cogently enough, but then lapse into camp, which substitutes comic derivation for Romantic originality. The medley of high-sincerity genres in *The Orators* dramatises a number of these self-imploding speakers: the hurried dignitary at a prize-day, paranoid cult leader, surrealist prelate, lucidly mad political pamphleteer and stomach-turning confessee. Other works fashion purposely unsympathetic, overbearing or preposterous personae designed to arouse resistance. Relevant here are the oddly compelling yet insidious voices of 'The Watershed', 'Venus Will Now Say a Few Words', section III of 'The Witnesses', and 'Lady Weeping at the Crossroads'. These figures later evolve into the gentle ironists of 'Atlantis', 'In Praise of Limestone', and 'Dame Kind'.

But it is also possible to trace Brechtian parallels in Auden's use of non-dramatic and lyrical genres. As suggested above, Brecht favoured a harsh lighting which exposed the hasty carpentry and clumsy painting of the sets. Poems too have atmospheric effects and scene changes, but to reveal the artifice needed to construct context Auden used a technique of mimetic substitution. He replaced the description of a subject with a summary of the norms often found in its representation. 'Fish in the unruffled lakes' does not depict a scene so much as illustrate how to encode various scenic effects: teeming life (instead of portraying the outlines of the fish, just show their colours); perfect beauty (have swans in flight); innocent strength (put a lion, alone, in a grove); and time's inescapable destruction (select the instant when a wave collapses into itself).

Yet a poet's repertoire of disenchantment must also include resources which, though not beyond a playwright's reach, are more at home in works principally designed to sustain multiple rereadings rather than propel a live performance. If studied with care, these more intricate tactics of achieving disillusionment hold the promise of a new field for Auden studies. As a case in point, the evident polemic of *Spain* strikes many as a betrayal of the poet's repeated warnings against works of art having a 'message'. But the poem can also be approached as a dialectic of representation and syntax which effectively disclaims a precondition for absolutist paradigms, whether on the right or left, namely a master narrative. To identify his discursive target, Auden borrows a device from the religious oratorio, a petitionary chorus. The voices of the poor yearn for some myth of inevitable progress to exonerate them from responsibility for their lives. But yearning turns to cynicism in the subsequent antiphon, where the nations supply the desired myth with a rearward march from Athenian democracy to the 'city state of the sponge'.

Having framed the problem, Auden responds with techniques that draw readers into a game of designing their own myths of history, or if that fails, then at least recognising how others do it. The six 'Yesterday' stanzas set aside chronology for an unsequenced hodgepodge of skills such as taming horses, navigating trade routes or feuding about theology, and inventions such as the abacus, prehistoric megaliths, filing systems or weirdly chiselled rain-spouts. Unlike a history which features specific agents and events, or a political theory which illustrates guiding ideas, Auden uses repeated nominalisations to eliminate people from the picture, freezing the action of a verb into the static condition of a noun. Instead of medieval masons who build cathedrals, there is 'the carving of angels'. Misogynist celibates disappear into their propaganda weapon, the 'Sabbath of Witches'. By cutting the expected narrative into a congeries of changeless and dehumanised states, the nominalisations foster an opposing imaginative impulse, somewhat like the syntactic equivalent of an after-image. Each abstracted vignette demands a plot to give it context, conflict, characters and conclusion. Yet each one might also be developed in myriad ways. Thus the position that would otherwise be occupied by subject and verb, a controlling narrative, yields to a vast catalogue of attendant tales, as if Auden the schoolmaster had listed writing topics for a class: abandoned folk gods, tracks across colonial deserts, adored madmen, each addition dissecting the premise of a definitive history into countless points of view.

Auden's literary theory guides his poetic practice, and together they work to achieve an actual social result. There can be little understanding of one without the other. In all his writing, he sought to encourage a broadly applicable recognition and wariness of the interpretative paradigms that would deny individual freedom. 'What does the song hope for?' asks the poem 'Orpheus'. However criticism replies, it must fairly acknowledge the question.

# 12

JOHN LUCAS

# Auden's politics: power, authority and the individual

In one of his very last poems, 'A Thanksgiving', Auden directed a wry backward glance over his life, for each stage of which, so he claimed, he chose to be directed by different masters. At first, when moor and woodland were sacred, Hardy, Edward Thomas and Frost were to hand. Once love struck in, Yeats and Graves proved a help. Then, without warning, 'the whole / Economy suddenly crumbled: / there, to instruct me, was Brecht'. And when Hitler and Stalin did 'hair-raising things', Kierkegaard, Charles Williams and C. S. Lewis 'guided me back to belief'. This necessarily concertinas a wide stretch of years. More interestingly, it avoids mention of the name that, during the period of the crumbling economy, meant at least as much to Auden as Brecht did – Karl Marx. This is not to say that Auden was ever a wholly committed Marxist. Though in 1932 he wrote a poem called, on first publication, 'A Communist to Others',[1] he never joined the Communist Party of Great Britain, nor did he waste time on flat, ephemeral pamphlets or boring meetings. Nevertheless, during the 1930s he made much use of Marx's ideas, as he admits in *New Year Letter*, where at one point he notes that 'We hoped; we waited for the day / The State would wither clean away, / Expecting the Millennium / That theory promised us would come. / It didn't.' Stan Smith has noted that the 'abrupt reversal on the enjambment enacts the dialectical process, setting up an antithesis of theory and event' (Smith, p. 135). This is not therefore so much a dismissal of Marx as a recognition that his theory is itself part of the dialectical process in which 'we' believe.

That Auden came eventually to turn his back on Marx is not to be doubted, even if he was never entirely able to rid himself of a manner of arguing, a way of thinking, that took for granted the complex engagement of individual with, in the loosest sense of the word, history. There is no space here to track the changes in Auden's political thinking throughout the course of his writing life. This has been ably done by Smith and others. My aim is more modest. It is to speculate on the extent to which Auden retained a curiosity about the nature of power and authority, how he saw these as affecting or expressed through *communitas*, and what this means for the individual.

To use this word at all may seem to beg the question. Isn't individuality subsumed into the collective 'we' of *New Year Letter*? And surely anyone at all committed to Marxist thinking would be sceptical of liberal claims to the integral selfhood which individuality implies? Yes and no. Auden has been accused of changing ideas as often as other men changed hats, as though he didn't really believe in anything, or was, in Tom Paulin's words, fascinated by politics and psychology as part of a 'voracious quest that would satisfy him long enough to write a poem. Once the poem was written he either jettisoned the structure or tacked on a new idea.'[2] There is some truth in this, but I don't necessarily see it as implying any dilettantism on Auden's part. 'What daffodils were for Wordsworth, death is for me', Philip Larkin reportedly said. Cross out 'death' and insert 'ideas' and you have the key to Auden's inspiration. And this is so whether he is fox or hedgehog, or playing, as at different times he does, Prospero or Ariel.

Play is crucial. In England there is a long tradition, which comes from Nonconformity, of identifying radicalism with an unremitting seriousness in which there is precious little room for fun. But Auden belongs to a rival tradition, one characterised by its first great spokesman as that spirit of 'opposition' for which he said he was born. Such opposition is inseparable from an *élan* endlessly at the service of what might be called a principle of delight. 'Letter to Lord Byron' is Auden's act of homage to his true forebear. As he says at the opening of Part III, 'I like your muse because she's gay and witty', and Byron himself can be praised as 'a good townee, / Neither a preacher, ninny, bore, nor Brownie'. The adroit, comic rhyme both is and testifies to delight.

Those words were written in August 1936, at precisely the moment when Franco's Falangist troops began a war against Spain's democratically elected government. Ten years earlier, the undergraduate Auden had, like many of his fellow students, lent a hand at the time of the General Strike. Nearly all those volunteers chose to help the Conservative government by acting as police-men or by driving buses. Auden however decided to support the strikers. According to Humphrey Carpenter, Auden's decision was influenced by his friend David Ayerst, who was Chairman of the Oxford University Labour Club, 'and had nothing to do with any political sympathies' (Carpenter, p. 52). To substantiate this, Carpenter refers to Auden's review of Evelyn Waugh's *Autobiography*, in which he recalls that he volunteered to drive a car for the TUC and that on one occasion he was required to deliver R. H. Tawney to Mecklenburgh Square. As a cousin married to a stockbroker lived nearby, Auden invited himself to her house for lunch. They were just sitting down when the husband discovered that, far from being a special constable, his wife's cousin was working for the other side. 'Whereupon, to my utter astonishment, he ordered me out of his house. It had never occurred to me that anybody took the General Strike seriously' (*F&A*, p. 514).

Although these words were written in 1965, nearly forty years after the events to which they refer, I am not about to accuse Auden of revising history. Samuel Hynes quotes Isherwood's recollection of the Strike as the opportunity for a 'tremendous upper-middle class lark', and MacNeice's as 'the occasion for a spree'.[3] On the other hand, we know that Auden's fellow undergraduate Norman Cameron was outraged by the assumption that he would be in favour of strike-breaking. According to A. J. P. Taylor, with whom Cameron had gone to help the strikers in Preston, When 'a very superior person called the strikers "poor, ignorant people"', Cameron stood very tall: '"You little shit! You bloody little prig! Those people" – and his voice roared over Preston – "are worth a thousand of you."'[4] It is likely that Auden's experience at Mecklenburgh Square helped him to realise how deep his opposition to the world of respectability ran. It is worth noting that in the same year, 1926, he became openly opposed to his mother's bourgeois values. Hence her letter to an Oxford friend in which she complains of her son that 'I cannot help feeling that self-sacrifice, self-discipline (self-control even), are looked upon with scorn' (Carpenter, p. 50). 'Be happy and you will be good', Auden was shortly to insist was the true path: in Blake's words, 'Damn braces, bless relaxes'.

'Paid on Both Sides' (1928) is, in part at least, the product of Auden's recognition that the braces were worn by all those people and institutions he had grown up to know as Authority. It is here that an emerging politics first shows itself. There are, for instance, Auden's lampoons of Authority's different voices; more significantly, perhaps, there is the choice of form that he adopts and then adapts for his own purposes. 'Paid on Both Sides' he calls 'A Charade', and its abrupt switches of style, of fragmented narratives, of wide-ranging allusiveness, between them provide a mélange, or, it might be more accurate to say, a collagist work which is radically modernist in denying to any voice or manner true, as opposed to assumed, authority. None of these voices is reliable. The mockery of those certainties voiced by John Nower in his speech about not betraying the dead – 'Can we be deaf to the simple eloquence of [their graves'] inscriptions' – reminds us that, in Richard Wilbur's words, Auden, like others of his generation, felt that 'a whole lot of old guys had sent a lot of young guys off to die for nothing'.[5]

Old guys, old style. The new styles of architecture implicit in 'Paid on Both Sides' are as radically anti-realistic as the last section of Sylvia Townsend

Warner's novel, *Lolly Willowes* (1926), in which, as the heroine breaks away from the stultifying bourgeois containments of family life, the novel's register switches from drawing-room realism to lively fantasy. The same holds true of Edgell Rickword's verse masque, 'The Happy New Year', which appeared in his 1928 collection, *Invocations to Angels and the Happy New Year*. Rickword's masque opens as a pastiche of received poetic style and ends with the phantasmagoric vision of a city of death. The use of masque makes evident his intent to connect emergent political and social energies with new, or newly revived, cultural forms.[6]

In invoking the names of Townsend Warner and Rickword in the context of Auden's early work I have no wish to argue for influence. The point is rather that for all these writers, radical political thinking goes hand-in-hand with consideration of formal radicalism. Hence, Auden's ceaseless ranging among forms and poetic mannerisms. That this regularly required or at least encouraged an opportunism is obvious. But unlike many commentators I see nothing in this that needs to be defended. There has been much wrangling over a poem that Auden came to call '1929', although it is usually referred to by its opening line 'It was Easter as I walked in the public gardens', and when it appeared in *Poems* (1930) it was simply numbered 'XXIV'. The poem has been discussed at some length by Michael Kilby and I don't intend to rehearse here either his argument or those of such commentators as Edward Mendelson, John Fuller and Stan Smith, with whom he takes issue. All four recognise that between sections I and II, written in April and May, 1929, and III and IV, written in August and October, there is a noticeable switch of meaning. My contention is that Auden is content with this switch. He *means* it. Easter is at once the time of death and rebirth. The last section begins, 'It is time for the destruction of error.' Kilby refers to John xii. 24. 'Except a corn of wheat fall into the ground and die, it abideth alone: but if it die, it bringeth forth much fruit.' It doesn't really matter whether we interpret this death and rebirth in terms of the dialectic of history or, more specifically, as the entropic declension of the 'old guys'; what does, is the poem's openness to new life, even if that requires 'The old gang to be forgotten in the spring'. Kilby sees the closing lines of the poem as embodying a perception 'that events are entirely governed by historical inevitability, imperturbable in the face of religion'.[7] Well, yes, but while death and rebirth are inevitable, and declare history's cyclic pattern, the *nature* of what is born is nevertheless unpredictable, and testifies to history as change.

For an older generation change was bound to be for the worse. It would usher in hooded hordes, the rough beast itself. What makes the young Auden so exhilarating a poet is his readiness to turn doom back on its prophets. As with the artist James Boswell's visionary drawings of 1933 entitled

*The Fall of London,* there is an unmissable relish about Auden's warnings of imminent downfall, whether he adopts the minatory glee of poem XXXI of *Poems* ('Get there if you can') or the aloofly diagnostic tone of XXX ('Consider this and in our time'). The opening lines of the latter poem are among the finest Auden ever wrote. Considering 'as the hawk sees it or the helmeted airman' is clearly prompted by his awareness of aerial photography and how that made available panoramic shots of England seen from above. (Aerial photography fascinated English artists of the time, especially perhaps John Piper.) But a helmeted airman may also be piloting a bomber plane. Several years before Auden wrote his poem in March 1930, London had staged a number of pretend air-raids in order to alert the public to the danger of war from the air.[8] Aerial photography lays the body of England bare to dispassionate scrutiny much as a torso on the operating table is bare to the eye of the surgeon. As the surgeon then concentrates on the infected part, so the camera's eye can zoom in on tell-tale signs: of 'cigarette-end smouldering on a border' or 'the insufficient units / Dangerous, easy, in furs, in uniform'.

There is nothing of random observation in Auden's method, no hapless recording of social ephemera. What we are given are synecdochic details, clues by which to read society's ills. Auden, in common with many of his generation, had no doubt about its malaise. One manifestation of this was the Great War. Another could be inferred from 'the intolerable neural itch' (*EA*, p. 36). Others in the present book will wish to enquire into Auden's reading of Freud, his fascination with the psychosomatic explanation for illness associated with such mentors of his as Homer Lane, Groddeck and John Layard. Here, it is enough to suggest that Auden synthesises and variously rearranges the events of recent history and the cause-and-effect inferential claims of psychologists in order to arrive at his own version of both the cause of and cure for civilisation and its discontents.

It was this grand claim he would eventually turn against, regretting, so he said, his too-frequent adoption of the preacher's loose, immodest tone. In fact, he went on being a preacher all his life, though the manner of address certainly shifted from the public and hortatory towards the more relaxed utterance of the private priest. But the 1930s was a decade which uniquely seemed to require writers to speak out. In the leading article of *New Verse* no. 3, published in May 1933, Charles Madge asserts that 'We must certainly be on our guard against political feelings taken at third hand. But the remedy is as certainly not to be found in keeping out of politics. It is not a question to be decided by our two standards of subtlety and vitality; but by a third standard, that of competence, which includes originality' (p. 3).

Not 'political thinking' but 'political feeling'. It would be wrong to lay a great deal of emphasis on what may have been a casual phrase, but this in itself alerts us to the fact that for much of the 1930s there was precious little by way of informed theory behind the decade's political radicalism, in Britain at all events, and what little there was lagged well behind anything being written on the European mainland. Edgell Rickword confessed that even after he became a member of the CPGB in 1934 he read no Marxist theory except for 'the historical part of *Das Kapital* and the *Manifesto*', although he greatly admired Caudwell's 'general articles on studies in a dying culture'.[9]

How much Marx Auden knew is difficult to judge, especially as he absorbed and adapted ideas with the kind of rapidity that left everyone else far behind. But certain of his poems register political feeling more profoundly than any other writing of the 1930s. 'O what is that sound that so thrills the ear', first published in book form in *Look, Stranger!*, is an instance. At a glance, this ballad-style poem, about the sudden menace of soldiers who act not as guards but an invading army, seems to apply to such contemporary events as Mussolini's invasion of Abyssinia or, at a pinch, Franco's invasion of democratic Spain. But Mendelson dates its composition to October 1932, which means that it was written before even Hitler came to power. Yet no poem more fully captures that feeling so prevalent in the decade, of the abandonment of their responsibilities by Western liberal governments, of their betrayals, their obeisance to the jackboot. The poem could well have been written after the *Anschluss* and the invasion of the Sudetenland, both of which happened in 1938. 'Were the vows you swore me deceiving, deceiving? / No, I promised to love you, dear, / But I must be leaving.' Léon Blum deciding after all not to come to the aid of the Spanish Republic? Chamberlain at Heston airport? Neither, of course, and yet both. It is part of Auden's genius that he should renovate the ballad form in order to turn fable to contemporary account, to evoke the deep uneasiness of all those who yearn for the self-sufficiencies of private love at a time when these are threatened by forces over which individuals have no control.

This collision between private and public is a matter he returns to in several key poems, never settling for one position, never repeating himself in either manner or matter. If I single out here the poem known either by its first line 'Out on the lawn I lie in bed' or by the title 'A Summer Night' it is not because I think it definitive but because it plays so wonderfully well with the necessary tensions between what E. M. Forster called the inner world of personal relationships and the outer one of telegrams and anger. Forster's belief in the integrity of individual selfhood is one of the poles – the other being historical inevitability – between which Auden's poem moves. It opens as a celebration of *Agape*, a lyrical evocation of entire well-being, of consonance between outer and inner weather: 'Equal with colleagues in a ring / I sit on each calm evening'. The verse's supple ease, varied metrics, the assurance with which it uses both masculine and feminine rhyme, imply technical abundance as its own principle of joy: 'eyes in which I learn / That I am glad to look, return / My glances every day'. But by a brilliant coup, the moon that seems to bless the 'colleagues' does not shine on them alone. 'She climbs the European sky / . . . And blankly as an orphan stares / Upon the marvellous pictures.' Auden was subsequently to alter the word 'orphan' to 'butcher', and the implications of this will be considered later. For the moment, I want merely to note that the image marks the beginning of the poem's turn towards the outer world, where, under the same European sky that apparently shelters the few whose privileged existence the poem has so far celebrated, 'Poland draws her Eastern bow', and 'violence is done'. This prompts the further awareness that we, the 'gentle', do not ask 'what doubtful act allows / Our freedom in this English house, / Our picnics in the sun'.

'Gentle'. The word has a double meaning: the gentility, the genteel, a class of people, but also those who are mild and kindly disposed. Under pressure from the 'gathering multitudes outside', hidden by the 'creepered walls', even these latter qualities become suspect. What, after all, can 'Our metaphysical distress, / Our kindness to ten persons' claim to offer when confronted by 'the crumpling flood' of insurgent forces that 'Hold sudden death before our eyes / Whose river-dreams long hid the size / And vigours of the sea.' The sea strikes with all the unopposable power of historical inevitability. But the river-dreams are not, even so, to be discounted. The opening stanzas have testified to the legitimacy of such dreams. Apocalyptic flood-waters threaten, but when they retreat and 'stranded monsters gasping lie, / And sounds of riveting terrify / Their whorled unsubtle ears', the rebuilding of a juster world may include 'this for which we dread to lose / Our privacy', 'this' being all that is meant by river-dreams. But 'may' acknowledges the impossibility of forejudging the future, of knowing exactly what stranded monsters will be thrown up by the forces of change. Nor can we know what they will become, how they will evolve. As a poem written at much the same time remarks, 'men are changed by what they do' ('Here on the cropped grass').

'Out on the lawn' is an extraordinary accomplishment: intricate, considerate, and, perhaps most important, unpanicked in its response to forces that by the time of the poem's composition in June 1933 were all too obviously emergent. Auden's variation on Burns's 'flyting' stanza is a kind of debonair flourish, a way of showing how to hold your poise. This needs to be said, because there is a critical line, almost amounting to an orthodoxy, that argues for 'new styles of architecture' as requiring more than Auden can offer. Hence, Antony Easthope's claim that while 'the programme of the left poets of the 'thirties was anti-bourgeois and anti-liberal', in fact 'both in theory and practice the 'thirties poets failed to push far beyond the limits of reformism'. This failure, Easthope concludes, amounts to 'a failure to confront and eradicate an englobing liberalism, a privileging of the individual and his "experience"'. So, although Easthope is prepared to acknowledge Auden's virtuosity, this apparently 'surrounds a conventional centre. The typical line is iambic, even pentameter.'[10]

But 'Out on the lawn' no more has a centre than it is typically iambic. In one sense its movement is impeccably Marxist: history, both personal and social, is seen in terms of thesis, antithesis and synthesis. In another, Auden's refusal to welsh on the private values of love and companionship is crucial, as it is in many of his finest poems. Easthope thinks Auden should have set out to 'eradicate an englobing liberalism', though quite how is not clear, given that poems, unlike weedkillers or Agent Orange, can't really eradicate anything. As for the claim that Auden should have denied the 'authenticity' of individual experience, it's this very authenticity that 'Out on the lawn' so finely establishes, even though in other poems – for example 'Easily my dear, you move, easily your head' – he probes at the compulsions and insufficiencies of erotic love which 'except at our proposal, / Will do no trick at his disposal'.

This is sceptical, anti-romantic, but still fully aware of love's power. Throughout the thirties Auden continued to make poems out of his questioning of the private versus public, of individual versus social desires and forces. In this context *Spain* is therefore crucial. According to Peggy Garland, Auden remarked that '"A poet should be in the thick of things . . . Right in the middle of wars and troubles and weddings and birth and death – the lot." . . . He said he must and would go to Spain, but was afraid of what he might see – he dreaded seeing wounded people in pain.'[11] Auden did indeed make the journey to Spain, but *Spain* is entirely free of personal testimony. It may even be his refusal to romanticise the poet as presence that caused Orwell's infamous jibe about him being the kind of person who is always somewhere else when the trigger is pulled. The testimony provided in Auden's poem is not of the order of 'I was the man, I suffered, I was there', but of the writer as Everyman for whom History matters, that History which 'to the defeated. / May say Alas but cannot help nor pardon'. History, as Stan Smith notes, is for Auden a collective experience: it is *our* thoughts that have bodies, the menacing shapes of *our* fevers that are precise and alive (Smith, p. 95).

Recognition of this brings with it the recognition of agency. Hence, that most eloquent of all Auden's near-lyric poems, 'Look, Stranger!', with its appeal to 'stand stable here'. We are all strangers, and afraid, in a world we never made, but we can nevertheless help change that world. And those who stand stable may serve the cause by refusing to be panicked into retreat. 'Look, Stranger!', which was written in November 1935, is keenly aware of impending crisis. Ships that 'Diverge on urgent voluntary errands' may look back to the far-called navies of Kipling's 'Recessional', but where Kipling's ships 'melt away', as though anticipating dissolution – the pre-eminent symbol of Empire lured to destruction by siren voices – the ships of Auden's poem have somewhere to get to: they are agents of history rather than its victims.

Nevertheless, the urgency with which the ships choose to embark on their errands signifies that time is short. It has become even shorter in *Journey to a War*, from which comes a key sonnet sequence, 'In Time of War'. This was prompted by Auden's and Isherwood's finding themselves willy-nilly pitchforked into the Sino-Japanese conflict. Here, Auden considers history as, among other things, an unfolding of the potentialities for evil that result from imperialist ambitions: 'And maps can really point to places / Where life is evil now: / Nanking; Dachau.' The perspective is necessarily world-wide.

It may therefore seem odd that Auden chose to preface the book with a sonnet to E. M. Forster, and even odder that he then in later versions tacked the sonnet on to the end of the sequence. Certainly most commentators appear perplexed by Auden's decision, either choosing to say nothing about it, or like John Fuller, finding it something of a Forsterian anti-climax: Auden 'ends by locating the "international evil" in the genteel prejudices of the English middle-class that Forster exposed in his novels' (Fuller 1970, p. 128). But Auden knows what he is doing, even if he seems to be conscripting Forster to a larger cause than the novelist would wish to serve. 'Just as we are closeted with madness', Auden says, 'you interrupt us like the telephone.' In other circumstances, the telephone might be a call from (and to) the world of telegrams and anger. Here, it breaks in on the solipsistic insanities of those for whom social responsibilities have become meaningless, for, the poem acknowledges, we are all Lucy, Turton, Philip, Forster's characters, we all wish international evil, are keen to join the ranks of the benighted, denying reason and ignoring love; but Miss Avery, in the very moment that 'we swear our lie . . . / Comes out into the garden with the sword'.

In *Howard's End* the sword had been wielded by Charles Wilcox, the militarist son of the businessman, Henry Wilcox, and aimed at Leonard Bast, the near working-class lover of Helen Schlegel, sister to Henry's wife. Major Turton is one of the administrators of *A Passage to India*; both Philip Herriton of *Where Angels Fear to Tread* and Lucy Honeychurch, the heroine of *A Room with a View*, try to deny the rightness of their and others' sexual love. The 'armies of the benighted' is a phrase that occurs in the latter novel and is applied to all those who deny 'the holiness of the heart's affections'. 'We', Auden says, indicting himself together with others, typically wish evil rather than good.

'More substance in our enmities / Than in our love', Yeats had said, in 'Meditations in Time of Civil War'. Auden says very much the same thing. In an essay first broadcast in 1938 under the title 'Two Cheers for Democracy' (part of a BBC series of talks called 'What I Believe', the title he later gave to his own contribution), Forster reproves the cult of great men. They spread a desert of uniformity and very often a pool of blood, too. He mentions no names, though he invents an Admiral de Toma whom he imagines as staging a coup, failing, and so retiring from history. The Admiral fails with a completeness no artist or lover can ever know, Forster says, 'for with them the process of creation is its own achievement, whereas for him the only possible achievement is success'. But de Toma-like ambitions threaten to overwhelm the world. Force and violence amount to 'the ultimate reality of this world', but the reality does not always get its own way. 'Some people call its absences "decadence"; I call them "civilisation" and find in such interludes the chief justification for the human experiment.' Contemplating a coming darkness, Forster comments that 'the greater the darkness, the brighter shine the little lights, reassuring one another, signalling: "Well, at all events, I'm still here. I don't like it very much, but how are you?" Unquenchable lights of my aristocracy! Signals of the invincible army! "Come along – anyway, let's have a good time while we can." I think they signal that too.' Forster's aristocracy is, he has earlier explained, not formed from social rank, but from 'the plucky, the considerate, and the sensitive'.[12] It may all seem merely whimsical, yet I suspect that many of those who heard the original broadcast version of the essay, in the autumn of 1938, or who later read it in *The Listener*, were chastened by Forster's refusal to bend the knee to the forces of history. There seems little doubt that Auden was among them.

Moreover, Forster's statement that he hated the idea of causes, and if required to choose between betraying his friends and betraying his country, hoped he would have the guts to betray his country, delivered in that wry, unemphatic voice,[13] must have affected many. So that when Auden, by then living in New York, came to write 'September 1, 1939', his mention of those ironic points of light that 'Flash out wherever the Just / Exchange their messages', is plainly a bow towards the unquenchable lights of Forster's 'aristocracy', to all those who, composed of 'Eros and of dust . . . / Show an affirming flame'.

But what exactly is the flame to affirm? According to John Fuller, Auden blamed the anxiety of modern man 'largely on those thinkers of the Renaissance and the Enlightenment who were responsible for Economic Man' (Fuller 1970, p. 260). Smith argues that for 'any decent radical in the thirties, England was not a *patria* to be proud of but a burden of betrayal, shame and perfidy' (Smith, p. 118). 'There is no such thing as the State / And no one exists alone', Auden claims, 'We must love one another or die.' ('September 1, 1939'). On the face of it this is an impeccably Marxist statement. But in 'Two Cheers for Democracy' Forster had said that 'only Love, the beloved Republic', deserves three cheers. Forster's utopianism has little if anything in common with a Marxist vision. And it is this, I believe, that helped Auden to reshape his own political thinking during the next thirty years.

Of course, there were many false starts and casualties – 'September 1, 1939' among them. Nevertheless, it may be a mistake to argue that Auden's move to America triggered his betrayal of an earlier radical politics. It is rather that the move coincided with a reformulated desire to stand stable, to resist or at any rate challenge the unopposable power of Authority whose buildings grope the sky. Hence, the epigraph for *New Year Letter*. It comes from Montaigne: 'We are, I know not how, double in ourselves, so that what we believe we disbelieve, and cannot rid ourselves of what we condemn.' I do not believe in belief, Forster had said. Auden's newly found, or anyway, newly stressed scepticism, disavows all previously accepted versions of Authority, pre-eminently Marx and Freud, at the same time accepting that they cannot be entirely extirpated from modern ways of thinking or understanding experience. The task is, however, to discover 'To what conditions we must bow / In building the Just City now', knowing that everywhere civilians 'come to grief / In brotherhoods without belief / Whose good intentions cannot cure / The actual evils they endure' (*New Year Letter*). The sadness of this is distanced from a cynical denial of the legitimacy of belief; but it testifies to the difficulty of finding a sure ground for it.

This is why the tone of so many of Auden's postwar poems shifts from the swift motions of his work in the thirties, work which he unfairly condemned for its reliance on the preacher's loose, immodest tone. As I have already noted, Auden remained a Preacher – the more so if we understand the term as it is used of the author of Ecclesiastes: 'For in much wisdom is much grief: and he that increaseth knowledge increaseth sorrow.' The Preacher might be speaking of, or indeed for, 'The Shield of Achilles'. The greatness of this poem undoubtedly has much to do with its deromanticising of art. When Thetis looks over Hephaestos' shoulder, hoping to see 'Marble well-governed cities / And ships upon untamed seas', she is expecting art to endorse a heroic view of life. What she sees instead is 'A plain without a feature', where 'A million eyes, a million boots in line, / Without expression' are waiting for a sign. When the sign comes, it is carried by a voice without a face that proves 'by statistics that some cause was just / In tones as dry and level as the place'. Most commentators agree that the poem, which was written in 1952, is about Auden's disenchanted view of the post-Second-World-War world. This is so, but we should add that it is also about the need for art to confront the worst rather than seek refuge in dream. Its plangent dystopianism extends to all those who continue to find allure in the wished-for grandeur of conquest and subjugation, whether Agamemnon at Troy, Hitler, Stalin, Pol Pot or, most recently, George W. Bush.

In preferable contrast are the river-dreams of 'In Praise of Limestone' (1948). This moralised landscape is woven through with political aware-ness, although now it is an awareness in which the claims of individuality replace or anyway minimise those of 'Collective Man'. Its modesty of ambi-tion is opposed by 'the best and worst' who sought 'Immoderate soils where the beauty was not so external, / The light less public and the meaning of life / Something more than a mad camp'. The last phrase suggests that, at least tongue in cheek, Auden identifies his preferred way of life with a gayness that has no official purchase. He is still in opposition. And it also suggests why, soon afterwards, Frank O'Hara would remark, rejecting Yeats, that 'Our responsibilities did not begin / in dreams, though they began in bed' ('Memorial Day 1950'). But Auden is not yet consistently prepared to walk away from History into a cultivated privacy, although the signs are there. Hence, the brutal flippancy with which, in the 1945 *Collected Poetry*, he changed the moon's 'orphan' face (of 'A Summer Night') to that of a 'butcher'. He also omitted the stanza about the 'creepered wall', thereby diminishing any sense of guilt at privileged separation from the gathering multitude. Yet of his limestone landscape he remarks that it is 'not the sweet home that it looks, / Nor its peace the historical calm of a site / Where something was settled once and for all'. This of course cuts both ways. As a living place, not merely an archaeological wonder, it contributes to the ways we think about the lives we try to choose. And its connection to 'the big busy world' means that it is not to be thought of in terms of private vision, a dream freed from history. Auden's politics have not yet become the quietistic, despairing kind that more often than not characterise his last years.

## NOTES

1. The complicated story of this poem, of its revised titles and text, is rehearsed by Edward Mendelson, in *EA*, pp. 421–2.
2. Tom Paulin, *Ireland and the English Crisis* (Newcastle: Bloodaxe Books, 1984), p. 87.

3. Samuel Hynes, *The Auden Generation: Literature and Politics in England in the 1930s* (London: Faber, 1976), p. 34.

4. Warren Hope, *Norman Cameron: His Life, Work and Letters* (London: Greenwich Exchange, 2000), p. 53.

5. See 'Richard Wilbur on W. H. Auden', *ASN*, 12 (1994), p. 10.

6. See John Lucas, *The Radical Twenties: Aspects of Writing, Politics and Culture* (Nottingham: Five Leaves Publications, 1997), pp. 194–7.

7. Michael Kilby, 'Some Thoughts on "1929"', *ASN*, 15 (1996), pp. 10–15; this reference p. 15.

8. See John Lucas, *The Good That We Do* (London: Greenwich Exchange, 2001), pp. 159–61.

9. John Lucas (ed.), *The 1930s: A Challenge to Orthodoxy* (Brighton: Harvester Press, 1978), p. 9.

10. Antony Easthope, 'Traditional Metre and the Poetry of the Thirties', in Francis Barker *et al.* (eds.), *1936: The Sociology of Literature: Practices of Literature and Politics* (Colchester: University of Essex Press, 1979), pp. 331 and 336.

11. 'Peggy Garland's Memories of Auden', *ASN*, 16 (1997), p. 4.

12. 'What I Believe', repr. in E. M. Forster, *Two Cheers for Democracy* (London: Edward Arnold, 1951).

13. It can be heard on an ARGO LP recording he made in 1959.

# 13

ROD MENGHAM

# Auden, psychology and society

Auden's elegy for Freud uses a phrase that has passed into the language. Freud, he says, 'is no more a person / now but a whole climate of opinion'. By November 1939, the influence of the founder of psychoanalysis seemed to pervade the artistic and intellectual cultures of the West – even the literary culture of England, a country that talks a lot about the weather. In Auden's own work, however, Freud's centrality was not quite so assured; his significance was sometimes equal to, at other times actually less than, that of figures such as Georg Groddeck and Homer Lane. He would have found out about Freud, probably, in connection with his father's medical practice. According to Humphrey Carpenter, Dr Auden was 'paying a lot of attention' to Freud in 1925 (Carpenter, p. 40). Auden's introduction to the ideas of Groddeck and Lane, however, was effected by John Layard, who was living in Berlin when Auden made his first visit there in 1928. Although he was later to refer rather cruelly to 'loony Layard', this name-calling owed less to Auden's opinion of Layard's ideas than to his shock at being asked to finish the job when Layard bungled a suicide attempt. This troubled figure was an enthusiastic disciple of Lane, whose papers he collected and collated for what became Lane's only published work, *Talks to Parents and Teachers* (1928). His extra significance for Auden consisted in his simultaneous and complementary investments in both psychology and anthropology. Layard had travelled to Malekula in the New Hebrides in 1914–15 with W. H. R. Rivers, whose book *Conflict and Dream* (1923) was to supply Auden with material for 'Paid on Both Sides'.[1] Layard's own papers on the 'Flying Tricksters of Malekula' would inform the composition of *The Orators*. From the start of his career as a writer, Auden became used to thinking about psychological models in relation to the customs and rituals of an entire society, rather than exclusively with reference to the personal history of the individual.

His earliest writings show an understanding of the role of repression in both art and behaviour. He was notoriously fond of stressing the importance of neurosis in the formation of an artistic personality, but perhaps the most significant emphasis he places in his statements on the uses of psychoanalysis is on the need to politicise it: 'Freudianism cannot be considered apart from other features of the contemporary environment', he wrote in 'Psychology and Art To-day' in 1935, 'apart from modern physics with its conception of transformable energy, apart from modern technics and modern politics' (*EA*, p. 337). One year later, the pressure he brings to bear on psychoanalysis in 'The Good Life' lies in inducing it to find common cause with Communism. He considers that both 'regard thought and knowledge as . . . determined by the conflict between instinctive needs and a limited environment'; both, therefore, are 'concerned with unmasking these hidden conflicts' and both 'regard these conflicts as inevitable stages which must be made to negate themselves' (*EA*, pp. 351–2). Where Auden places a certain amount of strain on the relationship between psychoanalysis and Communism is in claiming that 'both desire and believe in the possibility of freedom of action and choice, which can only be obtained by unmasking and making conscious the hidden conflict' (*EA*, p. 352). Here, there is a certain degree of political utopianism that fails to acknowledge the revisionism inherent in the Freudian programme, the extent to which it seeks accommodation within the existing social and political framework.

In this respect, Auden became more excited by the radical promise he found in the teachings of Lane and Groddeck. Lane's main contribution was a revolutionary redefinition of the concepts of criminality, moral guilt and so-called unethical behaviour.[2] He was something of a pioneer in the fields of penology, education and psychotherapy, although he had no professional training and this helped to make him jealously resentful of established psychoanalysts, who in turn regarded him as something of a charlatan. At one point he was put on trial for deception and fraud despite the support of public figures such as the Bishop of Liverpool and Lord Lytton. Auden made it clear that he felt Lane had been unjustly victimised in his poem of 1930, 'Get there if you can', speaking of how 'Homer Lane was killed in action by the Twickenham Baptist gang' (*EA*, p. 49). In his collaboration with Isherwood on the play *The Enemies of a Bishop* (1929), Lane is the model for the heroic protagonist, whose enemies are exposed in the terms that had been applied by Lane's opponents. According to Isherwood, 'The Bishop is the hero of the play; he represents sanity, and is an idealized portrait of Homer Lane himself. His enemies are the pseudo-healers, the wilfully ill and mad' (Carpenter, p. 107).

Lane became best known as superintendent of the 'Little Commonwealth', an 'open' remand home set up in Dorset during the First World War. His basic ideas are easy to assimilate. Auden summed up his position in his own journal of 1929: 'Resist not evil; or as Lane puts it, "It is no good fighting evil as it only fights back and there is no energy left for creating knowledge"' (*EA*, p. 300). What most people would think of as evil, Lane was liable to regard as good, commenting that: 'a bad boy' was simply an example of good qualities wrongly directed, and that while Freud believed in original sin, he (Lane) I believed in 'original goodness'. The conviction which provides the basis of Lane's outlook is that all instinctual behaviour is good, not just in a biological sense but in a moral sense as well. This involves a drastic simplification and distortion of Freudian ideas, in which Lane regarded the conflict between the claims of the instincts and the demands of society as completely unnecessary. Instinctual desires are implanted by nature and are therefore inherently good. Instincts are derived from racial experience and comprise our most efficient teacher; Lane refers to them as 'Mother Nature'. Of course, if the instincts are acted upon without restraint of any kind, they may be a nuisance to others and even a danger to oneself. It is the function of parents and teachers to prevent such an eventuality. If the pressures of society that parents and teachers represent are brought to bear properly upon the child, this qualifies them to be thought of as 'Mother Law'.

But parental prohibitions – and this was the key for Lane – should never carry any moral connotations. The parent should never say 'Bad boy, stop that', or 'Naughty girl, don't do that', only 'Stop that', because if prohibitions are used as a means of inculcating moral standards this makes the conflict between instinctual wishes and society's demands intolerable. The child should be allowed to learn about moral standards only as a natural consequence of its own behaviour, which will enable it to understand the pragmatic value of morality. Adopting a morally disapproving attitude towards infantile misbehaviour creates in the child a fear and hatred of the unconscious, which may extend to all instinctual wishes whether creative or destructive and leads the child to the belief that to obey one's natural promptings is to forgo the love of mother, society, God.

Lane's attempt to put into practice the implications of all this resulted in a psychotherapy that tried to replace a moral attitude with what every child really needs, which is love that ignores the whole question of good and bad behaviour. Psychological disorders resulted from a failure of the loving relationship, and the remedy was its restoration. Lane believed it was essential that the analysand should feel himself or herself to be loved by the analyst, and it seems that this approach may have been taken somewhat literally on occasion; it was certainly the subject of a great deal of suspicion during Lane's trial. Another medically unethical practice he adopted was telling certain of his patients stories about other patients. In one way, this was scandalous, but it had a therapeutic purpose that was similar to that of the literary expression of psychological resistance explored by Auden and other writers in the 1930s.

There was a childishly optimistic side to Lane's own character which is partly what led him to believe that his own kind of treatment could effect a complete cure by producing 'harmony and synthesis' of the warring elements of the psyche. This is claiming a great deal more than orthodox psychoanalysis, which would have a more limited ambition, geared to bringing about a recognition that conflict exists and to devising some means of coping with the reality of conflict. Where Lane provides little purchase for Auden's political interests is in the belief that conflict is completely internalised, in the sense that external forces only symbolise internal states, so that there is no need to adjust the social environment, only to develop an inner harmony: 'external forces . . . will seem to be the real causes of the conflict which man wages; but the real conflict will not be between himself and something or someone else, but between himself and himself'.[3] What Lane does allow for is the emancipation from guilt, and the rejection of existing concepts of sin and criminality, while what Groddeck allows for is the extent to which these feelings can be inscribed in the body of the patient. What Groddeck provides is a focus on the meaning of illness, on the body in trouble, on physical symptoms.

Groddeck's most famous theoretical move was the conceptualising of the 'It'. It has been argued plausibly that Freud derived his understanding of the Id from his Berlin-based colleague's characterisation of the It. But the It is not the name of something in opposition to the Ego; it does not represent the forces of the unconscious as opposed to the conscious. Both unconscious and conscious comprise the psyche, and the psyche as a whole forms only one part of the It. The It is to be thought of as that force which motivates the whole of humankind's activity as technologists, artists, worshippers, patients, etc., as Groddeck wrote in *The Unknown Self*: 'The It is not the Unconscious, but conscious and unconscious combined; it holds absolute sway over the activities of the brain, over consciousness. There is no opposition between the ego and the It, rather is the ego a phenomenon of the It.'[4] One of the most important means the It has of expressing its intentions is illness. Illness is seen as the body's form of protest against the conditions in which the human organism is forced to sustain a burden of repressed guilt: 'Illness is often only a means of flight from something not understood, and a defence against what is unbearable.'[5] In this sense, illness is health (and this is the kind of inversion that reminds us of Homer Lane), although for Groddeck it is illness that does the same kind of work as art, not the treatment of illness. Illness tells the same kind of story as art about the reality of hidden conflicts: 'sickness is nothing abnormal . . . its nature is not essentially different from building, or poetry-making, or walking, or health'.[6]

Where Groddeck provides some leverage for Auden's political requirements is in admitting the extent to which illness might be a reaction to external constraints: 'whoever finds life too hard, sometimes external life, still oftener his private mental life, can easily drop all his difficulties, at least for a time, if he gets ill'.[7] It is 'still oftener' the private mental life that creates difficulties, so that Groddeck is at most indecisive about the role of external constraints, but that kind of hesitation gives Auden enough leeway to emphasise the extent to which humankind is, in the formula Auden used in his elegy 'In Memory of Ernst Toller', 'lived by' forces outside itself. In the Journal of 1929, Auden makes reference repeatedly to the doctrines of Freud, Lane and Groddeck. For the most part, Groddeck's thought is mimicked in a fairly straightforward fashion: 'Infectious diseases: a sign of the unconscious sense of unity between men' (EA, p. 299). Lane and Freud, on the other hand, are echoed problematically, sometimes in ways that make them seem interchangeable: 'It is the body's job to make, the mind's to destroy . . . The development of consciousness may be compared with the breaking away of the child from the Oedipus relation. Just as one must be weaned from one's mother, one must be weaned from the Earth Mother (Unconscious?)' (EA, p. 298). Sometimes they are echoed in ways that show a desire to refute Freud: 'The error of Freud and most psychologists is making pleasure a negative thing, progress towards a state of rest. This is only one half of pleasure and the least important half. Creative pleasure is, like pain, an increase in tension' (EA, p. 299). Edward Mendelson quotes, from an unpublished part of the Journal, Auden's rebuttal of the psychoanalytical project of delving into the patient's past 'for the origins of division': 'Freud says it is better to recollect infantile experience than to repeat this. This is wrong. Recollection does nothing' (Early Auden, p. 50).

By April 1930, in the poem 'Get there if you can and see the land you once were proud to own', Auden was prepared to discriminate between the deceptive benefits of Freud's teachings and the more reliable prescriptions of Homer Lane. Freud is included in a list of names of literary, philosophical and scientific analysts whose apparently penetrating diagnoses of society are misleading, beguiling, insidious. Their 'compelling logic' acts as a lure and a seduction. By contrast, Lane is one of a much smaller band of radicals – 'Lawrence, Blake and Homer Lane' – whose uncompromising frankness had led either to their alienation or their victimisation. Part of the problem that Freud represented for Auden was his very authoritativeness, his effective dominance of intellectual culture. In the writings of Groddeck, the rejection of authority is a prerequisite of the movement towards health. However, for

Groddeck, the erosion of dependence is a project focused on the need to separate from the mother. Groddeck's most notorious essay deals with the expression of this repudiation of the mother in the figure of Jesus nailed to the Cross, with his back to, facing away from, the embrace of the mother figured in the Cross itself. This is to give a cultural reference to the need for separation. Auden gives it a characteristically historical application as early as in his 1929 Journal: 'The real "life-wish" is the desire for separation, from family, from one's own literary predecessors' (*EA*, p. 299). Paradoxically, it was precisely because Auden was dependent on Freud for insights of this and other kinds, that he felt the need to disaffiliate himself from certain aspects of the Freudian agenda.

Freud was most incomplete in the area that Auden's generation had given priority to, the necessity for political revolution. Already in the late 1920s, Auden was anticipating the need to supplement a Freudian diagnosis with Marxist prognosis, as he wrote in a journal: 'Freud's error is the limitation of neurosis to the individual. The neurosis involves all society' (*Early Auden*, p. 52). This widening of scope of individual symptoms to embody the structural problems of whole societies, was exploited busily in Auden's poems and plays of the early 1930s, especially in *The Orators*. But there was also a sustained interest among both psychologists and Marxists in the possibility of forging a historic alliance between the two methodologies. Alistair Browne's essay on 'Psychology and Marxism' (1937), based on clinical experience in the East End, reaches conclusions very similar to those of Christopher Caudwell's Marxist assessment of the uses and abuses of psychoanalysis in his essay 'Freud: a Study in Bourgeois Psychology' (1938).[8] Auden was strongly sympathetic towards the idea of subordinating Freud to Marx, but he was no member of the Party, and was capable of moments of pessimism and misgivings over the value of subordinating the individual to the collective.

The first person plural point of view of the 1936 poem 'Certainly our city' (*EA*, pp. 165–6) registers a series of small jolts of self-recognition, the desiderata of psychoanalysis. But this salutary adjustment of focus is happening too late. The moment seems to have passed to have made proper use of the 'candid studies' of Groddeck and Freud, and already a doomed future is unfolding that leads inexorably towards a scenario in which 'the wish to wound has the power'. The dispositions of past, present and future anticipate the structure of *Spain*, composed exactly a year later, although that poem's appeal to its readers to assist in changing the direction of history draws the opposite conclusion to its predecessor. By 1939, writing 'In Memory of Ernst Toller', Auden's sense of the failure to grasp the forces of history is compounded by the suspicion that European culture is now 'too injured to get well'. The transatlantic perspective makes this condition less fraught than it might otherwise have seemed, but does not eradicate the bleakness with which Auden measures the correlation of external and internal pressures:

> We are lived by powers we pretend to understand:
> They arrange our loves; it is they who direct at the end
> The enemy bullet, the sickness, or even our hand.

The elegies of 1939 draw a line under the attempt to make workable a constructive synthesis of psychological and sociological viewpoints. Before that moment is reached, Auden's intention is to develop in his writing the sense of a situation in which the cure of the individual is irrelevant in the face of the power of ideology that can go on reproducing the same conditions. The implication is that poetry can distil critical reflections on the ideological process. In 1935, he provided in his essay 'The Good Life' (*EA*, pp. 342–54) a description of the mechanism of repression which makes it clear he regards repression chiefly as a historical stage in the development of humankind; it is an instance of the work of ideology which, seen from this historical perspective, is at least theoretically reversible.

The 1929 Journal had associated the damage inflicted by repression with the military fiascos that have since become an important feature in the cultural memory of the First World War: 'A colonel captures a position, after receiving severe wounds himself and the loss of three-quarters of his regiment, to find that the enemy are his own side. Repression is equally heroic and equally foolish' (*EA*, p. 300). In the poem 'It's no use raising a shout', also written in 1929 (November), the estrangement of unconscious knowledge from conscious awareness is figured in closely similar terms: 'In my spine there was a base, / And I knew the general's face: / But they've severed all the wires, / And I can't tell what the general desires' (*EA*, p. 43). The use of apposition and metaphor suggests a mere parallel whereas Auden perceives a direct, aetiological connection between the social history of the First World War and the neurotic anxieties of his own generation.

In the years since the Armistice, perhaps the most significant historical event to galvanise awareness of the links between individual psychology and what Charles Madge was to call the 'mass-wish' was the abdication of Edward VIII in December 1936. According to Madge, the sequence of events leading up to the abdication disclosed the threshold between desire and repression in the public sphere: 'Millions saw the emergence of their own thwarted and concealed desires.'[9] What is especially fascinating about the timing of the abdication is its close coincidence with the founding of Mass-Observation, the nation-wide sociological survey movement of which Madge was a founding member. The anthropologist Bronislaw Malinowski was in no doubt about the intimate connection between the two events, noting that Mass-Observation started work in conditions of 'national stress . . . which compelled every man and woman to think and feel, to react towards a definite issue'.[10] Mass-Observation's first major project involved coverage of thoughts and feelings about the coronation of George VI, a ritual event that would repair the damage to the national fabric. Malinowski saw it as the means by which the British could restore their 'cultural credit'. The methodology of the new movement was to assemble a variety of responses to given themes and issues and to work out a statistical average that would approximate to the national social consciousness. A number of poets were involved from the outset, most notably Madge himself, Humphrey Jennings and David Gascoyne; but not Auden. Nonetheless, it was little over a year before the emergence of Mass-Observation that Auden had been utterly absorbed in collaborative work for a mass medium, in the shape of his contributions to the GPO. Film Unit. His forms of address were changing in response to the need to engage with the social consciousness of a public much broader than that of readers of poetry. He may not have taken part directly in Mass-Observation's experiment of listening to the voice of the people, but after the composition of *The Orators*, his poetry began to echo the voice of the people with an increasing sense of purpose.

Just as the poetry of Surrealism moved during the 1930s from an enthusiasm for automatic writing to the language of research into the surrealism of everyday life, so Auden's work, in a parallel tendency, relinquished its early embrace of the parable form, and gradually withdrew from the densely encrypted style suitable for the expression of highly idiosyncratic preoccupations, in favour of a more civically minded emulation of the techniques of a popular, oral tradition specialising in forms such as the ballad. Madge had argued in 'Press, Radio and Social Consciousness' for the value of the mass media as a means of reflecting the 'unconscious fears and wishes of the mass',[11] despite their being compromised by issues of ownership.

'Letter to Lord Byron' (1936) explored Auden's own psychological history in a self-consciously conversational idiom, obviating an intense confessional mode with an entertaining flippancy, intended to emulate the worldliness of his addressee, a poet who flourished at a time when the reading public for poetry was larger than it ever has been, either before or since. All the usual references to Groddeck, Lane and Freud are there, but they are made curiously weightless by having to contribute to the relentless maintenance of epigrammatising wit. Despite the fact that Auden is describing symptoms, registering fixations and recalling his earliest memories, the free associations of the talking cure are replaced by the strictest regulations of verse form, syntax and control of meaning. In the later 'In Memory of Sigmund Freud' (1939), the organising structures of poetry are judged to perform the same function as the talking cure in identifying formative moments of pressure. Freud wasn't clever at all: 'he merely told / the unhappy Present to recite the Past / like a poetry lesson till sooner / or later it faltered at the line / where long ago the accusations had begun'. But neither in the poem to Byron, nor in the elegy to Freud, is there a faltering line, unless deliberately contrived. In the earlier text, Auden expresses with some bravado his total opposition to any therapy aimed at cure: 'Let each child have that's in our care / As much neurosis as the child can bear' (EA, p. 193). The vulnerability epitomised here is rendered totally inaccessible by the verbal armature. Just as 'Letter to Lord Byron' matches the expertise of Byron's sarcasm, so the elegy speaks continuously with the 'rational voice' it attributes to Freud. In the world of the Freud elegy, 'Impulse' behaves with decorum, while Eros is credited with responsibility for the social fabric. The ambitious coordination of the poem, its flawless choreography of measure and syntax, is a demonstration of the rehabilitated consciousness that presides over Auden's transatlantic broadcasts in the post-1939 period. Although the subject of the poem is celebrated for his intimacy with the night and its inhabitants, there is no hint of unillumined meanings in the poem, whose overriding aim, like Freud's, is to 'serve enlightenment'.

The homage to Freud is not only an elegy for an individual, it is also a formal separation from Auden's earlier manner of writing in response to the workings of the unconscious. The most vivid passage concerns the retrieval and restoration of forgotten components of the self, 'long-forgotten objects' lying in the grass of our neglect, which revealed by Freud's 'undiscouraged shining', can be 'returned to us and made precious again'. Even while it celebrates the enshrining of memory, the poem as a whole enacts the abandonment of the kind of psychological resistance for which Auden's poetry first became known. And if its gravitation towards social consciousness is enacted in the afterlife of the poem – in Auden's success rate at making phrases we use without knowing their source – that resonance is achieved at the cost of muffling the sound of fear and desire that Auden himself does not want allayed.

## NOTES

1. In the later years of the Great War, W. H. R. Rivers treated the neurasthenia of Auden's soldier-poet heroes, Robert Graves, Siegfried Sassoon and Wilfred Owen at Craiglockhart Hospital, Edinburgh.

2. Information about Lane's life and ideas has been drawn from two sources: Homer Lane, *Talks to Parents and Teachers* (London: Allen and Unwin, 1928); E. T. Bazeley, *Homer Lane and the Little Commonwealth* (London: Allen and Unwin, 1928).
3. Lane, *Talks to Parents and Teachers*, p. 102.
4. Georg Groddeck, *The Unknown Self*, translated by V. M. E. Collins (London: Vision Press, 1951), p. 84.
5. *Ibid.*, p. 45.
6. *Ibid.*, p. 73.
7. *Ibid.*, p. 71.
8. Alistair Browne, 'Psychology and Marxism', in C. Day Lewis (ed.), *The Mind in Chains* (London: Frederick Muller, 1937), pp. 167–84; Christopher Caudwell, *Studies in a Dying Culture* (London: John Lane The Bodley Head, 1938), pp. 158–92.
9. Charles Madge, 'Press, Radio and Social Consciousness', in *The Mind in Chains*, p. 160.
10. Bronislaw Malinowski, 'A Nationwide Intelligence Service', in Charles Madge and Tom Harrisson (eds.), *First Year's Work 1937–8 by Mass-Observation* (London: Lindsay Drummond, 1938), p. 108.
11. Madge, 'Press, Radio and Social Consciousness', p. 160.

# 14

RICHARD R. BOZORTH

# Auden: love, sexuality, desire

A comprehensive treatment of the subject of this chapter would involve much of what made Auden an influential writer, conceivably touching on nearly every poem, play and libretto he wrote, as well as a fair proportion of his prose, published and unpublished. Little of his writing from the 1920s and 1930s does not involve 'desire', even restricted to its psychological meanings, and with his extensive reading of Sigmund Freud, D. H. Lawrence and Georg Groddeck, among others, Auden did much to adapt psychoanalytic thought for Anglo-American modernism. If he wrote some of the most memorable love poetry of his time, this also constituted a sophisticated engagement with a body of erotic and Romantic writing stretching from Plato through Petrarch and Dante to Shakespeare. Along with T. S. Eliot, he ranks as one of the most important English-language religious poets of the last hundred years, for whom the interrelation of Eros and *Agape* was an abiding concern. It is easier, in other words, to say what Auden wrote that does *not* impinge on love, sex and desire, than what *does*.

But however one might delimit the subject, the rise of academic lesbian and gay studies presents a further challenge: how to grapple with the fraught relation of Auden's sexuality to his life and work. With the exceptions of Gertrude Stein and E. M. Forster, it is hard to name another gay or lesbian writer who achieved anything like Auden's stature in modernist literature, and a list of younger poets, many of them gay or lesbian, whose work reflects his influence would be a lengthy one. But unlike Stein or Forster – or, for that matter, Christopher Isherwood, with whom his life and career were so intertwined – Auden has not figured significantly in histories of modern gay and lesbian writing. This is partly a matter of historical timing: he lived, after all, for just four years more after the 1969 Stonewall Riots in New York's Greenwich Village, the event that has come to signify the inauguration of modern gay liberation. Still, Isherwood's 'coming out' in *Christopher and His Kind* was published only a few years later, in 1976, and even Forster, born in 1879, lined up for gay rights with the posthumous publication of

*Maurice*, his only explicitly homosexual novel, in 1971. Auden, by contrast, made no effort to be identified with the cause of gay liberation and decidedly discouraged biographical responses to his work by asking in his will that all recipients of his letters destroy them.

During his lifetime, Auden's homosexuality had something of the status of an open secret: known to some readers, to be sure, but either ignored by commentators in print or addressed only by implication or innuendo. A tacit ethic of 'Don't ask; don't tell' overwhelmingly governed his reception by reviewers and academic critics, and in this arrangement, cultural mores coincided not just with his own assumed wishes but with reigning literary-critical methodologies. Given the sway of Formalist approaches in English studies in the decades following the Second World War, scholars found it congenial to consign his homosexuality to the realm of extra-textual irrelevance. Even as late as 1983, a critic could dismiss the matter with the observation that 'Most of Auden's published work may be read for its artistic, psychological, or philosophical interest as one might read E. M. Forster's masterpiece, *A Passage to India*, without any awareness of its author's homosexuality.'[1] The implication is that because Auden did not compel readers to attend to his homosexuality, it can reasonably be placed outside the bounds of meaningful critical or interpretive response to his work.

With the rise of lesbian and gay studies and 'queer theory' in the academy, such a view carries much less force than it once did. Changes in sexual politics have combined with evolving critical approaches to yield new insight into literary portrayals and expressions of same-sex desire, from the ancient world to the present. An indispensable axiom for this work has been that the cultural force of the closet has been such that absences and silences must not be taken at face value, and it has become clear that since the advent of modern categories of sexual identity, roughly in the late nineteenth century, much literature has found ways to give voice to homosexual desire and identity in spite of official moral opprobrium and legal sanction.[2] Sodomy was for centuries the sin 'not to be named among Christians', but for writers as different as Shakespeare and Emily Dickinson, Gertrude Stein and Oscar Wilde, compelling cases have been made for the use of coded discourse and other linguistic strategies to articulate the socially unspeakable.[3]

Using similar approaches, recent work on Auden has elucidated a thoroughgoing concern with homosexual desire and love that was largely ignored or unseen by earlier critics.[4] That such arguments do not respect his own wishes on this score is, in fact, far more debatable than may first appear. Throughout his career, Auden's work reflects an abiding sense of literary meaning not as a singular, stable entity but as the fluid effect of an interactive verbal performance – what in later years he called 'a dialogue between the reader and the words of a poem' (*SW*, p. 114).

From his early poetry, with its tropes of espionage and atmosphere of embattlement and paranoia, to his later concern with secrets and reticence, Auden was incessantly fond of blurring distinctions between the unspoken, the unspeakable and that which goes without saying. In '"The Truest Poetry is the Most Feigning"' (1953), for example, he offers ostensibly frivolous professional advice to the aspiring love poet. Rather than sincere self-expression, Auden prescribes a poetics of unashamed Petrarchan artifice, which will not only make the poem more appealing to those with different erotic tastes, but offer protection on that day when 'Poets are suspect with the New Regime'. All that will be needed is to 'Re-sex the pronouns' to turn the love poem into a 'panegyric ode which hails . . . The new pot-bellied Generalissimo'. Auden concludes with the paradoxical proposition that not just love, but 'truth in any serious sense, / Like orthodoxy, is a reticence'.

This blending of provocation and obscurantism, seriousness and playfulness, is a characteristic gesture for the later Auden, and coming at the end of a poem, it implies something deeply serious and revealing in the frothy verbosity of light verse. The poem, in fact, unsettles the distinctions between 'orthodoxy' (literally, straight doctrine) and subversion, reticence and revelation, suggesting that in love and in art, the ostensible impersonality of convention can also enable intimate disclosure. There is a complex sexual-political subtext to this poem as well, so much so that Alan Sinfield has located here a virtual 'gay aesthetic' for the later Auden.[5] But even when engaged in apparently dispassionate critical commentary, Auden's assertions on the relation of life to a poet's art involve similar manoeuvres, so that his habitual condemnations of personal or biographical approaches to literature are much more sly than has often been assumed. An arguably paradigmatic declaration on the subject occurs in what must be among his most widely available and most widely read essays: the introduction to the 1964 Signet Classics paperback edition of Shakespeare's sonnets.

Appropriately, in 'Shakespeare's Sonnets', Auden provides a good deal of historical, formal and thematic commentary to assist a likely readership of secondary school students and undergraduates. But he opens with a dismissive assertion that seems designed to provoke such readers to think about what is involved in responding to lyric poetry: 'Probably, more nonsense has been talked and written, more intellectual and emotional energy expended in vain, on the sonnets of Shakespeare than on any other literary work in the world' (*F&A*, p. 88). While this is an exercise in vanity because, he notes, virtually nothing is known about the circumstances of the sonnets' composition, the very absence of information has been a boon to critical narcissism, as readers have used the sonnets to project their own self-interested theories about Shakespeare's sexuality. Such readers, he asserts, belong not to 'the sheep . . . who love poetry for its own sake' but to 'the goats . . . who only value poems either as historical documents or because they express feelings or beliefs of which the reader happens to approve'. To approach poetry in this way is more than just intellectually misguided, Auden suggests. It is wrong: 'A great deal of what passes today for scholarly research is an activity no different from that of reading somebody's private correspondence when he is out of the room, and it doesn't really make it morally any better if he is out of the room because he is in his grave' (F&A, p. 89).

How convincing such claims would be depends at least partly on what one might know about Auden and his other work. He was, as a young man, notorious for reading his friends' mail, and in later years, he reviewed quite a few literary biographies and editions of writers' journals and letters. Among these, his 1969 essay on J. R. Ackerley's memoir *My Father and Myself*, 'Papa Was a Wise Old Sly-Boots' (F&A, pp. 450–8), found it an occasion for elucidating the psychological meanings of various sexual practices among gay men. But even within his Shakespeare introduction Auden contradicts his very own principles. He argues both against those who want to exonerate Shakespeare of sexual 'abnormality' and against 'the homosexual reader' determined to have Shakespeare for a gay icon (in Auden's words, a member of the 'Homintern' – a usage he borrowed from Isherwood and Cyril Connolly). Instead, we are to see the erotic as merely the 'medium' for Shakespeare's deeper concern with 'the Vision of Eros': love as a spiritual experience transcending sex and corporeality – the subject of Plato's *Symposium* and Dante's *Vita Nuova*. But having made this point, Auden also comments that the sonnets are extremely unusual in Elizabethan poetry because of 'the impression they make of naked autobiographical confession' (F&A, p. 104), and he even infers a directly biographical narrative: 'The story of the sonnets seems to me to be the story of an agonized struggle by Shakespeare to preserve the glory of the vision he had been granted in a relationship, lasting at least three years, with a person who seemed intent by his actions upon covering the vision with dirt' (F&A, p. 103).

Notwithstanding his condemnations of prurient readerly speculation, Auden's introduction is as much a document in his own personal reactions to the sonnets as it is a dispassionate scholarly introduction. Like Oscar Wilde, whose 'Portrait of Mr W. H.' likewise engaged questions of what the smitten reader would like to believe about Shakespeare and the Young Man, Auden too recognises the subjectivity of criticism. The sonnets are, in his view, so revealing of the personal that Shakespeare must have been 'horrified' at their unauthorised publication, since sodomy was grounds for execution (*F&A*, p. 105). And despite his scorn for the biased homosexual reader who ignores the unambiguously sexual poems to the Dark Lady, Auden's inferred 'story of the sonnets' makes no mention of her either. This is, in fact, not just a biographical account but, as Edward Mendelson has argued, an *auto*biographical one – a version of Auden's embittered narrative of the early years of his own relationship with the young Chester Kallman (*Later Auden*, pp. 466–8). Eighteen years old when they met in 1939, Kallman had occasioned Auden's own Vision of Eros, which was subsequently undermined by Kallman's infidelity and Auden's own jealousy. By 1942, the relationship had ceased to be sexual, and the bitterness of the 'Crisis' (as Auden termed it in his private letters) left his mark not only on his poetry then but on his work for years to come – including here.[6] Despite the ostensible moral of his Shakespeare introduction, in other words, Auden was offering a distinctly personal response in keeping with his views elsewhere, both in conversations and in lectures, that Shakespeare's sonnets contain a paradigmatic tale of the emotional and psychological temptations and dangers facing homosexual love.[7]

As so often in his later work, Auden's essay is playing a game about the personal, in which – as Edward Mendelson aptly puts it – 'he was leaving his secrets hidden in plain sight' (*Later Auden*, p. 450). This was a practice that he had engaged in throughout his career, in the spirit of his epigraph to *The Orators* (1932), which extolled 'Private faces in public places'. The canon of high modernism has traditionally positioned Auden as an heir of T. S. Eliot, and his apparent early advocacy of an aesthetics of impersonality and his theoretical interest in psychoanalysis have made it easy to miss how directly his artistic investigations of desire followed from his personal concerns with love and sex. Far from indifferent to his sexuality, the young Auden spent much time and energy trying to make sense of the psychological and social meanings of same-sex desire and homosexual identity, and this project left an imprint on his early work that readers were free to see. Rife with sexual innuendo, 'Letter to Lord Byron' portrayed his early life as a journey driven by neuroses, and his Byronic 'airy manner' conveys a rebellious distrust of all forms of conformist coercion, from political authoritarianism to capitalist mass media to that 'Goddess of bossy underlings, Normality', who governs the upbringing of the modern bourgeoisie (*LFI*, p. 207). He himself, Auden writes, greeted the matron at his first school with the comment 'I like to see the various types of boys' (*LFI*, p. 205); went to an Oxford dominated by aesthetes who 'made new glosses on the noun Amor' (*LFI*, p. 209); and found his way to Weimar Berlin, where he imbibed the ideas of John Layard (disciple of the eccentric English educator Homer Lane), D. H. Lawrence and André Gide. Together, they taught him 'to express my deep abhorrence' of 'anyone preferring Art / To Life and Love and being Pure-in-Heart' (*LFI*, p. 210). Later outlined in Isherwood's 1938 memoir, *Lions and Shadows*, the gospel of the Pure-in-Heart extolled impulse as God, unjustly imprisoned by the false deification of the devil Reason: a philosophy that owed as much perhaps to the Blake of *The Marriage of Heaven and Hell* as to Lawrence or Lane.[8] In citing Gide as an influence, Auden insinuates that this philosophy of the Pure-in-Heart involved a sexual-political element to justify an embrace of his own homosexuality in Berlin, and for those willing to hear, the sexual implications of lines like these would have been clear: 'He's gay; no bludgeonings of chance can spoil it, / The Pure-in-Heart loves all men on a par' (*LFI*, p. 210).

But to judge from his private, unpublished writings and his poetry of the late 1920s and early 1930s, Auden was far more troubled than 'Letter to Lord Byron' lets on by what homosexuality meant for him personally and by the significance of same-sex erotic bonds in modern culture. The remarkable journal he kept in Berlin in early 1929 records, on facing pages, a diary of his love life and sexual relations with various young men he met in Germany, and a complex theoretical engagement with the work of Freud and Lawrence and the ideas of John Layard. The boy bars of Berlin apparently offered a therapeutic venue to fight the devil of control and practise being Pure-in-Heart, and in poems like 'Sentries against inner and outer', 'Upon this line between adventure', 'What's in your mind, my dove, my coney', and 'It's no use raising a shout', he portrays the closeting effects of neurotic self-consciousness. His ambitious four-poem sequence from this period, later titled '1929', cites two boyfriends by name as exemplars of a psycho-spiritual health to which to aspire: 'my friend Kurt Groote' and 'Gerhart Meyer / From the sea, the Truly Strong Man' (*EA*, p. 37). The 'truly strong', in the Auden–Isherwood usage, would be free of any neurotic need to prove his masculinity, and from passages like these, the poem's ideal of a healthier future gains a distinctly homoerotic cast. But it is clear from his journal that Auden saw his homosexuality as rooted in neurotic doubts about manhood:

> All buggers hate each other's bodies as they hate their own, since they all suffer under the reproach, real or imaginary of 'Call yourself a man' . . . Lack of skill in games at school, or anything that tends to make him feel 'I'm not a he-man' makes him fall in love with hookers. If not hookers, small boys[.] Sex relation an act of sympathetic magic.[9]

In keeping with his sense of homosexuality as a disorder, '1929' ends in an apocalyptic prophecy of 'the destruction of error', declaring (in a telling reference to Gide's sexually revealing 1924 autobiography, *Si le grain ne meurt*) that 'Love' necessitates 'Death of the grain, our death'. The implication is that he himself is among the incurables whose wandering from the straight and narrow path requires some sort of death and rebirth.

What Auden's Berlin journal makes apparent is that some of his early poetic diagnoses of psychological and social disorder manifest the tangled, contradictory attitudes about homosexuality he was grappling with at the time, and that he was using poetry itself as a quasi-psychoanalytic discourse for making sense of the meanings of desire. The riddling poem 'Before this loved one' (1929), occasioned by Isherwood's infatuation with an impoverished, beautiful boy he had met in a Berlin bar, diagnoses in the relationship 'an instinctive look' and 'a backward love', ever glancing over its own shoulder, so to speak, at its inescapable ancestry in earlier loves and, ultimately, in 'family', in 'history', and in 'ghost's adversity' (*EA*, p. 31). Here as so often in his early work Auden portrays love as all but irremediably defined by the past – as the very expression of the weight of a psychic inheritance from the living and the dead. In his explicitly Oedipal versions (as in the relation between John Nower and his vengeful mother, Joan, in 'Paid on Both Sides'), Auden is not simply rehearsing a Freudian cliché about domineering mothers and their homosexual sons, but expressing a tragic sense of desire itself as fatally infected by the inertial weight of the past: a form of arrested psychic development. In this same period, his journal was obsessively analysing his own sexuality in just such terms, writing of one relationship as a 'substitute and incestuous' coupling with his own 'son'; in another tracing his homosexuality to 'lack of breast-feeding'; elsewhere interpreting it as 'criticism of the mother as a love-object'.[10] Arguing with himself about these things, with Freud about matters like sex and the death instinct, with Proust about the homosexual as *homme–femme* and the dangers of strict gender binarism in children's upbringing, Auden's journal writing constitutes a singular document in gay literary history. For it shows him having absorbed what Foucault famously termed the 'medicalisation' of homosexuality: the modern theorisation of homosexuality as an identity subject to intellectual analysis and social control.[11]

If homosexual desire was troublingly contradictory from a psychoanalytic angle, so were its political valencies for Auden. The tropes of espionage and subterfuge that pervade his early work have been interpreted in a variety of ways: adolescent rebellion against the adult world, the internal psychological dynamics of desire and repression, the embattlement of the Auden group as Leftist products of bourgeois England, and Auden's own struggle with division itself as a conceptual and artistic problem. Read as allegories of the closet, early poems like 'Control of the passes was, he saw, the key',

'Who stands, the crux left of the watershed' and 'From scars where kestrels hover' imply Auden's fascination with the idea that sexual marginality can lend itself to a subversive detachment from mainstream culture. Auden's most elaborate investigation of this attitude occurs in Book II of *The Orators*, 'Journal of an Airman'. Using John Layard's anthropological fieldwork on the 'Flying Tricksters' of New Guinea (believed by their tribe capable of transforming themselves into birds) and their homoerotic initiation rites, Auden constructed the Airman as one of a group of subversives at war with 'The Enemy'. Although never quite stated openly, the Airman's homosexuality is strongly implied and has long been assumed by critics. Indeed, his sexual marginality is deeply tied to his rebelliousness. He is initiated into the cult of airmen at age sixteen by his maternal uncle, through whom he traces his deviant ancestry; he is obsessed with signs of secret identity; he makes cryptic references to a certain 'E', evidently his lover.[12]

In making the Airman a practical joker at war with an ever-present 'Enemy', Auden seems to have been indulging and critiquing his own pretensions as a politically subversive homosexual poet. The Airman's suicidal demise comes from his realisation of inescapable complicity (he calls it 'infection') with the Enemy. He thus implies Auden's ultimate dismissal of such ambitions as symptoms of an arrested development bred by mainstream culture. Here, as in 'Paid on Both Sides' and many of his early poems, Auden's portrayals of embattled groups are suffused with an aura of schoolboy homoeroticism and war-gaming. As a matter of theory, Auden seems to have been influenced by Freud's analysis of the conservative power of sublimated Eros in *Group Psychology and the Analysis of the Ego* (1921), but the theory was persuasive because of his own experience. In 'The Liberal Fascist' (1934), written for an essay collection on English public schools, he criticised his own otherwise progressive school, Gresham's, for the pernicious effects of its honour code, which prohibited smoking, swearing, and indecency, and which required enforcement by the boys themselves. Such a system constituted, Auden wrote, a virtual 'fascist state', inculcating group loyalty to disastrous effect on 'all those emotions, particularly the sexual, which are still undeveloped' in a boy. Denied expression, such emotions 'will not only never grow up, but they will go backwards' (*Prose I*, p. 59). For all the political seriousness with which the young Auden's poetry was taken, his portrayals of subversive rebellion in shorter poems like 'From scars where kestrels hover' and 'Look there! The sunk road winding' and in *The Orators* are both satirical and fatalistic, for such ambitions, he seems to imply, are merely the rebellious fantasies of immature psyches shaped by the very institutions the would-be revolutionary is trying to overthrow.

After *The Orators*, which many found all but impenetrably obscure, Auden seems to have made a conscious effort to cultivate a more accessible poetic style. Nevertheless, this work contained the seeds of ideas about art and Eros that informed his developing aesthetic theories in the 1930s and beyond. Early in the obsessive, cryptic theorising that constitutes much of his Journal, the Airman defines love as 'awareness of difference' and identifies himself as the 'AGENT OF THIS CENTRAL AWARENESS' (*EA*, p. 75). In these terms, his war on the Enemy is actually a war of love, for his tactics of subversive practical joking aim to expose the Enemy's foolish assumption that everyone and everything is what he thinks it is: it is an agenda of exposing difference. This is also a good description of the readerly experience of much of Auden's early published work, which characteristically portrays a realm that seems recognisably a physical place (the landscape of industrialised northern England) but is obscurely charged with dramas of intense conflict and embattlement. They are works that seduce the reader's interpretative desire in imagery and style that notoriously resist pinning down in referential terms. In the Airman's terms, they enforce awareness of difference in a challenging aesthetic of difficulty.

By the mid 1930s, Auden's work became much less aggressively avant-garde, making use of conventional forms like the sonnet, ballad and ode, and developing a more accessible lyric voice. But the 'awareness of difference' remained central to his published views about poetry, even as he began to stress explicitly the ways in which it functioned therapeutically for both poet and reader. 'What we call evil is something that was once good but has been outgrown', he wrote in 'The Good Life' (1935), describing the mechanism of repression (*Prose 1*, p. 114). In 'Psychology and Art To-Day' (1935), he employed related terms for discussing the value of psychoanalysis and art: 'Cure consists in taking away the guilt feeling, in the forgiveness of sins, by confession, the re-living of the experience, and by absolution, understanding its significance.' Psychology works, however, only insofar as it recognises differences. It is 'opposed to all generalisations', and so is art: 'You cannot tell people what to do, you can only tell them parables; and that is what art really is, particular stories of particular people and experiences, from which each according to his immediate and peculiar needs may draw his own conclusions.' Both psychology and art, at root, engage the 'central awareness' of 'difference' that the Airman defines as love (*Prose 1*, pp. 102–3).

In seeing psychology and poetry in this way, Auden was portraying a relation that, quite often, his love poetry focuses on for its *absence* in actual erotic relations. Typically, his love poems from the 1930s offer guilt-ridden confessions of an actual failure to love that is disguised in the poet/lover's manifest expression of desire: 'Such dreams are amorous', Auden writes in one poem, but 'no one but myself is loved in these' (*EA*, p. 145); 'It is an enemy that sighs for you' (*EA*, p. 147); 'I may be false but O be true to me' (*EA*, p. 150); and most grotesquely, 'the voice of love' pleading for erotic and emotional authoritarianism: ' "Be Lubbe, Be Hitler, but be my good / Daily, nightly" ' (*EA*, p. 153). All of these verses come from poems – many of them sonnets – addressed to the same young man who later inspired the oft-anthologised 'Lay your sleeping head, my love'. At one point Auden even seems to have contemplated an entire sequence in the manner of Shakespeare, and like Shakespeare's sonnets, much word-play in his love poems involves a profound sense of the moral and psychological duplicities of desire: neither the cynical poet/lover nor the apparently naïve young man he addresses should be believed, for both are playing coercive emotional games with emotions. Such an implication also haunts 'Lay your sleeping head, my love', which Mendelson has termed 'the first English poem in which a lover proclaims, in moral terms and during a shared night of love, his own faithlessness' (*Early Auden*, p. 233). The rhythmic verbal music of this 'Lullaby' (as later titled) is so compellingly handled that we are apt to forget the basic irony of the poem: it is a sincere confession of faithlessness that goes unheard by the beloved, who is of course asleep. What Auden's poems imply is impossible in life – a true confession of love – is paradoxically what they offer in art: a recognition of the differences between two people that the lover narcissistically seeks to erase through emotional domination, wishful thinking or simple lies. They are 'parables' drawn from Auden's own, inarguably dark view that homosexual love was especially – though not uniquely – given to envy and the will-to-power. But they do not enforce the particularity of his sexuality on readers, and in this, they seek to leave readers free to respond according to their immediate and peculiar needs.

With Auden's turn to Christianity after his emigration to the United States in 1939, his poetic theory took on a vocabulary drawn less from psychology and more from theology. But he consistently described poetry in ways that suggest he saw it as modelling a non-coercive love only theoretically possible in social bonds or actual personal relationships. 'In a successful poem', he wrote in 'The Virgin and the Dynamo', 'society and community are one order and the system may love itself because the feelings which it embodies are all members of the same community, loving each other and it' (*DH*, p. 69). Behind this proposition would seem to be the notion that poetic form can exemplify a reconciliation of human sameness and difference through its negotiation of the semantic multiplicity of language itself and the emotional multiplicity of the poet. Were such patterned arrangements actually carried out in society, Auden acknowledges, the result would be totalitarianism, but precisely because art is gratuitous – pointless, unnecessary – it provides what he calls an 'analogy' to 'paradise' or 'the forgiveness of sins'. Poetry is, in other words, an emblem of what Auden liked to term 'The City' in Augustine's sense – the City of God. Such verbal and emotional orders, however, are radically at odds with modernity, which the later Auden habitually attacks for the destructive sameness compelled by totalitarian systems and capitalist mass culture. Poetry's voice may amount to no more than that of a 'suburb of dissent', but its marginality makes possible an intimacy that modern mass society would not otherwise tolerate. Ultimately, for Auden, Eros and Agape seem to merge in his views of poetry. In *Secondary Worlds* (1968), he defined poetic meaning as 'the outcome of a dialogue between the words of the poem and the response of whoever is listening to them', a deeply interpersonal process yielding 'the kind of knowledge implied by the biblical phrase "Then Adam knew Eve his wife": knowing is inseparable from being known' (*SW*, p. 114). From this angle, all poetry can be read as love poetry, for all poems bear the potential for intimate self-revelation, by both poet and reader.[13]

Considered in sexual-political terms, it is hard to know whether Auden's propositions about love, sexuality and poetry mark him as deeply conservative or radical. Although he never in his adult life sought to live or to be taken as anything but homosexual, nor does he ever seem to have abandoned the attitude that homosexuality was psychologically or morally suspect. Nor does his poetry force the reader to confront his homosexuality directly. Because he resists easy appropriation as an affirming voice for gay sexuality and identity, Auden is therefore unlikely to figure as largely in gay male literary history as, say, Walt Whitman or E. M. Forster. At the same time, his views of love, sex and desire are so thoroughly shaped by his grapplings with the psychological workings and political implications of homosexuality in particular, that his career constitutes an important chapter in literary history that bridges Oscar Wilde and the relative decline of the closet in literature after Stonewall. Within these parameters, Auden's career appears as a remarkably lengthy, sophisticated effort to make sense of homosexual desire and identity, as well as an endless combat – by turns anarchic and subtle – against the constraints on speakability that enforce the closet. 'The blessed', he writes in one of his greatest, most intensely homoerotic love poems, 'In Praise of Limestone', 'will not care what angle they are regarded from, / Having nothing to hide'. The lines are at once coy and revealing, and their coyness about what Auden is hiding is also an invitation to the reader to speculate. Here, as so often, he proffers poetry as allowing for love in 'awareness of difference', conjuring what remains a utopian, liberal vision, in which identification with others does not collapse difference into sameness, but honours it.

## NOTES

1. Edward Callan, *Auden: A Carnival of Intellect* (New York: Oxford University Press, 1983), p. 36.
2. See Eve Kosofsky Sedgwick, *Epistemology of the Closet* (Berkeley: University of California Press, 1991), pp. 67–90.
3. See for example, Bruce R. Smith, *Homosexual Desire in Shakespeare's England: A Cultural Poetics* (Chicago: University of Chicago Press, 1991); Paula Bennett, 'The Pea That Duty Locks: Lesbian and Feminist-Heterosexual Readings of Emily Dickinson's Poetry', in Karla Jay and Joanne Glasgow (eds.), *Lesbian Texts and Contexts: Radical Revisions* (New York: New York University Press, 1990), pp. 104–25; Catherine Stimpson, 'The Somagrams of Gertrude Stein', *Poetics Today*, 6:1 (1985), pp. 67–80; Christopher Craft, 'Alias Bunbury: Desire and Termination in *The Importance of Being Earnest*', *Representations*, 31 (1990), pp. 19–46.
4. See Richard R. Bozorth, *Auden's Games of Knowledge: Poetry and the Meanings of Homosexuality* (New York: Columbia University Press, 2001); Robert Caserio, 'Auden's New Citizenship', *Raritan* 17:1 (1997), pp. 90–103; Edward Mendelson, *Early Auden* (London: Faber and Faber, 1981) and *Later Auden* (London: Faber and Faber, 1999); Gregory Woods, *Articulate Flesh: Male Homo-Eroticism and Modern Poetry* (New Haven: Yale University Press, 1987). For important earlier analyses that touched on homosexuality and Auden, see Randall Jarrell, 'Changes in Attitude and Rhetoric in Auden's Poetry', in *The Third Book of Criticism* (New York: Noonday Press, 1971), and James Southworth, *Sowing the Spring: Studies in British Poetry from Hopkins to MacNeice* (Oxford: Basil Blackwell, 1940).
5. See Alan Sinfield, *Cultural Politics – Queer Reading* (Philadelphia: University of Pennsylvania Press, 1994), p. 60.
6. See Bozorth, *Auden's Games of Knowledge*, pp. 198–220.
7. See W. H. Auden, *Lectures on Shakespeare*, ed. Arthur Kirsch (Princeton, N.J.: Princeton University Press, 2000), pp. 97–8; Howard Griffin, *Conversations with Auden* (San Francisco: Grey Fox Press, 1981), pp. 98–9.
8. See Christopher Isherwood, *Lions and Shadows: An Education in the Twenties* (New York: New Directions Publishing, 1977), pp. 239–41. For an argument about the relevance of Layard's ideas for Auden's views of sexuality and the intellect, see Bozorth, *Auden's Games of Knowledge*, pp. 56–62. Blake's text is a major influence on Auden's posthumously published study of 1939, *The Prolific and the Devourer*.
9. W. H. Auden, *1929 Berlin Journal*, unpublished manuscript journal (Berg Collection, New York Public Library).
10. *Ibid.*; for further analysis of Freud's developmental theories of erotogenic organisation, and their influence on Auden, see Bozorth, *Auden's Games of Knowledge*, pp. 69–80.
11. See Michel Foucault, *The History of Sexuality*, trans. Robert Hurley (New York: Vintage Books, 1990), pp. 36–49.

12. See Bozorth, *Auden's Games of Knowledge*, pp. 123–31; Peter Edgerly Firchow, *W. H. Auden: Contexts for Poetry* (Newark: University of Delaware Press, 2002), pp. 70–119.
13. For an astute analysis of the relationship between Auden's views of Eros and Agape, see Alan Jacobs, *What Became of Wystan: Change and Continuity in Auden's Poetry* (Fayetteville: University of Arkansas Press, 1998).

# 15

GARETH REEVES

# Auden and religion

Auden liked systems. He liked to categorise and pigeonhole, but invariably with the awareness that all systems and categories only work on their own terms, that the systematiser is implicated in his creations, that consciousness, while freeing us to explain ourselves to ourselves and to each other, also imprisons us in the explanations we have framed. There can be no one to stand outside and watch (except God). Hence the provisionality, audible in all his poetry if carefully listened to, of the various systems of belief he entertained one after the other, Freudian, Marxist, liberal humanist, even and finally Christian – although this last came to seem to Auden the one that gave him the most room to manoeuvre. Such freedom within restraint characterises also, and especially, Auden's attitude to poetry. Poetic form may be arbitrary, but within its limits and limitations it permits, or rather induces, quest and discovery, although the object of discovery, especially for the Christian Auden, is always out of reach. The limits of poetry make us aware of what lies beyond, as he wrote in 'Un Homme d'Esprit': 'The formal restrictions of poetry teach us that the thoughts which arise from our needs, feelings, and experiences are only a small part of the thoughts of which we are capable' (*F&A*, p. 364). Poetry came to be for Auden the most serious game of *homo ludens*. His 'Ode to Terminus' thanks the god of limits 'for giving us games and grammar and metres'. But disaster happens when one system encroaches on another, the artistic on the political, say: in 'The Poet and the City' Auden argued that a 'society which was really like a good poem, embodying the aesthetic virtues of beauty, order, economy and subordination of detail to the whole' would be a horrific dictatorship practising brutal eugenics, and gave a tongue-in-cheek demonstration of the petty-tyrant poet's method of composition, his verbal 'selective breeding' and 'extermination', the dictatorial techniques of rephrasing, transposition and cuts (*DH*, p. 85). 'Poetry makes nothing happen', he famously wrote in 1939, but he also wrote in the same poem that it is a 'way of happening'; and even, perhaps especially, in the face of his espousal of Christianity in 1940, he needed to demonstrate, to himself as much as to his readers, the nature and importance of poetry's particular way of happening.

Auden's account of his conversion reveals that he knew he had always needed to entertain systems. With some condescension he writes that the various 'kerygmas' – preachings – of Blake, Lawrence, Freud and Marx taken up by him and his contemporaries in the 1930s, 'were all Christian heresies'. At least they were all based on the religious belief that 'matter, the natural order, is real and redeemable . . . and historical time is real and significant' (*Pilgrims*, p. 38). Psychoanalysis, Freudianism, Marxism, are all partial and monistic explanations, whereas Christianity is complete. He quoted approvingly Nietzsche's view of Christianity as 'a system, a view of things, consistently thought out and complete. If we break out of it a fundamental idea, the belief in God, we thereby break the whole into pieces' (quoted in RD-H, p. 202). Christianity subsumes all other systems; it is the system to end all systems. This way of thinking reverses even as it is consistent with earlier Auden, who, in an essay called 'The Good Life', published in 1935, attempted to synthesise religious, scientific, philosophical and political systems, and concluded by finding Christianity wanting in comparison with the other systems when faced with the challenges of the modern world. One can imagine an older Auden with the benefit of hindsight finding the seeds of his religious conversion in the questions posed in the essay, 'If our desires are mutually incompatible, which are we to choose? i.e. what ought we to desire and do, and what ought we not to desire and do?'[1] These questions were to be given a Kierkegaardian Christian-existentialist answer, where that 'ought' becomes a Christian imperative, and our freedom to choose an unknowing 'leap of faith'. So when Humphrey Carpenter emphasises the rationality behind Auden's religious beliefs, writing that his 'conversion had apparently been an exclusively intellectual process rather than a spiritual experience', he is pointing to a deep-seated tendency that had been with Auden from early on (Carpenter, p. 298). That rationality eventually involved the recognition that Christianity paradoxically requires the exhaustion of all reasonable explanations and a leap of faith into the unknown and unreasonable.

Hence *New Year Letter*, which reasons its way towards Christianity, quotes St Anselm's '*credo ut intelligam*', 'I believe in order that I may understand' (*NYL*, line 422), for absolute and irrational belief permits, because it goes beyond, the exercise and play of that most human of faculties, the reason that accompanies understanding. Characteristically, Auden 'the double man' (the work's original, American, title), the categoriser and qualifier who sees himself in the mirror and on the other side of every argument, must use reason to get beyond reason. Moreover at this time (the poem was written between January and April 1940) the internal struggle was urgent, for Hitler's domination of Europe and the start of war signalled for Auden the failure of reason, the stand-by of the liberal humanist. As he was to remember sixteen years later, 'the liberal humanism of the past had failed to produce the universal peace and prosperity it promised, failed even to prevent a World War' (*Pilgrims*, p. 40). And in 1940 he wrote that 'The whole trend of liberal thought . . . has been to undermine faith in the absolute' by trying 'to make reason the judge', an argument he read in Reinhold Niebuhr's book *An Interpretation of Christian Ethics* (1936) and which must have weighed heavily on an intellect as active as Auden's.[2]

'Historical time is real and significant' for Auden because the Christian's belief in 'a personal God implies that the relation of every human being to Him is unique and historical', as he wrote in *Canterbury Pilgrims* (p. 32). So History must be schematised to see where I am now, at this moment in History. One statement in 'The Good Life' which the Christian Auden would have found proleptic acknowledges the point of view that the 'existence [of evil desires] in us is to be explained by the Fall – an inherited defect in our nature, which, since God is good, must be attributed to a volitional act of rebellion at some period of human development' (pp. 34–5). As Carpenter points out, this view of the Christian doctrine of the Fall as 'a representation of a fact of human psychology' became characteristic of Auden's religious thought: he saw the Fall 'as a symbol of the point in history where Man developed self-consciousness and became aware of the possibility of freedom and autonomy' (Carpenter, p. 299). Thus *New Year Letter* focuses in on this central and distinguishing fact, that 'Man faulted into consciousness', that alone of all creation we know who we are and what we are doing, knowledge which is the ground of our freedom and our responsibility to choose. The poem thus gives a Christian twist to the existentialism of the sonnet sequence 'In Time of War' from *Journey to a War* (1939), with its evolutionary version of History to the point where we are 'now' ('Yes, we are going to suffer, now', sonnet XIV; 'Where life is evil now', sonnet XVI), when 'We live in freedom by necessity' (sonnet XXVII), a phrase which conjures up in an intriguing blend of elegy and expectancy Engels's dictum, 'freedom is the knowledge of necessity'. From here the way for Auden led to Kierkegaard: 'As a spirit, a conscious person endowed with free will, every man has, through faith and grace, a unique "existential" relation to God, and few since St Augustine have described this relation more profoundly than Kierkegaard'. *Canterbury Pilgrims* (pp. 41–2), from which this derives, explains that one reason for the attraction of Kierkegaard (other reasons, not unrelated, were his humour and his 'talent . . . of making Christianity sound bohemian') was the capaciousness and generosity, the paradoxically unsystematic nature of his system, for it comprehends all that makes us human. Kierkegaard's view of humanity as made up of conscious beings perpetually obliged to exercise their free will to choose from an infinity of foreseeable possibilities, means that each individual presents his unique case.

But for Auden poetry's way of happening cannot be existential, for it deals in things completed, not things foreseeable; it is art, not life:

> Art in intention is mimesis
> But, realized, the resemblance ceases;
> Art is not life, and cannot be
> A midwife to society,
> For art is a fait accompli.

These lines occur near the start of *New Year Letter* in the context of contemporary Nazi anarchy, and the 'task', both in 'Art and Life' is to 'set in order'. 'Midwife to society' flirts with a jocularly dismissive tone, raising the question of whether such a fate for poetry is desirable, for the orders of art are potentially dangerous in the ways described in 'The Poet and the City'. But the poet never allows himself to give up on the possibility of poetry's efficacy, and characteristically the opposed view is allowed a sly look-in. In the parabolic model of poetry which this verse-paragraph goes on to describe, 'unique events that once took place', when used in a poem, change into

> An abstract model of events
> Derived from dead experience,
> And each life must itself decide
> To what and how it be applied.

The style of *New Year Letter* sounds reasonable, but the reasoning is often slippery. Here the poet holds his cards close to his chest with 'And': the necessity thus to 'decide' shows that poetry is either ethically neutral, or that it is ethically invigorating since we are compelled to exercise choice. Substituting 'But' for 'And' would tend to tip the balance in favour of the first alternative, emphasising the gap between art and life: '*but* it is up to us as to how to apply art's model to life', rather than '*and*, as a consequence, we are able to apply'. Poetry reads us as we read it. It becomes a parable of our freedom to choose, of our moral being.

How we receive poetry depends on our predisposition. Thus in *New Year Letter* the devil has 'no positive existence': as our self-projection and double agent he is only our 'recurrent state / Of fear and faithlessness and hate'. As such he does not tell lies 'But half-truths we can synthesize: / So, hidden in his hocus-pocus, / There lies the gift of double focus.' As Stan Smith points out, Auden is here 'turning his favourite trick on the word "lies", changing its grammatical function from noun to verb as its semantic function too is converted from language to physical position' (Smith, p. 130).[3] That change artfully demonstrates how by indirections we may, so the poet hopes, find directions out: by tempting us with half-truths the devil presents us with the possibility of truth. Thus poetry is like a 'magic lamp', 'utterly impractical, / Yet, if Aladdin use it right, / Can be a sesame to light.' The utter impracticality of poetry has its guiltily negative aspect ('For poetry makes nothing happen'), but not being a midwife to society may not be such a bad thing if it can be a doorway to the 'light' beyond, a means of leaping. A note to these lines intimates this tension between guilty aesthetic delight and ethical aspiration, its optative mood: 'The Devil, indeed, is the father of Poetry, for poetry might be defined as the clear expression of mixed feelings. The Poetic mood is never indicative.' The synthesising poetic intelligence has to deal with 'mixed feelings', but, as the lines of poetry with which the note ends say, 'The Truth is one and incapable of self-contradiction; / All knowledge that conflicts with itself is Poetic Fiction' (*NYL*, p. 119). Something that is 'incapable of self-contradiction' is not the stuff of poetry, which needs the 'half-truths we can synthesize' for its very existence. There is no room here for something called Poetic Truth: all poetry is by definition fiction.

Aesthetic delight is so dominant in a poem like 'Leap Before You Look' that its intensely mixed feelings risk going unnoticed. But then its manner is beguilingly polite, as if in fear of offending. The poem plays around with language in a self-consciously formal manner, the delight in its own proce-dures affecting the tone unsettlingly. The greater the demands on the poet of its formal game, the smaller the demands on the reader, or so it seems, for its expression is deceptively clear. A seductively deliberate fait accompli, its message is that lack of deliberation is the order of the day. Its ludic arena is highly restricted, a fact that makes the proposed leap all the riskier. John Fuller, pointing out the poem's 'ingeniously' artful 'pseudo-villanelle' form, argues that 'such technical shadow-boxing' gives the poem a 'sense of circumspection [which] nicely underlines the "danger" which is the sub-ject of the poem'. Fuller also writes that the subject of the poem is 'the risk involved in making the existential choice of life, more specifically the suggestion that Kallman might follow him in becoming a Christian' (Fuller 1998, p. 397). That circumspection takes the form of a deference ('Much can be said for social savoir-faire') which, it proposes, must be put at risk; and beneath the social niceties is an awesome Kierkegaardian 'solitude ten thousand fathoms deep [which] / Sustains the bed on which we lie, my dear'.[4] The social savoir-faire of this address knows that it is playing artfully with its (poetic) audience, those being wooed to take the recklessly unsociable leap, even as it contemplates the loneliness where 'no one is watching' and where questions of audience are beside the point. The cosily friendly 'my dear' plays with and off those friendless fathoms with artfully polite circumspection. The poem sounds like an invitation expecting circumspectly polite resistance, and Kallman never did accept the invitation (Carpenter, pp. 300–1).

Poetry is time-ridden, it belongs to History and our fallen condition, but it can make us, within its enclosed arenas, its parables, conscious of the timeless. The 'Coda' to 'Archaeology', one of the last poems Auden wrote, concludes with the assertion that 'History / is nothing to vaunt of' since it is 'made . . . by the criminal in us', whereas 'goodness is timeless'. Just as poetry is born of our devilish mixed feelings, so History is the child of 'the criminal in us'. Only in myths and rites, we have just been told, can we escape our time-bound individuality ('Only in rites / can we renounce our oddities / and be truly entired'), the pre-eminent instance being the 'abominable' rite of the crucifixion. That rite, with its attendant criminal in us, Auden contemplated at length in 'Horae Canonicae'. The rest of this chapter will be devoted to this sequence, for the crucifixion presented the poet with a challenge that focused his mixed and guilty feelings about the role of poetry.[5]

In his commonplace book *A Certain World* Auden insists on the impossibility of Good Friday as a subject for poetry: 'Christmas and Easter can be subjects for poetry, but Good Friday, like Auschwitz, cannot. The reality is so horrible . . . Poems about Good Friday have, of course, been written, but none of them will do.' He goes on to sketch in an argument that underpins the progress of 'Horae Canonicae': 'Just as we were all, potentially, in Adam when he fell' – which is the idea motivating the first poem, 'Prime' – 'so we were all, potentially, in Jerusalem on that first Good Friday' – which is the motive for 'Terce' and 'Sext'. The puzzle behind the whole sequence, and its central poem 'Nones' in particular, is indicated when Auden goes on to imagine himself as a witness to the crucifixion, 'a Hellenized Jew from Alexandria visiting an intellectual friend'; and 'averting my eyes from the disagreeable spectacle, I resume our fascinating discussion about the nature of the True, the Good, and the Beautiful' (*CW*, pp. 168–9). The poetry of 'Horae Canonicae' spends its time averting its eyes from the disagreeable spectacle, elaborately circumventing the subject. At the heart of the sequence is the intractability of the crucifixion as a subject for poetry: its meaning is that it cannot get at the meaning. And the larger implication is that this is what happens every day of our lives: we do not, we cannot, because it is 'so horrible', think about Christ's martyrdom, even though, or indeed because, it informs everything we do and are. That is why Auden called the sequence 'a series of *secular* poems based on the Office' (Fuller 1998, p. 456, emphasis added) because the focus is the life lived, and not lived, in the shadow of, and necessarily despite, the Cross.

In approaching the events of the crucifixion in relation to the daily life of the individual with his temporal 'oddities' and to mankind's guilt and suffering, 'Horae Canonicae' takes its cue from that pre-conversion poem 'about suffering', 'Musée des Beaux Arts', turning it, with the benefit of hindsight, into a proleptically Christian poem. Fuller has pointed out the 'rich double meaning' in this poem's first word, 'for it is Bruegel's very circuitousness of approach ("about" in a different sense) that Auden is interested in . . . In Bruegel's *Landscape with the Fall of Icarus*, the painter presents a momentous event in a world of diurnal unconcern' (Fuller 1998, p. 266).[6] Likewise Auden approaches his subject circuitously, for before his poem gets round to mentioning the Brueghel painting in line 14, it notes, as if in passing, the world's unconcern both at 'the miraculous birth' (the word 'Christ' being studiedly circumvented) and, almost in the same breath, at the crucifixion: 'They never forgot / That even the dreadful martyrdom must run its course / Anyhow in a corner . . .' The whole matter of the Incarnation passed barely noticed on the stage of History. 'Horae Canonicae', then, is 'about' the crucifixion in the same way that 'Musée des Beaux Arts' is 'about suffering'. Running its course anyhow in a corner is how the dreadful martyrdom is presented in the sequence, or, rather, extensively circumvented among a world of richly elaborated diurnal unconcern. As ever, Auden as entertainer of systems shadows the sequence, for the Offices of the canonical hours along with many other tables of categories, either borrowed or invented (historical, theological, anthropological, social, physiological, personal), provided the poet with systems to be imaginatively exploited, affording him the opportunity to exercise his fallen nature, the criminal in him, to give the devilish father of poetry his due (see Fuller 1998, p. 457).

This 'Poetic Fiction' is 'knowledge' that knowingly, and often with surprising humour, 'conflicts with itself'. It is also a quiet tour de force, a literary performance that knows it is performing, though never ostentatiously so. The sequence confesses abundantly to feelings of guilt, of forgiveness, of the possibility of redemption, without coming across as 'confessional'. 'Prime' achieves this effect by hauntingly enacting the individual's waking from sleep – in so doing intimating Auden's notion of the Fall as a psychological fact, 'Man fault[ing] into consciousness' – in a mysterious lapse into consciousness, where the acting subject of the seductively welcoming opening adverbs is at first uncertain: 'Simultaneously, as soundlessly, / Spontaneously, suddenly / As, at the vaunt of the dawn . . .' Does the second 'as' have the same function as the first; is one perhaps comparative, the other temporal? With the 'dawning' of consciousness comes the self's implication in and resistance to historical guilt and responsibility, to the criminal in us. History may be 'nothing to vaunt of' ('Archaeology'), but here the self is caught in the act of vaunting before it has become conscious enough to know better, 'at the vaunt of the dawn'. That phrase typifies the artful artlessness of 'Prime'.

The internal rhyming and assonance, the patterns of sound weaving through each of the three long sentences that form the poem's three stanzas, give an air of automatic writing, *homo ludens* at his most playful, appropriate to the re-enactment of an Everyman consciousness lighting out at its inno-cent dawn: 'and I / The Adam sinless in our beginning'. That phrase sounds like an innocent jingle, though the echo of 's*in*less' in 'be*gin*ning' holds what is in store. The fortuitousness of this art is part of our (fallen) humanity, is the implication, one to be spelt out in 'Nones', where the poet happens upon the chanciness of the rhyme 'will' and 'kill'. 'Holy this moment, wholly in the right': one chime, happy at the start of the second stanza, plays off against another, not so happy, at the end of the poem, where the poet's 'name / Stands for my historical share of care'. Individuation, the decline from the general Adam to the particular named person, brings with it conscious-ness of self and other, of individual and society, of inherited guilt and respon-sibility, the world of time, the 'living' and the 'dying', of all that makes us human.

From the poet's Christian perspective this is to state the obvious – 'Paradise / Lost of course' – but the triumph of the poem has been to create a simulacrum of time suspended, a timeless now, this holy moment, before the onset of History and being in time. Thus in the first stanza the sense of timelessness comes in large part from the spiralling syntax, those sus-pended 'as' adverbs giving way to clauses that take in even as they pass over what is to come, what has been left behind, and, disarmingly, what is, or is to become, the sequence's central subject, intimated with circuitously ironic understatement as 'an historical mistake', a way of putting it that conjures up an aversion 'from the disagreeable spectacle'. Not until the stanza's end do we arrive at the main clause, and the moment out of time 'Between my body and the day', between sleeping and waking, self and other, unconsciousness and consciousness. This moment which becomes the existential 'presentness' of a new world in the second stanza, which also ends, via a similar syntactic spiralling, timelessly where it began, suspended in the 'holy' time before the original sin, 'wholly in the right', and before the onset of History. To say that this Edenic moment is re-created in the optative mood is to empha-sise the knowing fictionality of this seductive literary wish-fulfilment. The knowingness is in the playful phrasing: 'the vaunt of the dawn' teeters on the edge of self-parody, 'the nocturnal rummage / Of its rebellious fronde' sounds as if the submerged political analogy ('fronde' refers to aristocratic French insurrectionaries) is being mildly ribbed, and so on. Such moments are always poised to slip into graver images and sounds. The effect unsettles, questioning the numinousness of the experience. The wavering tones belong to a poet with an irremediably (and perhaps in his own eyes irredeemably) worldly and ironic intelligence, even, or especially, when approaching the numinous and otherworldly.

As a series of 'secular' poems 'Horae Canonicae' gives the devilish-criminal in the poet ample scope, especially when it comes to the next poem, 'Terce', with its thumbnail sketches of those, including the poet, who are inevitably to participate in the crucifixion, sketches drawn at times amusedly, at times laconically, the worldly tone turning world-weary. As in 'Musée des Beaux Arts' life will continue willy-nilly while the abominable rite occurs, and some details from that poem carry over into this: in particular the hangman's comically friendly dog recalls the earlier poem's dogs with their 'doggy life'. The earlier poem's daily unconcern gets transmuted in 'Terce' into the disregard of the small and large deities who 'Cannot be bothered with this moment'. That casual tone has turned by the last line into the deadly irony of 'knows that by sundown / We shall have had a good Friday' (more deadly than Eliot's 'in spite of that, we call this Friday good').[7] The stifling by brackets of the knotty and central theological paradox of free will and God's omniscience underscores the intransigently secular perspective: '(that is what / We can never forgive. If he knows the answers, / Then why are we here, why is there even dust?)'. Does the speaker know he is echoing the Bible ('For dust thou art, and unto dust shalt thou return', *Genesis* iii.19)? The poet must know, but in this fictional enactment his persona evidently does not. What, asks the casual parenthesis, is the point of it all, the meaning of life no less? 'Sext' likewise indulges a worldly-wise manner in its portrayal of the three components of any civilisation (a section of the poem for each) that make possible the crucifixion: those with a vocation, the executives, the crowd. But each section, written in the poet's most characteristic and lively diagnostic mode, is brought up short by an absolute and unanswerable paradox. The first section asks where society would be without those who have a vocation; and yet, it abruptly ends, without them 'there would be no agents' for the crucifixion. It is not just that we are stymied by the paradox; we are perplexed by the sudden negation of the poet's imaginatively inventive art that has but a moment before been wittily creating and categorising a society.

If 'Horae Canonicae' is not confessional in the manner of, say, Lowell's 'Life Studies', the figure of the poet is throughout intermittently but continually implicated and questioned in the stylistic ways this account has been suggesting. If the poet, as he is imagined in 'Terce' to have been before the crucifixion, does not know who he is to write about that day, he realises it only too well in his aubade after the crucifixion, in 'Prime'. If coming to consciousness brings with it all the world of knowledge, endeavour, responsibility, guilt and death, it brings with it also an awareness that that Truth has been told and fictionalised in poetry only too famously: 'I draw breath . . . / . . . and the cost, / No matter how, is Paradise / Lost of course and myself owing a death'. Suspending Milton's epic across the line-break like this enacts the opening up of the Edenic moment only to experience its immediate withdrawal as the contingent world of time and guilt impinges. It also underlines the literariness of this experience: it is a story told often before. At the same time, the implication of the poet in this sinful world casts a shadowy guilt over his literary endeavour. A curiously covert link exists between sin and poetry here, created by the way in which the line elides *Paradise Lost* and the guilty poet with not so much as a comma between them. And if the 'breath/death' echo makes its point with too obvious an audibility, that could be the point: 'of course' the story is only too familiar, at any rate to the card-carrying Christian.

To the poet, that presents a particular challenge, as is evident from the hauntingly powerful 'Nones'. At the heart of this heartfelt poem, which is central (in both senses of the word) to the sequence, is a massive absence, an emotional blank. Where we are now, at this moment in History, is nowhere; and in the midst of this absence we encounter the poet's *Doppelgänger*. After evoking the post-crucifixion sense of existential desolation ('We are left alone with our feat', a bitterly laconic circumlocution for the abominable rite) and the now meaningless world of human action, the poet fleetingly includes his former poetic self, for among the 'discarded' artefacts are snatches of poetry ('Abandoned branch-lines', 'Grindstones buried in nettles') that recall Auden's prelapsarian youthful poetic landscapes (which even then were on the verge of lapsing), the post-industrial 'watershed' of 'dismantled washing-floors, / Snatches of tramline'.

Apprehensions of the numinous and timeless may be explained only 'too well' now by the fact of the Incarnation and its culmination, and the crucifixion may have the potential to make sense of History, but for the time being our guilt-ridden existence will continue inexplicably, is the implication, however we 'misrepresent' or 'use this event' (including using it in poetry). But the poet would escape his sense of desolation in an emotionally exhausted aversion of eyes and mind. However, 'our dreaming wills' only 'seem to escape', for what follows in the penultimate stanza is a series of increasingly nightmarish imagery which, as it proceeds, in Anthony Hecht's words, 'takes on the somewhat vulgar contrivances of an unconscious with

the taste and standards of grade-B movies'. Hecht is evidently not intending to be negative, for, as he implies, the encounter at the end of the stanza
puts the nightmare into ironic perspective, 'the arch-villain' of the movie
turning out to be the poet's *Doppelgänger* 'in Poe-like seclusion'.[8] In his
self-absorption the poet-figure has been inventing cinematic scenarios that,
however compelling, come across as all too knowing rewrites of early Auden
again, with an eye for would-be diagnostic details, mysterious antagonists
and significant landscapes, and an ear for the fast tone and authoritative air. If
phrases like 'latent robbers' and 'hostile villages at the heads of fjords' sound
clichéd, they do so partly because early Auden, as its supreme practitioner,
has accustomed us to this idiom of urgent sinister-comic threat ('latent robbers' is a good joke: they lie hidden and, being robbers, are potential liars).
The dream comes across as out of place in this poem, but that is the point:
the *Doppelgänger* poet is being shown up.

For the dream belongs to the 'will' and is therefore the product of a mis-
placed effort to explain and rationalise. When the will relaxes there ensues
in the final stanza a poetic release, undesolate and distinctly lacking the tonal
games of the previous stanza, in the spirit of these words by Auden about
the world of nature, the un-Kierkegaardian (he insists) unconscious world
of universal being:

> every man has a second relation to God which is neither unique nor existential:
> as a creature composed of matter, as a biological organism, every man, in
> common with everything else in the universe, is related by necessity to the God
> who created that universe and saw that it was good, for the laws of nature to
> which, whether he likes it or not, he must conform are of divine origin.
>
> (*Pilgrims*, p. 42)

If these words sound preachy, their equivalent in 'Nones' does not. The
final stanza prays that our 'biological organism' may restore 'the order we
try to destroy', in an ignorance different from the poem's earlier vexed and
desolate incomprehension. In the poem's concluding vision, of creaturely
care and universal law, the poet can make his point about the natural order
while allowing himself a chuckle of envy with a joke about hens in 'pecking
order'. And as ever he cannot resist seeing his earlier poetic self in a new
light: the youthful line 'As the hawk sees it or the helmeted airman' arro-
gantly (or so the later Auden might have supposed) paralleled human and
creaturely panoptic perspectives, whereas here in 'Nones' 'the hawk' gazes
on our fallen world 'without blink', with a quasi-divine unillusioned but
caring indifference.

In 'Compline', the last service before sleep, which returns the sequence to
the state of unconsciousness with which it began, the poet asks, 'Can poets

(can men in television) / Be saved?' The parenthetical phrase puts the poet on a par with all who have to do with an audience and a public, which is everyone, since, though all individuals, we are all responsible (immediately after the crucifixion, in 'Nones', 'we have lost our public'). The poet admits that he can make no sense of what happened 'between noon and three', the hours Jesus hung on the Cross, instead recollecting 'Actions, words, that could fit any tale, / And I fail to see either plot / Or meaning'. But if his poetic fictions cannot fill his amnesia satisfactorily, this means that the only recourse is to fall back on prayer, which the end of 'Compline' proceeds to do. This prayer, like all prayer, must learn to accept the given, numbering the poet, humorously, as one of the ineffectual 'poor s-o-b's' who desires to be spared 'in the youngest day', which, Fuller surmises, 'may be both the Last Day and the ever-present Now' (Fuller 1998, p. 461). 'All knowledge that conflicts with itself is Poetic Fiction': even if prayer would see beyond this, having to accept that 'facts are facts', always the poetry knows that it can never get further than a 'clear expression of mixed feelings', can never reach 'the Truth'. Both the Last Day and the ever-present Now, the existential moment which is no sooner present than past, are beyond poetry, words even. And the ineffable is precisely, in the words that begin 'Nones', 'What we know to be not possible', a way of putting it that undoes itself even as it is uttered.

## NOTES

1. 'The Good Life', in John Lewis, Karl Polanyi and Donald K. Kitchin (eds.), *Christianity and the Social Revolution* (London: Victor Gollancz, 1935), p. 31.
2. Quoted in Carpenter, p. 283. See Carpenter, pp. 306–7, for Niebuhr's influence.
3. Smith is developing a deconstructionist argument about the radical challenge of *New Year Letter* to the notion that 'language has to correspond to a fixed reality and its sole purpose is to ensure that fixity'.
4. For Kierkegaard's 'ten thousand fathoms', see Fuller (1998), p. 397.
5. 'Prime' and 'Nones' first appeared as separate poems in *Nones* (1952). The whole sequence was published as the third and final section of *The Shield of Achilles* (London: Faber and Faber, 1955), pp. 61–80.
6. Fuller also (1998, p. 267) hazards a proleptically Christian reading of 'Musée des Beaux Arts': 'To what extent, the reader wonders with biographical hindsight, was the poet himself "reverently, passionately waiting / For the miraculous birth"?'
7. T. S. Eliot, 'East Coker' iv, *Four Quartets*, *Collected Poems 1909–1962* (London: Faber and Faber, 1963).
8. Anthony Hecht, *The Hidden Law: The Poetry of W. H. Auden* (Cambridge, Mass.: Harvard University Press, 1993), p. 347.

# 16

PAOLA MARCHETTI

# Auden's landscapes

Humphrey Carpenter and friends such as Brian Howard and Lincoln Kirstein have suggested that Auden had no visual sense and little interest in the visual arts. His topographical and pictorial iconography has, possibly in consequence, been largely overlooked. But the depiction of landscape, both real and symbolic, is a recurrent feature of his poetry. His approach to the physical landscape and to painters such as Daumier, Picasso, Cézanne, Dürer, Titian, Brueghel, Salvator Rosa, Poussin and Piero di Cosimo, consistently transforms the perceived world into symbolic, allegorical and metonymic modes, as vehicles for intellectual and moral ratiocination. Not for nothing is one of his early poems called 'Paysage Moralisé' (1933).

Auden consistently projected his bipolar vision, working through a complex series of opposites, on to his landscapes. His early approach to topographical imagery, shaped by a Romantic sense of the contradiction between reason and feeling, was gradually transformed into a postmodern acceptance of duality as a 'unity-in-tension' (*DH*, p. 65) of different modes of being. His poetic landscapes are haunted by the opposition of the wilderness and the city, reflecting a divided human nature, engaged in a historic quest in which the ideal is repeatedly threatened with relapse into barbarism. Landscape forms the backdrop for such journeying along an unending road, with a great city behind and unexplored regions ahead.

Many of Auden's poems are posited on such metaphorical journeys through symbolic landscapes. Others deploy landscape allegorically to explore the relation of the mind and body to their habitat, viewed in psychological, historical, anthropological and social terms. On occasion, Auden reverses the traditional device, in which the natural world is anthropomorphised. Instead he 'naturalises' the human body, viewing it as a natural landscape. He uses allegory and symbolism as the poetic counterpart of the basic duality he perceived in human nature between Logos and Eros: allegory being a more active and rational approach to the world (via analogy); symbolism a more passive, visionary expression of a primary world of perceptions.

If duality is the key to Auden's poetry, the multiple perspectives offered by the image of parallel and coexisting geological strata, or of overlaid layers of paint in a painting, are the key to understanding his landscapes. His early works express the struggle between the body, constrained by natural and inescapable laws of cyclical repetition, and a mind which resists and seeks freedom from necessity. The image of the journey is developed as the search for the right place, the Just City, where true existential freedom may be realised. This place initially has political connotations, but is transformed in the 1940s and 1950s into a spiritual locus beyond time and space, St Augustine's 'City of God'. In his later years a balance is reached and the body reconsidered as a human landscape.

In the early poetry, natural and human perspectives converge or collide. One perspective derives from Thomas Hardy, from whom Auden learnt to see reality from a great distance, as in the view *sub specie aeternitatis* of *The Dynasts*, reproduced in the hawk's eye view of 'Consider this and in our time'. The other perspective derives from T. S. Eliot, whose work taught Auden to see reality close up, from a particular, and often squalid, urban viewpoint. In his early works Auden combined these perspectives with images derived from the new sciences of psychology and anthropology, and from science in general, as represented by Darwin's and Huxley's visions of nature and culture. His early scientific and psychological stance investigated the human landscape, of mind, society, history, in the context of evolutionary natural processes.

Between 1927 and 1931, Auden created the parameters of his imaginative landscape: dark woods, abandoned mines, locked gates and chained-up orchards, remote valleys, limestone hills and mountains, silted harbours, fortified farms and besieged cities. The most pervasive image is that of places of passage, transit and division: frontiers, passes and watersheds. The landscape is inhabited by spies, secret agents and enigmatic heroes who possess incomplete maps of the country, and by adversaries, enemies, censors, hostile and retributive figures, who may be pursuing and even trying to kill the protagonist. 'The Watershed' describes a landscape 'comatose, / Yet sparsely living'. 'The Letter' speaks of coming down into a new valley, frowning at having lost one's way, and of crouching behind a sheep-pen to avoid being seen, without ever explaining the reason for such caution. 'Taller Today' speaks of a walk in an idyllic orchard, but undermines a 'peace / No bird can contradict' with the prospect of night and snow, visions of the dead howling under remote headlands, and of lonely roads where the traveller is confronted by a Sphinx-like Adversary who puts apparently easy but actually treacherous questions. 'From scars where kestrels hover' depicts a mysterious leader looking down into a happy valley he cannot enter, his companions doomed, dying beyond the border in a world of 'acrid' streams and 'driven sleet'. In 'The Secret Agent', the self is a trained spy out of touch with his base in an uncharted enemy region, led into a trap by a 'bogus guide', conscious that he will soon be caught and shot. The poem later called 'No Change of Place' speaks of anxious journeying from one place to another, only to reach the conclusion summarised in the title, forced to turn back in the foothills by a gamekeeper with gun and dog.

These are all real and symbolic loci in which a personal psychomachia unfolds. The land through which the spy travels is the *Ur-Mutter*, the primal mother, an impersonal nature with its unchanging laws of birth, generation and death that absorb the history of the individual into the history of the species. Death is defeated only by the powerful resistance of the life force – Eros, 'Dame Kind', 'Love', or evolution figuratively anthropomorphised as the goddess of 'Venus Will Now Say a Few Words' – a force sometimes associated with a stream feeding a turbine or with the ambivalent fire of love. Such energy is also a cultural form of imprinting, shaping the collective mind, as in 'Family Ghosts'. The natural world is for Auden a place of unfreedom. In spite of nature's incessant transformations, everything in it is inevitable and predetermined. The relationship of spy to alien landscape is a troubled one, as in 'To Ask the Hard Question', because the protagonist is aware of the dissociation between his body, the natural map of these poems and the journey the intellect initiates to free itself from the laws of nature. Though nature imposes limits, boundaries and 'chained orchards', the spirit refuses to acknowledge them during its uncertain journeying. The land to be explored is the protagonist's own body, as differentiated from that of both the Mother and Nature. This interpretation is confirmed by symbols which associate the earth with the body of a god in both classical and Norse mythologies. Further symbolic analogies are evoked by the poetry's derelict and depleted locations. Abandoned lead mines are a case in point. Lead, the *nigritudo* of alchemy, is matter in a state of unregenerate blackness and in need of fire for sublimation and alchemical transformation. Black coal represents a potential life which can be kindled by fire until its blackness turns into a fiery red. 'Love' in the early Auden is such a fire, the Lawrentian/Nietzschean force of Eros which offers a provisional way out of the impasse. Love is a seed which in the terms of Pauline paradox must die in order to create a new life.

Auden's early imagery still carries Romantic echoes: the poet stands between land and sea in poems such as 'No Change of Place' and 'The Wanderer', and has to start his journey to the sea from 'inland'. Initially he shuns responsibility and bows to the natural laws he would like to deny. This apparent calm, an anaesthesia of the will, is for Auden the modern malaise. If the individual is waiting for the regeneration represented by the water of love, the country, with its corrupted aristocracy, and the capital with its unscrupulous glittering elite, also await renewal. *The Orators* marks a break and starts Auden's self-conscious progress. John Fuller describes the work as a form of 'autotherapy': the poet banishes the ghosts of his own adolescence in deconstructing the rites of passage envisaged as school rituals. On a symbolic plane, passage requires the death of the old self, to let the new emerge.

These issues are sketched in the Prologue to *The Orators*, a poem subsequently published separately under the title 'Adolescence'. The adolescent boy wants to abandon a comforting maternal landscape that reminds him of his mother's body, but he does not turn his wish into action. The various sections of *The Orators* are allegorical descriptions of real places and events, many of them from Auden's immediate Scottish environment where he worked as a teacher in Helensburgh, Dumbartonshire. A key section, 'Letter to a Wound' describes his own psychological illness and associates it with different parts of the body, according to Lawrence's and his own ideas about psychosomatic illness. In 'The Journal of an Airman' he finally describes such illness as kleptomania, onanism and homosexuality. The Enemy the Airman wants to defeat has been interpreted as Lawrence (Mendelson), or the mother (Fuller), but one is inclined to think that he is both, and also Auden's own self. This seems to be confirmed by the Epilogue, with its intention to journey out of this forsaken landscape, passivity finally defeated by an active self which intends to go through the pass and travel beyond the wood.

*The Orators* offers the anatomy of a self sick in body and mind. On an allegorical plane, it depicts the sickness of the society which produced it, England in the 1930s. It is therefore an anthropological and social study of a sick body politic which transmits disease and neuroses through such institutions as its public schools. 'Ode v' depicts the school pupils as recruits on the side of repression in a wider cultural war. We, the soldier-pupils, observe the movements of the enemy in an embattled, First World War 'no-man's-land'. The young soldiers meet death anyway, going north and dying in the snow, a recurrent symbol of death for Auden, perhaps on the analogy of Gerald Crich's fate in *Women in Love*.

The symbolic self-destruction of *The Orators* is a salutary progress in Auden's own journey because it makes him aware of the positive function of limits and borders. In 'Now from my window sill' (1932), and in *The Dog Beneath the Skin* (1935) the poet prays to Blake's Lords of Limits and Lawrence's Witnesses, the ancestors, to protect him from what is beyond the border. These characters are versions of his *genius loci*, the guardians of doorways, copses and bridges, presiding over duality and over life and death as symbolised by the *limes*, or threshold, itself. The journey from the landscape of the unconscious body of childhood to the mature self-conscious body of the adult can now be seen as a journey towards the recognition of necessity. Auden's landscapes are the context for the journey of civilisation from its beginnings, the dark woods of, for example, Piero di Cosimo's depiction of primal anarchy, to its ideal cultural apex, the City.

The dualities of body and mind, nature and culture are crystallised in 'Paysage Moralisé' (1934) with its images of islands, shores, seas, in contrast to those of once 'learned' cities which are now 'starving' and 'unhappy'. 'Paysage Moralisé' is a key text in Auden's symbolic topography, and a link between the pre-eminently psychological landscapes of the 1930s and his historicised concepts of time and place in the 1950s and 1960s. If in the first sestina in *The Orators* ('Have a Good Time') the key words (country, bay, wood, love, clock and vats) stress the spy's personal discovery of his own body, the key words of 'Paysage' offer a larger historical perspective (valleys, mountains, water, rivers, islands, cities and sorrow). The valleys still represent the protection of the womb, the mountains again recall the masculine motive of the quest; water is still the power of life, regeneration and art. However, choices in history are seen as choices between imaginary and fantasy islands and the real, fallen and unhappy city which has to be rebuilt.

The text uses its key words allegorically, symbolically and historically, thus permitting parallel and complementary readings in accordance with a multiple vision which depicts the history of the individual and of civilisation. 'Man', the builder of cities, discovers that the impossible islands of his dreams are only the worlds of his mind, which rejects the reality of the body. In 'Paysage Moralisé' everything is double or has shifting and multiple meanings, reflecting humanity's divided condition. As the poet seems to indicate, such multiplicity can be perceived only when the poem is read as a picture which overlays synchronous events (the 'moralised' landscape of the title). The poem's final image is of a snow-bound landscape which, it hopes, will melt, gushing and flushing green these sorrowful valleys, making possible the rebuilding of 'our cities', that possessive adjective appropriating what was previously alien.

Islands, as either refuges in a pastoral dream of the past or goals of a future utopia, are a recurring symbol in this period. Iceland, in 'Journey to Iceland', is an imagined refuge away from Europe and history, though the traveller takes with him his duality, his personal history and his own landscape. Similarly, the question asked in the poem later called, questioningly, 'Whither', from the start of *Journey to a War*, as to whether a happy island exists, is answered negatively. Nevertheless, there remains the hope that the 'quick new West' of our false culture could be transformed (see, for example, 'Certainly Praise').

Love in these poems is seen as a force capable of transforming natural, primary narcissism into moral commitment in history by digging into the rich soil of the English tradition, as in 'O, Love, the interest itself in thoughtless Heaven'. As both a right to personal fulfilment (the 'language of love') and as a moral imperative ('the language of learning'), love is embodied in the physical landscapes of 'A Summer Night' and 'A Bride in the Thirties', the former seeing history as a sea scattering human debris on the shore, the latter casting it as an urgent journey under the 'sixteen skies of Europe'. Spiritual love is ambiguously invoked in 'Musée des Beaux Arts' (1938). Auden had already used Titian's allegory *The Three Ages of Man* in 'The Price' (1936). 'Musée' not only works through an indirect description of three paintings by Pieter Brueghel the Elder, *The Fall of Icarus*, *The Numbering at Bethlehem* and *The Massacre of the Innocents*, but also muses on art's ability to portray the historical world, contrasted with its inability to change it.

Brueghel's pictures depict human activities in landscapes where many stories are told simultaneously: Auden uses these stories as visual counterparts of his own reflections on 'man' as an individual and as a material and cultural being living in time. The first two pictures show an unredeemed humanity either in a state of nature (the mythical past of Icarus) or in the crowd of modernity (the city, the massacre). 'The Numbering at Bethlehem' suggests the possibility of an unselfish world of love redeemed by suffering. Nature is distant and indifferent while good and evil (the civilised and the primitive in us) seem to be the necessary agents of history. There are no heroes in these pictures: Auden has gone beyond his Romantic preconceptions to recognise that human existence in time requires art, like all other human endeavours neither innocent nor perfect, to rebuild the ruined walls of the city. Ready to set off on a new quest, the poet has to construct a physical and spiritual frontier between his former and his prospective self. The landscapes of Britain, even the symbolic white cliffs of home, become his past in 'Dover' (1937), a place merely of transit where happy and unhappy destinies intersect, disclosing to the traveller, quitting this 'island of minor importance', the whole wide Continent beyond. A similar moment occurs facing the energetic sea, recalling Monet, in 'Look, Stranger!', where ships go by like seeds 'on urgent voluntary errands', at the intersection of freedom and compulsion.

At one stop in his existential travels, New York confronted the expatriate poet with the image of Megalopolis, its 'blind skyscrapers' proclaiming 'The strength of Collective Man', the antithesis, it might seem, of the ideal city, but a place where two fundamental events contributed to changing Auden's ideological and personal paradigms. Love and faith become the cornerstones of this new mental landscape, where reality is accepted in all its incomprehensible otherness. The 1938 sonnet 'Chilled by the Present' speaks of sighing futilely after the innocent landscapes of 'an ancient South' of 'instinctive poise', but then redefines the human condition, in Engels's words, as that of living in freedom by necessity, a mountain people living amidst mountains. 'The Riddle' (1939) retells this story in terms of the loss of an Edenic landscape. Only the tree of life, of existence, the poem suggests, is real; the tree of knowledge is a mere subjective dream.

In the1940s, such ideas were rearticulated in terms of Kierkegaard's three existentialist stages, the aesthetic, the ethical and the religious. These reshape the human journey, no longer seen as Housman's 'long fool's errand to the grave', as a quest, defined in terms of the Christian myth of a primal Fall from unity into duality. Kierkegaard's three psychological conditions are also stages in humanity's journey through history. The aesthetic stage corresponds to a self subject to the laws of nature and the Fate of the Greek cosmos; in the ethical stage, the rational man of the Renaissance city rejects the childish universe of magic and enters time and space as a moral agent who aspires to order and truth. But order and truth are mined by ignorance and evil which cannot be overcome through historic action. The final stage necessary for salvation is that of religion, which, by encompassing and superseding both the previous stages, creates the prospect of a regenerated humanity. These three stages are not simply consecutive: they can be experienced simultaneously, a recognition which accounts for the multiple perspectives of Auden's mature poems.

Such an insight informs the topographical symbolism in the longer poems of the 1940s. The quest is a central theme in the sonnet sequence which concludes *New Year Letter* (1941). The quest is necessary ('The Way') in that it represents a moment of change, illumination and self-consciousness leading to personal decisions here and now. The restless protagonist of *The Orators* has become a Christian pilgrim whose meekness and patience make him a loser in Caesar's world ('The Lucky', 'The Hero'), losing the world, in traditional Pauline terms, in order to gain it.

In *The Age of Anxiety*, the traveller is associated in Jungian idiom with the four unredeemed faculties – thinking, feeling, intuition and sensation – identified with different parts of the body or with different ages of man. In "For the Time Being" the new religious dimension is symbolised by the journey of the Magi – scientist, philosopher and sociologist – who, crossing the deserts of the real to follow the star of the Annunciation, implicitly accept their own limits only to aspire to something beyond them. The quest in these poems of the 1940s does not offer permanent answers to a creature whose real condition is that of division. At the end of these partial illuminations, the travellers find themselves back at their point of departure. This is the fallen city, ruled by the barbarism of money and the machine, which in *New Year Letter* have transformed human community into an amorphous, disintegrated crowd. The city is now a place of spiritual paralysis created by the ethical, liberal man of the modern era, whose political and cultural utopias have failed, the pseudo-real New York of All Souls' Night, 1944, of *The Age of Anxiety*.

The desert, a void and barren landscape of metaphorical absences, gradually supersedes the city in Auden's symbolic topographies. The ideological function of the island is progressively transferred to the image of the garden (sometimes, the oasis), a powerful symbol associated with the religious and the aesthetic spheres, reflecting human self-division. The garden, the 'Nowhere-without-No' of *New Year Letter*, can be an ideal, otherworldly locus, beyond history, where human self-division is overcome and innocence restored in a New Jerusalem. From an aesthetic perspective, it is an ideal refuge, an earthly paradise where conflicts are resolved and order and beauty triumph over chaos and ugliness. In 'The Sea and the Mirror' such a place is a merely theatrical space, the stage where one is self-consciously an actor living two simultaneous lives, the imaginary theatrical one and the real one in abeyance for the duration of the play. In the poem, which is a serious meditation on the responsibilities of art, Ariel and Caliban represent man's double nature: the first as the Neoplatonic symbol of art and the mind, the second as that of the real body revolting against its tyrannous master. Ariel must be confined to the stage where reality is magically suspended and transformed into a world of possibility and general abstraction. Caliban, who represents multiplicity, violence and fragmentation, reminds the reader that our lives are lived offstage, in the actual, not the imagined world.

In *The Age of Anxiety* the mystical nature of the walled garden is emphasised by the references to medieval myths of the unicorn (last seen in glimpses at the end of *New Year Letter*) in the *hortus conclusus*, the rose garden of innocence before the Fall. (T. S. Eliot's *Four Quartets* are clearly intertexts of this extended 'eclogue', or pastoral poem.) The complex, symbolic world of art finds figurative counterparts not only in the Unicorn Tapestries in the Metropolitan Museum in New York, but also in the allegorical paintings of such Renaissance masters as Dürer, Piero di Cosimo, Pisanello, Gentile da Fabriano and Perugino. The garden is, among other things, the pastoral locus of opera, in particular of baroque opera (the gardens of Armide), a theatre of illusions and magic. It represents, for Auden, a space of conscious illusions where one can freely roam and where music is more important than words, because less burdened by historical and referential meanings (as in 'Song for St Cecilia's Day'). However, Auden does not reject commitment to the fallen historical world. Poems such as 'Memorial for the City', 'The Shield of Achilles' or the sequence 'Bucolics' depict problematic landscapes, where desolation presents a challenge to the human, or offer pastoral critiques of human waste, violence and destruction.

The traumatic experience of war in 'Memorial for the City' has created a symbolic landscape where civilisation has been replaced by the ruins and barbed wire of 'the abolished City'. The poem reflects on human cruelty, reminiscent of a primitive, pagan world where the possibility of choice and salvation posed by Christianity has not yet appeared. The poem, itself a journey through the different historical embodiments of the city, presents a human creature whose image has not been changed by history and who, no wiser, has produced our modern 'Metropolis' where other human beings 'can be counted, multiplied, employed' like money or 'in any place, at any time destroyed'. Here suffering and injustice are real, as they are in 'The Shield of Achilles'. But 'Memorial for the City' envisages a renewed City in which 'Our grief is not Greek' (that is, pagan, fatalistically pre-Christian) and time is not linear, endlessly repetitive and cyclical, but contains the possibility of a genuine break and discontinuity, into redemption and transcendence.

After the intense visionary and allegorical ordeal of the forties, Auden's poetry changes and acquires a more colloquial and relaxed attitude, inspired by Goethe but especially by the 'detached' commitment of a pastoral poet such as Horace, whose love for domesticity, the company of few friends, solitary meditation, realistic observation and fantastic invention Auden shares. He adopts Horace's terse conversational style, his pungent critical eye and his humorous indulgence. The motif of *carpe diem*, of the fugitive beauty of life which must be enjoyed while it lasts, is part of a stoic acceptance of what is given, together with the cultivation in keeping with the Horatian mode of such virtues as honesty, civil commitment and the pursuit of truth and balance in life and poetry. This new attitude is enhanced by Auden's rediscovery of the civilised Mediterranean landscape of Italy, where nature seems to have been more benign than in northern countries. The landscapes of 'In Praise of Limestone', 'Goodbye to the Mezzogiorno' and 'Ode to Gaea' introduce the more poised but still alert voice of the 'minor Atlantic Goethe' to be discerned in 'Bucolics' – the name applied to classical celebrations of idyllic pastoral landscapes.

Poems of this period voice a relationship with the landscape perceived as the physical context nurturing the lives and cultures of its inhabitants. The carved and chiselled limestone of Tuscan cities transforms the material world of nature into artful and urbane visions of order. The landscape seems to have been magically and effortlessly transformed into garden, vineyard, fountain, temple, palace and city. Here the mind has so shaped and transformed the world's body as seemingly to contradict Auden's 'anti-mythological myth' that art cannot improve the world. Leaving Italy after ten years, Auden felt compelled to contrast the northern cultures of guilt with the south's cultures of shame. He remained fascinated by a landscape whose vistas are a 'cure for ceasing to think', as he puts it in 'Ischia', where the heat and the language appear to render nugatory the idea of the quest. Yet the Mediterranean world seems nevertheless to be bound by the implacable laws of nature, the fate of classical paganism, as if choice and personal responsibility, founded in conscience and guilt, the mainstays of Protestant cultures, had been banned by the Catholic south.

The more detached perspective of these years is typical of a poet who, like the Airman of his 1930s writings, is a frequent flier, permanently, as the title of one later poem puts it, 'In Transit', and who can therefore look down on the earth in its magical and physical beauty from an altitude. In 'Ode to Gaea', the mother goddess Earth, daughter of Chaos, like Titian's Venus, admires herself in a mirror. Her body is enigmatically described according to the scientific perspective of the different realms of liquids (rivers/seas) and solids (mountain/plains), but also according to the mythical and psychological vision of ancient cartographers, who placed monsters and wild beasts at the extreme boundaries of the known world. Poets see the magic of life-giving water in all its possible metamorphoses, in a synthesising and panoptic vision that creates sequence and causality from all the minute particular observations of science, of hydrology and physical geography, following it from snow and ice, to small lakes, big river deltas, blue seas streaked by plankton and the white sea froth magically transmuted into myriads of white pebbles and birds. Humble, endlessly metamorphosing water is the unending source of life and hope celebrated in 'Streams' in 'Bucolics', while man is the little creature who, living in molehills, alters and changes the syntax of nature. What has been described as Auden's ecological consciousness makes him aware that nature cannot be reduced to geometry and that man is not only a rational creature but also an irrational, intuitive being who needs the magic of high places such as mountains. His early cartographic mythology is transformed in this new, poised perspective but, as in 'Musée des Beaux Arts', nature remains indifferent to man. The 'good landscape', the one we dream of, remains a fabrication and fantasy. The tension between civilisation, culture and art (the city) and the barbarous behaviour of natural man (the wood) becomes the theme of the sequence entitled 'Bucolics'.

Inspired by a series of pictures by Poussin and by Piero di Cosimo's cycle *The Early History of Man*, 'Bucolics' retrieves the complexity of the multiple vision expressed in 'Paysage Moralisé' but also transforms the pastoral tradition evoked by the title. Its seven poems ('Winds', 'Woods', 'Mountains', 'Lakes', 'Islands', 'Plains' and 'Streams') figure, in metonymic mode, the human characteristics Auden associates with them analogically. As in his earlier texts, the geography of a place suggests the idea of a journey into an imagined 'secondary world' and a return to the disenchanted here-and-now. The journey follows human evolution up to the present, evoking a landscape which is at once actual and figurative, associated with real historical events which simultaneously take on metonymically suggestive meaning. As in the 1930s poems, 'Bucolics' sees the history of the individual reproducing the history of the species, ontogeny recapitulating phylogeny. Auden's previously 'scientific' gaze is partially abandoned, however, for a more humane and intuitive perspective. The need for a reconciliation of the fractured human 'moieties' (Auden's word in *New Year Letter*) is here reflected in the ambivalent images, inherited from the pastoral tradition, of soft and hard primitivism. The soft, arcadian/utopian vision must coexist with the hard, scientific-rational point of view. The seven landscapes not only combine the four elements and their rich apparatus of contrasting symbols but also allude to different stages of technical and spiritual evolution from wood, to desert, to city. The desert plains of mass society is where all 'pointing' or aspiration has been dissolved. The only refuge for the poet is represented by the garden of 'Streams', a place of *concordia discors* inhabited by a *homo sapiens* who is also *homo ludens*, a world of pastoral innocence or the utopian realm of art which do not serve Caesar's realm. As in 'Paysage' or 'Musée', art illustrates human doubleness, but also promises choice and volition.

The major theme of Auden's late poetry is the cohabitation of Eros and Logos, body and consciousness, and the implicit acceptance of human duality. The body is revalued as the house of the spirit, which expresses its wish to shape and order the world through architecture. If the body is our primary home, the house, celebrated in 'Thanksgiving for a Habitat' as a private not public building, becomes our second body. The act of entering and leaving such a building implies the final dialogue established between subject and object, the material self and the conscious ego. Texts such as 'The Geography of the House', 'Grub First, Then Ethics', or 'The Cave of Nakedness', explain this new-found relationship as an *encomium* of the body itself, whose limits and needs can be transformed or apprehended as virtues. Thus the lavatory humorously demythologises artistic production by comparing it to excretion, while the kitchen reconciles body and soul by way of conviviality and the 'catholic' act of eating. The bedroom is the place of sleep, bodily regeneration and sexual reproduction of the species. Love has thus acquired a new dimension which may be summarised in Rosenstock-Huessy's observation that 'Sexuality throws no light upon love, but only through love can we learn to understand sexuality.'[1] Love is finally considered as both physical and spiritual, its duality acknowledged. If in the early poems the lover was the 'other', a body or landscape to be explored ('Easy Knowledge') and to get lost in, now he is still a 'you' different from 'I' ('The Common Life'), but also a dear place where one has roots ('Amor Loci'). The beloved mining landscapes of Auden's youth are redeployed in 'Amor Loci' to represent the loved one as a *locus amoris*, to be mined for the hidden ore of meaning and value.

'Ode to Terminus' retrieves the earlier image of the body as a place and the idea of a necessary boundary, now represented by death. The Lords of Limit are back. Yet, they no longer represent duality but rather intellectual humility, the awareness that knowledge and truth can be acquired only in fragments. The border, the extreme limit, is also associated with humanity's intellectual arrogance, represented by the modern Megalopolis. The city described in 'Ode to Gaea' or 'Atlantis' as either the unknown wilderness or the happy island, has become the spiritual desert, the 'gadgeted world' of boredom dominated by the press, networks and noise which 'shelters from the basilisking glare of nothing' ('City Without Walls'). Its history is retold in 'River Profile' by using the metaphor of the river's descent (the Fall) from the mountains to the sea. The lands the river runs through are phases of a civilisation but have also become a symbolic landscape leading to death. Human history is not evolution but degeneration in a still unredeemed, quasi-Wellsian universe: 'What they call History / is nothing to vaunt of, / being made by the criminal in us: / goodness is timeless' ('Archaeology'). Auden does not turn away from this view of the human, but regards it in a disenchanted double perspective where art and faith remain redemptive spiritual reference points. Once art is stripped of Romantic subjectivity, 'The Cave of Making' suggests, poetry may become the Horatian celebration of private and everyday life, in a landscape no longer corrupted and distorted by the Fall. In this perspective, the Platonic cave is humorously represented by Auden as our own mind, a place where 'silence is turned to objects' by language. In this 'Cave of Making', language translates, metaphorically shapes and projects ideas from the house of the mind on to the outside world, in the process creating a fully human landscape charged everywhere with spiritual significance.

NOTE

1. Cited in Fuller (1998), p. 493.

# 17

RAINER EMIG

# Auden and ecology

## Radical anthropocentrism

Auden's aversion to Romantic idealism, especially the Shelleyan mingling of spiritual sublimation and political radicalism, is well documented.[1] His nature images also reject Romantic models. For the Romantics, nature provided an imaginary framework enabling the self to overcome alienation. 'Nature' bridged the gap between childhood and adulthood as a quasi-religious power enabling the self to enter a higher plane than that of a mundane reality where actual, physical nature was increasingly sacrificed to the Industrial Revolution.

In Auden, images of nature are always man-made constructs. The early poem '1929' is telling. It contains a list of potentially Romantic nature images, frogs in ponds, 'traffic of magnificent cloud' across open sky, only to frame them in the urban context of a public garden and eventually of individual, social and political concerns. Already the term 'traffic' hints at a thoroughly anthropocentric perspective. In an essay on Robert Frost in 1936, Auden stated bluntly: 'Man is naturally anthropocentric and interested in his kind and in things or animals only in so far as they contribute to his life and sustain him; he does not interest himself in things to the exclusion of people till his relations with the latter have become difficult or have broken down.'[2]

'Paysage Moralisé' (1933) is another case in point. Already its title treats nature as a symbolic construction. Its focus is on the founders of civilisation and their increasing problems. Even its final image of a possible abandonment to nature ('Shall I melt? Then water / Would gush, flush, green these mountains and these valleys') rejects the Romantic sublimation of the self in a force beyond human control. Instead it returns to its initial mission and signals its inevitability for thinking human beings: 'And we rebuild our cities, not dream of islands'.

Auden's refusal to turn nature into an imagined escape, his insistence that it serve as a symbolic point of orientation for human beings who must embrace the tasks of civilisation, makes him an unlikely candidate for an evaluation in terms of ecocriticism. Developed from the 1970s onwards, mainly in the United States as a reaction to increasingly visible environmental problems, ecocriticism achieved some organisation during the 1990s in works such as *The Ecocriticism Reader*.[3] In its naïve formulations, ecocriticism is little more than traditional motif studies linked with equally old-fashioned moralism. Especially in its early phase it hunted for nature images in literature and evaluated their 'correct' representation. Genres such as 'wilderness writing' or 'nature writing' were its concern, and writers like Henry David Thoreau served as its patron saints. Since then, ecocriticism has struggled to evolve along similar lines as feminist theory – from an initial identificatory phase, via one resembling French *écriture féminine* in its search for ways in which nature might shape writing itself, to a third stage incorporating deconstructionist and poststructuralist ideas.[4]

Ecocriticism sets out to criticise anthropocentrism in human culture and literature. It defines it correctly as the product of a hierarchical opposition which enables humans to position themselves at the centre of their universe by constructing around them an 'environment' to be domesticated and governed. This is the reason why ecocriticism eventually abandoned the label 'environmental criticism'. In the course of the present chapter, however, it will become evident that 'ecology' is not free from anthropocentrism either.

The term 'ecology' was coined in 1866 by the German zoologist Ernst Haeckel.[5] From a term for systematising plants and animals, it soon evolved into an understanding of their relations in general. In the twentieth century, the term increasingly featured in writings on society, economy and politics, such as H. G. Wells's *Work, Wealth and Happiness of Mankind* (1932). Auden used the term only once, in *New Year Letter*, where it appears, tellingly, as 'The Catholic ecology' in a description of the speaker's journey through the 'Environment that keeps the soul' led by *Amor Rationalis*. Auden here emphasises rather than restricts anthropocentrism, by turning to the most anthropocentric construction of all: religion.

This might suggest the impossibility of applying ecocriticism to Auden's works. Yet he is frequently invoked in debates on ecocriticism and ecology. Robert Morrison, reviewing James C. McKusick's *Green Writing*, Lawrence Buell's *Writing for an Endangered World* and Jonathan Bate's *The Song of the Earth*, for example, starts with the famous line from Auden's 'In Memory of W. B. Yeats', 'poetry makes nothing happen'. He adds poignantly: 'Ecocriticism believes otherwise', and invokes Shelley's famous statement that 'Poets are the unacknowledged legislators of the World.'[6]

Auden is also quoted approvingly by natural scientists, especially his sceptical comments on the limitations of technology and rationality. Thus,

Guillermo Agudelo Murguía and Juan Sebastían Agudelo from the Human Evolution Research Institute in Madrid not only cite his 'After Reading a Child's Guide to Modern Physics'; they even call the first chapter of *The Sentient Universe*, their manifesto, 'Auden's Question, Gould's Answer'.[7] Auden's question concerns the usefulness of scientific knowledge – to which Stephen Jay Gould, an eminent palaeontologist, appears to provide an answer.

The present chapter will try to negotiate these contradictions. It will ask if Auden's poems can be read as ecological texts. If yes, what is their understanding of ecology? Rather than merely using ecocriticism as a tool, it will enquire whether Auden's works provide a productive critique of a strand of literary scholarship that only came into prominence after his death in 1973.

## Hidden laws: thinking in networks

It would be inaccurate to conclude from Auden's symbolic use of natural imagery that his poetry is rationalistic and ignores the physicality of human beings and their environment. His early works seek to control this environment rationally through the use of maps, aligning Auden with Thoreau, a surveyor by profession. Yet, as Rick van Noy argues, Thoreau's increasing frustration with cartography became the generator of idealised, 'sublime' anti-maps in his poetry.[8] Auden's early poems, in contrast, turn the environment into reified anti-sublime texts by creating linguistic maps out of place-names. Simultaneously, they acknowledge the status of a self divided between mind and body. Auden's 'clinical imagination' combines both. The son of a physician, Auden was fascinated by psychosomatic theories – to a degree that images deriving from them appear in menacing proportions in poems like 'The Questioner Who Sits So Sly'.

This is also noticeable in '1929'. After discrediting Romantic nature imagery, it elaborates its own model of human evolution by equating psychological maturation with somatic growth. Its second part contains two nursery rhyme stanzas outlining the progress of the individual from the mother's womb to the alienated maturity of colonialism, marriage and inheritance (a very British trinity). This common individuation has a negative counterpart in the poem's first section, where an isolated weeping male is described as 'Helpless and ugly as an embryo chicken'. Besides parodying conventional Easter symbolism, the line echoes popular theories of individual evolution of the 1920s, such as Rudolf Steiner's anthroposophy. Steiner's theories project the Darwinian evolution of the species on to individuals, ontogeny recapitulating phylogeny, turning presumedly scientific states into symbolic ones. From such anthropocentric symbolic thinking there appears to be no escape.

This is what the second part of '1929' concedes, ending with a problematic call to self-love as the basis for loving anything else: 'To love my life, not as other / Not as bird's life, not as child's, / "Cannot", I said, "being no child now nor a bird"'.

Auden's poem is more realistic than many ecocritical positions that pretend to 'speak for nature' or indeed to 'let nature speak for itself'. Not surprisingly, nature then tends to speak in the preferred symbolic modes of the ecocritic, in Romantic, moralistic or Thoreauesque phrasing. Auden avoids such muddled thinking by insisting that his speakers always speak from and for the position of the human. Nonetheless, his poetry is more than ready to accept the power of what exists outside humans, while recognising its conceptual dependence on human assumptions. There is no 'nature' in what we think of as nature, in the same way that 'landscape' is an invention of the thoroughly anthropocentric eighteenth century. In order to signal that his approach to any such 'nature' – external or internal, or oxymoronic, as in the concept of 'human nature' – is anthropocentric and thus deeply acculturated, Auden frequently presents it in mythological form. Nature features as a goddess in 'Venus Will Now Say a Few Words'; 'Dame Kind' in 1959 replays the medieval allegory of love and nature to stress its historicity and 'culturality'.

Yet seeing our representations of nature as inevitably anthropocentric does not make human rationality omnipotent. On the contrary, turning the construct 'nature' into an imaginary other by which to define the self ensures that 'nature' becomes a defining limit to human autonomy and power. The early poem 'Our Hunting Fathers' contrasts the 'sadness of the creatures', 'the lion's intolerant look' and 'the quarry's dying glare' with the love of personal glory, the gift of reason, liberal appetite and power and ultimately the rightness of a god. By positing 'nature' as irrational, we can perceive ourselves as miniature gods. Yet whether our 'rightness' is justified remains questionable, for the poem's construction of nature as inferior is evidently a projection of the human appetite for power. Lions' looks are no more intolerant than quarries' glare as they die. The poem ends with a completely anthropocentric task borrowed from Lenin, that imposes several constraints on the self: 'To hunger, work illegally, / And be anonymous'.

'The Hidden Law' (1941) takes further Auden's debate between human potential and limits. What this all-powerful hidden law represents remains opaque. Anthony Hecht, who makes it the title of a monograph on Auden's poetry, comes up with little more than Christian religiosity.[9] Yet it is by no means certain that the poem deals with anything remotely resembling Christian faith. Its self-consciously artificial form, that of a French *rondeau* normally reserved for light erotic verse, hints at complication. The random yet universal acceptance of the hidden law, its lack of reactions and answers, its reluctance to be codified and defined, could point towards scientific atheism as much as to any mythic system.

The poem could profitably be read as the ongoing, often libidinous attempt to come to terms with definitions of the self in, against or indeed *as* an environment in which the only reassurance lies in attributing 'utter patience' to any such hidden law. Once again, though, this patience might be as much a human projection as a transcendental guarantee. What becomes explicit in 'The Hidden Law' is a conception of existence as interconnected or 'networked', albeit with a tacit understanding that networks or 'laws' (Auden's term is clearer here) are thoroughly human, that is, symbolic, means for grappling with reality. As Auden observed in an essay in *Christianity and the Social Revolution* (1935), 'Man is an organism with certain desires existing in an environment which fails to satisfy them fully. His theories about the universe are attempts, whether religious, scientific, philosophical, or political, to explain or overcome this tension.'[10]

'Mundus et Infans' (1942), an occasional poem celebrating the birth of a son to friends, treats the issue in even more playful terms. Within the poem's jocular benevolence, praising the baby's vitality while also calling it a 'cocky little ogre', is a similar understanding of life as networked. The role of the mother for the baby is described in terms that also apply to the human relationship with the earth: she supplies and delivers 'his raw materials free'. The poem sides with the human when it calls the baby a 'pantheist', compares him with the saints and eventually invokes judgements (applicable to humans and deities), only to conclude that what the baby can teach us is the need to distinguish between hunger and love – impulses which connect us to the natural world and those which supposedly distinguish us from it. Human existence straddles a space that is as much divide as bridge.

In 'In Praise of Limestone' (1948) the shaping power of the law appears to be in the hands of nature, the limestone landscape that Auden loved. Yet what it shapes is ultimately not human, but itself. What might superficially be a Wordsworthian reminiscence of childhood and nature becomes an exercise in clinical detachment, and the seemingly personal (and Freudian) memories of mother and son, brothers, and juvenile rivals turn into a laboratory experiment in which soils are equated with personality types. 'In Praise of Limestone' is a comprehensive allegory of mankind (the masculine term is appropriate here) and its dominant characters. An allegory it remains, a complex symbolic construction representing abstract human qualities in concrete natural shapes. Almost like protagonists in a medieval morality play, the various soils possess voices and attempt to seduce the protagonists. A poem with qualities that more naïve examples of ecocriticism would appreciate – a celebration of nature that grants it a voice – thus ends up doing what all texts pretending to give a voice to nature do: it makes nature speak in human terms and for human purposes.

Auden recognised the dominance of this human perspective, what the title of one poem on this theme sums up as 'Our Bias' (1939). In 'Hunting Season' (1952) human activity periphrastically reduces 'Some feathered he-or-she' to a 'lifeless bundle'. Yet their practical superiority does not raise humans above generic impersonality. What enters the kitchen proudly with his catch is merely 'some / Example of our tribe'. This primitivism is then extended into Audenesque fairy tale, the roaring oven of a witch's heart, before the hunter is reincarnated as a lover whispering a woman's name. The allegorical association of hunting and love as 'venery' has a long history. Auden's poem takes it to its ultimate conclusion: the killing that is part and parcel of hunting is merely one of the more visible deaths resulting from our struggle to stay alive. Once again, the networked thinking is there, yet in a shape that, despite the dark humour of the poem, leads only to death.

## 'Nature' as radical other

'Ode to Gaea' is perhaps the most explicitly 'ecological' of Auden's poems, its title even recalling James E. Lovelock's 'Gaia' hypothesis, which views the earth as one single ecosystem.[11] Yet Auden's poem is hardly a simple hymn to a maternal earth, even though it speaks of the planet as 'Mother'. The ode remains firmly anchored in the Horatian mode, and its thinking is neoclassical rather than Romantic. Like all his nature poems, it starts firmly from within culture, specifying it here, in a reference to air travel, as 'this new culture of the air'. In 1954, before the era of space flight, Auden's poem already envisages an overview of the entire planet. This is not new: it recalls the detached, panoptic perspectives of his early poems, and prefigures those of 'Ode to Terminus' and 'Prologue at Sixty'. An ambivalent distancing in 'Ode to Gaea' permits the earth, allegorised as the 'nicest daughter of Chaos', a narcissistic gaze into a mirror. (The allegorising of the earth and nature as feminine is a crucial point in ecocriticism – and also frequently criticised by it.[12])

From this imagined narcissistic gaze emerges an interesting distinction: it permits the earth to see unnamed things worth admiring and 'what, in her eyes, is natural'. The conceptual problem returns: there is no 'nature' in nature. How could the earth admire that in herself which is 'natural' in her view? The text refers, of course, to the destruction human beings have wrought upon the planet. But it does not work through simple binaries of unspoilt nature and human destruction. It is we, explicitly, who watch, we who observe the earth's desolation in the form of oceans which are 'glamorously carpeted' with plankton. The poem's imagery is as complex as it is telling. The earth is personified, even allegorised as a mythological figure. It is the object of human observation, perception and categorisation. Some elements of the description seem identifiably man-made; the vastness and emptiness of others provoke us into making them manageable through such appropriating domestications as the image of a plankton 'carpet'. Domesticity will become important for the reassessment of ecology at the close of the present chapter.

Earlier times, the poem suggests, dealt with an incomprehensible earth by imagining its unknown reaches inhabited by dragons and wizards. But the knowledge provided by technology has not decreased earth's mystery. Here we have a glimpse of a recurring theme in Auden's later writings: his critique of scientific enthusiasm, technological advance, 'progress' – which to him is rarely matched by understanding. Yet 'Ode to Gaea' by no means rejects anthropocentrism. It puts human statements into the mouth of 'Mother' earth, as, for example, that '"of pure things Water is the best"'. Introducing this formulation as 'surely, a value judgment', however, reiterates the prissiness observable throughout the poem and signals once more that here is a human voice speaking for humans, not the planet. The text ironises its game further with whimsical speculation: 'but how does she rank wheelwrights?' Similarly, it is hard to image the earth caring for syntactic changes or the many 'sub-species of folly' which inhabit it. In the same way that 'The Catholic ecology' in *New Year Letter* poked gentle fun at the term 'ecology', 'Ode to Gaea' employs a characteristic eighteenth- and nineteenth-century approach to nature and the taxonomy of species, ironically to relativise human rationality vis-à-vis that which it needs to position outside itself to confirm its own existence: nature.

Very quickly the poem returns to a narcissistic anthropocentrism. Feeling 'neglected on mountain drives, / unpopular in woods' certainly owes little to nature and more to the individual. The supposed clash of 'the older lives' that Auden's poem reminisces about (nymphs, goddesses, etc.) with the rectangular symbols of 'a positivist republic', with the railroad as its contemporary symbol, is a mock battle. When contrasting it with 'the Devil's Causeway', a geological formation on the north-west coast of Ireland, and the pilgrims it used to attract, it is by no means clear whether the replacement of mythology and superstition by science and technology signifies an intellectual advance, or merely an exchange of paradigm labelling.

Even the present world with its crises and tapped telephones relies for its self-definition on the ability to distinguish man-made from what it labels 'natural', in the same way that it distinguishes between a mere rock formation (the poem calls it 'untutored' to signal that culture depends on learning) and the fortresses of the semi-mythological High Kings of Ireland. In fact 'Ode to Gaea' calls its own simulated overview nothing but a return to mythology in disguise. In the same way that the ancient Greeks imagined their gods to observe and direct humans from Mount Olympus, we now assume a similar position in believing we have achieved an overview of the planet. As long as this overview is a detached one, 'Ode to Gaea' suggests it does not differ significantly from superstition or myth-making.

Running up and down a gamut of quasi-mythological references and typically Audenesque in-jokes, the poem signals that it is concerned with the state of human culture, not with the planet. For this reason, Edward Mendelson calls the poem's title misleading, and argues that something has gone wrong with human attitudes towards the planet in 'Ode to Gaea'. But perhaps the poem merely acknowledges that human beings only ever operate within culture. 'Earth, till the end, will be herself', says its penultimate stanza, indicating that despite the inaccessibility of the earth or 'nature' to human concerns, its radical otherness continues to drive us to symbolic attempts to comprehend it, and ourselves. Auden's poem does not flatter when it calls the earth 'the real one' in its final stanza. Compared with the sheer presence of the earth, cultural constructs such as landscapes can only be lies. They are not even dangerous lies. When measured against earth's longevity, our cultures of the lie resemble children playing at being sensible, grown-up authority figures ('Bishop') in a space that accidentally grants us a temporary reprieve ('that tideless bay').

'Bucolics', with its complex mapping of natural phenomena (wind, woods, mountains, lakes, islands, plains and streams), operates on the same allegorical principle. I have argued elsewhere that, although these phenomena act as metaphors, the poems in the sequence refrain from turning them into facets of human character. Neither do they turn them into symbols which are larger than life, those of mythology and religion.[13] 'Dame Kind' (1959) takes this separation strategy to an extreme. It employs a medieval epithet for nature, one that combines maternal qualities with explicitly carnal ones. The 'kind' in 'Dame Kind' continues this ambivalence by evoking at once similarity ('of the same kind') and a problematic promise of care rarely evident in natural phenomena.

The poem is a mix of pseudo-scientific jargon and vernacular, oration and insistent questioning. It asks how human worship of nature emerged and if it has changed nature. Nature's semi-divine status is expressed by the capitalisation of its pronouns. Yet it is also treated casually, with one of the more colloquial lines observing that 'She mayn't be all She might be but / She *is* our Mum'. Nature is a rather distant and careless mother, unimpressed by sacrifices and cults as well as poetry and myths. Human technology might interfere with it – 'ONE BOMB WOULD BE ENOUGH' – a salient point in 1959, when the great powers were engaged in urgent discussions about nuclear test ban treaties. Yet as in 'The Hidden Law', the poem believes in nature's lasting power. Its laws indeed govern the most intimate realms. Stanza four, addressing the question of sex, euphemistically personifies nature as 'the Kind Lady who fitted you out', who, it suggests, will now 'fix you up'. The 'laws of nature' also affect what appears, superficially, to be most remote from nature, the human withdrawal into abstraction, and into the subjective realm of memories, hopes, fears. Stanzas five and six illustrate such forms of alienation in images resembling those of *Ash-Wednesday* and *Four Quartets* in their narcissistic sterility. Sterility is indeed one thing that nature cannot tolerate. Despite its lack of interest in human schemes and rituals, one way nature consistently enters into and disturbs our lives is by match-making: 'How much half-witted horse-play and sheer / bloody misrule / It took to bring you two together / both on schedule?' 'Horse-play' hovers between nature and culture; 'bloody' combines natural life-blood with political misrule, so that such cultural concepts as 'wit', 'play', 'schedule' are inextricably entangled with a nature they consistently strive and fail to turn into a mere symbolic accessory.

'Reflections in a Forest' (1957) is an even more explicit radicalisation of this relationship. It describes the feeling that forests generate in cultural terms, as 'nude august communities' and 'living statues', yet quickly realises that this is nonsensical: 'But trees are trees, and elm or oak / Already both outside and in'. Taxonomies of elm or oak are aspects of a conceptual system of which nature is ignorant and not in need. 'Tree' itself is a signifier whose signified is transcendental and conventionalised – and thus profoundly cultural. 'Already both outside and in' therefore hints at the theoretical borderline that nature occupies in human culture, that 'radical Other' spoken of above. Theorists such as Jacques Lacan and Julia Kristeva have located this borderline between the Imaginary and the Symbolic in the constitution of human consciousness, knowledge, 'truths'. Both theorists insist that the Imaginary can only ever be conceptualised in terms that already belong to its Other, the Symbolic, from which (as from consciousness) no way leads back. 'Reflections in a Forest' makes it clear that any 'truth' emerging from a supposed intercourse with nature would be solipsistic. Such encounters actually involve confrontation with an Otherness which 'Forbids immediate utterance'. Any way of speaking such knowledge would involve telling 'two different lies at once': the lie of nature and the lie of the self, both of them interdependent constructions without ontological guarantees.

'Et in Arcadia Ego' (1964) is an almost aggressive comment on this dilemma. Its sarcasm focuses on the apparent transformation in the modern era of the 'Earth-Mother' from uncontrollable virago and amazon to obedient housewife. Beneath its apparent domestication, however, lurks the old violence and barbarism. Once again, what the division into self and nature creates is not so much self-awareness as self-deception. It is no coincidence that this resident violence finds expression in the castrating gelding-knife of the poem's last line. The humanism that is sometimes uncritically attributed to Auden's later works is here explicitly countered with the reminder that it is only possible when based on a blindness about the problems at the root of human self-definition.

'Bestiaries Are Out' is a more playful reminder of the attractions and pitfalls of anthropomorphism, of seeing nature in human terms and vice versa. Using the example of bees, it moves from their appeal to primitive man, via use of their example as 'Civics Teacher[s]' in Renaissance political theory, to the current situation, in which 'bestiaries are out' because modern science recognises that such analogic thinking is 'Anthropomorphic and absurd'. The poem's finale cunningly resurrects the bees' appeal by raising an enigmatic half question (lacking a question mark) about how we 'children of the word' may interpret their behaviour in aesthetic terms, in an anthropocentric vocabulary ('code', 'catharsis', 'their biggest show', 'duel to the death') that pre-emptively links aesthetics with ethics. 'The Art of Healing', on the death of Auden's doctor, extends this reconciliation. First it defines healing as 'the intuitive art / of wooing Nature'. Yet it turns out to be a very different wooing from the domestication of 'Et in Arcadia Ego'. Rather than subsuming nature under culture, 'The Art of Healing' singles out the difference of human beings, whose concern with illness is always specific and individual, what the poem calls 'prejudices'.

'Short Ode to the Cuckoo' (1971) is paradoxical not only because 'short ode' is an oxymoronic contradiction in terms. Odes also commonly elevate rather than denigrate their object. The poem declares the cuckoo humanly relevant exactly in human terms. Even when the primitive beliefs in the bird's future-telling powers have vanished, when science has proved its ordinariness, some of the old 'mythic' magic still remains. The now apparently 'naturalised' bird's nesting habits (or rather, lack of them) still provoke moral outrage. The apparently demystified natural creature retains some of its traditional magic in the speaker's whimsical habit (recalling the legendary letter to the *Times*) of entering the first cuckoo of spring in his diary every year. Next to 'social engagements' and 'the death of friends', the bird becomes a reminder of a network other than the social, less absolute than death, yet still radically inaccessible, which forms the necessary other to the self's orientation in the world.

'Morality in an Age of Change', an essay in *The Nation* in December 1938, claimed that 'There are two kinds of goodness, "natural" and "moral". An organism is naturally good when it has reached a state of equilibrium with its environment. All healthy animals and plants are naturally good in this sense. But any change toward a greater freedom of action is a morally good change' (*Prose 1*, pp. 477–86; at pp. 477–8). Auden, however, quickly qualified this dangerous claim by placing it in a human and cognitive context which includes individual responsibility and morality: '*But* we are each conscious of ourselves as a thinking, feeling, and willing whole, and this is the only whole of which we have direct knowledge' and such experience 'conditions our thinking' (*Prose 1*, p. 479).

Auden's last poems reveal a surprising number of addresses to animals. In *Epistle to a Godson* (1972), 'Talking to Dogs', an occasional piece on the death by accident of a neighbour's dog, and 'Talking to Mice', form a triptych with 'Talking to Myself'. They represent a concern with the domestic and everyday already evident in *About the House* (1965). This would disqualify such poems for more naïve exponents of ecocriticism, whose focus is on 'wilderness writing'. Yet the very terms 'ecology' and 'ecocriticism' derive from the Greek root *oikos*, meaning household, the domestic sphere. Auden himself made this clear in a scathing review, 'Life's Old Boy', in *Scrutiny* (March 1934), of a book by Lord Baden Powell, founder of the Boy Scout movement: 'To say that the Backwoods life is natural and City life artificial is nonsense. The only possible meaning of "artificial" for this connection is "un-habitual"' (*Prose 1*, pp. 62–6; at p. 63).

Auden's domesticity and mundanity have, however, a deeper philosophical dimension, drawing on such thinkers as Heidegger, and combining with Auden's theological interests to foster a 'hallowing of the everyday'.[14] Such a hallowing, only superficially humorous, can be found in the poems to animals. 'Talking to Dogs' emphasises once more the otherness of animals: they expect food and fondling, not symbolic valorisation, from their human owners. In turn, their owners expect adulation from dogs, an adulation all the more gratifying because they lack the power to dissemble. In contrast to children, with whom their responses are frequently compared, dogs are 'complete' in themselves, as nature is also described in 'Ode to Gaea'; but it also exempts them from moral demands. Auden's essay on morality discussed above calls healthy animals and plants 'naturally good', but adds that 'In man, the evolution can be continued, each stage of moral freedom being superseded by a new one' (*Prose 1*, p. 478). The difference between 'human' and 'natural' therefore generates moral obligations.

The measuring of human life and morality against their natural other is also the theme of 'Talking to Mice'. In some senses, as 'domestic', part of the household, as dogs, but, as vermin, totally unintegrated into the human domestic sphere, mice occupy an intermediate location. The poem jokingly imagines training mice like children. As 'Good Little Mice', however, they would cease to be other, uncomprehending and incomprehensible. Beatrix Potter is the name associated with such fantasy domestications. Any quaintness her name invokes is dashed, though, by the poem's switch to realistic mode, speaking of the reproachful 'broken cadaver' of a mouse in a kitchen mousetrap. The poem concludes, not without irony, that this killing is not murder, for all householders behave according to the same 'moral' rules, the *Realpolitik* ('For *raisons d'État*') that 'every State' invokes 'when there is something It wants, and a minor one gets in the way'.

'Talking to Myself' turns the human body into an eco-sphere subject to the same moral-environmental investigations and tests as dogs and mice. It situates this body, a 'strange rustic object', in 'the about' (i.e. the physical environment around it) before acknowledging its primary status as home for the subjective being of the self ('My mortal manor, the carnal territory'). The body is also the speaker's tutor, which reverses the customary mind–body hierarchy. Yet such definitions only work when contrasted with examples from external nature. The body's relative passivity is measured by the absence of fangs, talons, hooves and venom. But no human beings, confronted with the scientific explanation of their individual genesis as a 'random event', hallowing selfhood, will believe anything other than that their own existence is a 'true miracle'.

More surprisingly, the self further declares its body to be an unknown quantity in many respects – and makes this lack of knowledge productive in exactly the same way in which nature's otherness became the generator of self and world in earlier poems: 'Thanks to Your Otherness . . . You can serve me as my emblem for the Cosmos'. Yet even this cosmic potential of the body as the closest ally and other nature has to offer to the self does not make it transcendental and truly universal. With typical ironic aplomb, the speaker demands that, should the time for dying come, his body should 'bugger off quickly'.

'Address to the Beasts' (1973), posthumously published in *Thank You, Fog* (1974) takes up this theme in imitation of St Francis preaching to the birds. Yet where Francis urged the birds to praise God, the poem expresses a certain envy of all natural creatures' groundedness in their environment and harmony with creation. Comparing them to humans, it asks sceptically: 'Shall we ever become adulted, / As you all soon do?' This seems unlikely. Humans destroy animals in the same way that they destroy what they call their environment, and are also likely to destroy themselves. With nuclear warfare in mind, the poem declares that 'one balmy day, / we might well become, / not fossils, but vapour'.

Auden's 'Catholic ecology' involves a relational anti-universalism. Ecological motifs in Auden's poetry are a far cry from romanticising and idealising nature as an ontological given. Defined at the start from a narcissistic human perspective, a radical anthropocentrism which turns it into a mere human projection, nature, still allegorised, then becomes a marker enabling the human creature to perceive its own limits. This move still turns nature into a radical other, a pole in the construction of what it means to be human. Only when the later poetry painfully and playfully acknowledges that difference at the roots of self and nature while simultaneously accepting their relatedness, can a communication emerge. As Auden says at the end of 'Talking to Dogs', 'Let difference / remain our bond', but in a context defined by 'the one trait / both have in common, a sense of theatre'. Out of this accommodation, respect and moral obligations emerge – the product of a system of 'difference' created by language, consciousness and culture, not as a consequence of natural and ontological givens. Humans do not become moral by becoming one with nature, but by accepting their differential relatedness to what they call nature. Ecology in Auden thus becomes a way of relativising universalist prejudices (including humanism) without creating new essentialisms and absolutes. This revisionary form of ecology, what we might speak of as a relational anti-universalism, makes possible a reconciliation of what is commonly and naïvely called 'human nature' both with itself and with 'nature' as its external counterpart.

## NOTES

1. See Alan Jacobs, *What Became of Wystan: Change and Continuity in Auden's Poetry* (Fayetteville: University of Arkansas Press, 1998), pp. 15–31.
2. Repr. in *Prose I*, p. 138. Auden's is the first of four untitled introductory essays commissioned by the publisher to enhance sales of the British edition of Robert Frost's *Selected Poems* (London: Rupert Hart-Davis, 1936). On this, see Mendelson's note in *Prose I*, p. 763.
3. Cheryll Glotfelty and Harold Fromm (eds.), *The Ecocriticism Reader: Landmarks in Literary Ecology* (Athens and London: University of Georgia Press, 1996).
4. *Ibid.*, pp. xii–xiii.
5. See Jonathan Bate, *Romantic Ecology: Wordsworth and the Environmental Tradition* (London and New York: Routledge, 1991), pp. 36–8.
6. Robert Morrison, 'Environmental Concerns: Ecocritical Landmarks, Textmarks, Benchmarks', *The University of Toronto Review*, 71:3 (Summer 2002).
7. The treatise has been published on the Internet under http://www.humanevol.com/imprimir/doc200302100410.html.

8. Rick van Noy, 'Literary Cartographers and the Spirit of Place', in Steven Rosendale (ed.), *The Greening of Literary Scholarship* (Iowa City: University of Iowa Press, 2002), pp. 181–206.

9. Anthony Hecht, *The Hidden Law: The Poetry of W. H. Auden* (Cambridge, Mass.: Harvard University Press, 1993), p. 463.

10. W. H. Auden, 'The Good Life', in John Lewis, Karl Polanyi and Donald K. Kitchin (eds.), *Christianity and the Social Revolution* (London: Victor Gollancz, 1935), pp. 31–50; at p. 31. Repr. in *EA*, pp. 342–54, and *Prose I*, pp. 109–23.

11. James E. Lovelock, *Gaia: A New Look at Life on Earth* (New York: Oxford University Press, 1979). Together with Sidney Epton, Lovelock first introduced his hypothesis in an essay entitled 'The Quest for Gaia', *New Scientist*, 65 (6 February 1975), pp. 304–6.

12. See Patrick D. Murphy, *Literature, Nature, and Others: Ecofeminist Critiques* (Albany, N.Y.: State University of New York Press, 1995), especially the chapter 'Sex-Typing the Planet: Gaia Imagery and the Problem of Subverting Patriarchy', pp. 59–69.

13. Rainer Emig, *W. H. Auden: Towards a Postmodern Poetics* (Basingstoke and New York: Palgrave, 2000), pp. 177–8.

14. For a detailed discussion, see *ibid.*, pp. 196–203.

# 18

IAN SANSOM

# Auden and influence

The description of Auden's influence usually concentrates on the work of a small core group during a limited period – what Samuel Hynes called 'the Auden Generation'. My intention is to extend the discussion to include several generations of English and American poets – what might be called, to pluralise Hynes, the Auden Generations.

The chapter does not purport to be a theoretical or practical-critical account of Auden's influence: it is not a set of hypotheses or close readings. Nor is it a list of writers who have obviously been influenced by Auden (although such a list would be useful, and it would be long). It is, rather, a descriptive mapping and selective interpretation of the reception of and responses to Auden's work, and an analysis of some of the significant ways in which Auden's influence has been mediated and made itself apparent. It should be acknowledged from the outset that Auden's influence has not always been positive. Auden has been blamed personally, and literally, for just about every failing in English verse over the past three-quarters of a century, and there undoubtedly are those individuals for whom his influence has been inhibiting, dispiriting or downright destructive. There have also always been those like Hugh McDiarmid, who regarded Auden as 'a complete wash-out', or like Truman Capote, who when asked what he thought of Auden's poetry replied, 'Never meant nothin' to me.'[1] Nonetheless, Auden's influence has been widespread, and, it is worth noting (since I will be restricting myself to British, Irish and American poetry), international in its scope.

My aim is to demonstrate how Auden's life and work have been constantly refigured in the work and imagination of other poets and thus how 'Auden' is, at the very least, what a semiologist might call a 'sign' of high semiotic intensity. My hope is that my mapping amounts to more than a mere plotting of signs and succeeds as a kind of brief cultural history, a sketch, or perhaps a story, about people reading poetry, and about how poetry can help us read people.

## The 1930s: 'Auden as a monster'

'It's odd to be asked today what I saw in Auden', replied John Ashbery to a wet-behind-the-ears interviewer in 1980, 'Forty years ago when I first began to read modern poetry no one would have asked – he was *the* modern poet.'[2] Nowadays people ask all sorts of pesky questions about Auden, not least about his absolute identification as 'the' poet of the 1930s. Adrian Caesar, for example, in *Dividing Lines: Poetry, Class and Ideology in the 1930s* (1991) has charged Samuel Hynes and Bernard Bergonzi, among others, with deliberately creating an Auden mythology which exaggerates Auden's importance as a thirties writer.

For those whom it affected, though, the Auden phenomenon was undoubtedly as disturbing as it was remarkable. The title of Geoffrey Grigson's contribution to the special 1937 *New Verse* Auden Double Number, 'Auden as a monster', is indicative of the fear and excitement generated by Auden's reputation: Auden's verse, writes Grigson, is 'monstrous'. Other contributors to *New Verse* were similarly impressed by Auden's peculiar strength and power: Edwin Muir described Auden's imagination as 'grotesque'; Dylan Thomas said he was 'wide and deep'; Bernard Spencer claimed that he had succeeded in 'brutalising' the language.

With its emphasis on Auden's 'monstrous' qualities, the *New Verse* Auden Double Number inaugurated a significant theme in subsequent figurations of Auden. There has been a persistent physiologism in writing about Auden: in reviews, essays and poems he is figured as a kind of predatory *Ubermensch* possessing great physical prowess and preternatural powers. Roy Fuller describes Auden, for example, as a 'legendary' monster; Patrick Kavanagh compares him to Shakespeare, gobbling up everything and leaving nothing for anyone else.[3] Such language admires as much as it is appalled, and descriptions of Auden as monster always seem to imply Auden as hero, and vice versa, an ambivalence which is of course characteristic of attitudes towards the heroic and the mythic. Edward Mendelson has made the point that there is no One True Auden, but most varieties of Auden do come in this monster/hero mould: his intelligence, it seems generally to have been agreed, is superlative, his insights premature, his appearance outlandish and his troubled career strangely exemplary.

Figured as hero/monster Auden has become an object of desire. The journalist Michael Davidson, for example, writes revealingly in his autobiography *The World, the Flesh and Myself* (1962) about being 'bewitched' by Auden, and many others have fallen under his spell. Charles Madge, in the 1933 *New Country* anthology, trembled with excitement at the thought of Auden and his poetry and Cecil Day Lewis in the same book ejaculated,

'Look west, Wystan, lone flyer, birdman, my bully boy!'[4] Joseph Brodsky, during the course of his Nobel Prize acceptance speech, managed to slip in a mention of his 'beloved' Auden, whilst Seamus Heaney proved himself a most receptive reader of Auden's verse when he wrote of the *Collected Poems* that 'in the end one assents with a "yes" as pleasured and whole-hearted as Molly Bloom's'.[5] These seductions testify above all to the seductive powers of Auden's poetry, but it is worth considering some of the other charms that made Auden so desirable, both during the 1930s and subsequently.

From the outset, what Auden looked like mattered, not just to his contemporaries at Oxford but also to later generations of readers, who have continued to respond in appalled fascination to what the poet John Hollander calls 'The Face'.[6] The most famous early photograph of Auden is probably the head and shoulders snap taken by Eric Bramall in 1928, showing Auden with head bowed, lighting a cigarette.[7] The image has been reproduced numerous times and it probably owes its enduring appeal to its ambiguity: the pose is simultaneously feminine and macho, coy and defiant; Bramall has in fact captured a gesture of exactly the kind that Roland Barthes discusses in *Camera Lucida* (1980), an image which suggests a privileged glimpse and which stimulates in the viewer an erotic thrill.[8]

There are also early portraits by Cecil Beaton, by the early 1930s a well-established fashion photographer and society portraitist. The mere fact that he was photographed by Beaton indicates something of Auden's early fame and notoriety. The pose in the most famous of the early Beaton photographs is rather more posed and consequently more awkwardly self-conscious than that in the Bramall snap, but there is the same seductive look, with Auden looking far off into the distance, like a seer.[9] Whether snapshots or professional shoots, the Bramall and Beaton photographs have come to signify not just Auden but thirties poetry in general; they have achieved the status of icons.

But really they are just adverts. Publishing has always been closely allied to publicity, and it is interesting to note how many of the early reviewers of Auden naturally resorted to the language of advertising when attempting to describe his work.[10] His publishers also did their bit, with their famous 'Vin Audenaire' ad in the *New Verse* Auden Double Number, and his work was also deliberately and determinedly promoted by the novelist Naomi Mitchison. Writing some thirty years after her notorious review of Auden's *Poems* Mitchison revealed that she had consciously decided to hype the book, and in her memoirs she admits that she also set out to persuade other 'top critics' of Auden's merits.[11] Mitchison, one might say, acted as a kind of tipster: she was midwife to the monster.

## The 1940s: 'Uncle Sam Auden'

After his trip to America in 1909 Freud is said to have remarked to Ernest Jones that he thought America was a mistake – a gigantic mistake, he admitted, but a mistake nonetheless. Auden's move to America in 1939 has often been viewed in similar terms, both by his contemporaries and by the literary historians and anthologists whose attempts to accommodate the move have obscured Auden's place in the literary histories of the two nations.

In his introduction to his 1970 anthology *British Poetry since 1945* Edward Lucie-Smith announced that he had decided not to include Auden because his residence in America made him an American rather than a British writer, a decision ratified by George Watson in his 1991 critical survey *British Literature since 1945*, from which Auden is excluded for being an expatriate.[12] That Auden fails the residency requirement for acceptance as a British poet is also stated clearly by David Daiches in the Introductions to English Literature series; after 1939, Daiches claims, Auden was an American poet and thus he belongs to American poetry.[13]

Unfortunately for Auden the official keepers of American poetry have been happy enough without him. For the mighty Norton Anthologies, for example, residence in America is simply not enough: Auden does not figure in the *Norton Anthology of American Literature* (1989); he is included instead in the *Norton Anthology of English Literature* (1986).[14] The *Heath Anthology of American Literature* (1990), on the other hand, with its self-consciously revisionist canon, cannot find room for an expat Brit like Auden amongst its many ethnic traditions. Excluded from British literary history because he left, and left out of American literary history because he's British – you might begin to think that Auden has fallen through the cracks.

Then again, it could be argued that just as his removal to America broadened his horizons, giving him an international point of view, so it also guaranteed his status as a kind of super-national poet. As an immigrant and expatriate Auden became a kind of bridge between two cultures. Literary histories and anthologies may have attempted to keep him out, but the evidence suggests that in the 1940s Auden's trans- or mid-Atlantic voice continued to find resonance on both sides of the Atlantic.

In England Auden's departure for America became a cause célèbre: according to Louis MacNeice writing in 1941, London was 'full of silly rumours' about Auden.[15] There were those, however, who felt Auden's departure as a matter of more serious consequence. During 1940 the pages of Cyril Connolly's magazine *Horizon*, for example, were given over to a long-running debate about the rights and wrongs of Auden's leaving England, and questions were raised in Parliament.[16] John Lehmann, a former friend and champion of Auden's work, expressed himself utterly dismayed by the attitude of 'Uncle Sam Auden'.[17]

Reaction against Auden in England supposedly took the form of the 'romantic' rebellion of the New Apocalypse school of poets, although many of these poets in fact inherited aspects of their style and ideas from Auden. The continuity between Auden and the younger English poets of the forties has been diligently traced by A. T. Tolley in *The Poetry of the Forties* (1985), which notes clear and specific instances of Auden's influence in the work of Lawrence Durrell, Anne Ridler, Julian Symons, Ruthven Todd, Drummond Allison and Roy Fuller, among others. At the very least, in England in the 1940s Auden was still setting the standard which other poets wrote against.

In the United States, though, he was revered. He took the oath of allegiance and became an American citizen on 20 May 1946. His *Collected Poetry* had been published in America by the American publishers Random House a year previously and had just gone into its fourth impression, having already sold over 14,000 copies. On this evidence Edmund Wilson pronounced that Auden had achieved 'almost the circulation of an American family poet'.[18]

Auden's influence in America has been widespread and long-lasting, affecting not only neoclassicists like Anthony Hecht and Richard Wilbur, but also confessionals like John Berryman and Karl Shapiro, older poets such as Carl Sandburg and many poets who were destined to make their mark outside the mainstream – including Robert Duncan, Frank O'Hara, James Schuyler, John Ashbery and James Merrill. Thus, in the 1940s the young Berryman was churning out Auden-influenced poems like 'World-Telegram' and 'Winter Landscape'; but then so was Ashbery a few years later in his first collection, *Some Trees* (1956), with its Auden-style eclogue, sestinas, pantoum and canzone, and so was Robert Duncan, who has described how Auden's images of disease in 'Journal of an Airman' enabled him, in his early poetry, to come to terms with his own 'dis-ease' as a homosexual.[19] Auden became a significant figure in American literary culture as editor of the Yale Younger Poets series between 1948 and 1959, when he was responsible for the publication of first collections by writers as various as Ashbery, Adrienne Rich and W. S. Merwin.

Auden's influence and impact in America are not, though, best summed up by the evidence of one single poem or significant friendship, but once again by an image, the famous Gotham Book Mart photo, in which, as James Atlas puts it, 'the temper of an era was captured'.[20] The photograph was taken at a party given by *Life* magazine for the arrival in America of Edith and Osbert Sitwell, which brought together many of the most important American poets and writers of the time, including Marianne Moore, Elizabeth Bishop, Tennessee Williams and Gore Vidal. The photograph shows Auden perched on a ladder high above the others: quite literally, as Geoffrey Grigson claimed in his 1949 anthology, *Poetry of the Present*, Auden 'arches over all'.[21]

## The 1950s: 'What's Become of Wystan?'

According to the cultural historian Robert Hewison in *In Anger: Culture in the Cold War 1945–60* (1981) postwar Britain was irritable, exhausted and lacking in self-confidence, and nowhere was this bad-temper and uncertainty more apparent than in reassessments of Auden's work by British critics and poets during the 1950s. F. R. Leavis inaugurated a decade of revaluations in 1950 with the 'Retrospect' to his notorious 1932 survey of contemporary poetry, *New Bearings in English Poetry*. In the 'Retrospect' Leavis stumbles through an explanation of why he had not included Auden in his original account and grudgingly admits that Auden had since made some advance in sophistication; but he then promptly dismisses sophistication.

Midway through the decade, Robert Graves also found Auden to be something of a stumbling block. In his 1954 Clark Lectures on 'Professional Standards in English Poetry' Graves launched a swingeing attack on literary idols, but was uncertain about Auden's status and settled for a jibe about his 'zinc-bright' influence.[22] In 1960, Philip Larkin presented his evidence for a revaluation in a review despairingly but affectionately titled 'What's Become of Wystan?'[23] In admonitory fashion Larkin reminded his readers that the 1930s had long gone and Auden's heyday with them. There was some faint praise for Auden in the *New Lines* (1956) anthology, the book which shaped and defined the Movement. In his introduction to the anthology, Robert Conquest admits that Auden's influence is apparent, but argues in mitigation that it is merely a 'technical' influence. Writing in *The Spectator* in 1954, Anthony Hartley described the spirit of the new British poetry as a joyful return to the 1930s. In the work of Empson and Auden, he claims, young poets had discovered their masters.[24] A couple of years later, however, Roy Fuller was pointing out that the young poets were far from happy about having Auden as master, since he had already said anything worth saying.[25] John Wain took the title for his first collection, *Mixed Feelings* (1951), from a famous phrase in Auden's *New Year Letter* ('poetry might be described as the clear expression of mixed feelings') and its sentiment nicely sums up the ambivalent regard in which Auden was held.

Mixed feelings about Auden's poetry during this period were matched by mixed feelings about his politics – in Britain, unlike America, interest in Auden's politics has been as enduring as the interest in his poetry. In 1957 Kingsley Amis's controversial Fabian pamphlet, 'Socialism and the Intellectuals', eschewed political action, citing Auden as his exemplar. According to

Amis, Auden connected directly with the intellectual climate of the fifties because his politics were nothing more than 'romanticism', which Amis claims is the natural state of socialist intellectual political thinking. Amis says he cannot really be bothered with politics, and Auden, he believes, sanctions his inaction.[26] There were those of course who disagreed with Amis's generous assessment of Auden's hand-wringing liberalism. In a review of 'Socialism and the Intellectuals', Paul Johnson condemned Amis's apathy and the failures of the thirties poets.[27]

Auden's politics seem to have been variously regarded, then, as an example to be followed or a mistake to be avoided. If in the 1930s Auden was generally regarded as a Leftist and in the 1950s praised and condemned as a Romantic and a liberal, so from the 1970s to the 1990s writers found him to be *engagé* and *dégagé*, according to personal taste. The poet Glyn Maxwell even went so far as to proclaim that Auden's example could provide an alternative to the sterile British two-party political system – Auden, in other words, as the much-talked-about Third Way.[28]

### The 1960s: 'Auden Aetat XX, LX'

Auden celebrated his sixtieth birthday in 1967. To mark the occasion *The Sunday Times* 'invited five admirers to send a birthday message'.[29] Two of the admirers, Stephen Spender and John Betjeman, were old friends and penned wistful, nostalgic odes, while Maurice Wiggins, the paper's television critic, managed to produce a pastiche, 'And Did You Once See Auden Plain?'. The poems by the other two admirers, Christopher Logue and Ted Hughes, are of rather more interest and significance. Logue's 'Notes made after reading Wordsworth's "Tintern Abbey" for Auden's 60th Birthday' is distinguished not so much by its quality but because Logue was associated with the radical poetic underground and his tribute might therefore be said to represent a younger generation's admiration for Auden. As for Hughes, Auden had already been of considerable assistance in his career, choosing *The Hawk in the Rain* as the winner of the 1957 Young Men's and Young Women's Hebrew Association of New York prize for the best first collection of poetry in English. The 1960s, one might say, like Hughes himself, owed a debt of gratitude to Auden which has been underestimated.

In the magazine *New Measures* Auden's work was appearing alongside that of younger poets such as Michael Horovitz and Tom Raworth, and the crown-prince of the counter-culture himself, Allen Ginsberg, not only made a pilgrimage to visit Auden in Ischia in 1957, but according to his biographer Barry Miles even attempted to kiss the hem of Auden's garments when visiting him in Oxford in 1958.[30] In 'Prologue at Sixty', the last poem in

*City Without Walls*, Auden asked 'Can Sixty make sense to Sixteen-plus?' The answer, apparently, was yes: the critic Eric Mottram, in his essay 'The British Poetry Revival, 1960–75' notes that Auden's poems remained an inspiration for poets such as John Ashbery and Lee Harwood, and Ian Hamilton, editor of the influential magazine *The Review*, said that part of the magazine's philosophy was 'going back' to Auden.[31]

In his biography of Auden, Humphrey Carpenter sets out the conventional view of the poet's failing fortunes during the 1960s. But in his obituary for Auden, Roy Fuller wisely recognised the changing context in which Auden's later work should be interpreted and understood. To understand Auden's continuing importance and influence in the 1960s, notes Fuller, one needs to pay attention not just to the sales of his books but to the wider phenomenon of his fame, and in particular to his crowd-pulling appearances at poetry readings and events such as London's annual Poetry International Festivals.

The Poetry Internationals institutionalised the ad-hoc poetry-reading 'event' and made it a familiar feature of mainstream literary culture in Britain. Auden had already done much to help establish the poetry-reading circuit in America, but his readings on the South Bank in the 1960s had a special significance. The South Bank Arts Centre was developed on the site of the 1951 Festival of Britain and was designed as a testament to the rebirth of British culture after the war: Auden's successes in the South Bank's Queen Elizabeth Hall marked his return to the heart of British establishment culture.

Between 1967 and 1973 Auden appeared at every Poetry International – the only poet to make such regular appearances – usually reading on the last night and drawing large crowds. Charles Osborne, in his diary of the 1970 Festival published in *The Sunday Times*, described Auden as the Poetry International 'mascot', and Alfred Lautner in his history of the Festivals claims that Auden's contributions were always the 'highlight' of the Festivals.[32]

Highlights from each Poetry International Festival were broadcast on the BBC Third Programme every year between 1969 and 1973, selected and introduced by the poet George MacBeth. Recordings of these broadcasts are an important but neglected part of the evidence of Auden's continuing popularity throughout the late 1960s and early 1970s.[33] In the broadcasts MacBeth introduces each poet, offering a few words of commentary and background information, and his prefaces to Auden always portray him as pre-eminent: in 1970 he describes him as Poetry International's 'star'; in 1972 as the 'father-figure' and by 1973 simply as 'the doyen'. The BBC knew it was on to a good thing with Auden's cult performances: in 1972 it broadcast a special half-hour programme called 'Auden in London', featuring all the poems read by him at the 1972 Festival, to mark his return to England. Over forty years after the publication of his first collection, Auden remained a star, or at least a star-turn.

## The 1970s: the 'undisputed master'

Auden was found dead in his hotel room in Vienna on 29 September 1973 and in the way of such things, in death he was instantly granted his immortality. According to *The Times* obituary, 'W. H. Auden, for long the *enfant terrible* of English poetry, who has died at the age of 66, emerges finally as its undisputed master.'[34] Elegists were soon queueing up to offer their profound assessments and conclusions about his achievement.[35]

After the initial rush of emotion and eulogy, however, interest in Auden's life and work has inevitably become of an increasingly trivial, occult or fetishistic kind. There is the inevitable trade in Auden merchandise and memorabilia, and rumours of hidden treasures and Holy Grails – the lost book of essays, the missing-link play, the holograph poems. Then again, there is also the more serious stuff: the manuscript collections, the bequests, the archives. In 1980 Dr Lola Szladits, curator of the Berg Collection of original Auden manuscripts at New York Public Library, enthused that there was enough Auden in the Berg to fill the whole library.[36] The creation of such massive collections encourages the regarding of a poet's work as an asset, a sign of the wealth, power and prestige of the collection's holders.

The spirit of Auden survives in such archives and objects, and also in places. Edward Lear, in Auden's poem, 'became a land'. Auden himself has become a street – actually, three streets named after him in Austria – and there are various memorials dotted around the world: a tablet in Christ Church chapel, another in Westminster Abbey, plaques at 1 Montague Terrace, Brooklyn and at the hotel in Vienna where he died. If nothing else, it seems poetry can make tourism happen. During the 1950s, according to Harold Norse, in the wake of Auden, the island of Ischia became a popular literary hang-out, and Kirchstetten, the village in Austria where Auden spent his summers from 1958, is also now an Auden-inspired holiday destination, strongly recommended by Richard Kellett in the Auden Society *Newsletter*.[37]

## The 1980s and 1990s: 'teaching Auden'

Even before his death Auden had long been on the syllabus – far too long, according to Robert Creeley, who complained that at Harvard back in the 1940s the courses he took in contemporary poetry were dominated by the teaching of work by Auden and Wallace Stevens and excluded Pound.[38] The academicisation of Auden's work has seen a steady progress since, with a procession of commentaries, treatises and variorum editions. Outside universities, though, most people's first and last contact with Auden is likely to be in a school anthology. Peter Sansom describes one such encounter from the teacher's point of view in his poem 'Teaching Auden' in which a young girl attempts to grapple with what 'exactly Auden meant'.[39] In the handful of anthologies traditionally used at GCSE level Auden is well represented, and his work continues to be promoted and mediated not only by schools and universities but by various other institutions including libraries, publishing houses and also, unexpectedly, by the British film industry. In the 1994 box-office hit *Four Weddings and a Funeral* Auden's poem 'Funeral Blues' was read as an oration at the funeral of a gay character, played by the actor Simon Callow. Faber and Faber rushed out a pamphlet of ten of Auden's poems, entitled *Tell Me the Truth About Love*, to cash in on the film's success and, according to Edward Mendelson, the pamphlet has sold about 275,000 copies. Not surprisingly, Faber also decided to produce a long-awaited paperback edition of the *Collected Poems*.

Readings from, quotations from, allusions to, and representations of Auden and his work in other people's books and in other media are therefore extremely important in maintaining his public profile, even if the public doesn't know it. Auden's words have been used without attribution in various contexts, notably in speeches by American politicians: Anthony Hecht points out that Peggy Noonan borrowed the 'points of light' from Auden's 'September 1, 1939' for the campaign speeches of the first President Bush, and Edward Mendelson recalls a choice example from the 1960s when the phrase 'We must love one another or die' was adapted for a campaign advertisement for Lyndon Johnson's 1964 election campaign.[40]

In England, Auden's words have tended to be put to more prosaic uses. The 1993 Annual Report for the Transport Users' Consultative Committee for Western England, for example, recorded the suggested development of twenty-eight park-and-ride stations providing a shuttle service to urban centres, and made its point with a quotation from Auden.[41] He has also proved useful to the compilers of English dictionaries. It was always Auden's wish to be included in the *Oxford English Dictionary*, and according to Toby Litt, in a survey of usage in the second edition of the dictionary, his wish was granted 724 times 'at least', with 110 possible coinages or first usages, including the phrase 'Age of Anxiety', defined by the *OED* as 'the title of W. H. Auden's poem applied as a catch-phrase to any period characterized by anxiety or danger', the adjective 'entropic' and the noun 'agent' abbreviated from 'secret agent'.[42]

Occasionally, Auden's continuing presence can be seen not just in print but on stage. In Paul Godfrey's *Once in a While the Odd Thing Happens*, for example, a play about the life of Benjamin Britten first performed at the National Theatre in 1990, Auden featured as a jealous despot, while Vince Foxall's *Strictly Entre Nous: The Life, Times & Loves of W. H. Auden* (1995) provided a rather more sympathetic portrait. The character of Hilary in Alan Bennett's West End hit *The Old Country* was also apparently based on Auden.[43]

Auden was first represented in fiction by Cecil Day-Lewis, writing as Nicholas Blake, as the detective Nigel Strangeways in the novel *A Question of Proof* (1935). In Stephen Spender's novel *The Temple* (1988) partly written in 1929, partly in the late 1980s, the fictional representation of Auden's character is doubly complex, with Spender's caricature of Auden, Simon Wilmot, becoming the character 'W' in a novel by another character, William Bradshaw (himself a caricature of Christopher Isherwood). More recently, Auden is the *éminence grise* of the Amanda Cross novel *Poetic Justice* (1970), a campus thriller in which Professor Kate Fansler, an amateur sleuth and English professor, is constantly quoting Auden, much to the bemusement of her friends and colleagues.

But by far the most astonishing aspect of the continuing use and representation of Auden and his work by other writers has been the continual flood of poems to, for and about him. The poems addressed to Auden are remarkable for both their abundance and their variety. Auden's work features in other people's poems in a number of ways – through allusion, quotation, imitation, parody and pastiche. The use of quotations from Auden often occurs as a prompt to poems, within poems and in the margins of poems, as epigraphs and as notes. Some poets, meanwhile, use Auden's own forms as a means of addressing him: Anna Adams's *A Reply to Intercepted Mail* (1979) for example, is a verse-letter to Auden in the rhyme-royal of his own 'Letter to Lord Byron'. Francis Spufford's 'A Letter to Wystan Auden, from Iceland' is the same, as is David Grant's *Letter to W. H. Auden*.[44]

The most common kind of tribute to Auden are those personal poems from friends and admirers, wishing him birthday greetings: Edmund Wilson and Louise Bogan's 'To Wystan Auden on his Birthday', Geoffrey Grigson's 'To Wystan Auden, 1967', Charles Causley's 'Letter from Jericho', William Meredith's 'Talking Back', and recording and remembering encounters, Anne Rouse's 'Memo to Auden', Lincoln Kirstein's '*Siegfriedslage*', Roy Fuller's 'Visiting the Great'.[45] Auden's death prompted a number of elegiac summings-up and assessments, and poets have continued to mine this vein: James Schuyler's 'Wystan Auden', Robert Greacen's 'Auden', Derek Walcott's 'Eulogy to W. H. Auden' and Clive James's 'What Happened to Auden', Elizabeth Jennings's 'Elegy for W. H. Auden', Karl Shapiro's 'W.H.A.', Paul Muldoon's '7, Middagh Street', Carol Ann Duffy's 'Alphabet for Auden'.[46] Other poets have written indirectly in praise of his inspiriting influence (Richard Wilbur's 'For W. H. Auden', Thomas Kinsella's 'Dedication'); or about their discovery of his work (Christy Brown's 'W. H. Auden').[47] The work of Gavin Ewart contains virtually all of these kinds of tribute, and a few that haven't been mentioned, such as the ribald 'The Short Blake-Style Gnomic Epigram', which readers may wish to consult for themselves in order to discover Ewart's memorable rhyme for the phrase 'bottle of hock'.[48] Of course, all of these are only poems which have been written *for* Auden. There are many more which have been written *because* of him, but that's another story.

## NOTES

1. Hugh McDiarmid, 'Metaphysics and Poetry' (1974), repr. in Alan Riach (ed.), *Selected Prose* (Manchester: Carcanet Press, 1992), p. 281; Truman Capote, quoted in Lawrence Grobel, *Conversations with Capote* (New York: New American Library, 1985), pp. 144–5.
2. Interview with Peter Stitt, 1980, repr. in George Plimpton (ed.), *Poets at Work* (Harmondsworth: Penguin, 1989), p. 395.
3. Roy Fuller, 'W. H. Auden, 1907–1973', *The Listener*, 4 October 1973, p. 439; Patrick Kavanagh, 'Auden and the Creative Mind', *Envoy*, 5:19 (June 1951), p. 35.
4. Charles Madge, 'Letter to the Intelligentsia', and C. Day-Lewis, 'The Magnetic Mountain', both in Michael Roberts (ed.), *New Country* (London: The Hogarth Press, 1933), pp. 231–2; 223.
5. Joseph Brodsky, *Index on Censorship*, 17:2 (February 1988), p. 15; Seamus Heaney, 'Shorts for Auden' (1976), repr. Haffenden, p. 496.
6. John Hollander, 'W. H. Auden', *Yale Review*, 77:4 (Summer 1988), p. 502.
7. The photograph is illustration 6 (b) in Carpenter.
8. See Roland Barthes, *Camera Lucida* (1980; trans. Richard Howard 1981; repr. London: Fontana, 1984), pp. 32, 16.
9. The photograph is illustration 57 in *Tribute*, p. 164.
10. See, for example, Haffenden, pp. 95, 132.
11. Naomi Mitchison, 'Young Auden', *Shenandoah*, 18:2 (Winter 1967), p. 14; *You May Well Ask: A Memoir 1920–40* (London: Gollancz, 1970), p. 119.
12. Edward Lucie-Smith, *British Poetry since 1945* (Harmondsworth: Penguin, 1970), p. 27; Watson, *British Literature since 1945* (Basingstoke: Macmillan, 1991), p. xiv.
13. David Daiches, *The Present Age: After 1920*, Introductions to English Literature series, vol. v (London: The Cresset Press, 1958), p. 48.
14. See the *Norton Anthology of English Literature*, vol. II (5th edn, New York: W. W. Norton, 1986), pp. 2293–306.
15. Louis MacNeice, 'Traveller's Return', *Horizon*, 3:14 (February 1941), p. 116.
16. See, for example, 'Comment', *Horizon*, 2:2 (December 1940), pp. 281–2; *Hansard*, 13 June 1940.

17. John Lehmann, *I Am My Brother: Autobiography vol. II* (London: Longman, Green, 1960), p. 290.
18. Edmund Wilson, 'George Grosz in the United States', repr. in *Classics and Commercials: A Literary Chronicle of the Forties* (New York: Farrar, Straus 1950), p. 345.
19. John Berryman, *Collected Poems 1937–1971*, ed. Charles Thornbury (London: Faber and Faber, 1990), pp. 20–21, 3; Robert Duncan, *The Years As Catches: First Poems (1939–1946)* (Berkeley, Ca.: Oyez, 1966), pp. vi, 5.
20. The photograph is repr. in Osborne, p. 261; Atlas, 'New Voices in American Poetry', *New York Times* Magazine, 3 February 1980, p. 19.
21. Geoffrey Grigson, *Poetry of the Present: An Anthology of the Thirties and After* (London: Phoenix House, 1949), p. 19.
22. Robert Graves, 'These Be Your Gods, O Israel!', *Essays in Criticism*, 5:2 (April 1955), pp. 129–50.
23. *The Spectator*, 15 July 1960, pp. 104–5.
24. Anthony Hartley, 'Poets of the Fifties', *The Spectator*, 27 August 1954, p. 260.
25. Roy Fuller, 'Poetry: Tradition and Belief', in John Lehmann (ed.), *The Craft of Letters in England: a Symposium* (London: Cresset, 1956), p. 7.
26. Kingsley Amis, 'Socialism and the Intellectuals', repr. in Gene Feldman and Max Gartenberg (eds.), *Protest* (London: Souvenir Press, 1959), pp. 299–315.
27. Paul Johnson, 'Lucky Jim's Political Testament', *The New Statesman and Nation*, 12 January 1957, p. 36.
28. Glyn Maxwell, 'Random Thoughts on my Debt to Auden', *Agenda*, 31:4–32:1 (Winter–Spring 1994), p. 222.
29. *Sunday Times*, 19 February 1967, p. 28.
30. See *New Measures* 1 (Autumn 1965); Barry Miles, *Ginsberg: A Biography* (London: Harper Collins, 1990), pp. 229–33, 242.
31. Eric Mottram, in Robert Hampson and Peter Barry (eds.), *New British Poetries: The Scope of the Possible* (Manchester: Carcanet, 1993), p. 22; 'Ian Hamilton and Peter Dale in Conversation', *Agenda*, 31:2 (Summer 1993), p. 8.
32. Osborne, p. 322; Alfred Lautner, 'The Nine Lives of Poetry International', *The New Review*, 1:5 (August 1974), p. 42.
33. The recordings are held at the British Library National Sound Archive, London – for details see Toby Oakes, 'A Handlist of Recordings Held at the National Sound Archive', issued as an addendum to *ASN*, 4 (October 1989).
34. *The Times*, 1 October 1973, p. 19.
35. See, for example, Stephen Spender, *W. H. Auden: A Memorial Address* (1973), repr. as 'Valediction', in *Tribute*, pp. 244–8; and Clive James, 'Farewelling Auden' (1973), repr. in *At the Pillars of Hercules* (London: Faber and Faber, 1979).
36. Quoted in Michael Leapman, 'Engrossing Record of Auden's Vigour and Achievement', *The Times*, 9 December 1980, p. 10.
37. Harold Norse, *Memoirs of a Bastard Angel* (London: Bloomsbury, 1990), p. 307; Richard Kellett, 'An English Visitor in Kirchstetten', *ASN*, 4 (October 1989), p. 3.
38. 'A Note on Ezra Pound', *The Collected Essays of Robert Creeley* (Berkeley, Ca.: University of California Press, 1989), p. 25.
39. Peter Sansom, *Everything You've Heard is True* (Manchester: Carcanet, 1990), p. 11.

40. Anthony Hecht, *The Hidden Law: The Poetry of W. H. Auden* (Cambridge, Mass.: Harvard University Press, 1993), p. 169; Edward Mendelson, 'Editing Auden', *New Statesman*, 17 September 1976, p. 376.
41. TUCC *Western England Annual Report: Year Ended 31 March 1993* (Bristol: no publ., 1993), p. 7.
42. Toby Litt, 'From "Acedia" to "Zeitgeist": Auden in the 2nd edition of the OED', *ASN*, 4 (October 1989), pp. 2–3.
43. See Alan Bennett, *Objects of Affection* (London: BBC Publications, 1982), pp. 217–20.
44. Anna Adams, *A Reply to Intercepted Mail* (Liskeard: Peterloo Poets, 1979); Francis Spufford, *London Review of Books*, 21 February 1991, pp. 10–11 (see also response by Stan Smith, *London Review of Books*, 4 April 1991, p. 4); David Grant, *Letter to W. H. Auden* (Axminster: Escargot Press, 1993).
45. Edmund Wilson and Louise Bogan, and Geoffrey Grigson, in *Shenandoah*, 18:2 (Winter 1967), pp. 43, 16–17; Charles Causley, in *A Tribute to W. H. Auden* (Menston: Scolar Press, 1973), unnumbered pages; Meredith, in *For W. H. Auden: February 12, 1972*, eds. Peter H. Salus and Paul B. Taylor (New York: Random House, 1972), pp. 70–1; Anne Rouse, *Sunset Grill* (Newcastle: Bloodaxe, 1973), pp. 62–3; Lincoln Kirstein, *Shenandoah*, 18:2 (Winter 1967), pp. 51–5; Roy Fuller, *The Reign of Sparrows* (London: London Magazine Editions, 1980), pp. 28–9.
46. James Schuyler, 'Wystan Auden', *TLS*, 28 March 1975, p. 826; Robert Greacen, *A Bright Mask* (Dublin: The Dedalus Press, 1985), p. 37; Derek Walcott, *The Arkansas Testament* (London: Faber and Faber, 1988), pp. 61–5; Clive James, *The New Yorker*, 2 November 1992, p. 84; Elizabeth Jennings, *Growing Pains* (Cheadle Hume: Carcanet, 1975), p. 44; Karl Shapiro, *Collected Poems 1940–1978* (New York: Random House, 1978), p. 281; Paul Muldoon, *Meeting the British* (London: Faber and Faber, 1987); Carol Ann Duffy, *Standing Female Nude* (London: Anvil, 1985), pp. 10–11.
47. Richard Wilbur, *New and Collected Poems* (London: Faber and Faber, 1989), p. 26; Thomas Kinsella, *Poems from Centre City* (Dublin: Peppercanister, 1990), p. 24. Christy Brown, *Collected Poems* (London: Secker and Warburg, 1982), pp. 128–9.
48. Gavin Ewart, *The Complete Little Ones: His Shortest Poems* (London: Hutchinson, 1986), p. 35.

# 19

NADIA HERMAN COLBURN

# Bibliographic essay and review of Auden studies

Auden's complete works are not yet collected and his papers and letters are divided among a number of libraries and private sources. Thanks to his literary executor, Edward Mendelson, the papers are in better order than those of many writers, and a project is currently underway to make his complete oeuvre available in thoroughly researched and accessible volumes. The most significant collection of Auden's manuscripts can be found in the Berg Collection of the New York Public Library. Other important collections can be found at the Harry Ransom Humanities Research Center, University of Texas, the Bodleian Library, Oxford, the Harvard Library and the British Library, London.

An extensive though incomplete bibliography compiled by B. C. Bloomfeld and Edward Mendelson, published in 1972, only goes through to 1969 (*W. H. Auden: A Bibliography, 1924–1969*. Second Edition). Mendelson's supplement, bringing it up to 1983, has been published in *Auden Studies 1*.

Auden published over twenty books of poems in his lifetime. The majority of the poems are republished in *Collected Poems* (1976; revised edition 1991). The volume is not however a Complete Poems, since it excludes some of his most famous, subsequently disavowed poems. The text reflects not the original published version, but Auden's later revisions. For original versions, 1929–39, see *The English Auden*. Katherine Bucknell's *Juvenilia* includes all of Auden's known early poems (1922–8) and provides helpful bibliographical and textual comments. Edward Mendelson is general editor of the multi-volume *Complete Works of W. H. Auden*, published by Princeton University Press (USA) and Faber and Faber (UK). *W. H. Auden: Critical Editions* form a subcategory of this series which, to date, includes an annotated version of *Lectures on Shakespeare* (2000) and *The Sea and the Mirror* (2003), both edited by Edward Kirsch. The former provides reconstructions of Auden's Shakespeare lectures, delivered at the New School in 1946.

Auden was prolific not only as a poet but also as a prose-writer, drama-tist and librettist, publishing five important volumes of prose: *The Enchafed*

*Flood* (1950), *The Dyer's Hand* (1963), *Secondary Worlds* (1968), *A Certain World: A Commonplace Book* (1970) and *Forewords and Afterwords* (1973). There is a large number of uncollected reviews and essays. Two volumes of Auden's prose have so far appeared in *The Complete Works*: *Prose and Travel Books in Prose and Verse: Vol. 1 1926–1938*, and *Prose: Vol. 11 1939–1949*. Auden's complete plays (mainly in collaboration with Isherwood) and libretti (mainly in collaboration with Kallman) are collected in a further two volumes: *Plays and Other Dramatic Writings, 1928–1938* and *Libretti and Other Dramatic Writings, 1939–1973*.

Several volumes record Auden's conversations, in particular Alan Ansen's *The Table Talk of W. H. Auden* (1991) and Howard Griffin's less reliable *Conversations with Auden* (1981). *Auden Studies 11* includes updated bibliographical information about interviews, dialogues, conversations.

Auden did not save his correspondence, but many friends have done. Several large editions are in preparation, but none is yet published. To date, the largest selection can be found in the issues of *Auden Studies*. *Auden Studies 111* contains Mendelson's bibliography of the published letters. Auden letters can be found in major collections of the papers of many of his friends, among them, Spender, Isherwood, E. R. Dodds, Eliot, Stravinsky and MacNeice.

Not as much has been written about Auden as about some other major twentieth-century poets, in part because Auden sometimes falls through the cracks – neither fully English nor American, modernist nor postmodernist. The work that has appeared tends to be of a high quality and generally trustworthy. Perhaps the three most comprehensive and indispensable books are John Fuller's *W. H. Auden: A Commentary* (1998), which expands on his 1970 *Reader's Guide*, and provides a commentary on all the mature published poetry and major plays, and Edward Mendelson's two studies, *Early Auden* and *Later Auden*, which together provide the most comprehensive and in-depth analysis of Auden's oeuvre.

For an overview of Auden's reception during his lifetime, John Haffenden's *Critical Heritage* volume is instructive, with excerpts from the most influential reviews, and a good introductory essay. Although from the first Auden was arguably the most prominent poet of his generation, he met with mixed responses. Two important anthologies, *New Signatures* (1932) and *New Country* (1933), placed him as the leader of a new group of politically minded poets, but his work also met with negative criticism from some of the leading critics of the age, including F. R. Leavis and later, Randall Jarrell, initially an admirer.

Pioneer studies include Francis Scarfe's *Auden and After* (1942), Richard Hoggart's *Auden: An Introductory Essay* (1951), the first book-length study,

Monroe K. Spears's still instructive *The Disenchanted Island* (1963), the first systematic, analytical account, and Barbara Everett's *Auden* (1964). By 1973, the year of Auden's death, roughly twenty full-length books had been written about him. With the exception of Joseph Warren Beach's *The Making of the Auden Canon* (1957), which though somewhat negative offers insights into Auden's revisions, most of the early books provided a general overview of Auden's career and assessment of the poetry. Among the best of these are Herbert Greenberg's *Quest for the Necessary: W. H. Auden and the Dilemma of Divided Consciousness* (1968), Justin Replogle's *Auden's Poetry* (1969) and François Duchêne's *The Case of the Helmeted Airman* (1972), which illuminates Auden's early work, as does Richard Johnson's *Man's Place* the later, 'American' poetry. More recently Anthony Hecht's *The Hidden Law* (1993) and Stan Smith's *W. H. Auden* (British Council Writers and Their Work series, 1997) have been among the best overviews of Auden's career. Smith's earlier *W. H. Auden* (in Terry Eagleton's Rereading Literature series, 1985), was the first reading fully informed by modern critical theory, an approach taken up more recently in studies by Rainer Emig and John R. Boly. Paul Hendon's *Reader's Guide* (2000) combines thoughtful résumés of the work with copious quotation from 'essential criticism', while Allan Rodway's *Preface to Auden* (1984) helpfully combines biographical and critical approaches.

The first full biography, Charles Osborne's entertaining *W. H. Auden: The Life of a Poet* (1980) has been to some extent superseded by the mass of new information in Humphrey Carpenter's *W. H. Auden: A Biography* (1981), and Richard Davenport-Hines's insightful *Auden* (1995). Other, more specific biographical works include Charles Miller's *Auden: An American Friendship* (1983), Dorothy Farnan's entertaining *Auden in Love* (1984) and Thekla Clark's *Wystan and Chester* (1995), personal memoirs focusing on Auden's relationship with Chester Kallman.

Several collections of essays and excerpts have been published. Among the best are Spender's *W. H. Auden: A Tribute* (1975), a collection of remembrances and personal essays about Auden published shortly after his death, Monroe Spears's *Auden: A Collection of Critical Essays* (1964), which is particularly good for early criticism, Ronald Carter's Macmillan Casebook, *Thirties Poets: 'The Auden Group'* (1984) and the collections edited by Alan Bold, Harold Bloom and George Bahlke.

Most Auden criticism, either implicitly or explicitly, addresses the distinction between Auden's English and American periods. Studies devoted to later Auden tends to examine the moral aspects of his work, while work devoted to the earlier Auden tend to examine its political dimensions. For many years, the majority of books that considered Auden, without focusing exclusively on him, addressed his 1930s poetry. Samuel Hynes's *The Auden Generation: Literature and Politics in England in the 1930s* (1992) remains one of the best of these studies. Other accounts include Donald Mitchell's *Britten and Auden in the Thirties* (2000), Lucy McDiarmid's *Saving Civilization* (1984) and Norman Page's *Auden and Isherwood: The Berlin Years* (1998), a biographical and topographical study. Books with a more general application include Julian Symons's anecdotal memoir, *The Thirties: A Dream Revolved* (1960; 1975), Frederick R. Benson's *Writers in Arms* (1968), on the literary impact of the Spanish Civil War, and Keith Williams's *British Writers and the Media, 1930–1945* (1996). Revisionist critics such as Adrian Caesar and John Lucas have questioned how central Auden is to the period.

More specialised aspects of Auden's life and work have been explored by Lucy McDiarmid in *Auden's Apologies for Poetry* (1990), which examines Auden's ambivalence about poetry, by Marsha Bryant writing on Auden and documentary (1997), and by Richard Bozorth, whose *Auden's Games of Knowledge* (2001) considers the implications of Auden's homosexuality for his writing by looking closely at his language as a conflicted discourse and Auden's sense of himself as an insider/outsider. Much recent writing in journals and essay collections examines Auden in relation, for example, to nationalism, exile, travel writing, poetic influence, modernism and postmodernism.

## Select booklist

Bahlke, George W. *The Later Auden*. New Brunswick: Rutgers University Press, 1970.

Bahlke, George W. (ed.). *Critical Essays on W. H. Auden*. Boston: G. K. Hall, 1991.

Bayley, John. *The Romantic Survival*. London: Constable, 1957.

Beach, Joseph Warren. *The Making of the Auden Canon*. Minneapolis: University of Minnesota Press, 1957.

Blair, John G. *The Poetic Art of W. H. Auden*. Princeton: Princeton University Press, 1965.

Bloom, Harold (ed.). *W. H. Auden* (Modern Critical Views). New York: Chelsea, 1986.

Bloomfield, B. C. and Edward Mendelson. *W. H. Auden: A Bibliography, 1924–1969*. Second edition. Charlottesville: University Press of Virginia, 1972.

Bold, Alan. *W. H. Auden: The Far Interior*. London: Vision Press, 1985.

Boly, John R. *Reading Auden: The Returns of Caliban*. Ithaca N.Y.: Cornell University Press, 1991.

Bozorth, Richard R. *Auden's Games of Knowledge: Poetry and the Meanings of Homosexuality*. New York: Columbia University Press, 2001.

Bruce, Cicero. *W. H. Auden's Moral Imagination*. Lewiston, N.Y.: Edwin Mellen Press, 1998.

Bryant, Marsha. *Auden and Documentary in the 1930s*. Charlottesville: University Press of Virginia, 1997.

Bucknell, Katherine. *W. H. Auden, Juvenilia, Poems 1922–28*. London: Faber and Faber, 1994.

Bucknell, Katherine, and Nicholas Jenkins (eds.). *The Map of All My Youth: Early Works, Friends and Influences (Auden Studies 1)* Oxford: Oxford University Press, 1990.

*The Language of Learning and the Language of Love: Uncollected Writing, New Interpretations (Auden Studies 2)*. Oxford: Oxford University Press, 1994.

*In Solitude, for Company: W. H. Auden After 1940: Unpublished Prose and Recent Criticism (Auden Studies 3)*. Oxford: Oxford University Press, 1996.

Buell, Frederick. *W. H. Auden as a Social Poet*. Ithaca, N.Y.: Cornell University Press, 1973.

Caesar, Adrian. *Dividing Lines: Poetry, Class, and Ideology in the 1930s*. Manchester: Manchester University Press, 1991.

Callan, Edward. *Auden: A Carnival of Intellect*. New York: Oxford University Press, 1983.

Carpenter, Humphrey. *W. H. Auden: A Biography*. London: Faber and Faber, 1981.

Clark, Thekla. *Wystan and Chester: A Personal Memoir of W. H. Auden and Chester Kallman*. Second edition. London: Faber and Faber, 1995.

Cunningham, Valentine. *British Writers of the Thirties*. Oxford: Oxford University Press, 1988.

Davenport-Hines, Richard. *Auden*. London: Heinemann, 1995.

Davison, Dennis. *W. H. Auden*. London: Evans Bros, 1970.

Deane, Patrick. *History in Our Hands: A Critical Anthology of Writings on Literature, Culture, and Politics from the 1930s*. London and New York: Leicester University Press, 1998.

Duchêne, François. *The Case of the Helmeted Airman: A Study of W. H. Auden's Poetry*. London: Chatto & Windus, 1972.

Emig, Rainer. *W. H. Auden: Towards a Postmodern Poetics*. London: Macmillan, 1999.

Fenton, James. *The Strength of Poetry*. New York: Farrar, Straus & Giroux, 2001.

Firchow, Peter Edgerly. *W. H. Auden: Contexts for Poetry*. Newark: University of Delaware Press, 2002.

Fuller, John. *W. H. Auden: A Commentary*. London: Faber and Faber, 1998; Princeton: Princeton University Press, 1998.

Gingerich, Martin E. *W. H. Auden: A Reference Guide*. Boston: G. K. Hall, 1977.

Greenberg, Herbert. *The Quest for the Necessary: W. H. Auden and the Dilemma of Divided Consciousness*. Cambridge, Mass.: Harvard University Press, 1968.

Griffin, Howard. *Conversations with Auden*, ed. Donald Allen. San Francisco:Gray Fox, 1981.

Haffenden, John (ed.). *W. H. Auden, the Critical Heritage*. London: Routledge & Kegan Paul, 1983.

Hecht, Anthony. *The Hidden Law: The Poetry of W. H. Auden*. Cambridge, Mass.: Harvard University Press, 1993.

Hendon, Paul (ed.). *The Poetry of W. H. Auden: A Reader's Guide to Essential Criticism*. Cambridge: Icon Books, 2000.

Hoggart, Richard. *Auden: An Introductory Essay*. London: Chatto and Windus, 1951.

*W. H. Auden*. London: Longmans, Green, 1957.

Hynes, Samuel. *The Auden Generation: Literature and Politics in England in the 1930s*. Princeton: Princeton University Press, 1982; London: Pimlico, 1992.

Jacobs, Alan. *What Became of Wystan: Change and Continuity in Auden's Poetry*. Fayetteville: University of Arkansas Press, 1998.

Jarrell, Randall. *Kipling, Auden & Co.: Essays and Reviews 1935–1964*. Manchester: Carcanet Press, 1981.

*The Third Book of Criticism*. London: Faber and Faber, 1975.

Johnson, Richard. *Man's Place: An Essay on Auden*. Ithaca, N.Y.: Cornell University Press, 1973.

Lucas, John. *The Radical Twenties: Writing, Politics and Culture*. Nottingham: Five Leaves Publications, 1997; New Brunswick, N.J.: Rutgers University Press, 1999.

Marchetti, Paola. *Landscapes of Meaning: From Auden to Hughes*. Milan: Università Cattolica, 2001.

Maxwell, D. E. S. *Poets of the Thirties*. London: Routledge and Kegan Paul, 1969.

Mazzaro, Jerome. *Postmodern American Poetry*. Urbana: University of Illinois Press, 1980.

McDiarmid, Lucy. *Saving Civilization: Yeats, Eliot, and Auden Between the Wars*. Cambridge: Cambridge University Press, 1984.

*Auden's Apologies for Poetry*. Princeton: Princeton University Press, 1990.

Mendelson, Edward. *Early Auden*. New York: Viking; London: Faber and Faber, 1981.

*Later Auden*. New York: Farrar, Straus & Giroux; London: Faber and Faber, 1999.

Mitchell, Donald. *Britten and Auden in the Thirties: The Year 1936*. Woodbridge: Boydell Press, 2000.

Nelson, Gerald. *Changes of Heart*. Berkeley and Los Angeles: University of California Press, 1969.

O'Neill, Michael, and Gareth Reeves. *Auden, MacNeice, Spender: The Thirties Poetry*. Basingstoke: Macmillan, 1992.

Osborne, Charles. *W. H. Auden: The Life of a Poet*. London: Macmillan, 1980.

Page, Norman. *Auden and Isherwood: The Berlin Years*. London: Macmillan, 1998.

Replogle, Justin. *Auden's Poetry*. Seattle: University of Washington Press, 1969.

Rodway, Allan. *A Preface to Auden*. London and New York: Longman, 1984.

Scarfe, Francis. *Auden and After: the Liberation of Poetry 1930–1941*. London: Routledge & Sons, 1942.

Smith, Stan. *W. H. Auden* (Rereading Literature). Oxford and New York: Basil Blackwell, 1985.

*W. H. Auden* (British Council Writers and Their Work). Plymouth: Northcote House, 1997.

Smith, Stan (ed.). *Auden* Special Issue, *Critical Survey*, 6:3. Oxford: Oxford University Press, 1994.

Spears, Monroe K. *The Poetry of W. H. Auden: The Disenchanted Island*. New York: Oxford University Press, 1963.

Spears, Monroe K. (ed.) *Auden: a Collection of Critical Essays*. Englewood Cliffs, N.J.: Prentice-Hall, 1964.

Spender, Stephen (ed.). *W. H. Auden: A Tribute*. London: Weidenfeld and Nicolson, 1975.

Strong, Beret E. *The Poetic Avant-garde: The Groups of Borges, Auden, and Breton*. Evanston, Ill.: Northwestern University Press, 1997.

*W. H. Auden Society Newsletter*. Irregularly published, currently from Columbia University: New York, N.Y.

Whitehead, John. *A Commentary on the Poetry of W. H. Auden, C. Day Lewis, Louis MacNeice, and Stephen Spender*. Lewiston, N.Y.: Edwin Mellen Press, 1992.

Williams, Keith. *British Writers and the Media, 1930–1945*. London: Macmillan, 1996.

Wright, George Thaddeus. *W. H. Auden*. New York: Twayne Publishers, 1969.

# INDEX

Auden's works are subdivided below into *Poetry* (volumes and individual poems), *Plays* (including libretti, radio and film scripts) and *Prose* (volumes, essays, chapters). The latter includes prose passages from 'mixed' volumes of verse and prose, where such extracts have individual titles and are discussed separately in the text, and anthologies edited by Auden, whether of prose or verse. Poetry and prose collections and critical and biographical sources are indexed only when they are discussed in their own right, but not when identifying references. Where there are alternative titles both are indicated. The poet himself is not indexed.

# CAMBRIDGE COMPANIONS TO LITERATURE

## CAMBRIDGE COMPANIONS TO CULTURE

CPSIA information can be obtained at www.ICGtesting.com
Printed in the USA
LVOW092145101111

254479LV00002B/61/P